CURATORIAL DREAMS

Curatorial Dreams

CRITICS IMAGINE EXHIBITIONS

Edited by Shelley Ruth Butler and Erica Lehrer

McGill-Queen's University Press
Montreal & Kingston | London | Chicago

ISBN 978-0-7735-4682-0 (cloth)
ISBN 978-0-7735-4683-7 (paper)
ISBN 978-0-7735-9854-6 (ePDF)
ISBN 978-0-7735-9855-3 (ePUB)

Legal deposit second quarter 2016
Bibliothèque nationale du Québec

Printed in Canada on acid-free paper that is 100% ancient forest free (100% post-consumer recycled), processed chlorine free

McGill-Queen's University Press acknowledges the support of the Canada Council for the Arts for our publishing program. We also acknowledge the financial support of the Government of Canada through the Canada Book Fund for our publishing activities.

Library and Archives Canada Cataloguing in Publication

Curatorial dreams : critics imagine exhibitions / edited by Shelley Ruth Butler and Erica Lehrer.

Includes bibliographical references and index.
Issued in print and electronic formats.
ISBN 978-0-7735-4682-0 (cloth). – ISBN 978-0-7735-4683-7 (paper). – ISBN 978-0-7735-9854-6 (pdf). – ISBN 978-0-7735-9855-3 (epub)

1. Museums – Philosophy. 2. Museum exhibits – Philosophy. 3. Museum techniques – Philosophy. I. Butler, Shelley, 1964–, author, editor II. Lehrer, Erica T., author, editor

AM7.C87 2016 069 C2015-908385-0
C2015-908386-9

Set in 10/14 Sina Nova with Gill Sans Nova
Book design & typesetting by Garet Markvoort, zijn digital

CONTENTS

Part Two: Breaking Frames

Part Three: Activating Art and History

Part Four: Establishments Revisioned

ILLUSTRATIONS

ACKNOWLEDGMENTS

We developed *Curatorial Dreams* in the context of the Centre for Ethnographic Research and Exhibition in the Aftermath of Violence (CEREV) at Concordia University in Montreal, where we have enjoyed a lively community of scholar-curators including Lon Dubinsky, Sharon Gubbay Helfer, Heather Igloliorte, Florencia Marchetti, Cynthia Milton, Monica Patterson, Joseph Rosen, Anna Sheftel, and Stacey Zembrzycki. We also benefited from conversations hosted at CEREV with guests Cory Kratz, Ruth Phillips, and Bob White. Two of our contributors, Lucian Gomoll and Lissette Olivares, organized a seminal conference, "The Task of the Curator: Translation, Intervention, and Innovation in Exhibitionary Practice" at UC Santa Cruz in 2010. There we encountered inspirational projects and "collected" two additional contributors to the present volume.

We thank our editor Jonathan Crago of McGill-Queen's University Press for his enthusiasm for this project, Concordia University and the Canada Research Chairs program for financial support, Ozren Stambuk and Kimberley Moore for editorial and administrative assistance, and Mary Caple for her excellent project management. We also remember Roger Simon, who was a key inspiration for our vision of curating as an important form of critical thinking.

Chera Amlag

Hood famous Cafe + Bar

Strengthened fillipino American community

Goals & methods:
constructive scholarship. interdisciplinary practice
Public Humanities

Method where

CURATORIAL DREAMS

Academics imagine exhibitions
as a creative and critical response
to research

Hypothetical – but serve as thought
experiments

What it offers? Scholars new modes of research
dissemination theory application
Challenge institutional norms in museums
inspire new forms of engagement

INTRODUCTION

Curatorial Dreaming

SHELLEY RUTH BUTLER and ERICA LEHRER

In contrast to the nocturnal dream, that of the daytime sketches freely chosen and repeatable figures in the air, it can rant and rave, but also brood and plan.
Ernest Bloch[1]

This is a book about imagined exhibitions. These "curatorial dreams" were conceived by a diverse group of humanities and social science scholars whom we challenged with the task of drawing up blueprints for exhibitions that reflect their particular research and respond to their own critiques of exhibits or of broader social landscapes. This is an unusual approach; scholars are highly trained in analysis and critique, but are generally unpractised at offering constructive solutions to the problems they identify, let alone in the form of a public exhibition. The robustness of the field of critical museology is a testament to the ferment around museums and exhibitions as key sites of cultural politics, both as enacted by museum practitioners and as objects of academic study. Yet Shelley Ruth Butler's 2001 conference panel in Montreal on "imaginary exhibitions," which prefigured the present volume, highlighted the deep cognitive boundary between the two groups; an attempt to develop a conceptual meeting ground revealed the ingrained nature of arm's length, rational critique among scholars.[2] Although invited to "dream," the academic panelists at the conference described brave new museological experiments and critiqued status quo exhibitions, but did not propose creative responses of their own.

Public humanities theorist Julie Ellison asks whether scholars, in our "necessary skepticism," have made analysis and hope, theory and action, "strangers to one another."[3] In response to Ellison's profound question, and inspired by the laboratory, the design studio, and the architectural charrette[4] – spaces and methods for thinking creatively, conceptually, collaboratively, and concretely – we propose curatorial dreaming as an innovative method of engaged cultural analysis and critique. Our idea is that working outside our comfort zones, in a constructive rather than deconstructive mode, can be a productive departure for scholars and academics, an important addition to our toolkits.[5] Such dreaming asks us to diversify our methods, while offering an opportunity to engage with wider audiences in new ways. This volume is the fruit of our contributors' efforts – as well as our own – to curate our arguments, shifting our scholarly subjectivities beyond the insular world of academic writing to the open civic space of the exhibition.

As editors we encouraged creativity and thinking "outside the box." Yet we also gave our contributors exacting guidelines for what, in our view, constituted a fully developed curatorial dream. Beyond titles and venues, they outline their curatorial goals, discuss the theoretical, substantive, or museological issues that prompted their work, and offer evocative descriptions of key exhibitionary moments. And they describe and analyse specific curatorial strategies and processes of exhibition development. The combined result is that the broader practical and political contexts and negotiations of curatorial work – generally unseen in the final exhibitions that audiences encounter – are rendered visible and significant.

Complementing contemporary museological theory, which takes the possibilities and constraints of specific exhibition spaces into account, *Curatorial Dreams* proposes exhibitions in a wide variety of display environments, whether traditional or unconventional. These include city art galleries, colonial-era and "universal" museums, theatres, an architectural destination, and a memorial site, as well as vernacular spaces such as a library, a heritage festival, an airport lobby, an organization headquarters, a hospital, and a trailer stationed outside a county art gallery. The contributors come from a multitude of disciplines and interdisciplinary fields of inquiry – African American studies, anthropology, art history, Canadian studies, cultural studies, history, Latino studies, media studies, and museum studies, and their work is situated in Australia, Barbados,

Canada, Chile, the Netherlands, Poland, South Africa, Switzerland, and the United States. Despite their disciplinary and geographic diversity, however, the curatorial dreams presented here form a coherent set, in that they collectively experiment with inclusive, critical, democratic, participatory, reflexive, multi-vocal, and socially relevant exhibition design. The exhibits are shaped by theoretical concepts regarding – and debates surrounding – translation, identity formation, critical race theory, hybridity, cultural memory, affect, reflexivity, critical pedagogy, queer theory, and the conciliatory potential of heritage, among others. And, with each site being implicated in its own social constellation, the imagined exhibitions also work through ethno-cultural and class relations, aboriginal and disaporic communities, and transnational networks.

We are not blind to the potential pitfalls of critical or explicitly theoretical exhibitions. There is a growing literature that documents failed, flawed, and fraught attempts at critical and reflexive curatorship.[6] *Into the Heart of Africa* at the Royal Ontario Museum, *The West as America: Reinterpreting Images of the Frontier, 1820–1920* at the Smithsonian American Art Museum, and *Imaginary Coordinates* at Chicago's Spertus Institute of Jewish Studies generated high-profile controversies and accusations of elitism and partisan political correctness.[7] But we agree with Ruth Phillips, who notes that the controversies were valuable for unsettling modernist museums and for demonstrating that exhibitions are much more than sites of representation.[8] Exhibitions, it is clear, are also scenes of social and political action and the performance of culture and community.[9] This sense of the exhibition as a public site and an event, rather than a static text divorced from historical legacies and real world struggles, is implicit in many of the contributions to this volume.

As anthropologists specializing in museums and heritage who came of age professionally in a moment of disciplinary crisis amid calls for experimental ethnography, we are drawn to curatorial work as a valuable methodology that simultaneously embraces research, analysis, cultural representation, creative expression, social intervention, and dialogue with broad publics. We offer curatorial dreaming as an alternative mode of critical, intellectual practice – a form of "theorizing in the concrete."[10] In the spirit of civically engaged research, and in support of new kinds of knowledge production arising from the crossing of disciplinary and professional boundaries, we hope that *Curatorial Dreams* will speak not only to critical museum scholars or to a broader field of humanities and social science researchers, but also to curators and other museum practitioners such as educators. Further, we hope that *Curatorial Dreams* will inspire these differently situated experts to speak to each other.[11]

Dreaming as Method

As we tell our students, all exhibitions are arguments. They make assertions about history and aesthetics, about what counts as progress, and about the actual and appropriate relationships among people and between people and things. Exhibits naturalize particular ways of looking at the world. They can also clear paths for new ways of seeing. Critical humanities scholars know this only too well and have taken it as their task to illuminate, deconstruct, and demystify museum worlds.[12] But is this the only relationship scholars can have with exhibition arguments? By tapping into the power of aspirational imagination to propel cultural theory and museum practice forward and grapple creatively with pressing social, cultural, and political concerns, *Curatorial Dreams* proposes a new method of academic knowledge production. We go beyond the vagueness associated with much utopian thinking, and avoid the common pattern of enacting "good works" at disciplinary margins while leaving core modes of practice and inquiry unquestioned.[13] Instead, we explore the concrete process of designing exhibitions as a mode of thinking, theorizing, researching, experimenting, and argumentation that reconsiders the forms these can – and perhaps should – take.[14]

We are influenced by scholars who, spurred by their dissatisfaction with current models and enticed by the possibilities suggested by new social and technological realities, have proposed visions of radically altered museums.[15] Eilean Hooper-Greenhill imagines an emancipated, collaborative, spatially fluid "post-museum," noting that, whereas the "modernist museum was (and is) imagined as a building, the museum in the future may be imagined as a process or an experience."[16] Elaine Heumann Gurian's "Blue Ocean" museum responds to the cyber age with its vision of an open sea of knowledge in which visitors freely immerse themselves, and explores the administrative and curatorial changes that this concept of a museum would necessitate.[17] Julian Spalding's communicative "poetic museum" envisions objects telling larger, interconnected stories, and evoking wonder in visitors by channelling the passion of the curators who chose to exhibit them.[18] Such visionary theoretical literature reflects the urge to break free from established museological traditions and call out to the possible. And museums are indeed changing, in tandem with these writings and shifts in technology and public culture.[19] Some are compelled to address inherited elitism and colonial collections, while others are emerging anew in fresh political and social contexts such as democratic post-apartheid South Africa, or newly prosperous China. Our curatorial dreams are informed by these developments, and inspired by them to envision new ways in which museums might position themselves in relation to their own collections, constituents, and histories.

Rather than theorize broad institutional shifts, *Curatorial Dreams* proposes specific new exhibitions. We are cognizant that our project enters terrain fraught with tensions that divide museological theorists and museum practitioners. Scholars claim that museums present simplistic versions of culture and history.[20] But they too often overlook the specialized knowledge that museum practitioners possess about the workings of their institutions and the way their visitors use them. Further, critical museum theorists rarely value or even acknowledge the optimism expressed by many museum professionals (and stated in their institutions' mission statements), all of which are motivated by the potential for museums to contribute to an inclusive and enriching public sphere.[21] Scholar-critics are also largely ignorant of the practical and political constraints that museum curators and educators face in their own attempts to innovate.[22] Nor have critics been sensitive enough to the specificities of museum collections and institutional histories.[23] Museums and their exhibitions are often viewed as monolithic structures, removed from complex intra-institutional workings and the broader web of forces that shape their final forms. In response, *Curatorial Dreams* offers an "insider-outsider" perspective, with scholars imagining exhibits in relation to the problematics and possibilities of particular institutions, sites, communities, audiences, and social and political contexts. We begin not from abstract ideas, but by asking, "How can we communicate, using *these* materials, in *this* place?"

We are aware that our curatorial dreaming cannot truly bridge the theory-practice gap, since the process stops short of actual curating. Despite this limitation, a fundamental goal of our volume is to enrich dialogues between academics and museum practitioners, and to develop an understanding of the particular "interface" between specialized scholarly information and the diverse publics that exhibitions assemble. Curatorial dreaming is an important exercise for the museological imagination that, we argue, benefits both scholars and practitioners. It inhabits an in-between space, free from the constraints that real exhibitions regularly face on account of politics, hegemonic templates for presenting culture, available technologies, bureaucracy, and funding. Volume contributor Roger Simon reflects on the value of this approach: "For centuries, pure wishful images have discredited utopian dreams as mere fantasy, yet this cynicism misses core potentials in dreaming as a mode of generating possibility ... Such a mode can and does embody the seriousness of laying out the conditions for the possibly real. Daydreams imagine a praxis, a way of getting beyond existing norms and conventions to achieve something new."[24]

Some of our contributors reflect directly on specific challenges presented by their dreams. Manon Parry, for instance, discusses the political, legal, and ethical obstacles and objections that could be elicited by her imagined exhibition about the role of medicine in defining human normality, past and present. Yet, as Parry notes, such "speculative discussions of the problems of mounting such an exhibition may also allow for a more honest conversation about the political forces that frame museum work than accounts of real projects ever can." Indeed, to the extent that they are impossible to implement, curatorial dreams function analytically, laying bare the constraints, embedded values, and conditions of possibility in particular museums and spaces of display. At the same time, while this volume presents the curatorial dreams of academics, we envision the dreaming process as an enriching, exploratory method for museum professionals to use as well, thanks to its emphasis on process, creativity, and "thinking outside the box" of pragmatic constraints.

What can curatorial dreams created by scholars offer museum practitioners? Our contributors have deep investments in their research sites; they have conducted fieldwork and archival research, and mined literature, performance, popular culture, and visual arts for resonant and provocative materials. Consequently, their curatorial dreams can offer curators and other museum workers fresh resources for use in future exhibitions. Blending pedagogical and curatorial concerns is an approach much touted by museums, but less frequently realized in them. To our contributors, who are educators as well as researchers, that fusion is familiar. But in traditional, hierarchical museums, achieving an integration can be next to impossible. Moreover, many museum education programs are linked to narrow school curriculum goals. In the context of curatorial dreaming, however, the institutional struggle between curating and pedagogy can be sidestepped, enabling a freedom of expression that independent curators and artist-curators may be more able to enact. For curators in large establishment museums that must mount blockbuster exhibitions to balance the budget, temporary, independent exhibitions are the icing on the cake, the place where experimentation can more often take place.[25] The curatorial dreams presented here are precisely those kinds of projects, and it is no wonder that many of our contributors are inspired by previous experimental and theatrical exhibitions, not to mention interventions by artist-activist-curators such as Fred Wilson, Michael Nicoll Yahgulanaas, Coco Fusco, and Guillermo Gómez-Peña.[26]

For scholars, curatorial dreaming offers other benefits. The most basic is that exhibitions spur our thinking about local, place-based forms of research dissemination to wide audiences. Curating may provide the best approach to a given question or issue, a unique mode of address, a form of pedagogy, and a means of social intervention that has particular communicative, visceral, and affective qualities that are both meditative and informative, appealing both to our intellects and to our emotions. Further, curating is an opportunity to propose solutions to problems we identify through our own research – problems such as insular memory politics, rigid and essentialist categorizations of human communities, or patterned silences in the telling of history – and an occasion to intervene in public debates about them. Imagining an exhibition can be seen as a form of "constructive criticism" that affirms the underlying hopes, investments, and aspirations that may have drawn scholars into their fields in the first place. The process of curating offers respite from the often closed system – however valuable – of relentless academic critique, and satisfies the desires of many of us to use all our sensory faculties and creative impulses, and take advantage of a variety of public venues, to communicate the fruits of our research and make a tangible difference in the world.

Curatorial dreaming also challenges scholars to consider a range of factors – including materiality, space, emotion, the senses, and sociality – as we translate our work into exhibition form. Anthropologist Mary Bouquet describes the second-order translation inherent in making exhibitions based on anthropological theory – the uniquely generative ways in which theory is manifested beyond text, in objects, images, space, and design. She terms "implicit theory" the serendipitous discovery of new concepts during the concrete, spatial, collaborative process of exhibition making – the recognitions and reactions that can come, for example, from placing two objects next to each other, or the way that the social space of an exhibit can prompt individuals to share private thoughts. While the majority of the curatorial dreams presented here are unrealized, they anticipate connections, collaboration, and conversations with different audiences, communities, and stakeholders. They can also be read as invitations to future collaboration with museums and communities.

When we began this project, we envisioned working with "pure" museology critics and academics who had no previous experience with curating. We wanted contributors to experience a fundamental paradigm shift; the academics would need to set aside their linear models of knowledge dissemination and insert themselves into the complex world of exhibition making, which involves the "bringing together of unlikely assemblages of people, things, ideas, texts, spaces, and different media."[27] But we soon discovered that boundaries between academics and museum practitioners are already blurring, especially in relation to temporary exhibitions and the rise of the independent curator. Artists too are complicating the simple binary model that pits theory against practice, as they curate and create in response to critical theoretical discourse and to specific museum exhibitions and sites. As Irit Rogoff sees it, "the old boundaries between making and theorizing, historicizing and displaying, criticizing and affirming have long been eroded."[28] Some of the contributors to this volume already straddle academic and curatorial positions, or are en route to doing so. As we write this introduction, two of the curatorial dreams presented here have already seen their first iterations as concrete public exhibitions – in the World Trade Organization headquarters in Geneva (George Marcus), and in the Seweryn Udziela Ethnographic Museum in Kraków (Erica Lehrer).[29] While these developments may "contaminate" the purity of our model, they bode well for the productiveness of curatorial dreaming as a more far-reaching project that seeks new pathways for innovative, theoretically informed, and research-oriented exhibition creation.

While our contributors remain academics with primary professional identities as researchers, theorists, teachers, and authors, some of us, it turned out, already had secret lives as curatorial dreamers. While writing her ethnography of *Into the Heart of Africa*, a controversial exhibition about colonialism and collecting, Shelley Ruth Butler had assembled a collage that juxtaposed the imperial nostalgia found in the exhibit's promotional materials with excerpts from *Looking for Livingstone: An Odyssey of Silence* by African Canadian author Marlene NourbeSe Philip. The collage was later published, to suggest how a visual, curatorial intervention might critique ingrained Eurocentric, exclusionary, and authoritative habits of establishment museums.[30] Erica Lehrer, as a student, had created and disseminated reworked tourist materials such as postcards and maps, made from excerpts from her research interviews and photographic data. Her goal was to engage tourists and local residents of her Polish fieldsite in thinking critically about historical memory, and to communicate in a sensory way the complexities of the site to North American colleagues.[31]

Contributor Matti Bunzl confessed a love affair with contemporary art that had led to fieldwork in Chicago's Museum of Contemporary Art, where he curated an exhibit in his head as he "observed the MCA's real curatorial staff conceiving, revising, abandoning, reconceiving, financing, and eventually installing their exhibits."[32] Bunzl's "phantasmic show" is presented in this volume. Finally, we solicited Margaret Lindauer's curatorial dream upon encountering her essay "Critical museum pedagogy and exhibition development: a conceptual first step," in which she had created hypothetical, theoretically informed captions for photos included in *Inventing the Southwest: The Fred Harvey Company and Native American Art* at the Heard Museum in Phoenix, Arizona.[33] Our volume responds to what we identify as a broadly emerging zeitgeist characterized by a sense of peering over ivory tower walls, and a longing to translate, explore, and enact theoretically informed research in public settings.

Curating as Public Scholarship: Collaboration, Research, Pedagogy

From some quarters of the academy a call has been emerging for "public scholarship," or "scholarly or creative activity that joins serious intellectual endeavor with a commitment to public practice and public consequence."[34] Spurred by demands for relevance in higher education – and reflecting the origins of many of the social sciences in practical social issues and reform movements[35] – civically engaged scholars increasingly share a desire to move beyond academic criticism. They want to "give back" – or speak back – to communities with whom they work; they are openly self-reflexive about their personal cultural and political investments not only as scholars but also as members of various communities and publics, which they themselves help constitute; and they see the humanities as encompassing "doing and making as well as thinking."[36] Public scholarship is infused as well by an aspirational quality that is nonetheless critical and political. Accordingly, a notion of social justice informs many of the curatorial dreams in this volume, from Monica Patterson's exhibition of children's art and experience in a South African hospital, to Roger Simon's comparison of geographically and temporally diverse cases of government abuse and neglect of citizens.

A core trend among the present generation of public scholars is to question the directionality of the traditional knowledge production economy. Many challenge the model whereby raw materials are extracted from communities and delivered to the academy to be refined into theory, debated and incorporated into professional discourse. Civically engaged scholars recognize non-academic publics as valuable sources of expertise and as partners in knowledge creation, rather than as passive recipients of expert academic scholarship. In public history programs, for instance, academics acknowledge the "shared authority" they must negotiate with their research subjects.[37] In such a climate, research, pedagogy, and public work are pursued in tandem, and the collaborative project is becoming a new key "unit of knowledge production" in the humanities.[38] Exhibitions are fundamentally collaborative and sociable enterpris lent opportunities for the evolution of many tenets of Because of their arrangement as collectivities of peo social events, and as occasions for merging theory an Bouquet calls exhibitions "the form par excellence t emy and museum."[39] As a mode of mobilizing knowledge, on scholarly research form visible, criticizable traces of research that may implicate diverse publics. This is the premise of Manon Parry's imagined exhibition for the National Library of Medicine outside Washington, DC. While this gallery has moved beyond traditional celebratory exhibitions of medical accomplishments, it has never highlighted science itself as a contested, open-ended process with a spectrum of consequences, and this is precisely what Parry proposes, in order to empower audiences to evaluate science as a social process.

Museums are not, of course, unproblematic public spaces of knowledge production, given their legacies of elitism, paternalism, and social exclusion. Like the academy, museums are "going public" in new ways. With the advent of participatory and "new" museology, visitors are no longer considered passive audiences of didactic, authoritative presentations but are implicated in an ongoing process of knowledge production and debate, and increasingly seen as advisors, stakeholders, collaborators, and co-producers.[40] In this new model, collaboration involves negotiating power relations within and among institutions and communities. How to engage with publics as co-authors of exhibits remains an open and fraught question. Some of our contributors engage with this problematic, but have found it challenging to articulate a concrete curatorial dream for an exhibition envisioned as an ongoing collaborative co-production. Joshua Cohen notes that his proposed exhibition and multimedia performance on Guinean arts is provisional in nature, since "much of the specific archival, thematic, and traditional material to be incorporated into the production is to be determined via a collaborative process between artists, researchers, designers, and other participants ... a definitive description would undermine the project's fundamentally collaborative intent."

Our understanding of an exhibition as both product and process proved to be a conceptual challenge for us as editors too; we respected our contributors' theoretical commitment to process, but pushed them provide specifics. Butler takes a different approach to the problem, anchoring her curatorial dream in a "curatorial collective" – a model she develops as an alternative to community consultation models that risk paternalism.[41] She workshopped a draft of her curatorial dream with colleagues engaged with black history and culture in Canada, and invokes the dialogic nature of that encounter in her text. While it cannot substitute for the future work of a curatorial collective, Butler's textual strategy both highlights and models her collaborative intention, as well as reflexively documenting the exhibition-making process, which will itself be incorporated into the (anticipated) future project.

The "in-betweenness" of scholars who participate in the production of public representations has been noted, and particularly the way they are pulled into unique, sometimes uneasy subject positions from their standpoint between analysis and creation.[42] We see the exhibition as a communicative mode that can accommodate complex understandings of cultural difference and empathy. But public scholars have also learned that they cannot control the ways their exhibitions are received and used in real world cultural and political struggles. Their attempts at subtlety and multi-facetedness may be stymied by individuals or community groups who find more limited, hegemonically formatted representations of culture, history, or identity to be politically expedient.[43] Perhaps we would do well to think of the publicly engaged scholar as a "culture broker" who "enable[s] important transactions, interrelationships, and exchanges ... bring[ing] audiences and culture bearers together so that cultural meanings can be translated and even negotiated" in efforts at social transformation.[44] We believe scholars should work to make their voices heard alongside those of the community groups and corporate entities who currently dominate the field of public cultural representations. Real world politics notwithstanding, we suggest that exhibits can facilitate multifaceted, multi-perspectival communication across social boundaries, create connections among social groups, "seek out and cultivate ambiguity and complexity," and highlight the contingent nature of all claims to authenticity.[45]

If exhibits are, in practical terms, a form of public expression for scholars who hope to reach broad audiences, they can also be potential research tools that make use of auto-ethnographic, crowd-sourced, or other participatory forms of collaboration with their research subjects in the process of generating data. Exhibits are more than just sites to manifest preconceived theory; they can also be arenas for collaborative exploration of new ideas in particular situations with invested publics, a practice that may generate new knowledge for both academic and public purposes. Calls to democratize power relations in practices of research and representation in humanities and social sciences have led some scholars to experiment with the tools of art (particularly new genre public art, installation, and performance) in order to forge new aesthetics of research and "scenarios of practice."[46] Anthropologist George Marcus, for instance, describes how curated spaces might function as experimental research sites; his curatorial intervention at the World Trade Center headquarters, is designed to further his extensive ethnographic fieldwork on the subject of institutional and bureaucratic transparency. The in-situ public exhibition entices employees into exploring the "rules of the game" of diplomacy and trade negotiations. Such an approach rethinks the classic fieldwork "scene of encounter" and the "situated collaborative work" that takes place there.[47] Rather than replicate the standard, naturalistic "observer-observed" paradigm, these jointly created sites and spectacles provide provisional cultural configurations that can be conjured anywhere and subjected to mutual curiosity.[48]

The ability to physically inhabit the kind of "curated arguments" that exhibitions represent allows audiences proximity to scholars' primary objects of analysis, thereby offering the public an active role as co-investigators with multiple viewpoints. Lehrer's exhibition in Kraków (and its virtual afterlife) is designed to bring together potentially conflicting views on the meaning of controversial Jewish figurines. Her research informs the exhibition, but research and exhibition are informed by visitor responses, as real and virtual publics engage with the anthropologist curator, with each other, and with the figurines and the various ways in which they have been framed in different historical periods and by different constituencies. Exhibitions such as this one, which contain built-in research and self-documentation components, also give museum scholars an opportunity to substantiate (or disconfirm) increasingly common claims that museums can help communities "confront and counter prejudices, engender support for human rights and promote respect between communities."[49]

The dreams presented in this volume express optimism about engaging audiences in critical and relational thinking about histories of exclusion and legacies of the past, and – going a step further – in recruiting and engaging audiences as co-producers of knowledge for display. A number of our contributors develop curatorial strategies designed to move audiences to positions of empathy, historical or cultural interconnectedness, political critique, and concern about human rights abuses and colonial exploitation. Audiences are also given opportunities to publicly share their opinions and respond to specific questions that arise from an exhibition.

In our selection of projects, readers will recognize biases that reflect our sense of what counts as important, publicly engaged work. The collection also reveals our disciplinary orientations. All our contributors are engaged in interdisciplinary research that addresses contemporary cultural and political issues, and many are committed to explicit pedagogical concerns that are apparent in the exhibitions they envision. Our respective engagements with public history, "difficult knowledge," and community work are also evident; the curatorial dreams here address legacies of AIDS (Hernández), dictatorships in Chile and Argentina (Olivares and Gomoll, Simon), colonial violence in North America (Lindauer, Simon), the Chernobyl nuclear explosion (Simon), and contemporary racisms, prejudices, and inequalities (Bhimull, Butler, Iervolino and Sandall, Lehrer, Lindauer, Patterson). While there is a heaviness to these materials, many of the imagined exhibits immerse visitors in stories of resilience and creativity in the face of hardship.

The curatorial decisions behind these dreamed exhibitions have been carefully designed to activate and inhabit history in ethical ways. In some instances those decisions involve addressing "archival silences"[50] and providing alternatives to narratives of progress that are the purview of traditional museums. But discourses and acts of resistance are subtle, specific, and sometimes contradictory. Lisette Olivares and Lucian Gomoll, for instance, in their curatorial dream of re-conjuring numerous ways that a folkloric dance has been activated as a tool for public mourning and resistance in Chile, demonstrate the importance of respecting various actors' self-understandings, using juxtaposition to create a layered sense of the different agents, subjects, and meanings potentially involved.

Yet there is a countercurrent in the volume that resists the pedagogical impulse and disciplining effects of scholarship – these chapters propose exhibitions that valorize curiosity, wonder, and affect. While seeking to present Guinean arts in a manner attentive to political and social history, Joshua Cohen strives to protect the Guinean arts he curates from being reduced to an emotionally flat "social sciences" project. Matti Bunzl refuses "normative" critical museology in another way. His deconstruction of how value is conferred on contemporary art stops short of didactically exposing and explaining these elitist framings for visitors. As editors we pushed for a clearer exposé of the economically self-interested system of the art world, asking for signposts that would lead visitors to understand how authenticity, quality, and fame are produced by and for a moneyed elite. Bunzl resisted our democratizing impulse, and his curatorial dream consequently has a trickster quality that sits somewhat askew of the implicit ethic of the larger volume. He valorizes open-ended visitor experiences of excitement, curiosity, and exploration, but his critique of the discourse of an insider art world is ironic in tone, rather than revelatory. Janice Baker's exhibit also works against long-standing traditions of visitor edification. Her curatorial dream immerses museum-goers in a fantastical shadow-side of museums and the potential of hidden forces latent in their objects, envisioned here as running amok. Her dream is to create affecting encounters between visitors and artifacts in the gallery via the projection of films that themselves evoke transgressive scenes of chaos and carnival in museums. While the exhibition is accessible for a general audience who will be tickled by encounters with favourite movie moments, it simultaneously enacts a critique of the academy's anthropocentric and rationalistic approach to the value of museums and collections.

Finally, we envision curatorial dreaming as a pedagogical strategy for the classroom. As teachers, we have both made use of the method in our courses, in the context of in-class exercises and exams, as well as having students develop curatorial dreams over the course of a semester. We take inspiration from literary scholar Michael Rothberg's course assignment that provokes students to recognize the stakes of memory and cultural production by way of a Holocaust memorial design task that puts them in the position of "active participants in the construction of knowledge" rather than analysts of manifestations of it.[51] Questions invariably arise regarding which groups to include among the victims, where to place the memorial, the extent to which genocide can be visually represented, and what meanings might be taken away.

The Exhibits

Our curatorial dreams are presented in four parts. We begin outside museum walls to signal our commitment to thinking about curating in the broadest terms. Part One of the book, "Curating in the Vernacular," focuses on curatorial interventions that anthropologists have envisioned for their research sites. These projects question "the written word as the locus of anthropological knowledge,"[52] and make use of everyday spaces, attentive to the resonance of local landscapes and the power of commonplace artifacts to transmit and reinforce cultural meanings. Inspired by the recent proliferation of analytical and creative engagements that examine and blur the boundaries of art and anthropology, our contributors to this section use curatorial techniques to intervene in the flow of local social life, reframe workaday settings, or connect museum galleries to broader spaces in the city.

Making Transparency Visible by George Marcus uses the sober headquarters of the World Trade Organization to display its own (partially screened) internal documents, with the goal of drawing employees into reflexive organizational analysis. In *Most Disturbing Souvenirs* Lehrer explores whether ethnonationalist legacies of a traditional nineteenth-century ethnographic museum may be destabilized by linking objects and narratives in and outside the museum, using curatorial practices like highlighting, framing, and juxtaposition to reconsider quotidian landscapes – like shops in Kraków that sell Jewish figurines – in new ways. These curatorial dreams re-imagine public institutions and urban sites as display spaces, transforming their everyday occupants into accidental audiences.

Public spaces such as airports and hospitals are powerful sites for exploring inequalities embedded in taken-for-granted middle class life experiences like travel and health care. *The Alchemy of Flight* by Chandra Bhimull is a multimedia, multi-sensory exhibition about airline travel in the African diaspora, whose power derives from its location in the Grantley Adams International Airport in Barbados. Not your typical promotional airport exhibit, this curatorial dream is a concrete, critical response to the celebratory "Barbados Concorde Experience" exhibition-cum-shrine housed in a hangar beside the airport. Inspired by literature and oral narratives, *The Alchemy of Flight* provokes in-situ reflection on race, history, mobility, and freedom. Monica Patterson's *By and For Children*, situated in a children's hospital museum in Durban, South Africa, explores interconnections between children's health and legacies of apartheid. Recognizing the value of varied expertise, the exhibit includes the participation of children and families, social scientists, and community health professionals. It traces a careful line between critical history and the imperative of healing for its primary audience of sick children.

Part Two proposes art installations that take us into specific cultural worlds. These include Chicano avant-garde art, contemporary Guinean art and performance, and the production, circulation, and reception of contemporary, global-elite conceptual art. We call this section "Breaking Frames"; while treating very different substantive topics, each curatorial dream is fuelled by a desire to push the limits of "the gallery." These chapters in turn: interrogate the selective way in which Chicano art has been canonized in recent years in the United States by excluding histories of AIDS; engage with the problematic history of categorizing African arts according to Western disciplinary boundaries that separate dance, music and fine art; and highlight the tacit rules and insider codes that govern the seemingly pluralistic, democratic field of relational aesthetics and contemporary conceptual art.

Frozen World/Mundo Congelado by Robb Hernández begins at the Los Angeles County Museum of Art, or more precisely, in a trailer stationed outside the gallery. Influenced by postmodernism, Hernández's exhibition space "quotes" other examples of activist, mobile galleries created to promote cultural preservation and community-based protest. His curatorial dream is an intimate, restorative exhibition about Mundo Mezo, a gay Chicano avant-garde conceptual artist whose oeuvre was confiscated and possibly destroyed by his family following his death from AIDS. Against this destruction, Hernández affirms the etymological link between curating and "caring for," tracing Meza's life and art through photos, newspapers, paintings, ephemera, and oral histories. Informed by queer theory, the project explores archival practices that can illuminate alternative sexual identities and practices.

A similar institutional problem of selective inclusion shapes *The Play* by Joshua Cohen. His title cites a culturally specific Guinean practice of referring to dance and music performances as "play places." Cohen combines the roles of curator and theatre director, twinning a gallery and a theatrical staging space to point toward the kind of multi-sensory, multimedia performative context that brings Guinean masks alive by their users in Guinea and in the diaspora. Familiar binary classifications such as indigenous versus international, and visual versus performing arts are destabilized.

Classification is also at stake in Matti Bunzl's playful exposé of art conventions. In But Is It Art?: *Not Really*, each display copies a piece or installation by a famous conceptual artist, including, among others, Andy Warhol and Rirkrit Tiravanija. We appreciate Bunzl's combination of passion for and puzzlement by conceptual art; perhaps his intervention will vindicate anyone who has felt alienated by its contemporary codes of appreciation.[53]

Part Three, "Activating Art and History," explores how we might curate materials that participate – and implicate viewers – in painful histories of racism, government neglect of human rights, hatred, and genocide. The challenges of curating such "difficult knowledge" have in recent years been the subject of a growing field of scholarly interest that has addressed the subject on macro and micro levels, from memorial and human rights museums, exhibits about genocide, and the development of "sites of conscience" to the possibilities and challenges of looking at disturbing photographs or listening to troubling eye-witness testimonies.[54] Silke Arnold-de Simine notes that "museums – especially but not exclusively those that are privately funded – need their customers to approve of the exhibition rather than feel challenged beyond their comfort zone."[55] But as confidence in the transparency of memory and its promises as an ethical and political panacea have dwindled,[56] new curatorial strategies are being sought that might create sites of reconciliation, empathy, and a sense of implication or unsettledness, or inspire action.[57] It can be a tough balance, as museums that have opened the door to democratization must address multiple audiences with many different historical experiences at once. Discussing attempts to curate in critical, reflexive ways, Butler has emphasized that "the experience of viewing ... exhibitions should not be alienating for people who have personal and political ties with the histories of objectification and exclusion carried out by the very institutions we seek to transform."[58] Yet what may be most difficult about "difficult knowledge" is its uneven distribution: the pain caused by history and its traces is not universally shared – either across group boundaries or uniformly within them, across time, as sentiments shift even within individuals.[59] Given the diversity of audiences, what risks should one take? How to curate "between hope and despair" or between "critical" and "optimistic" museology?[60] Contributors to this section engage contested historical records, memories, and artistic productions that respond to legacies of political repression in Chile and Argentina, colonialism in the United States and Canada, and government abuses in the aftermath of Chernobyl.

For *Intervention/Resurrection* Lisette Olivares and Lucian Gomoll curate multiple performances of *La Cueca*, a traditional folkloric partner dance used by Pinochet's regime in Chile and re-appropriated by artists and activists as *La Cueca Sola*, a solitary version that involves mothers of the disappeared who transformed it into an act of public mourning. This curatorial dream traces culturally specific, intergenerational community and artistic responses to political crises, as well as intimate questions of identity. In *The Terrible Gift*, Roger Simon brings together archival materials and artistic productions pertaining to the Chernobyl nuclear explosion of 1986, the forced relocation of Inuit to the High Arctic in the 1950s, and political repression during the Argentine dictatorship between 1976 and 1983. His is a bold experiment in exploring how dispersed difficult histories might confront each other without misreading or reducing any of them. His comparative method avoids authoritative didacticism by using databases to enable visitors to explore deeply, cross-referencing and connecting divergent materials.

Recognizing the power of place, Margaret Lindauer situates *Reading the World* at the Fort Sumner Historic Monument in New Mexico, once a US military site where thousands of Navajo were imprisoned in the 1860s. Inspired by critical pedagogy, Lindauer juxtaposes archival images, artifacts, and film to investigate how Navajo and others make sense of a history of dispossession. Her exhibition explores the contradictions in the ways some Navajo have negotiated and even thrived in contemporary contexts of tourism and uranium mining. To create a dialogic atmosphere, Lindauer experiments with a curatorial strategy of posing questions, as opposed to using didactic exhibition panels.

In Part Four, "Establishments Revisioned," authors' imagined exhibitions infiltrate "the belly of the beast" in monumental, establishment museums such as the Tropenmuseum in Amsterdam, the Royal Ontario Museum in Toronto, the National Library of Medicine in Washington, and the Western Australian Museum in Perth. In the wake of three decades of critical museological theory, shifting demographics, and evolving social ideals, some establishment museums are striving to re-invent themselves as they compete with other educational and entertainment venues for limited resources and visitor attention. These curatorial dreams are thus articulated not so much in opposition to establishment museums as in conversation with their own efforts at democratization and reform. Serena Iervolino and Richard Sandell's *The World in One City* is staged in the famous Tropenmuseum, a colonial-era ethnographic museum of "the Tropics" that has itself undergone a decades-long process of reflexive transformation in light of the post-colonial critiques and demographic changes in Amsterdam due to historical and contemporary migration. Building on the museum's commitment to resisting established dichotomies of self and other, and in response to contemporary local Islamophobia, *The World in One City* is notable for its proposed use of diverse forms of expertise – a social worker, a filmmaker, an urban anthropologist, local artists, immigrants, and migrant workers – in order to evoke and enact aspects of everyday life in the city. The museum is to be transformed into an activist-oriented forum, a reflective dwelling space, and a dialogic salon. Butler's *Museum without Walls* takes a related approach in its examination of the Royal Ontario Museum. Both exhibitions take place in major urban centres with colonial pasts and post-colonial presents, and both rely on the power of personal encounters in museum spaces. *Museum without Walls* is a collaborative curatorial project that invokes the alienation that black Canadians experienced over two decades ago in response to the museum's famously controversial exhibition *Into the Heart of Africa*. But the project also responds to the contemporary marginalization experienced by black Canadians, and attempts to present the African gallery as part of contemporary Canadian culture. Guided by facilitators, youth participants inhabit the Canadian and African galleries in unconventional and creative ways, to generate ideas and images on the themes of belonging and exclusion.

The aim of the two final curatorial dreams in this section is to create engaging and affecting encounters in venerable nineteenth-century scientific institutions. In *abNormal: Bodies in Medicine and Culture*,

Manon Parry addresses the question: Who decides what is normal and what factors inform that decision? The exhibition explores scientific representations of gendered and racialized bodies, the medicalization of homosexuality, and the construction of disability, relating them all to social inequality. In a departure from display conventions of medical museums, audiences are given opportunities to respond personally to content, explore views of other visitors, comment on current trends, and use art and mass media materials to deconstruct and reconstitute popular and scientific images of bodies. Such individualized engagement is also the approach of Janice Baker's curatorial dream, *Reel Objects,* a cinematic installation staged in the monumental, dramatic Hackett Hall at the Western Australian Museum. *Reel Objects* immerses visitors in a non-linear, anarchic, and playful cinematic environment that reveals objects and things as being "out of place" in museum spaces. The intervention emphasizes affective, carnivalesque, macabre, and transgressive qualities of museums and their collections. The adoring responses to Christian Marclay's 2010 travelling cinematic art installation *The Clock* suggest there is a niche for exhibitions that immerse audiences in reverie, far removed from didactic categories or critical analysis.[61] Museums, like history, can be inhabited and activated in unpredictable ways.

Curator and cultural critic Barbara Kirshenblatt-Gimblett concurs. Her reflections, which close the volume, evoke the liberating possibilities of curatorial dreaming, as she remembers childhood reveries at the Royal Ontario Museum, and finds solace in imagination in her multiple perches in Polish public institutions, whether state-run hospital bed or state-of-the-art museum.

We have proposed an itinerary through *Curatorial Dreams* that is organized by sites – vernacular terrains, art galleries, commemorative spaces, and establishment museums. There are other ways to traverse this constellation of imaginary exhibitions. Close attention to participatory museology and audience engagement, for instance, could link contributions across these sections, as could themes such as critical race theory and inequality, intercultural dialogue, multi-vocal interpretation, healing, activism, and social critique. We leave this work of path finding and interpretation to you, the first audience for our gallery of curatorial dreams.

PART ONE

Curating in the Vernacular

CHAPTER ONE

Making Transparency Visible: Centre William Rappard, Headquarters of the World Trade Organization, Geneva

GEORGE E. MARCUS

My curatorial dream originates in the substantial challenges of conducting ethnographic fieldwork at the World Trade Organization (WTO). It should be understood primarily as an experiment in ethnographic method, inspired by the imagination and practices of installation artists. My exhibition design is thus the plan for a kind of machine to elicit what ethnographers most seek from those among whom they work: engaged thought and interpretations of the latters' own conditions. The artist is perhaps interested in something similar and even shares an ethnographer-like curiosity in designing site-specific installations, but artists' installations, in my view, tend to be more oriented to spectacle, broader publics, and perhaps transcendent values.[1] My installation uses ethnographic insight to produce more of the same by actually generating the kind of material and interactions that tried and proven participant observation fails to provide in the tightly controlled diplomatic and bureaucratic culture of the WTO. It creates art in aid of ethnography, and in so doing, has value for both.

The WTO, with 159 nation-state members, is a key international organization that furthers a vision of global governance through the encouragement of free trade. It emerged in 1995 out of the GATT (General Agreement on Tariffs and Trade) arrangements that followed the Second World War, and has been a centre of controversy ever since its founding;

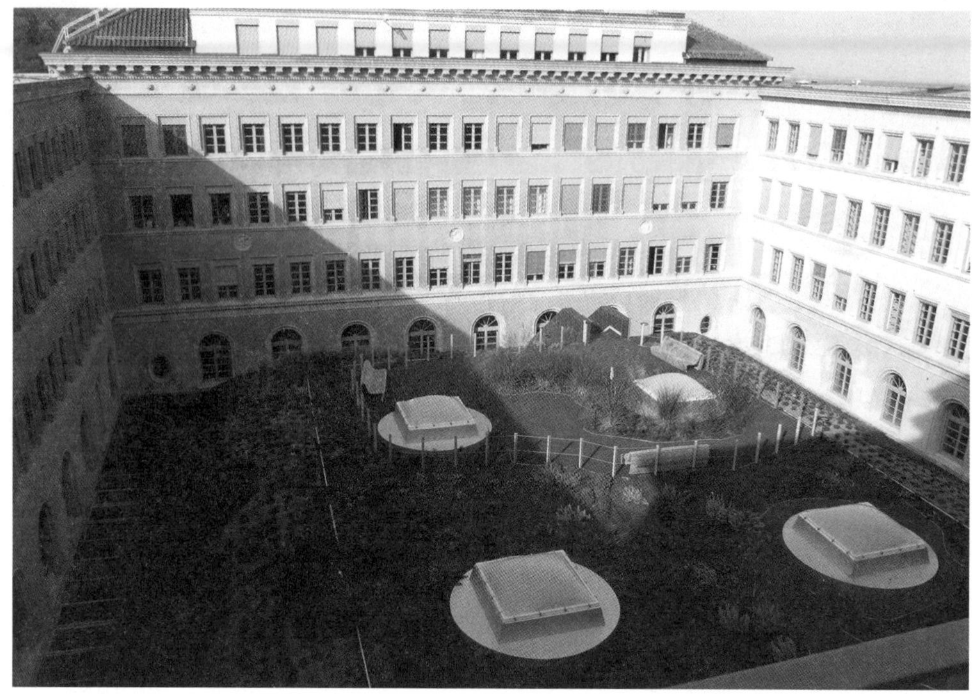

1.1 | The interior courtyard of the Centre William Rappard.

its ministerial meetings have attracted mass, and sometimes violent anti-globalization demonstrations, most dramatically in Seattle, 1999. A self-governing organization with several divisions, its administration is overseen by a secretariat of six to seven hundred diplomats, lawyers, economic researchers, and staff, under a director-general who, between 2005 and 2013, was the prominent French technocrat and previous economic minister of the European Union, Pascal Lamy. The secretariat is housed in the Centre William Rappard, a classical Florentine-style villa built in 1923, perched majestically over Lac Léman in Geneva (see figures 1.1 and 1.2). The building first housed the International Labour Organization (ILO) during the League of Nations period, then the GATT, and now the WTO.

The WTO has had a record of mixed success, and certainly has aroused much self-doubt, especially over the past decade, as it has been unable to resolve the Doha Development Round (DDR) despite repeated efforts.[2]

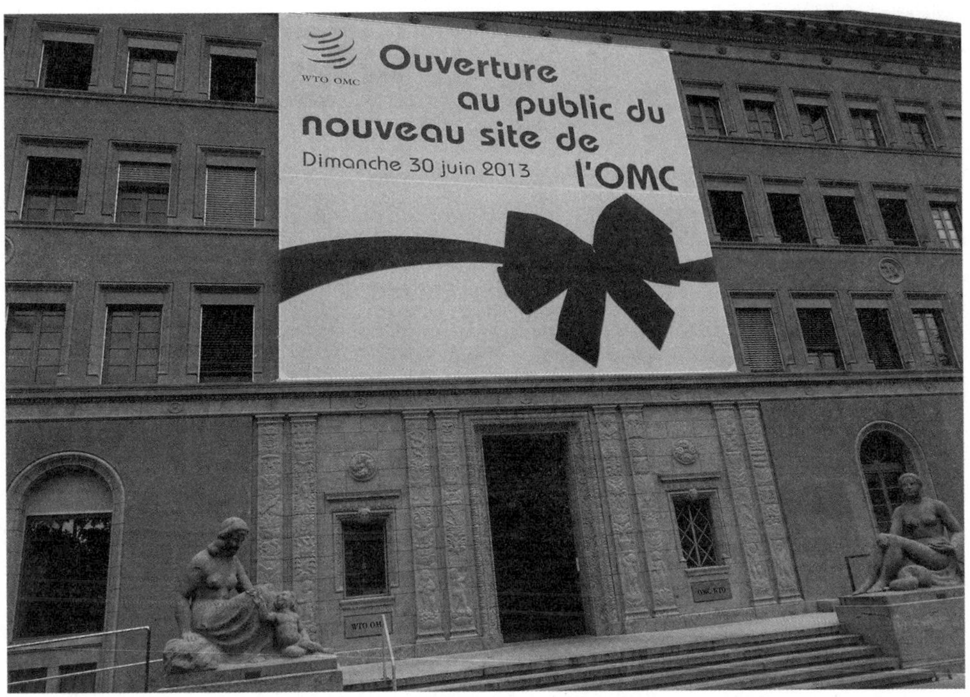

1.2 | The remodelled entrance to the Centre William Rappard.

Initiated in 2001 in Doha, Qatar, the DDR was intended to set goals for a new phase of global trade agreements that would address – for the first time – questions of development and North-South inequalities in the world trading system. Long dominated by European powers, and especially the United States (English is the WTO's official language, and some are impressed by the British "feel" of the everyday life of the secretariat bureaucracy), WTO processes are now complicated by a vastly expanded membership, including new and rising economic powers such as Brazil, India, and China.

The WTO has a well-functioning judiciary to resolve trade disputes regulated by previous agreements. But forward movement on new major agreements – the basis of the organization's perceived prestige – has been frustratingly slow, as it depends on achieving consensus around one issue at a time; Lamy once famously called the WTO's deliberative procedures "medieval." In the hope that anthropology might have insights to offer regarding the organization's internal workings, Lamy invited Professor Marc Abélès of the École des Hautes Études en Sciences Sociales in Paris to join an international team that he would recruit, to undertake ethnographic research at the WTO headquarters.

The research took place from 2008 through 2010, a period of increasing concern about the relevance and future of the organization.[3] In 2009 a major ministerial meeting took place at the WTO headquarters to resolve the Doha Round with new agreements, but it failed. During the severe world economic recession, with its precipitous drop in trade, the WTO was very much on the sidelines. During the period of our research, a certain evolution seemed inevitable; an organization that had focused on narrow economic subjects in its work of negotiation, regulation, and expert advice was challenged to address and encourage virtually unlimited areas of social concern. We observed the WTO's efforts, for instance, to connect issues of trade to global climate change, a domain that had generally been the purview of NGOs.

The effects of WTO rules and agreements are experienced throughout the world in virtually all areas of trade, including intellectual property and pharmaceuticals. Negotiations – as well as the less visible background work of lawyers, ministers, staff, interested parties, and delegations – occur in a variety of venues around Geneva. Yet in the Centre William Rappard – the focus of the organization's activities and the site that sets its mood – very little appears to be going on. Its labyrinth of identical offices, conference rooms, and rather gloomy open spaces formed the *mise-en-scène* of our ethnographic inquiries. Despite a schedule of constant meetings, conferences, and delegation visits, the atmosphere does not crackle with news or gossip (so much the worse for the anthropologist bred on village studies!). Private meetings, the production of reports in offices, coffee breaks – and smoking – are routine. Yet, negotiations go on continuously, decisions are made daily that affect the movements of goods and services throughout the world. So where, in such a milieu, can a participant observer find a foothold?

Each researcher specialized in an area of WTO operations of his or her own choosing. We had unusual access to WTO activities, but by no means carte blanche; attendance at moments of actual negotiation was off limits. We had to learn to read the organization through its other modes of self-presentation, however self-consciously minimalist, in order to master trade issues for their social and political implications, to cultivate relationships with certain subjects, and to appeal to their own reflective, ethnographer-like curiosities and insights about their work culture.[4] Most of the researchers made periodic visits to the WTO lasting from several days to two weeks; two took up residence in Geneva and were on-site at the Villa Rappard for a year. I chose to focus on the operations of the director-general's office, and the sources of its real, apparent, and limited powers (as defined by the WTO charter).

No topic has been of more general importance to our research – as well as to the WTO's public- and self-image – than that of transparency. Indeed, since the end of the Cold War and the spread of neoliberal principles of corporate organization, transparency has become an explicit "best practice" for all formal organizations, public and private, as both a performance and a measure of their accountability and virtue. This is particularly true for high-profile international organizations and regulatory agencies. Transparency as a term or concept connotes an absolute quality – outsiders to organizations should be able to see their internal workings, and internal actors should see their organization's own range of activities with full clarity. But the reality is that the performance of transparency takes place in a context of veiled institutional cultures based on discretion, secrecy, and tacit assumptions about everyday operations in which insiders are complicit. Transparency doctrines meet particular challenges in diplomatic institutions where trust depends as much on carefully modulated secrecy and discretion in the negotiations phase as on compliance with complete openness and visibility in regulatory oversight once agreements are reached.

In the interests of transparency, the WTO makes an immense amount of documentation available on its website; symbolically, the doors to its many offices along its corridors are always left open, even on weekends; and despite security monitoring of all who enter and leave the building, one does not feel surveilled once inside. Given the stakes of trade agreements for everyday lives across the globe, the WTOis motivated to fulfill "best practices" of transparency. But given its diplomatic habits of work and its role in encouraging the progress of negotiations and managing disputes, the boundaries of transparency and its performance of "best practices" must be constantly and deeply qualified. There is a politics to the everyday workings of the organization that requires exclusions and deceptions.

In contrast to the openness of the building, the entrance to the director-general's suite is controlled by an attendant. Within this suite is the space, both symbolic and actual, of secrecy in the organization. Into an elegantly appointed chamber, known as the Green Room – reputedly named for the offstage, intimate spaces in theatres where actors await their call to performance – select trade representatives are called to hash out and struggle over the details of agreements, in all-day-and-all-night sessions presided over by the director-general, who during stalled moments calls particular parties to his private office for one-on-one consultations, referred to as "confessionals." In organizational terms and to the public looking on, the Green Room symbolizes the opposite of transparency. Yet among the most powerful inner circle, it is the place of intimate displays of ultimate transparency.[5]

To excluded insiders, the public, and anti-global critics of the WTO, these norms and ethics are suspect. It is a short step from the assumption and acceptance of professionally practised discretion and secrecy to the popular perception of conspiracy.[6] The promise of transparency, its performance, and its qualification at the WTOhas been a deeply salient bind for our project's ethnographers as well; we have been invited inside by its head, but at every turn we have had to negotiate a bureaucratic culture more committed to secrecy and to the diplomat's professional norms of discretion than to transparency. Not irrelevantly, as participant observers, we also desired a kind of transparency, in the sense of being present while being invisible.[7]

Making Transparency Visible

My imagined exhibition takes place in the open halls of the Centre William Rappard, using the site itself to make visible and explicit the boundaries between transparency, its opposites, and its qualifications in the operations of the WTO administration. This exhibition is open to a curious and perhaps suspicious public as well as to those who work in the building and who enter and leave it on business. On the one hand, the exhibition materializes ethnographic data and curiosity about the lived and closely observed relationships – sometimes contradictory, sometimes not – among full, partial, and suppressed exposures of activity in this organization. And on the other, it develops a function of critique and self-critique by provoking explicit discussion and assessment of issues around the question of transparency.[8] WTO personnel are more than willing to qualify and nuance in interviews and conversations any simple ideal of "pure" transparency, but this exhibition makes them look (literally) more closely and reflexively at their own practices. Institutionally, the WTO is by design not a very reflexive organization – it does not have self-probing conferences, nor has it paid much attention to writing about itself. While its bookstore displays a voluminous literature on the WTO of the technical and passionately polemical varieties, little of it seems to have made an impression on its internal actors. My hope is that an installation in the midst of the organization's daily goings-on might more viscerally elicit what reports, meetings, studies (including perhaps the one that we will produce) do not. For the WTO project ethnographers, the imagined exhibit is an experiment in delivering the results of our research through engaged response, produced in the scene of fieldwork, by other than the usual textual means.[9]

The WTO ethnography and my imagined exhibition build upon and integrate my past lines of research. My work on dynastic lineages of wealth[10] led me into art connoisseurship and collecting as a marked interest and legacy of dynastic wealth. At the same time, I have been involved with the study of genres of cultural description, analysis, and expression – especially ethnography.[11] At the intersection of art, anthropology, and ethnography,[12] I have become especially interested in forms of ethnographic representation and performance, and their parallels in art genres.[13] Yet, despite various resonances with my past ethnographic and theoretical work, *Making Transparency Visible* is most inspired by artworks of a similar nature, including Hans Haacke's critical installations on corporate capitalism and Neil Cummings and Marysia Lewandowska's installations at the Bank of England and the Tate Modern.[14]

If the Villa Rappard were not the WTO headquarters, it could easily be home to a museum or art exhibition space; further along the lake on the path toward downtown Geneva there are similar buildings that have become museums, such as the Museum of Science and Technology. Indeed, in a recent project with a critical edge similar to my own,

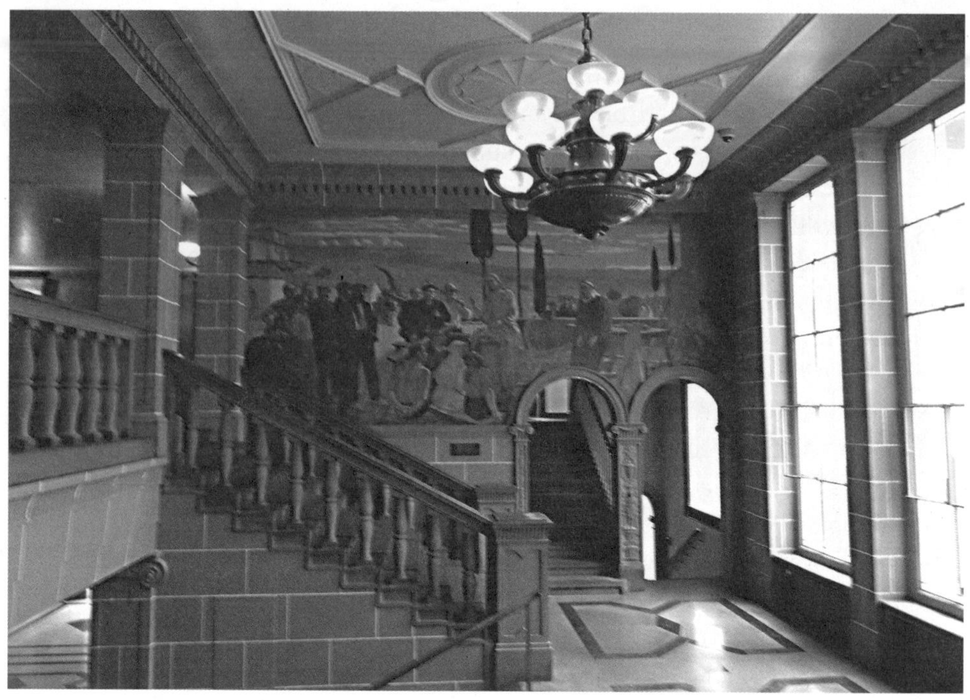

1.3 | A typical hallway with mural panels in the Centre William Rappard.

one of Pascal Lamy's two *chefs de cabinet*, a Brazilian career diplomat responsible for personnel and internal relations at the WTO as one of his assignments, supported the uncovering and restoration of several large murals, paintings, and tiled panels that had adorned the building during its earlier ILO, League of Nations existence, but had been obscured or dismantled in various renovations and additions over time. These works of art are now on display in the open interior, which was previously devoid of artworks (see figures 1.3 and 1.4); their novelty, along with the publication of an attractive pamphlet on the works, gives the space the air of an exhibition.[15]

The reasons for the removal and obscuring of this artwork over time are ambiguous, and it is unclear how much of an intentional provocation their reinstatement was meant to be (or, of course, how much attention is paid to them by daily passersby). But given that the conditions of labour are their key theme, their re-emergence in the heart of an organization

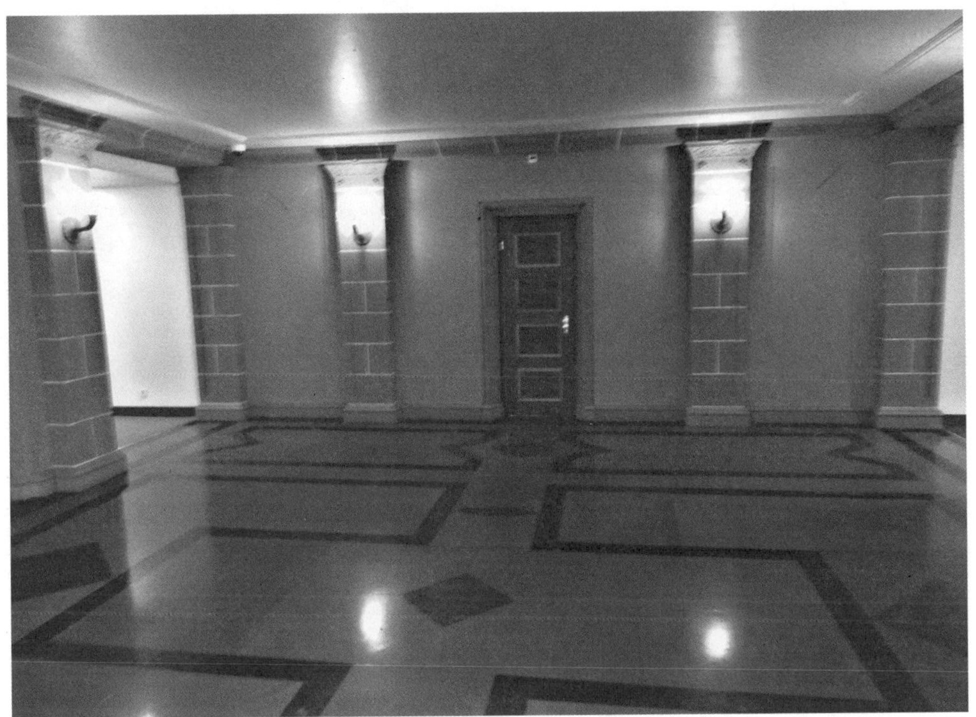

1.4 | An unadorned hallway of the Centre William Rappard.

devoted to the idea of free trade seems consistent with the WTO's current broadening of its concerns to include such topics as the inequalities and social displacements generated in part by free trade rules and policies. The *chef de cabinet*, it seems safe to say, had at minimum a rather playful sense of the murals' critical potential.[16] Like much in the spirit of WTO transparency, they have meanings that hide in plain sight.

Making Transparency Visible is situated in relationship to these artworks, to heighten and extend their mundanely subversive act of transparency. It is not a thematic relationship that I am seeking (although such associations may suggest themselves to viewers); my goal is to concentrate and enhance critical attention through the ambience of these locally novel representational forms. Mounting an installation in front of the murals might, for example, focus new attention on them on the part of building denizens and visitors; one or two displays might be situated in front of the Gustave-Louis Jaulmes murals in the Salle des Pas-Perdus

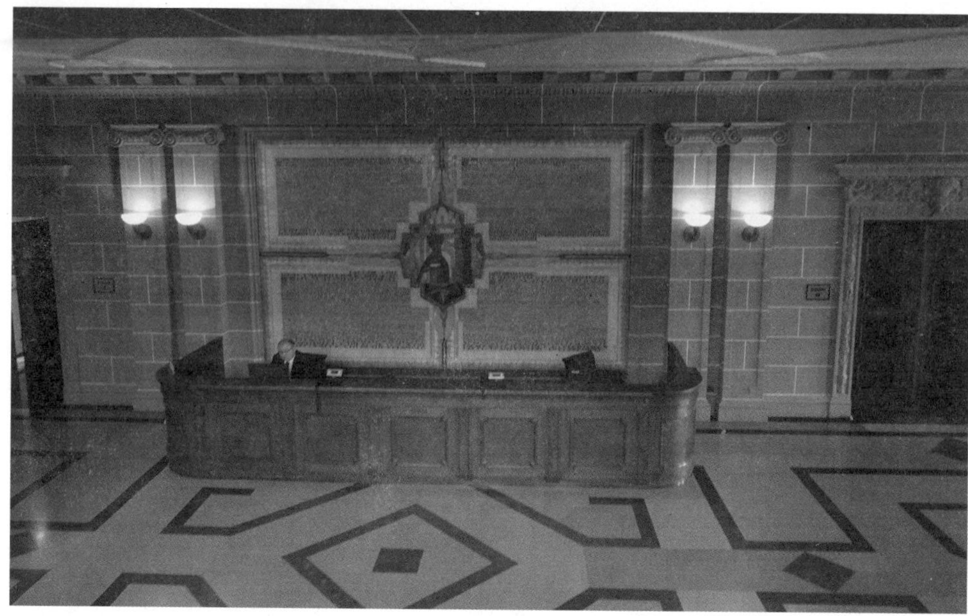

1.5 | The Delft Panel in the interior of the Centre William Rappard.

in the coffee bar area of the ground floor of the Villa Rappard, while others would be placed in proximity to Maurice Denis's *The Dignity of Labour* and the Delft panel (see note 5) that hangs in the foyer across from the large staircase of the building (see figure 1.5). If the murals communicate something critical about the WTO's role in the world, the installations are designed to draw this critique closer to home, and to focus on the internal conditions of the WTO process and experience itself. The gamble is that the juxtaposition of the two forms of art would heighten each of them in the act of viewing. But the installation also defines its own puzzles about the transparent, the opaque, and the shadows that surround the WTO.

Installation Design

The imagined WTO installation places assemblages of objects and images behind vertical plastic panels that act as screens of varying degrees of transparency: from clear to translucent to opaque. Individual screen panels are embedded with areas that magnify what is visible, or create degrees of shading and subtle gradations of blurring. The norm of organizational transparency that prevails at the WTO is thus probed by producing variations on literal, material transparency – or its opposite. Acts of viewing take place, as noted above, in relation to wall art (murals, paintings) that constitutes a deliberate, if ambiguously critical project of restoration and exposure. Viewers look through large panels of perhaps nine feet by four feet, arranged singly or in series of two or three depending on their content.

A key communicative effect of the design hinges on the variable transparency of the screens, making particular "scenarios" (single documents, photographs, objects, or images, or combinations thereof) easy, difficult, or impossible to see. The attention and curiosity of the viewer (who might otherwise pass the installation with little notice as she often passes the murals or, indeed, electronic bulletin boards) will be captured by varying the difficulty or ease of viewing what is behind the screens, as well as by unpredictably changing the scenarios behind the screens from one week to the next. This process is designed ideally to keep CWR workers, staff, and regular visitors attuned to the exhibit, and increase the amount of corridor and coffee break conversation about it and the issues of transparency it raises.

The exhibit will be on site for two to three months – to be extended if there were demand – and on an ad hoc schedule the scenarios and contents behind the screens will be shifted among the display sites as well as exchanged for surplus materials. Some of the shifts and changes will be made in direct response to discussions, reactions, and comments that arise among viewers. The goal, as noted, is for spectators, especially those who inhabit the building or visit it repeatedly, to develop an interest in the screens and a habit of looking through them as they pass, to satisfy their curiosity about what has been altered.

If feasible, an anonymous committee will meet periodically – perhaps on weekends when the building is usually deserted – to plan and make the ongoing shifts in the behind-screen scenarios, as well as to adjust the arrangement of the screens themselves. The committee will be composed of members of the ethnographic team from whose research this project arises, in collaboration with WTO personnel with whom we have worked, and who have developed their own appetite for critical, reflexive ethnography in their conversations with the anthropologists. Having insiders and outsiders collaborate on the design would suggest more general (if experimental) standards for other projects of institutional reflexivity, in the name of art (and culture) – a pursuit that the austere WTO seems to open to modestly entertaining at this juncture in its history.

In the interests of the experimental probing of the norms of transparency, this curatorial committee might devise and present a scenario of its own "behind the scenes" work during the final phase of the exhibit. The meta-message of this gesture would serve as a reminder that any regime of transparency, even as it comments centrally on the norm of transparency itself, is entwined with a regime of opacity. The dynamics behind the scenes of the exhibit would also be disclosed in a final reflexive act.

The exhibition has two constituencies in mind: those who work at the WTO and pass through on business, and the general public. The more sustained and engaged constituency for the proposed exhibit is the WTO staff, who pass by daily, and whose interest in it will be sustained by the ad hoc changing of the scenarios behind the plastic screens. It will also attract and engage the interest of the lawyers, delegations, and personnel from trade ministries around Geneva who depend on the organization's culture of discretion, formal, normative transparency, and the swirl of gossip and rumour around it, to conduct their affairs.

During the second half of 2009, two events highlighted the "general public" constituency of the WTO. Normally, the WTO is not a tourist or visitor destination (though one of our researchers who was studying the circumstances of China's accession to the WTO noted that Chinese tourists liked to come to the WTO and have their photographs taken outside the gate). However, in anticipation of a local decision to be made by the Geneva city government to allow the WTO to further expand its quarters, the previously mentioned Brazilian *chef de cabinet* arranged an "open house" to the community on a particular weekend. The doors and grounds were opened, and over five hundred citizens of Geneva wandered through. The *chef* reported that it was a great success (and shortly thereafter, city authorities granted the permit to build). Even on workdays, there is not much action, activity, or "atmosphere" at the WTO. Certainly there is not much to see (other than the artwork). When "action" occurs, it is more likely to happen outside the gates: at the end of November 2009, a few months after the open house, there was a mass demonstration in front of the WTO along with some rioting on nearby Geneva streets, as trade representatives from across the globe converged for one of the periodic "ministerials" at the Centre William Rappard.

In line with halting moves within the WTO administration to make itself more open to a general public, and as a self-interested performance of transparency designed to counter its longer-standing function as a rallying point for international activism, the proposed exhibition will be accompanied by a promotional campaign to encourage visits by local and tourist publics. The transparency theme is a sophisticated, ironic element in this campaign, in the spirit of art or installation exhibits in general.

Scenarios

Finally, then, what of the content behind the screens? Conceptually, the configurations of objects and images that make up the scenarios are intended to suggest the following twists: secrets that are not really secret but are sustained as such by deeply ingrained habits of discretion; self-conscious replaying of agreements and negotiations; the circulation of key documents (but not others) as performative acts of transparency; the politics of strategic or tactical disclosure that both trumps and demonstrates transparency; the demand for formal transparency as a violation of, or pressure on, public secrets (the economy of knowing what not to know and articulate). The installation suggests in visual or material terms that these features of social action accrue around the current formal norm of transparency at the WTO. The physicality and visuality of the installation mode, I argue, is unique in its capacity to illustrate the multiple ways in which transparency is ideally an embedded and sustained process rather than merely a symbolic act, a ritual, or a performance. Further, this form of communication can complicate, while still making legible, the complex embedded ethics of accountability that the idea of transparency as a norm and policy of "best practice" is meant to address.

There is a serious constraint on the material development of the scenarios. To conform to the quiet of the open halls of the CWR, no sound or moving images are permitted. This leaves photographs, artifacts, and documents, which can be enhanced by doodles, sketches, and cartoons. The most common forms of artifact produced at the WTO are documents, and a major modality of the installation will be "informed play" with their content. The challenge is to make what is already presumed to be an instrument of transparency more so, or rather more critically so.[17]

This austerity might be augmented during special occasions like the "open houses" mentioned above, perhaps even occasioning more animated content such as video footage of WTO protesters juxtaposed to recordings of speeches and interviews, as well as cuttings from press coverage over the years. But the discretion that defines the bureaucracy of diplomatic service carries over to the spare, minimalist character of the building's interior. The Villa is a quiet place; it can tolerate murals, but not sound. Perhaps consistent with the sensory emphasis of transparency itself, the exhibit content must first be noticed and then seen.[18]

The content of the installation tests the intellectual achievement of our fieldwork and validates its success at the classic ethnographer's task of interpreting "the native's point of view" from within to produce something compelling out of what is normal for our subjects. But true to an age where we do ethnography not only among, but increasingly for, those who are socially proximate and similar, our goal is for our subjects to see something both resonant and newly enlightening in the mundane stuff of WTO bureaucracy. We want them to notice what they might otherwise take for granted, to prick their common sense, to make familiar artifacts and situations interesting in new or provocative ways. From the point of view of transparency, the themes would be opacity, hiding in plain sight, and contradictions when what is shown itself obscures and what is obscured may actually reveal.

Scenario Ideas

I conclude this proposal with three sketches of particular exhibit scenarios. Their specifics, of course, will be worked out among committees composed of members of the team of ethnographers, in consultation with the subjects with whom they most closely worked at the WTO. A rich store of material for these scenarios comes from the massive WTO archives housed on the organization's in-house and public websites. The one literal norm of transparency to which the WTO adheres has been the meticulous exposure of its document trail. This exhaustive compendium is generally formal (no memoranda or early drafts) and it is of interest only if one knows what one is looking for. This trove is where insider knowledge and ethnographic competence might intersect to demonstrate the "hiding in plain sight" aspect of transparency's opacities and secrets. Here I will briefly note examples of the provocative form that such content might take in designing this exhibit.

Documents of Accession

A division of the WTO administration is devoted to the accession of new member states to the organization. The negotiations typically take years; there is no more powerful mechanism for a detailed reshaping of the inner workings of the political economies of nation-states according to a neoliberal vision of global order and governance than through the organization of a state's national economy as it prepares for participation in a free trade regime. The accession agreements of particular states bring nations, especially the economically most powerful, into the WTO under very different and often distinct conditions. For example, China's 2001 accession brought it into the WTO with exceptions that define its presence in the organization as rather understated compared to its economic growth and ambition and the unique role it has played in trends of world trade.

The documents of accession are of variable length, and technical. They are available to all, but they are probably read only by scholars or experts trying to resolve legal cases or hearings. Yet, within them lies some of the starkest evidence of power hierarchies, their various roots, and the consequences in how the memberships of different countries have been differently structured. *Making Transparency Visible* displays these documents strategically, by using screens to shade, blur, make clear, and magnify them to passing viewers, whose attention is manipulated by the precise design of the screening.

The exhibition includes a selection of member-states drawing from among the most as well as the least powerful. The selection is based on ethnographic knowledge of the current, past, and shifting reputations of members during the period of the research. A content analysis of the accession documents highlights critical pages and passages, pointing out the special conditions negotiated. These pages are reproduced in working draft form, typical of WTO documents when they are being negotiated. Passages are underlined and marginal notations are added, as is also typical of proposals, documents, and drafts being read and worked on in WTO deliberations. Screens are used to blur or shadow certain segments, to make others clear and transparent, and perhaps to use magnifiers in the screens to call attention to certain words, phrases, or figures. The sequencing and juxtaposition of these ethnographically read documents follows what is known about the recent histories and current reputations of the member-states selected for each scenario. As previously mentioned, the arrangement and composition of documents will be strategically shifted and altered in the course of the exhibit.

Training in the Art of Negotiation

The WTO administration regularly offers short-term courses, both at the WTO and in member countries, on the principles and practice of trade negotiation for members of missions. These are often lower-level personnel in trade delegations, and officials from developing and recently accessioned countries. I did not attend such a course, but colleagues who resided in Geneva did, and have written about them. Since courses are a key context for teaching WTO ideology and culture, including the norm of transparency (as well as a rather routine activity), they are good candidates for exhibit scenario source material. Text passages and documents from the curriculum are highlighted and notated, and when possible, doodles and cartoons from course students are included anonymously.

Photos or videos (without sound) of class sessions are positioned behind transparent screens and juxtaposed with images of meetings in the Green Room (other than negotiations) viewed through heavily shaded screens. Highlighted instructional texts about negotiations are juxtaposed with anonymous interview passages communicating "common, veteran wisdom" about WTO negotiation. These courses, often presented to personnel who may remain tangential to trade negotiations but are treated as if they will or might participate, are themselves a prop in the performance of transparency, despite being among the organization's most discreet processes. Creating an informed constituency for the private activity of negotiation creates a culture of (partial) familiarity and thus some degree of transparency. Such moments of the "socialization of transparency" around the most opaque of the WTO's processes form an ideal exhibit scenario.

WTO "Elitelore"

When the lack of progress of the Doha Round is raised by the media as a measure of the WTO's effectiveness and importance (or its deficiency in these domains), insiders often respond with admiring accounts of the organization's well-functioning system for articulating and adjudicating disputes among members on a broad array of trade issues; no other international organization, they say, has such a routinely functioning authoritative mechanism that produces results for its members. These disputes and the issues they raise form a record of the granular, real-world engagements and impacts that the WTO has had,[19] and the controversies surrounding them are among the most common topics of daily corridor talk at the Villa Rappard. They also represent the "backbone" of institutional memory and lore, integrated anecdotally into conversations and interviews with the most veteran, elite members of the organization's administrative, expert, and diplomatic circles. Stories of famous or recent disputes are thus a genre of "elitelore" – reminiscent of how ranked players recount the moves and moods of famous chess matches – in which insiders regularly produce their own "para-ethnographic" observations on the dynamics of transparency and its contradictions or paradoxes.

So this is another highly cogent subject for a set of exhibit scenarios. Select items of elite lore culled from interviews allow us to frame famous cases from the past with present resonances, and documents from the archive of dispute settlement are curated in a manner similar to the course material described above. Since outcomes of disputes and their resolutions have real-world consequences in the implicated localities, regions, and countries typically unseen in Geneva, *Transparency* displays selected collages of photographic or video images from these places alongside trade figures, to illustrate the outcomes of famous cases for the affected populations.[20] We juxtapose, for instance, documents illustrating WTO rulings and decisions on anti-dumping, or intellectual property in pharmaceuticals, with visual documentation (photos, videos, objects) of the local effects of these policies on key industries or on HIV-AIDS treatment programs. In this way – by mindful juxtapositions and deployment of screen modality – both the intended and unintended consequences of WTO decisions and agreements are highlighted as yet another crucial domain for considering the meaning of transparency.

Envoi

Dear Readers,

In the hope that this proposal might at some point lead to something more than a curatorial dream, I invite your comments, critiques, and suggestions. Please send them to the contact email address on the website of the Center for Ethnography, University of California, Irvine (http://www.ethnography.uci).

Here are excerpts from two readers' creative and analytical responses to my design, sent to me as personal communication. The first is from Hadi Deeb, a member of the research team, and the second from anthropologist Michael Fischer.

Deeb:

- Maybe lighting can do some work. Unpredictable illumination of both aspects of the installation and of those who go through it. Spotlighting in a sense, and therefore also shadowing …
- Sound: I know you mention not having sound and why. But what about something with whispering? Something audio that goes with the visual you describe – barely audible, inaudible, sometimes audible.
- Separation: What if some panels were set up in a way that physically separated staff and/or visitors as they went through, in some fashion moving some/one of them to an "inner" circle/path and others/the other of them to an outer?

Fischer: The three scenario examples are excellent to understand why folks might be interested in what lies behind the screen. For me it is these things (accession, teaching how to negotiate, insider/backstage/

elite knowledge) that are interesting, not the notion of transparency itself. One more device to play with the literal and metaphorical transparencies (screens, processes): have the screens be surfaces on which one can also write (either a transparent smart board, or a strip of white board for pinning up notes) on which people can comment, especially insiders with explanations and/or memories.

Apart from what happens inside the building, there's what happens outside, and that could be yet another set of photos, video screens juxtaposed to the negotiations at the time.

TER TWO

Most Disturbing Souvenirs: Curative Museology in a Cultural Conflict Zone[1]

ERICA LEHRER

Museums, particularly ethnographic museums, are paradigmatic sites for testing the limits of tolerance of, for, and within, minority cultures.
Reesa Greenberg[2]

Among the many historical sites which Poland must unearth as it comes to terms with itself and learns to situate itself with respect to its neighbouring "others," one in particular seems to me to be extremely promising and central – the interaction of Jewish and Polish memory.
Diana Pinto[3]

5 September 2010
Dear Tourism minister,
I have just returned from Poland, where I was a guest at a Catholic wedding of friends. While visiting the market at Zakopane (Krupowki Street), I saw on a number of stalls many samples of the most disturbing souvenirs. These were wooden carved figurines depicting religious Jewish men, dressed in clothes worn traditionally on the Sabbath and religious festivals, and wearing traditional head covering. They were all ugly with over-sized long noses, and holding sacks full of gold coins. These are familiar anti-Semitic images used for generations to demonize Jews. I was shocked and saddened. I saw similar figures in Krakow market (Rynek Glowny), and was most surprised to see sim-

ilar ones made from other materials on sale at Krakow International Airport, in a souvenir shop on the first floor.
[...]
Yours Sincerely,
Dr Rivka Robinson

Most Disturbing Souvenirs is a bilingual (English-Polish) exhibition that uses controversial Polish figurines depicting Jews to promote inter- and intra-ethnic dialogue and both analyse and challenge its limits. These figurines – a more-than-century-old tradition that has exploded in popularity with the rise of the post-socialist tourist trade[4] – exist against the backdrop of divergent memories of Poland's Jewish history.[5] While much Polish discourse tends toward either nostalgic visions of ethnic coexistence or ambivalent views of Jews as essentially unassimilable, Jews more frequently recall (at times with mythic generalization) their own exclusion, persecution, murder, and expropriation at the hands of Poles, which culminated in, but not did not end with, the Holocaust.

The fraught field of Polish-Jewish relations revolves most heatedly around questions of complicity, heroism, victimhood, and loyalty during and shortly after the Second World War, and government sponsored anti-semitic campaigns under communism. Since the 1960s the "relations" have played out mostly in the symbolic realm, in images of the other that have been strikingly enduring. These images have been enhanced by the passage of time, communist historiography, intergenerational silences, and the Cold War lack of contact between the two groups, although after communism fell in 1989 a process of difficult historical revision began. In the last two decades, Jews and Poles[6] have also begun to re-encounter each other, mediated by the Jewish heritage industry, whose rise has accompanied the transition to democracy. Here, "Jewish culture" is increasingly publicly celebrated in Polish festivals and artistic, theatrical, and culinary offerings, and other commodified forms of culture.[7]

The figurines are a lightning rod in Poland's present reckoning of its historical "bill of conscience" vis-à-vis its Jewish minority, because they link past conflicts to present-day culture. They elicit strong feelings among foreign Jewish visitors to Poland on "roots" or Holocaust-oriented trips whose structure often predisposes such travellers to expect and experience anti-semitism. Local Poles, by contrast, who tend to see them as harmless or even complimentary, more frequently display indifference or defensive reactions to criticism of them.[8] Not only can they be found by the hundreds in tourist shops and stalls, but they also stand on shelves or by cash registers in restaurants, gas stations, and shops across the country. While Catholic Poles may view the figures as folkloric trinkets reminiscent of a colourful past or as good luck charms for financial success, many Jews feel that their humorous poses, exaggerated features, and the gold coins they more recently often clutch, echo longstanding anti-semitic stereotypes. Between these two limits there is a range of perspectives: beginning in late communism some progressive Poles employed Jewish figurines as statements of philo-semitic resistance against government-sponsored cultural homogeneity or Polish ethnonationalism, while others – including some Jews – continue to admire them as moving memorial icons of a lost world. Despite their cultural and emotional potency, there has been a dearth of public discussion about them.[9]

In the continuation of the above letter to the Polish minister of tourism, the Israeli-born British author describes her Polish Jewish grandfathers and their families who were killed in Nazi concentration camps during the Holocaust. She emphasizes that the figurines are offensive and racist, that they perpetuate anti-semitism and envy, and that they are based on myth rather than truth. She demands that they be outlawed and removed from the shelves of all market stalls, and that their production be stopped.[10]

As this letter illustrates, the figurines can embody key mismatches in Jewish and Polish perspectives and thus form a line in the cultural sand. But I have observed in them another potential; namely, as a kind of talking stick – a generator of stories, a tool for the specification of feelings and the formulation of questions, a catalyst for discussion.[11] I have often brought one along when I have given talks about Poland's Jewish heritage, and passing it around among the audience has elicited a remarkable range and depth of expression.

Rather than silence these potent objects – as the writer of the above letter demands – my curatorial dream is to allow them to speak. To do so, I extend the letter writer's notion of the figurines' "disturbing" character. I wish to acknowledge not only the figurines' distorting and disempowering aspects, but also ways in which they may productively "disturb" common notions: that Jewishness (or anti-semitism) is firmly relegated to

Poland's past; that objectifications of ethnicity are exclusively destructive; that "Poles" and "Jews" are discrete and antagonistic communities; that tourist *tschotschkes* are superficial forms of cultural expression devoid of ethnographic relevance.[12] I see these objects as *uniquely* disturbing – like grains of sand in an oyster, around which pearls of insight may grow. They are "souvenirs" in many aspects of the word: cheap trinkets that are reductionist, stereotypical, and reassuring ("kitsch"), as well as unsettling reminders, bearers of conflicting memories, touchstones for place and time and difference. My curatorial goal is to harness the emotional and mnemonic potency of these objects and the conflicts surrounding them; and to forge a "curative" space where visitors can participate in the creation of self-reflexive and inter-subjective knowledge – about the figurines, about the individuals and communities to whom they matter, and about themselves, in the context of history.[13]

The Museum

Most Disturbing Souvenirs will take place in Krakow's Seweryn Udziela Ethnographic Museum. Situated off the beaten Jewish tourist track on the edge of Kazimierz, the city's historical Jewish quarter, this essentially nineteenth-century museum (est. 1905) is home to an impressive collection of Jewish figurines (as well as Jewish costumes used in Polish Christian folk rituals). Indeed, the museum's permanent display of these materials was a key inspiration for this curatorial dream.

Ethnographic museums have been criticized in post-colonial terms for producing ideas about culture based on othering, racism, ethnic essentialism, and evolutionary thinking, in the service of empire.[14] Today's East European countries were without classical colonies (and indeed long without sovereignty) and thus possess only piecemeal "foreign" collections. Ethnography here focused instead on the regional peasantry, an internal, class-based "exotic," celebrated as the source of the essential cultural self.[15] Peasant technologies, arts, rituals, and lore were documented to provide an empirical (and later, under communism, an ideologically appropriate) basis for a mono-ethnic "national culture" that would underpin claims to nationhood and consolidate the citizenry.[16]

In the Krakow museum – whose current permanent exhibition of folk culture was installed in 1968, the year of a major government-sponsored

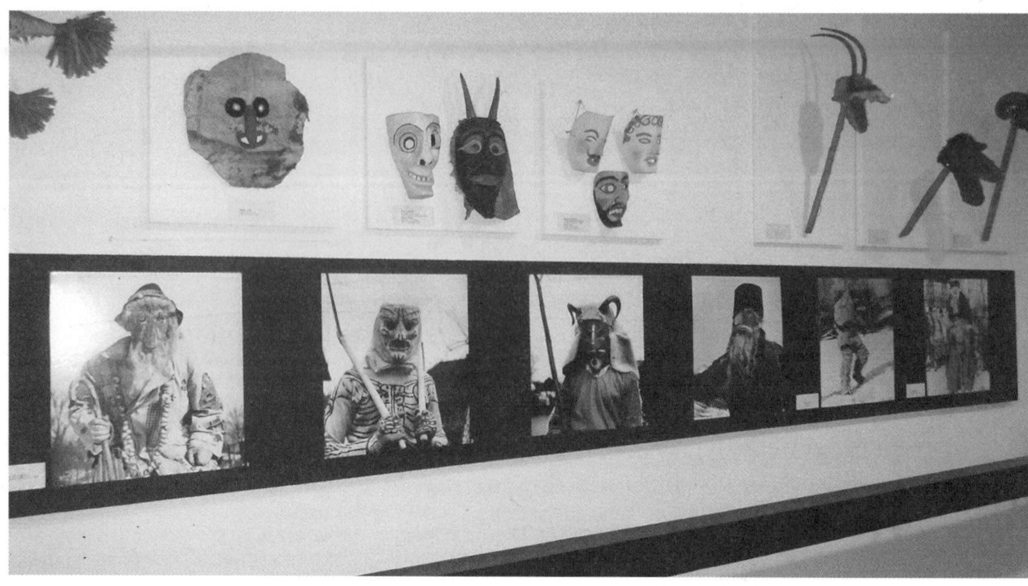

2.1 | One wall of the "Winter Customs" room, Seweryn Udziela Ethnographic Museum, Krakow, 2014.

anti-semitic campaign that decimated what was left of postwar Jewish presence through forced emigration – Jews are at best peripheral to the nation imagined by the displays.[17] In arrangements of photos and artifacts illustrating village social and economic life, in a cabinet of Polish regional costume, and most clearly in the content of the large galleries dedicated to seasonal rituals, the Poland envisioned by the museum is fundamentally a Slavic, Catholic one.[18] Jews appear most visibly through the gaze of their ethnic Polish neighbours, as costumes and masks donned for carolling (see figure 2.1), as puppets in Christmas crèches, as "Judas" effigies to hang, beat, burn, and drown at Eastertime, and as figurines – toy Jews who play music, read cryptic texts, and rock or bobble in a comic simulation of Chasidic prayer.[19]

The minimal interpretive texts for these materials – where they exist at all – range from brief, authoritative, symbolic readings that frame Jews in terms of their magical, mediating role in peasant cosmologies, to Polish-only labels saying simply, *Żyd* ("Jew"). There is a sense of self-evidence in these displays. The tone of the labels, and the information presented and excluded, constructs viewers as normative Catholic Poles – familiar, self-affirming, and unquestioning.[20] The museum's colourful catalogue featuring the wooden toys suggests that viewers might feel "appreciation" and "amusement" in looking at them – but not, for example, pain, shame, offense, or even the stirrings of memory.[21]

If the museum's Jewish figurines are framed outside both history and politics – blissfully untouched by the explosive debates about past and present Polish-Jewish relations that have gripped the nation in the last fifteen years – they are also cut off from their modern contemporaries: figurine Jews in a range of shapes and sizes, sold by the hundreds in shops just outside the museum walls. The bucolic world of "peasant customs" portrayed by the museum renders actual Jews invisible both as former neighbours and as potential contemporary museum visitors.[22] It also suggests that the trade in miniature Jews – and the Polish magical thinking connected to them – is a thing of the past.

Most Disturbing Souvenirs curates around the museum's collection in a way that circumvents knee-jerk reactions of easy dismissal or passive acceptance. Rather, its aim is for both non-Jewish Poles and Jews to gain an appreciation for the diversity of the figurines and the complexity of their social lives: the histories of their creation, circulation, and deployment, the different genres of representation and commemoration in which they partake, the textures of lived experience to which they speak, the reasons that they are embraced or rejected, the way their forms are changing in response to domestic and tourist economies, and the often exclusive worlds of meaning in which they are suspended. It also allows for a range of memories of, and responses to, Poland's Jewish heritage, and creates a space for communication and exchange about the forms such heritage may take. In assessing the legacy and future of Jewish Poland, this curatorial dream provides space not only to highlight patterns of prejudice against Jews but also to explore and discuss the human consequences of living in the wake of their murder. Pain and anger require space for expression. But so do less frequently acknowledged and more difficult to articulate emotions, those associated with cultural and social losses, shifting group identities and identifications, shared pasts, and many layers of nostalgia, shame, curiosity, hope, and fear.

Exhibition as "Cure"

Since a change of directorship in 2008 – part of a more general process of post-socialist institutional restructuring and reorientation – Krakow's ethnographic museum has begun reinventing itself. Rebranding ethnography in terms of introspection, dialogue, and "respect for cultures," the institution has initiated a number of contemporary, participatory projects involving community research and cultural creation. The "Spring" gallery, where the Jewish figurines were displayed, has also been partially re-installed, although to date the figurines themselves remain in storage.[23] The museum has hosted five visiting temporary exhibits on Jewish topics, two of them on "touchy" subjects of Poland's repurposing of monumental heritage like synagogues and cemeteries.[24] But given the economic situation and a generational inertia (an older guard of socialist-era–trained curators still presides over many collections), changes in approach have not permeated the institution. The museum's new slogan, which hung on a large banner on the main building's façade, is, "My museum, a museum about me." I designed *Most Disturbing Souvenirs* to make those words ring true for the wide range of visitors who may feel implicated by the museum's collections and displays, and particularly for those I hoped to draw to my exhibit.

One of my goals for *Most Disturbing Souvenirs* is to aid Krakow's ethnographic museum in fulfilling its new mandate. The exhibition draws conceptual tools both from current anthropological theory and from critical museology: inter-subjectivity; self-reflexivity; multi-vocality; attention to transnational cultural flows; fluidity and hybridity of identities; intracultural fractures and tensions; issues of power; a desire to both enlighten and unsettle established meanings; and a tolerance – even an appreciation – for the uncertainty and ambiguity surrounding cultural forms that exist at the intersection of manifold forces and worlds of meaning.

My curatorial dream is to serve the museum by bringing multiple historical contexts and a range of memories to bear on its timeless, idealized portrayal of Polish folk culture by opening the figurines to broader contexts of meaning. At the same time I want to make use of the special technology of the museum – the rarefied quality of looking that it engenders, the way it draws strangers together in shared meditation, the trustworthiness it is often accorded – to create an experimental "clinic" for a broader social ill.

Metaphors of "illness" have frequently been used in connection with both Polish and Jewish relationships to the wartime past, whether in psychoanalytic terms evoking trauma or with physical metaphors like the pain generated by a phantom limb.[25] The relationships of foreign Jews to Poland – the site of all the German Nazi death camps – have been called "fossilized,"[26] and cultural critics have described how wounds of the Holocaust are ritually transmitted to new generations using Poland as a dramatic *mise-en-scène*, and produce collateral damage in the form of anti-Polish stereotypes.[27] For Poles the impacted layers of war, occupation, territorial loss, and the tormented status of being collectively both victim and perpetrator are compounded by a sense of being overlooked or misread by the West. On both sides, rigid, unidimensional, typically national templates of accusation and self-defence are widespread.[28] These mask a shared problem of "congested affect," whereby ambiguous feelings like shame, remorse, curiosity, or desire remain unspecified and unnamed, preventing more complex discussions about the intimacies of living in the aftermath of genocide and multiple occupations.

Through my curatorial dream I envision a museum or an exhibition as a civic space for difficult but needed "cultural therapy," a space that offers an alternative form of entry into an otherwise habitually trodden domain of ossified memorial postures, a space that allows a reconfiguring of relationships both to the past and to (ideas about) other people.[29] Such a space would acknowledge the shared and the divergent wounds afflicting this part of Europe – and the way pathologies are often perpetuated in public presentations of culture – without lapsing into incapacitating anger, anxiety, guilt, or fear.[30] Finally, it would document what is generally unspoken, and make the new knowledge it engenders available to enrich public debates about history, memory, culture, heritage, and pluralism.

The etymological root of curating in the notion of "care," typically seen in terms of stewardship or custodianship, has been frequently invoked in discussions of critical museology. But in the case of material culture that is highly disputed, where the cultural products and meanings of one community are deeply objectionable to another community (whereas these objections are either invisible or dismissed by the first community), the word's shared origins with the term "cure" may provide a better metaphor.[31] One thread of critical museology holds that exhibitions can function as "cultural self-help," and portrays museums as "contact zones" where objects can help "challenge and rework relationship[s]" among groups that are in dispute.[32] I envision a "therapy" that does more than simply ease pain, a therapy that gets at underlying disease – with all the discomfort that can suggest.[33] I have in mind a homeopathic[34] approach, whereby a carefully administered dose of "difficult knowledge" may cause a limited but productive disturbance, a crisis that promotes uncertainty and emotional release, accompanied perhaps by a temporary vulnerability and a loosening of the boundaries of the self.

The envisioned exhibition explores how curating might harness the affective force of the figurines, to access their unsettling qualities and capacities, yet avoid triggering the defensive symptoms of blame, self-protection, and in-group policing that trouble both Polish and Jewish communities and keep them confined to their own, well-worn points of view. The goal is to create an atmosphere of critical empathy – of "experiencing together."[35] With objects as over-determined as the figurines, the exhibit must work to undermine expectations – from both Polish and Jewish mainstream communal perspectives. There is a fine line to walk here, an attempt to decentre the thinking of two different communities at once, in different ways. This means creating what has been called a "third space," a space that is "unfamiliar to both [sides], in which different groups can share a similar experience of discovery" and "where individuals are permitted to cross the boundaries of belonging."[36] Within that space, the figurines form a "third object," an oblique yet concrete point of reference that allows entry into topics too difficult or volatile to take up directly or in the abstract.

The Holocaust had a massive impact on Polish demography. The prewar Jewish population was 3.5 million; today it is ten or twenty thousand. Poles (95 percent of whom are baptized Roman Catholic) rarely come into meaningful contact with Jews in their daily lives. In a climate of globalization and Europeanization, new questions are arising about how to curate for collective remembering across national boundaries.[37] The kind of curative experience I am proposing is something that neither Poles nor Jews can do in the absence of the other.

As Schneider and Wright have proposed, "exhibition sites and strategies ... dramatically influence the kinds of dialogues and audiences that are possible."[38] *Most Disturbing Souvenirs* has the potential to create a local, human-scale focal point for confronting otherwise abstract accusations and assumptions, enabling face-to-face encounters with material culture, and with other people and their thoughts and feelings. It will shift questions of painful history and accountability into the present day, illustrating how problems of national belonging, stereotype, myth, and envy are close at hand, and expanding our thinking on Polish culture and heritage industries in our homes and shops.

Whose heritage are Poland's Jewish figurines? While discussions of cultural ownership are today being complicated by museums' own problematic collecting histories because West European and "new world" ethnographic museums are linked to colonial domination, objects are often considered in terms of single communities of *origin*, or "source communities." But it is more productive to view Poland's Jewish figurines in terms of "communities of implication," as from the moment of their creation they entangle two social groups.[39] The potency of these objects today lies in their potential to re-link these groups in a shared and contested stewardship of memory. Framing the figurines in their ambiguous "in-between-ness" allows for a fluidity and multiplicity in classifications of culture and heritage, and challenges standard notions of community and identity, even as it offers opportunities to clarify the differing stakes of group identities and representations of them.

"Exhibiting the Problem"[40]

The first step in healing is to recognize the problem. Because the figurines are such a ubiquitous yet banal and dispersed part of the commercial landscape, local Poles tend not to *see* them. The simple act of concentrating them in an exhibition in their numbers and diversity wakens local viewers to them *as a phenomenon*. Regarding diagnosis, the gallery is intended as a space for public consultation; I appeal to local and visiting viewers to bring their own knowledge to bear on the materials on display. Rather than rely solely on didactic texts, *Most Disturbing Souvenirs* first confronts its visitors with questions:

- *Do those who are different from us possess magical powers?*
- *Can models of them be toys?*
- *May a souvenir memorialize the dead?*
- *How can an object hurt, and how might it heal?*

The purpose of this approach is twofold: to domesticate the uncanny (for those whom the figurines disturb), and to unsettle self-satisfaction (for those who have no issue with them). Estrangement, ambiguity, and uncertainty create the conditions for new meaning to be made.[41]

The exhibit space then opens into a small, darkened hallway that functions as a screening room through which all visitors pass on their way to the galleries. Two films are projected side by side, two small windows splitting the darkened wall. On the right runs a loop of archival film – a mix of black-and-white and some rare colour – of Jewish communities in pre-war Poland. The laughing, teasing, shyness, and curiosity before the camera in the first film shows both the vivacity and quotidian quality of Polish Jewish life, and the range of Jews who mingled together – the Chasidim in their black cloaks and beards, their modernized family in suit-jackets (both smart and worn), women and men, scholars and manual labourers. On the left is a reel of colour footage from the shelves of contemporary Krakow shops and market stalls, crowded with Jewish figurines. The poverty of the frozen faces of these wooden replacements is accompanied by the fluttering of fifty-zloty bills being exchanged from Polish buyer to Polish seller, hand-to-hand, over their heads. Yet viewers cannot help but notice the documentary quality of the black-cloaked, bearded figurines, however diminished – the kernel of historical memory that they do, in fact, possess.

The major part of the exhibit consists of a series of galleries, each containing a single "genre" of figurine. Included are related forms such as an eighteenth-century, life-sized "figural beehive" in the shape of an Chasidic Jew (bees fly in through holes in the groin) and Jewish puppets who appear in miniature Christmas crèche theatres, playing stock characters that are part biblical, part local stereotype; wise and wicked in turn. While one may argue that a nineteenth-century Easter toy is not the "same thing" as a twenty-first-century tourist souvenir, this framing gives the present-day phenomenon of Jew-with-a-coin figurines a broader historical and cultural context, illustrating both its novelty and its deep cultural roots. Today's figurines share significant traits both with pre-war Slavic Christian ritual objects and with postwar secular sculptures that were based first on personal memory and later on nostalgic popular cultural images such as the "fiddler on the roof." Rare examples of figurines that depict Jewish suffering and persecution at the hands of the Nazis are another crucial genre included in the galleries. This wide array of forms and contexts evokes the multiple co-existing valences of "the Jew" in Poland. Visitors are left free to assess for themselves the paradoxical co-existence of both breaks from, and persistence of, longstanding stereotypes and magical thinking in relation to Jews.

Selected pairs of objects will be juxtaposed to disrupt ingrained ways of looking. For instance, the pairing of a bobbling prewar Jewish toy figurine with springed legs together with a Catholic bishop made by the same craftsman shows that fun was poked at a range of distinctive local characters – these two stand facing each other, in profile, to reveal the interchangeability of their bodies and facial features. A classic Polish "pensive Christ" figure sits side by side with a thoughtful Jew replicating the cheek-in-hand pose, evoking a humanistic sense of inter-group similarity, as well as hinting at Jesus's own Jewishness (an often-elided fact in this strongly Catholic country). A black-cloaked, white shirted Chasidic Jew will be accompanied by a penguin made by the same carver, their similarities underlining the triviality in much of the figurine trade.

Despite the seriousness of the subject, such strategic "humour" is introduced into the exhibit at a few points, disarming visitors and activating their curiosity and receptivity to the range of new ideas they are confronting. The exhibition opens with a life-sized beehive in the form of a Jew, accompanied by an ambient audio track of buzzing bees, attuning visitors' sensibilities toward both the ethnographic and the surreal – rational inquiry and emotional response. There is something (tragically) comical in portraits of Jews with coins sold with instructions to hang them upside down so the money falls out of the Jews' pockets – so they hang this way on the gallery wall. A present-day "rocking" toy Jew from Krakow's 2013 Emaus church fair is bolted to a special shelf outside the display cases, with the words "Try me! Tap me lightly, and I rock!" I want visitors to experience the figurine's specific kinetic technology, and be complicit in making a wooden Jew bobble in mock prayer.[42]

A number of curatorial strategies and design techniques are intended to bring awareness of multiple viewpoints, obliging visitors to confront the layers of hidden humanity that both inspire and refract the figurines. As noted above, Jewish subjectivity, Jewish experience, and the sense of a Jewish gaze are a crucial missing component in both the Krakow museum and the broader discussion of the figurines in Poland. But the exhibition

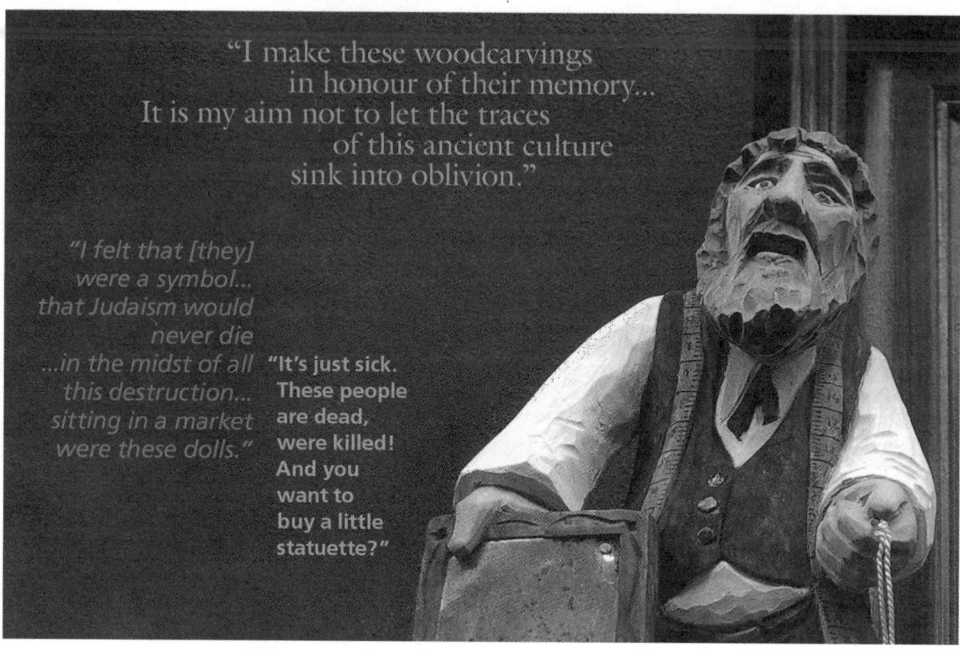

2.2 | A postcard experimenting with multiple perspectives on a carved Jewish figurine.

represents an attempt to leverage the "intersectional" quality of the figurines as memorial objects that implicate both Jews and non-Jewish Poles in significant ways, and open a space for dialogue. Thus, non-Jewish Polish voices – of figurine makers, vendors, and buyers – also play a vital role, making visible the psychological and emotional textures that circulate in the figurines' place of origin.

Video interviews done over many years of ethnographic research will be interspersed throughout the galleries, making visible the singular human hands that give rise to each figurine. A figurine holding a fragment of authentic torah scroll – for many Jews a combination that could provoke simple outrage – is made more complex when accompanied by an interview with its maker. He tells the ambiguous story of his childhood friend Srulik disappearing into the ghetto, of finding the scroll after the war, and years later meeting an Israeli tourist who taught him that cutting up a torah is desecration, prompting him to shift to photocopying. While perhaps not quite redemptive, this context allows the object to take on deeper memorial qualities.

To defuse the simplistic and volatile sensibility of many foreign Jews who see Poland's contemporary Jewish figurines as direct and unalloyed expressions of longstanding Polish attitudes of antipathy toward Jews – a framework that may provoke visitors to either defend or condemn them – *Most Disturbing Souvenirs* invokes multiple interpretive contexts. Today's Polish Jewish figurines can only be understood with simultaneous reference to the complex entanglement of religious, ethnonational, economic, visual-cultural, and memorial frameworks in which they are implicated. Wall texts discuss the impact of Poland's political, social, and economic history on the forms and trajectories of the figurines – the way state-sponsored ethnographic commissions as well as urban, sometimes foreign (including Jewish) collectors became arbiters of what constituted "authentic" folk art and the market they created influenced carvers' compositions. Using an art historical approach, the exhibition juxtaposes images to illustrate the broader visual history that the figurines share genealogically with longstanding tropes of modern art (images by Marc Chagall), religious iconography (portraits of saints and anti-semitic biblical illuminations), political propaganda (Nazi imagery), and Polish peasant culture (figurines of other local characters). These images suggest the social and cultural nature of carvers' influences and viewers' interpretations, and the well of common (and divergent) memory, tropes, and stereotypes that underlies the personal appraisals of both carvers and viewers.

Nonetheless, the personal experiences, memories, and reflections of individual Poles and Jews are crucial for bringing to light the intimate histories and the invisible emotional landscapes that the figurines traverse – how each "community" evinces both patterns and distinctiveness in its perspectives. Finally, the influence of international Jewish tourism and Polish economic anxieties must be taken into account if we are to understand the figurines' more recent transformations – their general proliferation, as well as their new emphasis as good luck charms.

A final display case titled "Only in Poland?" will contain selected figurines from other national and cultural contexts, such as an African-American "lawn jockey," an "Indian princess" kewpie doll, and Jewish figurines made in Israel, Italy, and the United States, to remind visitors that stereotypical ethnic miniatures are not exclusively a Polish phenomenon.

A core problem related to the representation of people in figurine form is that it literally "belittles" them. Figurines of ethnic others – which stand in for whole groups of people – not only freeze, simplify, and essentialize but they make these others "playable," inert toys in the hands of active human agents.[43] "You can make his head turn this way, or that – however you wish!" announces one videotaped figurine vendor, over the click-click-click-click of the neck's wooden ratchet cranking to and fro. To exhibit the small-scale Jewish figurines in display cases risks reproducing these unequal relations. The exhibit will therefore use an *Alice in Wonderland* tactic, so that viewers enter the figurines' world, at their scale, subject to their gaze and inquiries. Each figurine will have its portrait taken by a professional photographer, and these life-sized headshots will line the gallery walls at eye-level, demanding that visitors face them as equals – individual Jews with different features, expressions, and postures, looking back at them. While this tactic aims to unsettle Poles predisposed to thinking of Jews in stereotypical terms, it sends a message to Jews inclined to dismiss the figurines as simple evidence of Polish ignorance and anti-semitism as well. Up close, one sees the care put into some carvings, particularly the older ones. Some are thoughtfully rendered individuals, whether known, seen, or imagined: this one has blue eyes, that one red hair and a doctor's bag. Some look severe. Others sad. Rendering their *payes* (sidelocks), *yarmulkes* (skullcaps), *tsitsis* (ritual fringes), or *capotes* (traditional cloaks) requires some familiarity with Jewish tradition. Looking closely at the faces of the carved figures raises questions about what constitutes a caricature rather than a subtler evocation of ethnic distinctiveness – what is stereotypical and damaging rather than nostalgic or even artistic.

In a final tactic to deal with the issue of ethnographic and museum authority, *Most Disturbing Souvenirs* challenges the minimal, singular, detached, and seemingly neutral "museum voice" that ethnography museums have traditionally employed – the voice that effaces the cacophony of views, variety of trajectories, and terms of dispute that characterize the "social lives of things."[44] This exhibition contends that Poland's Jewish figurines are not reducible to any single perspective. These objects were born of and continue to be shaped by their "boundary" status, products of the ever-shifting intersection of cultures and communities. Their value as a collection consists of their ability to act as entryways into discussions about the frictions and connections across this border-zone. Thus a core methodology of the exhibition is to treat objects and displays to elicit as much as to provide interpretation: to "exhibit the problem" as museum anthropologists Ivan Karp and Cory Kratz put it.[45] While the entire exhibition is framed by questions, blank books are also positioned throughout the galleries, each with a specific question for visitors to consider. More than traditional "comment books," these are ethnographic fieldnote books, inviting collaborative investigation.

- *Do these figurines look to you like individuals, or stereotypes?*
- *What aspects of Jewishness do they represent?*
- *Do you think it is possible to commemorate the Holocaust in the form of a figurine?*
- *Do Jewish figurines bring luck? If you have one, does it work? And how, precisely?*

At the end of the path of the exhibition, visitors enter a separate "conversation room." In a previous installation I undertook in Poland in 2008, I observed how the creation of an intimate *public* space allowed, surprisingly, topics to be broached that had been impossible to discuss privately.[46] With a large central table and chairs, as well as clusters of comfortable upholstered benches forming cozy corners, this space is for unwinding, thinking, meeting other visitors, discussing, and further writing. Young bilingual volunteers act as sources of information, attentive listeners, and catalysts to conversation. The walls are lined with pinboards, each with an additional, broader question: How should we think about Poland's Jewish figurines? Are they toys? Do they allow us to communicate with our ancestors? How are they different from other racial and ethnic stereotypes? What makes them any different from nostalgic artworks, souvenirs, or popular culture made by Jews? How are they similar to anti-semitic imagery? And so on. These opportunities for visitors to register their responses to critical questions have the dual benefit of providing food for discussion and generating additional data for ongoing ethnographic research around the figurines, information which is difficult to gather in a naturalistic setting.

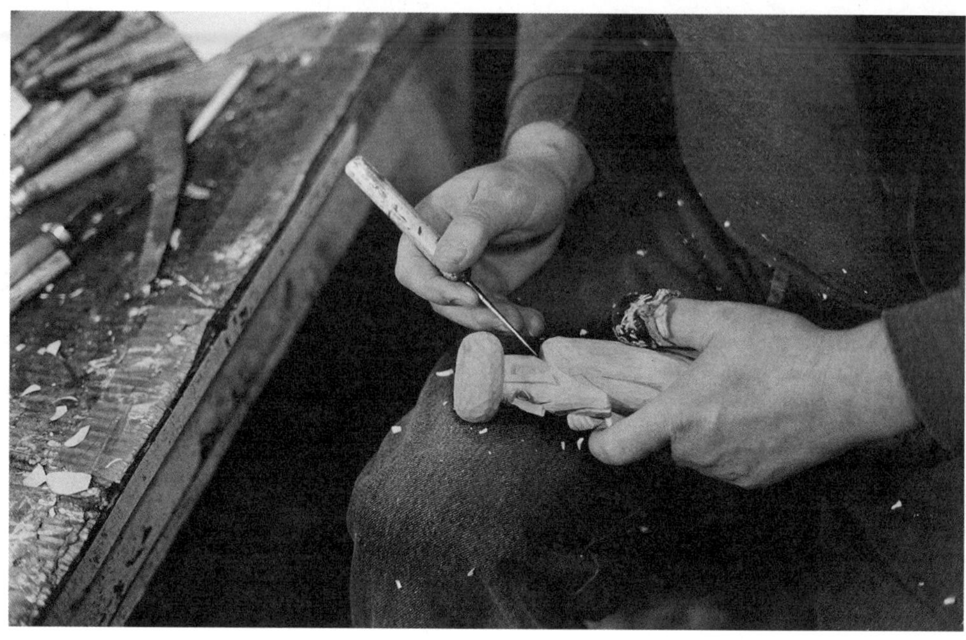

2.3 | Woodcarver Józef Reguła in his workshop, Połaniec, Poland.

The exhibition is designed to take place during Krakow's enormously popular annual Jewish Culture Festival, in order to divert some of the festival's temporary "captive audience" into the underused museum. Not only will these additional visitors broaden the range of conversation partners available to discuss this intercultural phenomenon – particularly with the addition of foreign Jews – but they will confront the ethnographic museum with the questioning presence of an unanticipated audience. At the same time, festival revelers will be prompted to connect lighthearted souvenirs and celebrations of Jewishness to problematic histories of representation. Indeed, to further extend the reach of the exhibition, the conversation, and the research, a participatory website will call for the submission of photographs of Jewish figurines wherever they are found – in their natural habitats in homes, in shops, in and outside Poland – along with information about their provenance and understood meaning.

A final element of this experience will be the presence in the exhibition space of Józef Reguła, a well-known woodcarver who sells his figurines in a nearby Jewish-themed shop. He has agreed to simply do what he does: carve Jewish figurines, and engage in conversation. Demonstrations by "authentic craft practitioners," a classic arrangement in the curation of folk culture, here fill a more ambiguous function. At a minimum, Reguła's presence will remind visitors that each figurine is the product of human hands – individual carvers, with their specific intentions and motivations, rather than faceless "Poles." He is unafraid of potential negative reactions, which I warned him that he may face from foreign Jewish visitors. He says he understands their concerns, and for him the goal is to exchange ideas.

The curatorial provocation I have proposed here is inherently risky. Given the volatile cultural-political landscape surrounding Polish-Jewish issues, my experiment could backfire, further deepening the divide between the two communities, closing down rather than opening up communication and dialogue. It could be misread, either as a further condemnation of Poles in blanket terms familiar in Western Jewish circles, or as a celebration of them that dismisses Jewish concerns and sensibilities.

But my gamble is predicated on my observations of the unique qualities that the newly "curated" Kazimierz neighbourhood itself engenders, which my curatorial dream hopes to expand and heighten: the drawing together of diverse individuals into a shared atmosphere of unsettlement, attentiveness, encounter, and self-questioning vis-à-vis the unrecognized symptoms of the difficult past.

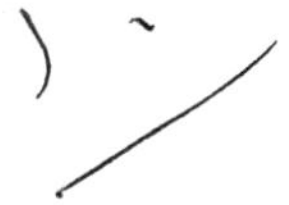

CHAPTER THREE

The Alchemy of Flight: Race, Mobility, Humanity

CHANDRA D. BHIMULL

I met History once, but he ain't recognize me,
. . . .
The jet that was screeching over the *Flight*
was opening a curtain into the past.
. . . .
'One day go be planes only, no more boat.'
'Vince, God ain't make nigger to fly though the air.'
'Progress, Shabine, that's what it's all about.
Progress leaving all we small islands behind.'
Derek Walcott, "The Schooner Flight"

When you think about flight, what comes to mind? The more ordinary airline travels become, the easier it is to take the experience of flight for granted. My imagined exhibition, *The Alchemy of Flight,* works against the inclination to normalize airline travel, a tendency that also screeches to a halt when explosions, hijackings, crashes, and other big bad things befall human life in the sky. It is an exhibition about race and airborne mobility, a pairing to shatter the myth that modes of transportation are merely means to an end. It curates extraordinary yet fleeting events that take place in airports and airplanes flying, in the confined spaces of the so-called in-between. I should note that my approach to the everyday life of flight addresses civil rather than military aviation, although the escalating number of deportation flights, air marshal services, and other such practices in the commercial aviation field are blurring the boundary between the two branches.

When people ask me what I study, they usually want to know why. Why do I study airline travel? How did a black woman get interested in that? As an academic, my answers to the why question are awkward at best. They include interest in the dynamic between the rise of airborne mobility and the upward expansion of empires; concern for how people in the air and on the ground experience the physical dimensions of artificial flight; curiosity about the social consequences of speed *up*; fascination with vertical life and white privilege.

My response to the how question is slightly more personal. As a citizen of the African diaspora, I feel at home in flight. A daughter of immigrants, I grew up going.[1] My mother is from Anegada. My father is from Trinidad. Like many Caribbean migrants they taught me that I am from elsewhere. Although born in New York City and raised on Long Island, I am from the West Indies by way of Africa, India, and Europe. I am displaced and dislocated in time and space, but I am not unique. I am part of a diaspora, a community of dispersed persons and distance.

What does this have to do with flying? Diasporas are about many things but, essentially, they are about movement. For centuries, transport technologies have made, maintained, and morphed diasporas; water- and land-based vehicles have tended to dominate discussions about the African diaspora in scholarship and the popular imagination. Slave narratives documenting the atrocities of the transatlantic triangle trade forged the link between sailing vessels and identity formation. Marcus Garvey pioneered a black-owned and -operated ocean liner enterprise as part of his "Back to Africa" initiatives. The Underground Railroad used transportation and communication lingo to connect travel, networks, and pathways to freedom. Paul Gilroy pointed out that any "image of ships in motion" across the Atlantic Ocean recalls Middle Passage for black elites.[2] The echoes of bondage rippling through George Lamming's thoughts about transoceanic workers expanded the image to include the broader black Atlantic world.[3]

What, then, do the mechanics and metaphors of flight reveal about race and mobility? What part does the airplane play in the African diaspora?

Why do airliners and other aspects of the commercial aviation industry feature so little in the stories we tell about what it means to belong to a society scattered around the world? What do routes not taken tell us about who or what moves when and where?

In what follows, I pursue these questions by imagining a public exhibition on flight through the lens of diaspora. On this creative journey, I seek indefinite considerations rather than definitive answers; I open up rather than seal off adventures in understanding how members of the African diaspora experience movement, which, unlike absolute motion, is a culturally driven way to change position. I begin by recounting my travels through two aviation museums. Each escapade generated real questions that shaped how I conceptualized my un-real exhibition, an undertaking I present in the second part of the chapter. I conclude by contemplating the broader implications of dreaming, a reflection that explains why stories about the ascension of scattered people matter.

Prelude to a Dream

My curatorial dream started after I toured and thought about two aviation museums and their dealings with race. The first is an online museum about African Americans and airline travel. It is a virtual place that delinks the image of the modern black traveller from the image of the bygone black traveller, the slave. The second is an aircraft museum that presents the history of supersonic flight. In a storage facility on Barbados, visitors can faux-fly a Concorde for fun and a fee. They can learn about Britain's efforts to use aviation to advance its former Caribbean colonies.

In both arenas, I felt awkward and excluded. The versions of flight on offer were about the legacies of an empire-state and the entitlements of a nation-state. The tales being told about being black put forth a profoundly fixed identity that was anchored without, beyond, or outside history. They thwarted the possibility of envisioning diasporic journeys.

I am not blaming the museums. They designed their exhibits for a different kind of visitor: tourist, elite, aviation buff. I had entered, experienced, and interpreted them anthrohistorically.[4] I am trained to attend to missing stories, stories about nonetheless mobile people who do not, and cannot fit into the chronicles on offer. My curatorial dream started there, in the non-presence of narratives dealing with the skyward motivations and mid-air movements of a people uprooted and strewn.

www.blackatlas.com

In the early fall of 2009, American Airlines launched Black Atlas, a "social networking site" intended to augment black interest in travel. Nelson George, a well-known commentator of and contributor to African-American culture, is the "Travel-Expert-at-Large." Like a native informant, he helps visitors navigate photographs, videos, maps, and forums filled with globe-trotting tips and travel advice. The main colours of the site are blue and white. The palette invokes images of the sky and the sea to suggest that the modern black traveller is someone who transcends Middle Passage. She is literally *over* it.[5]

I entered Black Atlas a few months after the portal opened. The language of the site struck me at once. The atlas is a primer. Like an old-fashioned guidebook, it tells me what to do and how to do it. A site made for black users, the airline capitalizes on the lexicon of diaspora. Common commercial expressions like "explore a city" and "find a fare," phrases such as "a new way to look at travel," "bringing the black experience to every corner of the globe," and "our mission: a unique online community that offers travel insights from an African-American perspective" kindle ideas about journey, exclusion, dispersal, and kinship. They seemed selected to train my thoughts. What makes an encounter black? What is an African-American outlook and why is it distinctive? Who demarcates and belongs to this bounded group? Why do we need to abandon the old and seek a new way to look at travel, and what is the old way anyway?

I thought about the ancestors, people made black by being moved. Among them were Sarah Baartman, Ota Benga, and other individuals transformed by transoceanic voyages. In transit, they became immobile spectacles on display: the Hottentot Venus in nineteenth-century London and Paris, the twentieth-century Pygmy in the Bronx Zoo.[6] This profound historical connection among movement, racism, and oppression made me curious. How does Black Atlas handle the past?

As I roamed this world I felt self-conscious and reduced, catching myself comparing the site to colonial exhibitions and racist ad campaigns from centuries ago.[7] Black Atlas is not, after all, a conventional atlas. It echoes former times and harkens back to earlier mappings by paying particular attention to people and their practices rather than to places.[8] It features cities like Cape Town and Chicago and reveals what black travellers purportedly do there: smell smoked ribs in Detroit, listen to African-American music in Barcelona, and search for hair products in Brixton. It envisions its consummate user as a particular sort of black person: thirty years old, "world explorers," frequent flyers, "proficient with social networking," family oriented or business minded, "African American."[9] An archetype, the imagined operator's questions are stereotypical: "Where can I get my hair done in Paris?" "Are there any African historical sites in Prague?" "Is there a Baptist church in Madrid?"

I visited Black Atlas for more than a year. My personal and professional interests seemed to converge neatly in this domain. A site about airline travel, the atlas curates and celebrates difference.[10] It deals with the global spread of a diasporic people. There is, however, a problem. Its world lacks historical depth. On the one hand it promotes aviation as "an important connector" to "the black experience." On the other hand it presents a version of blackness that is rooted in "African American culture." Why, when, how, and by whom is this social group created and contained? As hyperlinks labelled "Exclusive Membership" and "In the Community" advertise the airline as a company "Giving Back," we need to understand what was taken when and by whom. Why would an airline need to redress? What does it seek to return?

I started to dream. I began to wonder what it would mean if I envisioned the site as a vessel and surveyed Black Atlas as a place. Toward the end of my stay there, I noticed two odd things: a passport and nearly no planes. Around the time when the website launched, American Airlines released a digital press kit. It contained an emblem of homeland and identity, a blue and gold forty-nine pages passport for blackatlas.com. The citizenship motif continued on the website's homepage, which broadcasts "Black Atlas: Your Passport to the Black Experience." On this website dedicated to airline travel, the image of the airplane hardly turned up. The omission led me to reflect on the relationship between the presence of the passport and the absence of the plane. I started to imagine the black airline traveller as someone who, for the price of a ticket, gains access to another world.[11]

Supersonic

There is a white metal hangar next to the Grantley Adams International Airport in Barbados. Alpha Echo is inside. Formally known as G-BOAE, Alpha Echo is part of the British Airways Concorde fleet. There are six other planes in the fleet, all of which were retired when the airline ended its famed supersonic services in 2003. After the company grounded its iconic jets, it sent the planes to airports and museums on both sides of the North Atlantic. Four planes stayed in the United Kingdom, two went to the United States, and one was sent to Barbados. The airline retains ownership of them all.

The Barbados Concorde Experience opened on 16 April 2007. It is a multimedia museum designed to store and show its mechanical namesake. Alpha Echo is located in the middle of the main gallery surrounded by nine other exhibition zones. From a replica of the Concorde departure lounge at Heathrow Airport in London to stories about supersonic speed breaking and going beyond the sound barrier, the areas contribute in turn to lauding the grounded jet.

I visited the museum a few months after it opened. As active aircraft moved payloads in and out of the working airport next door, I noted that the museum offered visitors a version of airline travel that was both opulent and motionless. I entered zone 1, "Flight Path." Like a jetsetter, I walked a red carpet and purchased a "boarding pass" from a ticketing agent; a ticket cost thirty-five Barbados dollars.[12] On either side of the walkway, brightly coloured banners recounted the early history of flight.

I entered the hangar. There was a security checkpoint between the first and second zones. The line was not long. I "cleared security" and, facing the jet's famous needlepoint nose, continued through zones 2 and 3 to 4. Zone 2, "Supersonic Flight," outlined the Concorde's origins and zone 3, "Engineered for Speed," showed a short film about aircraft design on the side of the plane. From there, I proceeded to the "Departure Lounge" in zone 4, and waited to walk another red carpet and board the jet in zone 5: "Flight Experience."

Together with a few other visitors, I enplaned. A uniformed attendant proffered several in-flight entertainments: leather seats, model meals, a feature film, famous cargo, and a cockpit tour. We then walked toward zones 6, 7, 9, 10, and 11 ("Aviation Barbados," "Flight School," "Tarmac," "Observation Deck," and "Boutique") to read about local aviation endeavours, use a flight simulator, listen to expert engineers, watch planes, and buy souvenirs. Zone 8 was an event centre facility.

When the tour ended, the guide approached and asked why Concorde fascinated me.[13] I explained my longstanding efforts to understand how British Airways shaped – just as it was simultaneously transformed by – the people and places of the former and current British Caribbean. We spoke for some time about tourism, empire, and return migration, noting rumours about the airline refusing to fly colonial workers after the Second World War. Toward the end of our talk, the guide escorted me back to the Observation Deck. We moved to the far end of the room, away from a tour group that had assembled there. Looking out the window, the guide pointed down and described the Barbadian women who helped build the old runway on the grounds of a former plantation. The guide left and I walked through the museum again. I scanned the displays, trying to track down traces of the information I had just been given in conversation, to no avail.

The Concorde Experience marks an achievement and recoups a failure. It pays homage to a special alliance between the reputed flag carrier of Britain and the so-called Little England of the Caribbean.[14] It honours and resuscitates a craft that was an economic disaster and environmental hazard. As aviation historian R.E.G. Davies reminds us, Concorde was "one of the biggest scams ever perpetrated."[15] I left the museum wondering why some failures matter. I seek a space where the violence of airborne mobility can be seen and heard.

The Alchemy of Flight

Curation seems simple. Sites like Black Atlas and the Concorde Experience mute stories that highlight the historically informed trepidation with which racially oppressed people move through the world. I want to assemble a multimedia, multisensory exhibition about airline travel in the African diaspora. I want to create an *exceptional* space that strongly encourages visitors to think intimately and reflexively about those who have been excluded from narratives about the power of airborne mobility.

I look for a venue that would allow me to disentangle the cultural concept of movement from the more natural phenomenon of motion. I opt to install the exhibition in the Grantley Adams International Airport. I select this location for several reasons: it is a major transportation hub for air passage to and through the Caribbean; it is a safe yet liminal place, a complex built to enable and ensure the secure transfer of airplanes and their payloads; it is also a dynamic arena where massive mechanical bodies speed up and slow down. Named for the country's first premier, the airport is an important post-colonial counterpoint to the supersonic British jet sitting in the hangar next door.

The anatomy of the airport is vital. It is a government-owned facility in Christ Church, a parish on the southeastern side of the island. Its long grey rectangular building is accented by the national colours of blue and gold, supported by exposed steel columns painted blue and white, and tented with a tensile white sheath. There are two terminals, named landside and airside. Their interior mood feels light, fluid, and uplifting. The landside station is an open-air structure with a departure lobby, an arrivals area, check-in counters, public seating sections, and places to purchase food. The airside terminal is a combined indoor and outdoor structure located beyond the security checkpoint. It has a shopping mall, a food court, a departure lounge, an in-transit area, an arrivals hall, a baggage claim, and an immigration and customs processing zone. The roof is a translucent membrane stretched above and across both terminals. It integrates the two sections. The security corridor is a conduit through which permissible people and property move from side to side.[16]

I divide the exhibit unevenly between the two terminals. Visitors on the airside have full access. Security measures like passenger-only restrictions prevent landside people from experiencing the entire exhibition directly. To deal with this asymmetry, I give all viewing audiences *Terminal*, a guidebook that resembles an inflight magazine and features a travel itinerary summarizing the entire show. A teaching tool, *Terminal* explains the spatial dimensions and directions of air travel, telling viewers what their respective vantage point does and does not allow them to do. The names of the exhibition's sections reinforce these ideas: landside is "On the Ground"; airside is "In the Air"; exhibition pieces found on both sides of the airport are "In Transit."

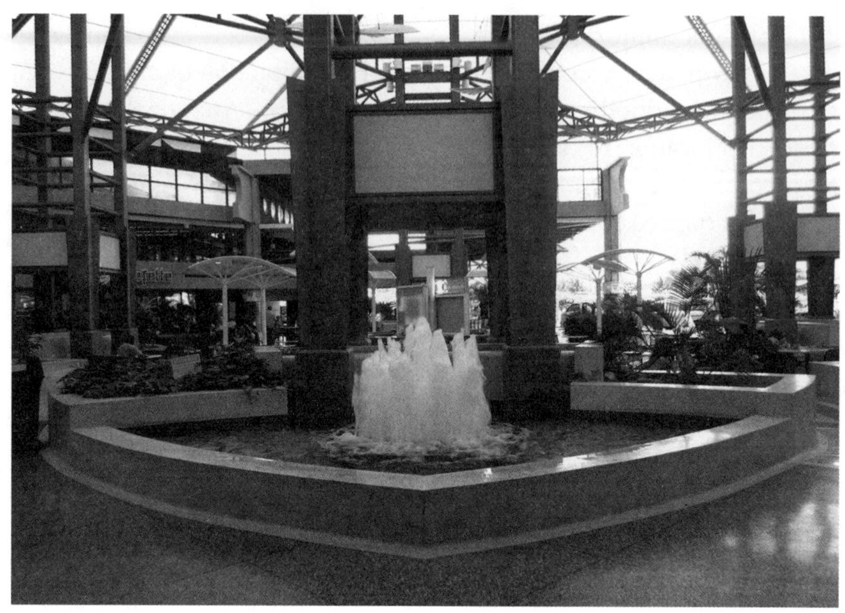

3.1 | Fountain in the food court of the Grantley Adams International Airport in Christ Church, Barbados.

The main display areas are water fountains and backlit lightboxes. They are scattered throughout the airport, helping to evoke some of the main diasporic elements of the exhibition: dislocation, passage, and fragmentation as connection. The upward flow and downward fall of fountain water and the scrolling feature of some lightboxes illuminate movement, one of the most important aspects of a diaspora (see figure 3.1).

The uneven allocation of displays poses a deliberate problem. The number and style of lightboxes vary dramatically between the terminals. The landside area has thirty-two lightboxes, none of which scroll. The airside section has twenty-three motionless and moving lightboxes. It also has vertical banners and clocks. In each terminal the displays are mounted on walls, suspended between steel columns, or hung down from rooftops. The flow of participants is also an issue. As noted, the landside spaces are relatively unrestricted in comparison to the airside arenas. The former are open to the general public, while access to the latter, which are located after security, is limited. To deal with these obstacles, I turn to Franz Fanon. In his early work on racial oppression and consciousness, he says, "O my body, always make me a man who questions!"[17] Unable to move their bodies, confined folks figure out ways to move their minds. They question.

In Transit

Landside and airside, the largest lightbox introduces the exhibition: *The Alchemy of Flight*. Under the title, a question asks viewers, "What happens to our humanity in the air?" Nearby, a phrase fades in and out on screens: "3° of Freedom."

"Three degrees of freedom" is a concept scientists use to evaluate movement through space. A combination of text and diagrams illustrates how people and things move forward/backward through space (one-dimensional, one degree of freedom), backward/forward, left/right (two-dimensional, two degrees of freedom), and forward/backward, right/left, and down/up in depth (three-dimensional, three degrees of freedom). Visitors also learn that all people need airplanes, submarines, and other mechanical devices to move with three degrees of freedom.[18] They then discover why degrees of freedom matter to members of the African diaspora, a meditation that pinpoints what happens when some people can rise above the limits of two-dimensional space and others cannot.

The second part of "In Transit" prompts people to think reflexively about flight. Visitors enter telephone-box-like computer booths. Each enclosure holds a person and a processor in a configuration that helps foster an intimate experience. The walls, ceiling, and floor are glass. To prompt thoughts about the sea and the sky, I lightly paint the surfaces blue and white, and play a soundscape softly in each box.[19] Soundtracks sample gusts, breezes, jets, propellers, mosquitos, bees, and other air transport audios from the Atlantic world. Meanwhile the terminal screen reads, "When you think about flight ... what comes to mind?" It asks visitors to answer in seventy-five characters or less. In real time, responses glisten and wane on lightboxes located throughout the airport. Imagined replies include winged things (birds, insects, fabled beings like fairies, and so on), trips, transportation, transcendence, lift, sky, light, swift, going up, and escape.

The third part of this section uses the water fountains. It is inspired by the underwater artwork of Jason deCaries Taylor, a sculptor of Guyanese and English parentage.[20] Taylor's haunting pieces, which he allows to decay naturally on ocean and sea floors, reverberate with the horrors of Middle Passage. Inspired by this work, I beam the epic words of Saint-Lucian writer and Nobel Prize winner Derek Walcott down from the airport roof. Under the undulations of recycling water, a tale of salvation and departure, ascent and loss manifests on the fountain floors:

> And God said to Achille, 'Look, I giving you permission
> to come home. Is I send the sea-swift as a pilot,
> the swift whose wings is the sign of my crucifixion.'
> ....
> Soundless, enormous breakers foamed across the pane,
>
> then broke into blinding glare. Achille raised his hand
> from the drumming rudder, then watched our minnow plane
> melt into cloud-coral over the horned island.[21]

On the Ground

Landside. Lightboxes are suspended between the blue steel columns (see figure 3.2). This part of the exhibition focuses on liberation, alienation, and duration. The first four screens, named "From Runaway to Runway," urge audiences to think historically and comparatively about the different kinds of freedom paths that members and descendants of Middle Passage sought, took up, and made. The selection of artifacts includes slave narratives, runaway slave notices, runway maps, maroon tales, and contemporary stowaway stories from the tarmacs of London and Conakry.

The second set of screens, called "From Overseer to Overseas," focuses on the power of verticality. Visitors consider aboveness, the ability to access and use an overhead vantage point from a seemingly disconnected distance to have an impact on those who cannot rise above the ground. From depictions of plantation elites *over*seeing slaves and disciplining bodies to airline passengers peering down on others from above, visuals prompt participants to question how the move from horizontal to sustained vertical travel transformed and reinforced social hierarchies. Afterward, monitors challenge onlookers to consider the geopolit-

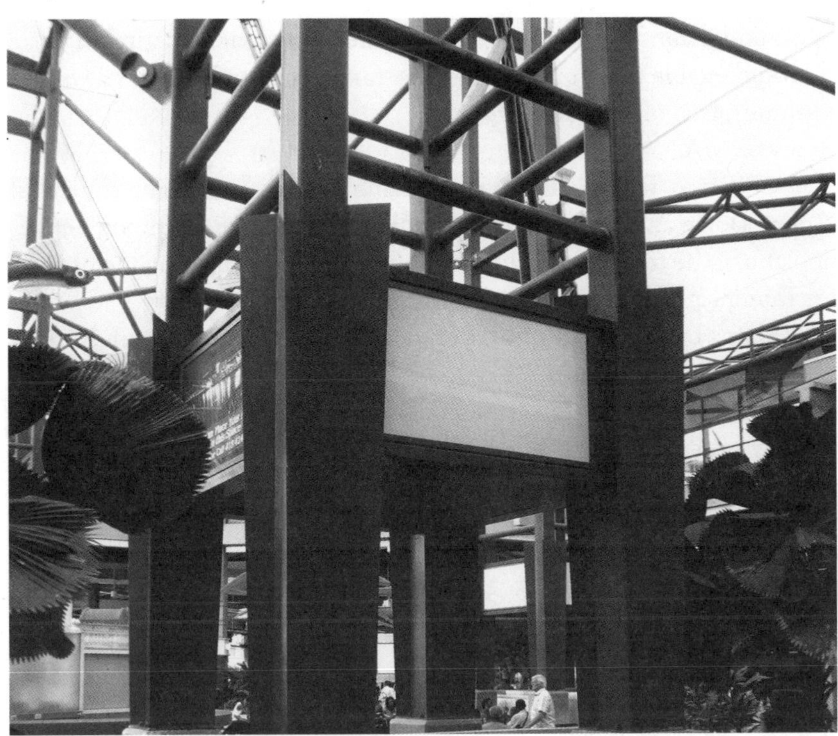

3.2 | Lightboxes in the Grantley Adams International Airport in Christ Church, Barbados.

ical consequences of this transition. A screen shows clips from *The White Diamond*, a film by Werner Herzog that follows a white airship gliding across the green treetops and misty waterfalls of Guyana. It gives insight into the imperial undertones of aerial survey work. Next to the screen, a sign reads:

> The Commission, appointed [in Britain by Parliament] to enquire into the question of a railway to the Mazaruni [a river in which the committee said "valuable merchandise" existed], reported that the knowledge of the mineral, timber and other natural resources of the Colony [British Guiana] was limited to certain areas adjacent to the main waterways below the rapids and to the diamond and gold mining areas above the rapids. Further surveys are,

> we understand, now in progress and the employment of aircraft would enable these operations to be carried out and extended with a minimum of time and effort.[22]

The human fallout and environmental damage of flight cohere in "Touch Down and Take Off." First, audio interviews and lightbox images depict bauxite miners and alumina refinery workers making metal parts for foreign planes in Jamaica. Aerial footage of the country's red mud lakes loops behind the portrait of the labourer, toxic pools built to store unrefined bauxite waste. Then, a second audio-video scene prompts visitors to think about forced removals and dislocation. In it, sixty- and seventy-year-old sisters talk fondly about two tall tamarind trees on Anegada, their flat island home. On a limestone and coral stretch nearly nine miles long, a mile wide, and twenty-three feet above sea level, those trees helped their father and other fishermen navigate around reefs and shoals to shore. These landmarks were felled for the first airstrip to be laid down.[23]

The final installation in "On the Ground" draws attention to gender. An area called "Rise Up" focuses on transatlantic migrations from the 1950s and '60s. Black-and-white photographs on clusters of screens show West Indians sailing to Britain as government-sponsored workers. The storytellers in this section are men for whom air passage is synonymous with protection. Advocating for employees to reach Britain in days instead of weeks by boat, their words, which stream on the screens, warn visitors: "A lot of females proceeding to England by ship get into the hands of some rather unscrupulous males and eventually find themselves pregnant on arrival in England. It would be almost impossible for this to happen if females proceed to England by air."[24]

As travellers on government tickets, black women rarely flew. Years later, they did. Narratives exposed in this unit trace their return migration. They pit the experiences of sailing against those of flying. There are glimpses of women feeling autonomous and liberated in the quickened detachment of vertical flight; a painful sense of individuality that was lost in accounts about faring the former slave-laden sea.[25]

> Out of the huts of history's shame
> I rise

Up from a past that's rooted in pain
I rise
I'm a black ocean, leaping and wide,
Welling and swelling I bear in the tide.

Leaving behind nights of terror and fear
I rise
Into a daybreak that's wondrously clear
I rise ...[26]

In the Air

The airside terminal is a transfer zone, with passengers coming and going. This part of the exhibition is about being en route. It concentrates on feelings central to the African diaspora: amputation, loss, and exile. It toys with words like "departure" and "arrival," terms laced with ambivalence. Individual flyers are brought into focus in a gesture that works against the mechanisms of anonymity imposed on slaves and inherited by their heirs.

In the departure lounge a lightbox declares "Higher Ground." Passersby walk among screens; soundtracks speak of soaring as survival, emancipation, and salvation in the face of relentless racial abuse. On a monitor an image of the black scholar and activist W.E.B. Du Bois appears. He asks us to understand oppressed people as travellers who cultivate a diasporic consciousness. It enables them to go elsewhere and elsewhen, a skill he sees as intimately tied to the terrains of domination and deliverance that uprooted people learn to negotiate.[27] Du Bois explains: "I had thereafter no desire to tear down the veil, to creep through; I held all beyond it in common contempt, and lived above it in a region of blue sky and great wandering shadows."[28]

Nearby, Toni Morrison is singing. In walkways and the in-transit area, she pipes through speakers. She riffs on the folklore of flying Africans, "New World" slaves who soared back to Africa and became ciphers of freedom in the Americas:

O Sugarman don't leave me here
Cotton balls to choke me

O Sugarman don't leave me here
Buckra's arms going to yoke me....

Sugarman done fly away
Sugarman done gone
Sugarman cut across the sky
Sugarman gone home.[29]

While the authoress sings, an air passenger arrives. It is a point of departure in the exhibition; the meaning of flight shifts from the liberation of a people to the ascension of a person. Meet Milkman, a projection. He is a fictional character from Morrison's world. He is searching for his identity. On a wall he writes: "When the little boy discovered, at four, the same thing Mr. Smith had learned earlier – that only birds and airplanes could fly – he lost all interest in himself."[30] Unable to fly, he loses his innocence. Later, he will take to the air and find the literal rise of the individual, intermingled with a dwindling sense of humanity. On an adjacent wall there is further text about Milkman:

> The airplane ride exhilarated him, encouraged illusion and a feeling of invulnerability. High above the clouds, heavy yet light, caught in the stillness of speed ... This one time he wanted to go solo. In the air, away from real life, he felt free, but on the ground, when he talked to Guitar just before he left, the wings of all those other people's nightmares flapped in his face and constrained him.[31]

Conversations about detachment and disengagement continue in the immigration and customs area, a space where surveillance, containment, enforcement, and other kinds of state-sanctioned forms of control manifest. Seven vertical banners hang in the hall. Images on them introduce airline passengers to their fellow travellers: asylum seekers and forced deportees. Photographs and short narratives tell basic facts about those in flight. They are women, children, and men who come from all over Africa and throughout the Caribbean to North America and Western Europe. They need help and are refused. Subsequently, governments of the global north hire guards from private security firms to escort rejected asylum seekers and other forced deportees home. National airlines and major carriers transport them.[32] Onboard, some airline passengers enjoy movies for entertainment while others suffer handcuffed wrists, tape-bound legs, and "carpet karaoke."[33] Sometimes, escorts abuse the guarded:

> Without warning [team leader] dragged detainee [who had been calmly sat down] to her feet and pulled us through some swing doors into a small foyer area out of sight of aircrew, ground crew and passengers. In here he pulled detainee and me to the ground and proceeded to tie her legs together with two pairs of restraints, of a kind I only ever saw him use. In doing so he rested his whole weight across detainee's upper body, which as I later learned carries with it a risk of causing positional asphyxia ... The flight passed off without incident, but on approach to Johannesburg detainee kept trying to unfasten seatbelt, and told child to do the same. Child was sitting in row in front with [another guard], who prevented her from doing so by first pulling the belt tight and then actually sitting on the little girl.[34]

At other times, deportees die. Asphyxiated en route, they are dead on arrival. Among those featured in the exhibition are Aamir Ageeb (Lufthansa flight 558; Frankfurt to Khartoum via Cairo; 28 May 1999), Jimmy Mubenga (British Airways flight 77; Heathrow to Luanda; 12 October 2010), and Semira Adamu (Sabena flight number unknown; Brussels to Togo; 22 September 1998).

Toward the end of the hall, there are two further lightboxes. One asks visitors, "What Would You Do?" Below, a placard invites them to see themselves as an airline passenger on a plane about to depart. Across the cabin sit three security guards and a forced deportee. The former start to use "excessive force" and the latter declares, "I can't breathe, I can't breathe." A telephone rings, and the caller notices, "That sounds really nasty – what's going on?" Ten minutes later, the deportee is unconscious and a guard anticipates, "He'll be alright once we get him in the air – he just doesn't want to go ... once we get him up in the air he'll be allright." The other lightbox asks again, "What happens to our humanity in the air?" The placard below pronounces the trip cancelled and the deportee dead. The remaining wall is blank. Visitors respond on tablet computers and their reflections fill the lacuna.[35]

Exit. Over the door leading out of this liminal place a sign announces, "Arrivals, Departures, Deportures."[36] Clocks delineate the designations; each clock keeps diasporic time: Bridgetown [Arrivals] Toronto [Departures] London [Deportures] Accra.

Waking Up

The Alchemy of Flight is ending. As visitors leave, lightboxes relay the violent affects and jarring effects of flying while black. Some screens list anti-immigration policies while others describe cavity search procedures. On one of them, an airport official in Barbados finger-rapes a woman on arrival from Jamaica. It is the passenger's first time off island, an outing to and from places where many diasporic people dwell. She takes this home with her, like a keepsake:

> When I bent over and spread my (private parts) I felt something enter my (private parts) and when I looked between my legs I saw her gloved hand in my (private parts). I screamed and stood up. She then told me if I obstructed her doing a cavity search she would have me locked up. I bent over again and spread. She again inserted her fingers and poked around. I felt like I was being raped. I was so hurt and ashamed. I felt dirty and defiled … I asked her who she was and she said, "I am your worst nightmare."[37]

Entry denied. She sleeps on a bare sponge mattress on a hard board cot sequestered in a small space. Stripped of options, she flies from Barbados in the morning.[38]

In the immigration screening room, there are many types of travellers. Among them, refused West Indians and other fictive kin wait to be sent away. They sit stigmatized on the notorious "Guyanese Bench." Stories told on airport tabletops recollect these remarkable flyers and their flights. The one about B757-200, a Boeing plane owned and operated by an African airline, stands out. Strikingly, it deals with discord *in* diaspora.

In 2001 the head of a Pan-African organization noted the lack of non-stop skyways between Africa and the West Indies. Without "a direct airline linkage between … the Caribbean and West Africa" citizens of the African diaspora cede power; in transit they loose speed. Decelerated and arrested, they are mediated by imperial networks as they move: "We have to go through either the United States or Britain, a very long journey through Britain."[39]

In 2008 travel conditions changed. A B757-200 owned by Ghana International Airlines took off in Accra and touched down in Barbados. It was the first direct artificial flight between Africa and the Caribbean.[40] It resounded with deep historical significance. The press used the language of diaspora to describe how air passage promised to "reconnect the umbilical cord after thousands were ripped from the womb of Africa." A charter, the airliner carried 149 round-trip passengers across the Atlantic, the return flight scheduled for fourteen days later. When the departure day arrived the return flight never turned up, grounding all the Nigerians and Ghanaians in Barbados for months. Some stuck passengers found work while West Indian and African governments grappled with the politics and price of removal. A few Barbadians fumed, impelling others to ask, "How come you welcome your oppressors over the years with open arms and hate your brother so?" The historic transatlantic trip turned into "The Great African Tourist Scam of 2008," the absent airplane revealing that diaspora still seems to depend on an ability to get up and go.[41]

Getting Up

Dream-states are imaginative communities formed in the face of empire-states and nation-states. And the ability to dream has long been part of how black people create powerful lives for themselves.[42] This curatorial exercise is an opportunity to dream. It invites us to harness and wield imagination. It turns us topsy-turvy into the un-real so that we can use uncertainty to pry open the conventions that create closed narratives.

I have always been suspicious of commands like "Wake Up" or "Get Up." They privilege event and prioritize certain versions of reality. I much prefer process: waking up and getting up. The tossing and turning, the stirring, that keep us connected to our dream-states.

CHAPTER FOUR

By and For Children: History and Healing in a Hospital Museum, KwaZulu-Natal

MONICA EILEEN PATTERSON

On 15 July 2010, a group of about two hundred children, health care workers, community activists, researchers, government officials, and members of the public celebrated the official launch of the KwaZulu-Natal Children's Hospital Restoration Project (KZN CHRP) in eThekwini (Durban), South Africa.[1] They gathered inside the hospital complex where the dilapidated main building still stood, encircled in white sheets that had been stitched together to evoke a giant bandage secured with a larger-than-life safety pin (see figure 4.1). Along the periphery of the grounds, a protective gate displayed enlargements of children's drawings and explanatory text on the hospital's origins. That day of hope was followed by months of frustration, as the project stalled, its projected cost skyrocketed, and unspent provincial funds earmarked for the restoration were returned to the National Treasury. But the initiative is once again moving forward, advancing the latest chapter in a century of struggle for the establishment and protection of a separate children's hospital in the region.

This chapter is situated between the unfolding developments of the actual KZN CHRP and my vision of one path that this and other children's hospitals might pursue.[2] Inspired by the project's visionary leaders, its future patients, and local South African initiatives that could be applied in a wide range of contexts, my curatorial dream presents the unique potential of an arts- and history-based hospital museum that is *by* and *for* children.[3]

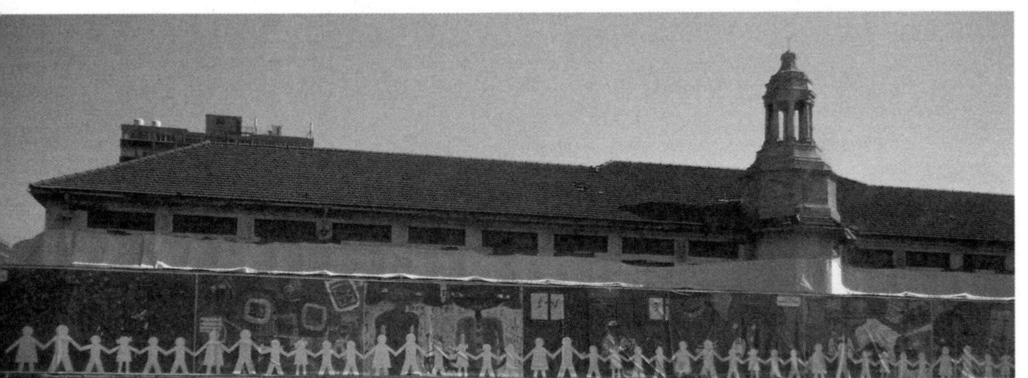

4.1 | KwaZulu-Natal Children's Hospital prepares for renovations, August 2010.

A wide range of actors, including children themselves, have long been active in the advocacy, activism, and engagement that led to the establishment of the originally named Addington Children's Hospital in 1931 and its planned resurrection some seven decades later. Located on the sunny shores of the Indian Ocean, Addington was the first children's hospital in South Africa. For decades before its full closure in 1984, a popular medical museum on the premises attracted local and international visitors alike.

Now flanked by uShaka Marine World theme park to the south and high-rise hotels and condominiums to the north, the renamed KwaZulu-Natal Children's Hospital (KZNCH) will serve as a crucial node in a broader and expanding infrastructure of healthcare, social services, education, and heritage preservation in the province and beyond.[4] With its aim of becoming an integrated children's wellness centre and a regional health precinct, KZNCH Trust CEO Arthi Ramkissoon hopes it will be a "one-stop facility for a whole range of child-related issues."[5] This chapter explores the vast potential of the unique presence of a museum space on a hospital premises. My curatorial dream, then, involves simultaneously re-envisioning what a children's hospital – and a museum – can be.

History of the Children's Hospital

According to popular accounts, when Durban Town Councilor Mary Siedle heard that a ten-year-old boy named James "Mickey" Freshwater died of dysentery in 1923 because of a lack of adequate facilities for children, she and other concerned citizens began plans to create a children's hospital "as a living memorial to youth and life through the alleviation of childhood diseases and suffering."[6] Leading the effort to establish a separate institution for sick children, Siedle was instrumental in securing the four acres of land upon which the hospital was built with grants from the town council (for 3.5 acres) and the provincial government (for 0.5 acres). She also collected over £23,000 GBP (a surplus of £9,000 GBP) as chairwoman of the fundraising committee, a group composed of provincial and city government representatives, healthcare professionals, and members of the public.

According to Catherine Burns, a leading historian, visionary of the hospital restoration project, and former advisor at MatCH, plans for the building were drafted by government architect John Stockwin Cleland, chief architect of the Public Works department, and designer of many other hospitals and health facilities in South Africa.[7] In accordance with a growing appreciation for the interconnectedness of psychological well-being, aesthetics, fresh air, and bodily health in the 1920s and '30s, the architect and planners aimed to make the wards as open and cheerful as possible to help speed children's recovery.[8] Large balconies were thus installed, with custom-made doors that could be fully opened on nice days, exposing the children to sunlight and the fresh sea breeze. Rendered in Union Period style, the six-ward, sixty-six-patient-capacity Children's Hospital was also equipped with an open-air sunbath, gardens, courtyards, and tennis courts for the nursing staff.[9] Planners commissioned South African artist Mary Stainbank and her British colleague and friend Wilgeford Vann-Hall to produce hundreds of works for installation, and the pair worked intensely between 1926 and 1930, creating statues, stained glass windows, ceramic pieces, relief panels, and glazed fountain figurines to grace the grounds.[10]

Attached to the main hospital, Addington opened its doors – to white children only – on 12 February 1931, some eight years after Mary Siedle first conceived of a separate children's hospital, attached to the main hospital.[11] Following the Second World War, the hospital admitted only children officially registered as White or Coloured, but a new outpatient section was established to extend specialized services to African and Indian children.[12] This movement toward broader racial inclusiveness eventually created problems for hospital staff, however, as in the early 1970s, when tensions between the *verlichte* (Afrikaans for "enlightened") Children's Hospital workers and the *verkrampte* (closed-minded, literally, "cramped") pro-apartheid establishment played out in intra-institutional battles over the relationship between the Durban Children's Hospital and the adjacent general Addington Hospital.[13] In 1971, citing the need for "budget cuts and savings," the operating rooms at the Children's Hospital were closed.[14]

In 1979 hospital staff began admitting children of colour, "non-whites" in the parlance of the times, further alienating the institution and its advocates from the Nationalist leadership in Pretoria. These were the years of "high apartheid," in which the government imposed major structural changes that stripped Africans of even more of their already limited rights and economic opportunities. But as Burns notes, even white children's needs were subordinated to the "louder voices of centralized planning and management-driven care," and in 1984 the Durban Children's Hospital wards were permanently closed.[15] The children's health services that were not dissolved outright were significantly downgraded or fractured, and relocated to the thirteenth floor of Addington Hospital. In particular, surgery was severely curtailed. In 1985 the state appointed Dr Mannie Steyn to chair a commission of inquiry tasked with investigating the future of the Durban Children's Hospital. As Burns comments, such official "one-man" commissions were a common tactic of the non-transparent, non-inclusive, and authoritarian apartheid state, and its findings were never released to the public.[16] Over the next several years, repeated requests to rehabilitate and reopen the building for people needing services were refused. From late 1991 to early 1992, as negotiations for the transition to democratic rule in South Africa began,[17] a group of long-time activists and progressive doctors at the Medical School in Durban formed a collective advocating for the "just and equitable use of this special space for the increasing needs of children of the city."[18]

After a solid decade of sustained organization and effort, the KZN CHRP was launched in June 2010 with a 118-million rand project budget. According to the project's website, the fundraising goal now sits at 540 million rand, or 50 million US dollars.[19] At the launch, officials projected a two-and-a-half year timeline to completion, which was later adjusted to five years.[20] Since it closed its doors in 1984, the hospital building has survived two fires (in which arson was suspected), and almost three decades of neglect and vandalism.

The Children's Hospital Museum

With its unique period artwork and architecture, and as South Africa's first hospital for children, the Durban Children's Hospital has been recognized by the Architectural Heritage Trust and Amafa, the provincial heritage conservation agency for KwaZulu-Natal, as a valuable heritage site. Of particular interest and importance to heritage conservationists – and to readers of this volume concerned with innovative curation strategies – is the presence of a small museum in the historic Nurses' Quarters at Addington, which opened in 1979. The Addington Centenary Museum collection includes archives and artifacts dating back to 1900. Housing a modest exhibit still listed on tourism websites as a popular site of interest (though for years no longer open to the public), the Addington Museum presented a well-worn narrative of the triumph of Western biomedicine over earlier and other forms of medical practice – complete with historical artifacts such as turn-of-the-century tools for tooth extraction.[21]

When I became aware of interest in preserving and updating the museum space in the overall renovation, it struck me as an ideal opportunity to address the interconnections between contemporary health issues and the history of apartheid, particularly as they relate to the under-acknowledged and over-simplified history of childhood in South Africa. This is a history of violence, racism, and sickness; but also of resilience and agency. In South Africa, apartheid produced a set of complex entanglements, contradictions, and inconsistencies that rendered black children at turns extensions of women, carriers of disease, beneficiaries of white custodianship, future labourers, pitiful innocents, targets of a security state, or simply invisible.[22] The consequences of these policies and practices still continue to unfold in the public health issues that face the country.

While the formal system of apartheid may have been officially dismantled more than two decades ago, countless legacies of this legally enshrined and socially upheld system of racial oppression endure. In the absence of significant socioeconomic change and psychosocial repair following the end of apartheid, a tiny (still disproportionately white) South African minority live in relative opulence while the vast (largely black) majority struggle to survive. This inequality continues to determine the distribution of resources in South Africa today, and hence the distribution of suffering among its people.[23] The HIV/AIDS epidemic has had a detrimental effect on many aspects of South African society in the post-apartheid era, including children's health. South Africa has more people living with HIV than any other country: more than 6 million in 2013.[24]

But there are particular challenges to the health and happiness of poor children in the province of KwaZulu-Natal, where the children's hospital (KZNCH) is located. With provincial prevalence rates of 37.4 percent reported among women attending antenatal clinics in 2011,[25] KwaZulu-Natal has long been considered one of the world's HIV/AIDS "hotspots." As a result, the country has the largest orphan population caused by AIDS in the world.[26] Children who have lost parents to HIV/AIDS are stigmatized to varying degrees within their communities as a result of their association with the disease. While most other parts of the world have seen drops in child mortality rates, as the KZNCH website notes, the rate in the KwaZulu-Natal region is rising, largely because of the prevalence of HIV, which contributes to 50 to 60 percent of deaths in children under the age of five.[27] The region, and South Africa more generally, is also plagued with a related tuberculosis epidemic featuring drug-resistant strains of the disease.[28] Another exacerbating factor for health in the region is that Durban is one of the most polluted areas in the world.[29] With its primary constituency of black, poor, sick children at the bottom of multiple hierarchies, how can the Children's Hospital Museum maximize its impact in the current socioeconomic reality?

To address children's health in South Africa today is to intervene in history. It requires attending to environmental, social, political, and cultural issues. Such work must interrupt the deeply entrenched conditions and structures of a political economy that has kept a poor black majority impoverished and marginalized, even in the post-apartheid era. A meaningful curatorial intervention would require a new way of conceiving of children, not as mere recipients of care but as valuable resources in today's society and active agents in larger historical struggles against poverty, inequality, and suffering. Achieving this deeper understanding of children's importance in turn demands greater recognition of the many ways in which South African children and youth were pivotal in toppling the apartheid regime: beyond their varied roles in the Soweto Uprising of 1976 they were and continue to be effective as local and international spokespersons on a range of issues, including children's rights. In addition, children have always been vital members of households, schools, communities, and economies, and though often un(der)acknowledged, their participation has a significant impact on these domains.

Re-imagining the Museum

Reflecting the racist underpinnings of colonialism and apartheid, museums and monuments in South Africa traditionally celebrated apartheid and its beneficiaries, while demonizing, belittling, or simply ignoring the black majority population. Post-independence, initial attempts to democratize such sites in terms of both access and content focused on correcting one-sided, often overtly racist representations to insert the experiences of South Africa's black population into the historical record and commemorative landscape. But many of these initiatives were designed and imposed from outside the communities they sought to represent, and lacked the kind of community involvement that should have driven the process.[30] Many have, for example, criticized the hegemony of ANC-centred interpretations, narratives, and key figures.[31] Furthermore, many of the new monuments, museums, and memorials in South Africa have catered to foreign visitors, and have emerged from an orientation in which culture and history are increasingly commodified for (tourist) consumption.[32] Finally, the dominant notion of inclusion has remained largely grounded in apartheid-era racial categories, which rarely allow for more textured or nuanced representations of differentiated black community.

The socioeconomic realities of contemporary, post-apartheid South Africa demand multiple, overlapping interventions, not isolated or temporary solutions. To that end, I propose that the mission of the KZN Children's Hospital Museum (KZN CHM) should be to provide visitors with a holistic encounter that will have a positive impact on their lives in ways that extend to their families, classmates, and communities, and continue beyond the time spent on the premises. Such an ambitious goal requires first and foremost that the patients of the Children's Hospital be recognized as a crucial resource in extending the museum's impact. In what follows, I explore possibilities for using the institutional space of the hospital museum to create a more dynamic, democratic, and participatory space of encounter and emergence. The museum I envision will directly engage with complexities around the roles, experiences, and participation of children in South African society, and their continued marginalization in many spheres. In so doing, the difficult task of animating South Africa's constitutional ideals into broader social practice and everyday thinking may be advanced in a small, unique way, and may serve more generally as a model for social justice in museology.

Two of the strongest impulses in the last twenty years in what has been termed "New Museology" are the calls for museums to democratize, and to evolve into more engaging, dynamic sites.[33] The KZN CHM is uniquely situated to build on these goals by becoming a museum not just *about*, but *by* and *for* children. Thinking across these three vectors – each with its own purpose, concerns, and constraints – opens new possibilities for more inclusive participation in a *living museum* defined as much by the activities, conversations, and experiences it fosters as by the content it may feature.

Re-envisioning the museum to address these three dimensions – about, by, and for children – requires an elaborate exercise in curating difficult knowledge.[34] This includes knowledge about racism, inequality, illness, poverty, suffering, and death. It demands that children be recognized as expressive agents, involved in acts ranging from the laudable to the unthinkable. Would it be possible to create a dynamic space that is nurturing for all children – including those who may never leave the hospital and whose lives may be cut very short – while simultaneously engaging with the painful historical realities that they faced, and often continue to face?[35] To do so we must ask: How can the history of childhood in South Africa best address the often silenced racism that erased black children from the picture (even while powerfully invoking universalist framings of "the child")? What insights from recent critical museology might address the cultural, historical, and political issues that define the situation of children in South Africa today? How can these be leveraged to engage suffering in ways that involve children as active contributors with their own considered perspectives?

Curatorial Strategies: Multifunctionality, Localism, and Constellation

My vision for the KZN CHM is based on three curatorial strategies: multifunctionality, localism, and constellation. Most commonly referenced in agriculture, *multifunctionality* refers to the capacity for a given activity to produce numerous benefits in different domains. Although it may not be named as such, the idea is increasingly driving the approach of many museums striving to survive. From the earliest days of its conceptualization, the original Addington and renamed KZN Children's Hospital functioned as a vehicle for a wide range of work: in addition to the employment and healthcare it provided, it was also a key site of artistic expression and philanthropic, memorial, museological, political, and human rights work. In the South African context, multifunctionality is a survival strategy for the millions who must eke maximum value from every resource. In the face of such privation, it is important that every aspect of the KZN CHM fulfill multiple needs of visitors and their larger communities. I therefore propose that the museum commit to multifunctionality as a primary methodology.

At the hospital's Restoration Project Launch in June 2010, the children's cause was used to morally frame and politically demand both abstract principles of human rights and specific state-provided services. As stated by KZN Member of the Executive Council (MEC) Sibongiseni Dhlomo:[36]

> The healthy growth and development of children is crucial to the future of this province and country. Health and wellbeing are an integral part of the child's right to life, survival, and development. The principle of human rights is universal and each child, including the adolescent, is entitled to fundamental rights and freedom. Our government's mandate is universal, as enshrined in our Constitution. It calls for equity: the enjoyment of the highest attainable standard of health is one of the fundamental rights of every

human being without distinction of race, religion, and political belief, economic or social condition.[37]

This fusion of nation building, health, human rights, and children's welfare invokes multiple, historically powerful (if sometimes empty) discourses, and performs multifunctionality on a discursive level: providing quality health care for children not only improves their lives individually but ensures the nation's future, while promoting freedom and equity. But on the ground, through a long history of grassroots activism, children's rights have proven to be a potent political node around which many broader sociopolitical and historical issues have cohered. Identifying the multifunctional possibilities in addressing these issues can yield a deeper understanding of their historical roots and present realities. For instance, during the last decades of apartheid rule, after political parties were banned and public gatherings were severely curtailed, community days were organized for children that both enabled their parents and caretakers to organize and to meet, and prompted reflection and action on the basic rights that children should enjoy. As far as the apartheid government knew, the events were simply creative workshops enabling children to express themselves through art, music, and theatre. But some of the cultural production that children created in these workshops circulated through local and global children's rights and anti-apartheid literature and drew attention to the deplorable conditions of black childhood in apartheid South Africa to wider publics. What started as highly localized efforts helped drive the global children's rights movement, and the movement's growing momentum symbiotically directed international attention and resources to a range of South African organizations. Today, similarly harnessing, utilizing, and directing the power of such multifunctional activities can also help galvanize efforts to manifest socioeconomic change.

With the (unrealized) hope of lasting economic stimulation promised by the proponents of South Africa's hosting of the FIFA-sponsored Soccer World Cup in June–July 2010, powerful local politicians and business people targeted the prime real estate upon which the old hospital sits for tourist development.[38] At stake in the ensuing debates, which still continue, are competing claims about the priorities of the ongoing project of nation building, the best way to address the needs of grossly underserved publics, and the comparative importance of local communities in these decisions as the consequences of apartheid policies and practices continue to reverberate in public health issues facing the country. Multifunctionality involves making every act, artifact, and activity beneficial in as many ways as possible, embedding maximum functionality and value into each component.

A strong case can be made for using scholarly research and community collaboration to intervene in social problems and to communicate with broader – particularly local – audiences about issues that affect them.[39] Drawing from existing local resources, initiatives, and ideas – what I call *localism* – not only helps to conserve effort and energy but also helps to ensure relevance and resonance, which are crucial for the long-term success of any public institution. With the increasing globalization and corporatization of heritage and museological production of many memory projects, local values and practices are not adequately considered or engaged. This neglect can result in lost opportunity, wasted resources, and feelings of resentment and alienation in host communities.[40] A commitment to localism must therefore drive the KZN CHM orientation at all levels.

My third curatorial strategy, *constellation*, involves looking outward with the goal of integration across disciplines and sectors: identifying, seeking out, and strengthening connections across expansive networks in order to actively position the museum within multiple broader contexts. Unlike networking, which maintains a core centre from which connections are made through various forms of outreach, constellation demands multiple versions of a single institution in relation to the assemblage of other units with which it is aligned. So for some visitors, the Children's Hospital may be a place for medical treatment and care, for others a site for health education, and still others an enjoyable diversion in a commuting itinerary, or the venue for the latest popular art exhibit.

The Children's Hospital and its unique museum are well positioned to connect and involve families, communities, nurses-in-training, social workers, educators, health workers, researchers, heritage workers, tourists, and children. On the premises there will be satellite offices for various NGOs, as well as the departments of Education, Social Development, and

Home Affairs. When it come to procedures like applying for and receiving disability grants, all these offices will be able to provide better services by constellating their efforts. The museum must situate itself within multiple clusters of related institutions such as the Red Cross Children's Hospital Trust, the Department of Health, the Children's Rights Centre, and the Provincial Treasury; and it will have the potential to capitalize on opportunities and places where the work it is doing on-site may be reinforced in the public realm, schools, government, health, and local communities.[41] Working with already existing infrastructure and institutions to complement and augment the museum's efforts is particularly important in a society plagued with extreme poverty and inequality.[42]

Combining the curatorial strategies of multifunctionality, localism, and constellation, the KZNCH includes plans for eco-therapy and environmental psychology components to the children's care and rehabilitation package. To this end, planners will consult with urban designers, play therapists, fitness experts, and children themselves to collaboratively design multi-purpose open spaces that help connect the Children's Hospital and Museum to other buildings and services in the precinct. Safe pedestrian walkways, bike paths, sidewalks, and conveniently placed, well-marked pathways and waiting areas for the People Mover public transport bus will link the various buildings. These areas will feature sculpture gardens, play areas, and scenic walks. The museum entrance will be easily accessible from the south beach's open new promenade, maintaining a sense of connection to life outside the hospital.

Planners have already committed to "greening" the spaces of the hospital grounds. As described by education specialists Janet Dymant and Anne Bell, greening is a growing international movement focusing "primarily on the design, use and culture of school grounds, with a view to improving the quality of children's play and learning experiences."[43] Their research has demonstrated the importance of environmental factors for children's physical activity levels, and for promoting active, imaginative, and constructive play, civil behaviour, and a better integration of physical activity into life more generally. By replacing some of the asphalt with a range of outdoor features (such as nature trails, trees, composting stations, art, mixed terrain, bird feeders, greenhouses, fountains, and food, flower, and butterfly gardens), they argue that children's "play repertoires" are also diversified, in turn increasing their opportunity for physical activity. Combining other kinds of terrain with asphalt, which provides even ground and allows wheelchairs to roll, will also enable a wider range of children to be active, and will expand the possibilities for play beyond the rule-based, competitive games that asphalt and sports fields tend to promote.

Dyment and Bell maintain that green spaces invite greater, more inclusive community involvement and an increased sense of investment.[44] In many ways, the application of greening practices is a return to the earlier visions of Mary Stainbank and the Addington Children's Hospital planners for the space as a place for nurturing and promoting not only physical but also social and cognitive health. Involving children as active participants in the process of greening can extend the benefits of such practices beyond the hospital grounds. Workshops on gardening, composting, and the use of indigenous medicinal herbs, for instance, could provide hands-on opportunities for children to learn skills directly related to the improvement and maintenance of their health and well-being.

Interventions and Exhibits

Restoration project planners have expressed interest in creating on the hospital site a lively new museum that is open to the public, drawing in tourists and locals alike. It is important to think expansively about constituency, and to recognize the many roles children embody: as potential patients, students, family members, community builders, expressive individuals, and agents with interests and agendas. Other populations, including family members, researchers, hospital staff, and members of various local communities, will also visit the museum or be influenced by its existence. The museum will include collaborative, community-engaged, interactive temporary and permanent exhibitions, using diverse multimedia presentation strategies, aspects I expand on below. The exhibits should focus not only on tangible but also on intangible cultural heritage,[45] and allow for multiple and emergent narratives (rather than closed, dominant, authoritative accounts). One of the best – and simplest – ways to facilitate these ambitious goals is to create opportunities for visitors to engage with and comment on the content that the museum presents. The exhibits should therefore be designed to promote and inspire dialogue, presenting the history of health and healing in South Africa dynamically, with particular attention to children's roles and experiences.

According to Burns, the new museum's permanent exhibition will "act as a magnet for health education, as well as [presenting] works that stretch and engage us around the complex history of health in South Africa, a lens through which to view so many layers of our history."[46] The museum collection contains the many pictures, letters, diaries, and medical and healing instruments featured in the Addington Hospital's original exhibit, in addition to original artworks, sculptures, and mosaics created by noted South African artists Barbara Tyrell, Mary Stainbank, and Wilgeford Vann-Hall. But the future exhibition is intended to present the long history of Western, African, and Indian healing traditions in the region, including content on the roles of traditional healers, nurses, midwives, and doctors, the rise of Indian Ayurvedic medicine in Durban and in KZN, and the achievements of the first professional nursing and medical elite among the amaKholwa (Christian converts) of the region.[47] Drawing from oral historical sources and using narrative framings that incorporate visual, audio, and other sensory materials, the exhibits will explore the social impact of disease and its context (poverty, race, gender, power, personal sacrifice, and striving.[48]

In my curatorial dream for the Children's Hospital Museum, a significant section of the museum will explore understandings of childhood itself. Such a topic is important at this site because children – particularly those who are hospital patients facing the possibility of death – need a space to engage with life in all its dimensions. Adults, too, must confront the realities of what it has meant to be a child in South Africa, in order to change this reality for the future. Through a critical history of children's rights in the country and abroad (with participating children's rights organizations as partners), my proposed exhibition will examine South African childhoods, the role of children and youth in the struggle for liberation, and local child heroes and heroines. The museum will address several questions relating to childhood, including: What is the history of childhood in this region where the infant mortality rate is rising, and where romantic imaginings and assumptions about childhood as a time of innocence, comfort, and freedom from labour and strife are often inadequate or even irrelevant? What is childhood like in South Africa today? What can it be?

Maximizing opportunities for multifunctionality, localism, and constellation, I envision that exhibit planners will work with local educators to ensure that exhibits augment and draw from primary and secondary school curricula to facilitate the integration of field trip visits from area school children throughout the school year.[49] Exhibit design should be generated through transparent and collaborative processes that involve community members, patients, and at every stage, children, taking them into account both as primary constituents and as resident experts. In addition, community organization and NGO partners, health care and social service workers, parents, and children themselves can help identify and recruit local children who might benefit from participation in hospital museum programming. Given that the definition of "child" is an open debate in South Africa, where the internationally sanctioned termination of childhood at the moment of reaching eighteen years does not adequately reflect the plasticity of more nuanced and context-specific social understandings of "child" and "adult," a generational approach to gathering young people in flexible age cohorts that reflect cultural and communal understandings of childhood is advised.[50] Interactive exhibits with the capacity to record visitor responses can double as vehicles for data collection and community forums, lending deeper insights into the question of what it means to be a child to various constituencies. I propose several "Community Days of Dialogue" a year: workshops organized around a single question such as "What are children's rights and responsibilities?" or "How do you practise good health?" Organized in partnership with local groups, these open community workshops will produce educational content, build community, connect patients with the outside community, collect data, and offer opportunities for self-expression and dialogue.

While democratizing the museum space and the processes leading to the creation of exhibits, I suggest that other spaces in the health precinct may include exhibit components such as plaques and informational panels that make visible the history of the hospital and the region, and installations of children patients' artwork in available spaces. Engaging and provocative public service messages concerning health and wellness should also be integrated into the health precinct's public spaces, particularly in the waiting areas. The museum can generate revenue through a coffee and gift shop that sells children's books and toys, and originals, prints, postcards, and catalogues of children's artwork. Local institutional partners such as the Killie Campbell Africana Library and Museum should be consulted for assistance with documentation and reproduction, and new opportunities for collaboration should be identified.

Children's Art Gallery and Art Production

First and foremost, the museum will be a child-centred space. Drawing from the field of art therapy, the KZN CHM will serve as a venue both for the display of children's original artwork produced by hospital patients on the premises and by children from the region, and for workshop-based discussions with the aim of creating friendships and allegiances across lines of difference. Creating art serves many functions for children. It can provide a means of creative self-expression, education, dialogue, memorialization, fun, and psychosocial repair. It can also help children deepen their cognitive, linguistic, creative, and social development.

Historically, children's art in South Africa has conveyed powerful messages to local communities and to the world about the harsh realities the artists have faced. During the 1980s and early 1990s in particular, children's art featured regularly in international and local anti-apartheid posters, calendars, books, and pamphlets as an indictment against a system deemed by the United Nations in 1973 to be a crime against humanity.[51] Several travelling exhibits became public, political rallying grounds as they toured South Africa and beyond.[52]

While my imagined core exhibit presents a brief history of the role of children's art and travelling exhibits in the struggle against apartheid, the hospital will also feature an adjacent art gallery that will allow something of the museum to spill out into the larger expanse of the hospital. Display parameters will privilege child viewers, with art displayed professionally, but lower on the wall to meet a range of children's eye-levels.[53] Labelling will not only include child-appropriate language (in several of South Africa's eleven official languages), but will involve audio components and various methods of recording viewers' reactions to the artworks. Children will participate in workshops to generate labels for the museum's works as a way to initiate dialogue, build self-confidence, encourage self-expression, and come up with better labels. Visitors will also be invited to create their own labels, and responses, and attach them to designated areas with adhesive notes. A guest curator program will invite children who are hospital patients to curate temporary exhibits, producing curatorial statements that explain their choices in the selection and arrangement of artworks. These exhibits will be digitized, and their works tagged and archived with open access for researchers and members of the public. Child-friendly (touchable, sit-able, climbable) sculptural works can also be incorporated into open spaces and along walkways.

Several local initiatives are already doing important work within the intersection of art, healing, and oral history, and their methods could be productively employed in workshops for children at the hospital.[54] Three examples come to mind. The first, South African artist Jane Solomon's "body mapping" process, was developed in 2002 as a form of art and narrative therapy through memory work for people living with HIV/AIDS in South Africa.[55] In a series of workshops, participants help each other to trace the outlines of their bodies onto large pieces of paper, sketching and painting in images and words to express their life experiences in personal, often intimate self-portraits. The body mapping process includes visualization exercises, group discussion, reflection, sharing, and community engagement, which could be powerfully combined with education about health and illness at the KZN CHM.

A second example may be found in the the Memory Box Programme, established in 2000 by the Sinomlando Centre for Oral History and Memory Work in South Africa. Combining artistic expression and oral history methodology, the project was designed to assist vulnerable children facing the loss of parents and loved ones to HIV/AIDS. Facilitators help to gather family life histories from sick parents or caregivers, and provide a recording and transcription of the interview to be stored in the child's "memory box." These decorated boxes contain the life story of the deceased, personal mementos, and the child's artwork and writing. The boxes are produced over a series of about nine weekly workshops with ten to twelve children participants, using techniques from play and art therapy.[56] The extended process of making these receptacles of memory helps build community, establish on-going support networks, document lost lives, and provide an outlet for children's self-expression. Most importantly, the project helps to foster resilience as the children come to terms with negotiating loss.

A third, similar, initiative is "The Suitcase Project," first organized by educationist and researcher Glynis Clacherty in 2001, to provide psycho-social support for refugee children in Hillbrow in Johannesburg.[57] In facilitated group settings, children come together to share their experiences of war and displacement, their struggles with identity and xenophobia, and their hopes and dreams for the future. Through a creative process of designing their own individual suitcases and with the support of art therapist Diane Welvering, the children explore questions of identity and reclaim memories. As Clacherty describes it, the suitcase is a powerful symbol and medium for immigrant children not only because it alludes to journeys but because it possesses both an open public face and a hidden interior. She hoped the suitcases could "help some of the children to reclaim the memories, both difficult and happy, that they were now choosing to hide."[58] Providing children with counselling, an outlet for personal and creative expression, education, and opportunities to develop their skills and support networks, the project is designed to help children counteract their sense of loss and displacement resulting from oftentimes forced migration from their homes. In addition to forming meaningful and often rare personal possessions for the children who produce them, the suitcases are also powerful artifacts, dense with meaning, symbolism, and cultural and historical information and, with their creators' permission, are worthy of exhibition and sustained engagement.

In connection with the KZN CH Restoration Project, associated children's groups have been participating in a child-initiated international program called "Room 13," a "social enterprise organization" started by a group of primary school students in Scotland. Room 13 helps to bring adult artists-in-residence to interested schools and communities to work in a mentoring capacity for children in art studios that they set up, work in, and administer. At the artists' discretion, prints and originals of some of the artwork they produce could be sold online and in the KZN CHM gift shop to generate funds for materials and operating costs. The agentive, child-empowering framework of this project is important and unique. As the participants in South Africa's fifteen partner schools in South Africa write:

> Room 13 is a place where our imagination runs free. It is a place for us to go to after school and express our creativity through painting, drawing, drama, poetry and storytelling, any form of artistic expression we desire. We run Room 13 ourselves – we have our own management team and we choose our artist-in-residence to act as our employee and run our studio like a business. Our biggest project yet was to let you know who we are and what we do, so we created our own website for you to see for yourselves … So check it out and see what our art lets us do.[59]

Original art is available for sale on the website and in Room 13 studios around the globe.[60] Constellating beyond the Children's Hospital Museum itself, with the artists' permission children's art produced in the Room 13 studio will decorate and enliven many other spaces in the hospital complex. Labelling and signage by children and adults will also help direct people in other parts of the precinct to the museum and gallery space.

In the past few decades, memorials for the dead have proliferated around the globe. They are often site-based, reflecting the value placed on the aura of authenticity and return: visitors want to "be there," in the place where loved ones last lived, as a way of (re)connecting.[61] Memorialization has been embedded throughout the Children's Hospital since its inception, with commemorative plaques honouring hospital donors' deceased family members installed in hallways, gardens, and above cots. Several rooms or wings were also named after the deceased.[62] But such approaches hardly exhaust the therapeutic potential for memorialization and commemoration in the hospital's unique space. A hospital is a place where death is institutionalized and commonplace, but also tragic. How might on-site commemoration both honour those who have passed and comfort the living – a group that includes family members of the deceased but also sick patients who are still receiving treatment at the hospital? What ethical issues are involved in mourning and memorializing loss of life when children are involved not only as mourners, but also as the mourned? And how can the KZN CHM protect space for the personal and culturally specific processes of mourning a child's death, while also acknowledging or even emphasizing that the circumstances of physical health and sickness are embedded in larger socioeconomic conditions?

Serving a broad demographic, the KZN CHM is a powerful place to address and make visible these often-obscured aspects of hospitals, as part of a holistic approach to treating health in all its dimensions: physical, psychological, emotional, historical, cultural, and social. I propose that a special Memorial Room next to an interfaith prayer and contemplation room provide a space for hospital visitors to think and talk about loss, death, and dying – as well as to remember and commemorate those who have passed. With the permission of their creators, products of the body mapping, memory box, and suitcase workshops may be displayed to facilitate exploration of these issues, offering an intimate entryway into larger social, cultural, and political challenges that other parts of the exhibit might address. The Memorial Room will also allow for a range of activities, including workshops and presentations by grief counsellors, culturally specific events, and memorial services with community members.

Conclusion

As South African author and activist Gabeba Baderoon has written, "What we choose to display in our public spaces, who curates our perspectives, who becomes visible to us in art – represents a national conversation [of] who 'we' are."[63] Museums can thus extend the parameters of visibility and engagement. As both communal and state institutions, they can serve as forums for important dialogue and debate. A site of potentially impactful intervention, today's newly named KwaZulu-Natal Children's Hospital Museum is a place where the powerful and fraught category of "childhood" can be publicly unpacked and leveraged *by* and *for* children, affording them a place in national debates not only as the subject of more serious discussion, but as sovereign participants in the conversation themselves. Through children's active participation in this unique institution situated at the interface of many needs and services, children and those who care for and about them can re-envision what a museum and a children's hospital can be. Drawing on the expertise, experience, and hopes of community members, academics, business leaders, members of government, and non-governmental organizations, planners have committed to private-public partnership – a groundbreaking approach in a country where the quality and availability of healthcare are still overwhelmingly determined by one's race and class. The history of the hospital parallels the larger story of apartheid, and offers opportunities to reopen and reconsider questions about children's agency, worldviews, and life circumstances. My curatorial dream envisions the KZN CHM as a potentially transgressive space for moving beyond those circumstances and their ongoing legacies, by taking South African children seriously not just as recipients of advocacy and care but as active participants who deserve space to express themselves and to shape the institutions that serve them according to their needs and wishes.

PART TWO

Breaking Frames

CHAPTER FIVE

Frozen World/Mundo Congelado: AIDS, Chicano Art, and the Queer Remains of Mundo Meza

ROBB HERNÁNDEZ

Little is known of artist Edmundo "Mundo" Meza. Born in Tijuana, Mexico, on 19 July 1955 and raised in Huntington Park, California, he is a forerunner of experimental performance, a genre more closely linked to the white male embodiment of Vito Acconci, Chris Burden, and Allan Kaprow in contemporary art.[1] With Robert "Cyclona" Legorreta and Gronk in 1969–72, Meza traversed the streets of East Los Angeles like a Neo-Dada barrio *flâneur*, rupturing banal urban landscapes in fabric swaths, found detritus, and attention-grabbing visages imbued with Kabuki theatrics, clown aesthetics, and androgynous masquerade.

Meza was a deeply influential figure among Chicano artists from Garfield High School, artists like Harry Gamboa Jr, Gronk, Willie Herrón, and Patssi Valdez who later founded Asco (Spanish for "Disgust") in 1972. Though Meza was invited to join the collective – making the legendary group of four, five – he instead embarked upon a promising commercial career in L.A.'s nascent art and fashion industry, mingling with Hollywood glitterati, fashionistas, and "New Wave" émigrés from the UK.[2] This environment nurtured an artistic vision predicated on *tableau vivant* settings, mannequin forms, taxidermy props, and photorealist still-lifes, a shocking pastiche populating his window display installations in trendy Melrose boutiques. This "frozen" vocabulary was an essential element of his oeuvre. However, his burgeoning career took a sudden turn. He was growing sick. Just months from his thirtieth birthday, Meza passed away from AIDS complications. And yet, it is the mystery surrounding the aftermath of his death in 1985 that serves as the impetus for this exhibition. The entire body of his work vanished, marking one of the greatest travesties wrought by AIDS on the Chicano art world. Through the trace of the artist and the imprint of his little-seen aesthetic, *Frozen World/Mundo Congelado* dares to resurrect the queer remains of Mundo Meza, telling a story never meant to be told.

In my curatorial dream, the above text comprises the opening statement of my show, a restorative archival exhibition that operates on three levels. First, the show illuminates the pervasive trace of Mexican American gender and sexual transgression in Chicano art history by confronting the ephemerality of "queer evidence" and finding its remains in art archives.[3] The outcome of this confrontation is to contest archives as impartial bodies of record, passive collecting units, and neutral venues. Second, the show narrates the devastating consequence of the AIDS crisis on Chicano avant-gardists in the early 1980s by presenting a collection of photographic, artifactual, and documentary remains of Mundo Meza's body of work.[4] By embracing the void of his paintings specifically, the exhibition magnifies this moment of crisis in contemporary Chicano art, using loss as the symbolic and cultural tool. Third, it recuperates Meza's interest in "frozen art" as a curatorial tactic, exploring his aesthetic through audience encounters with Photo/Book/Fossils, Installation Relics, and Phantom Gallery display. By exhibiting Meza's tenuous place in Chicano art at the intersections of liveness/stillness, presence/absence, permeation/glaciation, I dream his oeuvre from its end in ruin to a future of restoration and possibility.

Frozen World/Mundo Congelado emerges at a pivotal moment in Chicano exhibition history and the cultural politics of California more broadly. In the fall of 2011, the Getty launched *Pacific Standard Time: Art in L.A. 1945–1980*, drawing on 170 exhibitions from 130 partnering museums and galleries.[5] Their initiative marked an historic occasion for the city, boosting five Chicano art shows at major cultural institutions like the Museum of Latin American Art, UCLA Fowler Museum, and Autry National Center, a first in L.A. history. In particular, the historic retrospective, *ASCO: Elite of the Obscure*, opened at the L.A. County Museum of Art (LACMA) on 4 September 2011. The first Chicano art collective exhibition at LACMA since the Los Four show in 1974, the Asco retrospective examined the significant contributions of this renegade Chicano conceptualist art group, which initially consisted of Harry Gamboa Jr, Gronk, Willie Herrón, and Patssi Valdez, with its later iterations explored in other galleries. Facing the difficult task of curating conceptual-performance work, LACMA drew on photo-documentation, Super-8 film recording, and ephemera formulating Asco's confrontational and absurdist language in print material and performance props. Organized in a series of rooms, each area highlighted interventionist street actions, experimental image-text pieces, and shifting artistic perspectives. In a gallery entitled Art/Life: Expanded Collaborations and Networks, a cast of characters populating Asco's world are cited, including a cohort of gender- and genre-bending avant-gardists, among them Robert "Cyclona" Legorreta, Edmundo "Mundo" Meza, Joey Terrill, and Teddy Sandoval.[6] As provocation was likely a key curatorial goal for this retrospective – and was in any case achieved – divergent sexual identities, practices, and behaviours in the Chicano avant-garde were gestured at in the show, begging further aesthetic and historical explication.

Leaving ASCO: *Elite of the Obscure*, I found myself pursuing another line of inquiry. Because the retrospective was chronologically organized through the life of the collective in 1972–87, its reciprocal relationship to death remained unanswered. In its effort to reproduce and regenerate "presence" in the museum, it understates the way this timeframe was shaped by "absence," the absence of subjects, audiences, and documents devastated by the outbreak. I wondered: what impact did AIDS have on this generation of Chicano artists in the 1980s? If Asco formed the cultural centre of the avant-garde and symbolically anointed as such by a prestigious art institution like LACMA, what happens when we occupy its queer deathly margins?

These questions shed light on the power of the disease and its devastating consequences on Chicano contemporary art – not only on the artists' lives but also on the ways in which queer Chicano aesthetics, art networks, and audiences were obliterated by death. The careful examination of artists like Legorreta, Meza, Sandoval, and Terrill in ASCO: *Elite of the Obscure* has been surprisingly restrained, further supporting David Román's claims that in our present cultural context we get "the sense that AIDS is over."[7] In turn, we must intervene in a reified post-AIDS discourse in both the art museum and Chicano art history. AIDS as a curatorial endeavour needn't be a relic of the 1980s and 1990s defined by exhibitions that incited a range of emotion and mixed critical responses like Nicholas Nixon's *People with AIDS* photo retrospective at Museum of Modern Art in 1988, Nan Goldin's *Witnesses: Against Our Vanishing* at Artists Space in 1990, or the NAMES Project AIDS quilt shown in monumental scale on the National Mall in 1993.[8] This current reluctance to re-engage the AIDS archive is particularly profound in Chicano art history as contemporary art exhibits circumvent appraisals that, I argue, were intrinsic to a more nuanced and multicentric Chicano avant-gardism(s).[9] *Frozen World/Mundo Congelado* embraces this curatorial void using the vanishing wrought by AIDS to productively (re)member one of East L.A.'s most provocative artists, Mundo Meza.

Insurgent Archive Curation

Frozen World/Mundo Congelado – in an effort to speak back against this incorporation of the once-abject Chicano artist into the art museum-industrial complex and the all-too-easy circumvention of AIDS cultural analysis in Chicano curating – is a temporary, mobile archive gallery staged in a trailer that sidesteps the museum's authority by activating a migratory venue in the service of queer and Chicano art counter-publics, particularly in Southern California. While the roots of this "insurgent curation" recall the portability of Marcel Duchamp's *Boîte-en-valise* ("Box in a Suitcase"), they also reflect racial and queer curatorial tactics of art activism, cultural preservation, and community-based social practice. My alternative archival gallery shares important antecedents with the Barrio Mobile Art Studio, an outreach and art education program spearheaded by Self-Help Graphics in East L.A. in the mid-1970s. Converting a step van into a travelling arts classroom, Chicana/o artists like Linda Vallejo and Michael Amescua introduced artistic techniques and expressive practices to youth, elders and even gang members in the barrio.[10] This precedent was echoed in Ruben Ochoa's curatorial innovation, CLASS: C (2001), for which the interior of a 1985 Chevy van doubled as a nomadic gallery furnished with white walls, hardwood floors, boutique lighting, and art objects. It literally became an art delivery service riffing on his parents' restaurant business dispensing tortillas across the city.[11]

In queer terms, the ambulant capabilities of this format parlayed direct confrontations with institutional goliaths through insurgent archival counters. This practice was recently employed when Republican congressional leadership demanded the removal of gay artist David Wojanorwicz's video *A Fire in My Belly* (1986–87) from the historic *Hide/Seek: Difference and Desire in American Portraiture* exhibition at the Smithsonian National Portrait Gallery in 2009. In turn, art activists Mike Blasenstein and Michael Dax Iacovone restaged the video, along with a controversial timeline of alleged Smithsonian censorship, in a nearby trailer installation dubbed "The Museum of Censored Art," a curatorial response attended by sixty-five hundred patrons.[12]

Though misperceived as hostile and reactionary, Blasenstein and Iacovone's trailer venue shares a lineage with other queer and American ethnic curations. For instance, in June 2010 Julia Wallace and Alexis Gumbs founded the "Mobile Homecoming Project," to document, record, and broadcast oral histories of Black lesbian everyday life from their roving RV.[13] As a mobile repository, their vehicle is a collection unit that gathers artifacts, personal testimony, and private papers across the United States, challenging holdings in more systematic mainstream archives. The actions of Wallace and Gumbs stage new ways to transfer intergenerational Black feminist lesbian knowledge through a migrating and portable public history intake centre. In this way, the RV acts as an archive-generating machine, an alternative circuitry for queer information technology. The site itself is not prostrating in its treatment of Black lesbian pasts but rather generating in the documentation process through an intertextual play of sight and sound. These queer and racialized precepts inform my curatorial lexicon and the "frozen world" I stand to make.

From a distance, we see the mobile gallery approaching. Forty-five feet in length, this customized trailer commands attention as it advances. *Frozen World/Mundo Congelado* redefines the "travelling exhibition" in a more conventional museum vernacular by imitating the spectacular movement essential to Meza's formative performance actions with Cyclona and Gronk in the early 1970s. As Gamboa puts it, "[They] would oftentimes dress in long, flowing velvet robes layered with satin, silk, and lace clothing and promenade, arms interlocked, to a quick paced goose step, shoving pedestrians out of their way."[14] The trailer rolls with a similar transgressive motion, eluding the banal, disrupting the ordinary, and causing human traffic to freeze. Its movement is neither nomadic nor erratic. It negotiates sprawling L.A. neighbourhoods, strip malls, freeways, and even U.S./Mexico borderlands with glacial intent, highlighting loci central to Meza's brief life at each stop. Ranging from his birthplace in Tijuana, Mexico, to the site of his posthumous exhibition at the Otis-Parsons Exhibition Center near McArthur Park; from the apartment he once shared with his collaborator and former lover, Simon Doonan, at the Fontenoy in Hollywood, to the windows he dressed at Maxfield Bleu's, Melon's, and Flip's on Melrose, the travel schedule is a poignant metaphor for Meza's "frozen world." The trailer gallery occupies Southern California with "goose step" pace interjecting queer archival possibility in the urban geography.[15] That is, the exhibition's physical presence – if only temporary – actualizes queer absence to the viewer, crystallizing traces of Meza's life and death in the landscape. After all, ice moves and inevitably evaporates.

The rear of the trailer gallery opens, stairs drop down, and a posterior panel swings open, bearing the show's introductory statement on the reverse side. This text is paired with two images reproduced, horizontally arranged, and mounted on the wall. The first is a photographic portrait of Mundo Meza. The image, perhaps a familiar one to some Chicano art aficionados, depicts Meza dressed in a popular vaudevillian costume. Half of his profile is adorned in an elegant black tuxedo. On the other half he sports a blond wig, face make-up, strapless evening gown, and shimmering costume jewelry. Some may immediately conclude that Meza was a cross-dresser, entertainer, or actor in stage costuming. His fractional half-drag is a performative play with genteel masculine and feminine archetypes which suggests a predisposition to trick, shock, or tease, testing a social system of gender identity predicated on biological essentialist categories. His portrait is a similarly conflicting epidermis, a mixture of white and brown halves allegorizing his draggy *mestizaje*. Meza's eyes focus off-camera, on some activity outside the pictorial frame.

This enlarged photo reproduction is paired with a scrapbook collage mined from the papers of Robert "Cyclona" Legorreta. We see the same Meza portrait again, only recontextualized within the archival logics of personal scrapbooking.[16] The photographs are chronologically arranged on the page, taking the viewer through a sequence of preparations from the evening of November 1973, the night of Robert "Cyclona" Legorreta's "comeback party," an engagement hosted by fellow Chicano avant-garde collaborator Gronk.[17] According to Legorreta, October 1973 also marked Meza's first solo exhibition at the East Los Angeles Public Library when he was just eighteen, an exhibition that included a collection of large-scale paintings of rock and roll icons. Unfortunately, the work was unexpectedly stolen off the walls of the library, portending the loss that would plague the artist for the rest of his brief life.[18]

I frame Meza's portrait against the scrapbook, illuminating the broader themes of Chicano artistic collaboration, "live art" performance, and male-male intimacy conjured through self-image transformation.[19] In one scrapbook photo, we observe Meza's hand carefully applying cosmetics onto Legorreta's face, a blank canvas covered in a façade of ivory white. Transitioning race and gender with the end of his make-up brush, Meza's artistic exchange substantiates Legorreta's claim that he was a living art piece painted, designed, and sculpted by Chicano avant-gardist hands. My pairing accentuates the portrait's comparative relationship to the scrapbook photo collage, intensifying viewer attention to the commemorative and relational interaction between the two objects. The artifact couplet emphasizes the origins of the photographic material so that we can contemplate how Legorreta's custodial intervention and careful restorative efforts in the scrapbook medium actually protected a rare document of Meza's image, artistic practices, social relationships, and creative expressions. More to this point, the hang enhances the imprint of Meza's non-extant work, which is seen in the painting partially unveiled over the shoulder of Cyclona adorned in extravagant self-display. His work remains in memory, collage, and picture. This hints at the way his artistic innovation freezes in a multilayered assemblage of performance documentation, scrapbooking, and photo display.

As visitors enter the gallery space, they will encounter an environment reminiscent of Ochoa's CLASS: C (2001). Hardwood floors, white walls, and boutique lighting give the impression of a contemporary art space. However, my show allows for a curatorial exercise that confronts and embraces the paucity of ethnic and queer art-historical materials and contests the dictates of linear chronology in the retrospective genre, which presumes benchmarks of life, career, and pedigree; such conditions affected artists with AIDS in the 1980s quite differently. As a result, *Frozen World/Mundo Congelado* adopts Ochoa's curatorial setting to create an intimate experience with the non-extant. The show suggests the complexities of cultural memory, personal archiving, and AIDS discourse in contemporary Chicano art, finding possibility in the impressions of Meza's oeuvre in archival materials, materials largely rebuked by the more clinical and lineal presentation of the artist's life typical of museum retrospectives.

Photo/Book/Fossils

Inset wall mounts line the gallery with books and photos juxtaposed in a mélange of open shelving, plexiglass enclosures, and vitrine encasements. The icy veneer of these cubes showcases "photo/book/fossils" or photographic materials mined from the pages of books, newsprint, and, as evinced by the audience's first encounter in the show, scrapbooks. Each "fossil" ossifies personal, intimate, and androgynous portraits of Meza, picturing him and his little-known past. The resulting book collection is a compilation that makes cultural linkages to East L.A., queer urban nightlife, and gay and lesbian liberation in the city in 1960s and 1970s, broadening the "literature" of Chicano avant-gardism(s).

"Teddy Sandoval, Patssi Valdez, and Mundo Meza," a photograph by Harry Gamboa Jr, appears in *Urban Exile: Collected Writings of Harry Gamboa Jr* (1998).[20] Taken twenty years earlier in 1978, the "fossil" pictures a mature Meza beside Patssi Valdez. His gaze penetrates Gamboa's lens. Over Valdez's left shoulder, we see the late artist Teddy Sandoval, in mid-conversation with an unknown figure off left field. The image is a poetic view of Chicano avant-garde origins. Though Meza had his premiere solo exhibition at East Los Angeles Public Library in 1973, his first group show may have actually occurred at the Mechicano Art Gallery in East Los Angeles in 1971. The newspaper *El Chicano* reported that Valdez, who was twenty at the time, had a two-person show with sixteen-year-old Meza just prior to her turn in the Asco art collective in 1972.[21] Their age difference is remarkable, a testament to Meza's accomplishment early in life.

However, his first collaboration with Valdez likely occurred at *Caca-Roaches Have No Friends*, a bizarre rehearsal in sexually transgressive Chicano performance art written by Gronk and starring Robert Legorreta as "Cyclona." It was performed in East L.A.'s Belvedere Park on 20

November 1969, years before Asco's founding.[22] Fourteen-year-old Meza arranged set designs, painted the grotesque masks, and also performed in a simulated orgy on stage alongside Valdez and her sister, Karen.[23] Gamboa's photograph explicated Meza's presence within the creative circuits of Chicano avant-gardism(s) – a nod to his wild youth with Legorreta, Gronk, Valdez, and Gamboa on the streets of *el barrio*.

The open-book display underscores one of Gamboa's avant-garde narratives about AIDS, mined from *Urban Exile* and entitled "In Order of Disappearance," written in "memory of Teddy Sandoval, Jack Vargas, Gerardo Velasquez, and Mundo Meza."[24] Meza marks the end of the list, in a reverse chronology from the first act of disappearance in 1985 ("Nervous Gender" frontman, Velasquez, died in 1992, and artists Vargas and Sandoval died in 1995, respectively). The book sits alongside the Xerox reproduction of a *Los Angeles Herald Examiner* article by Pam King from Sunday, 20 January 1980 reviewing photographer Anthony Friedkin's social documentation of homosexual life and culture in L.A. and San Francisco in 1969–72. *Gay: A Photographic Essay*, Friedkin's show at Cameravision Gallery, she writes, presents a rare window into the hustlers in Hollywood, vice cop raids on bars along Santa Monica Boulevard, gay civil rights leaders on Wilshire, and even barrio youth in East L.A. In the *Herald Examiner* clipping, viewers will note that an image entitled *Jim and Mundo* (1972) is prominently featured beneath the headline. At the foot of the vitrine, we read the label text:

> *Jim and Mundo* is a product of Anthony Friedkin's photo documentation of queer East L.A., an idea prompted by his frequent visits to the gay dances at Trouper's Hall on North La Brea in 1969–1972, a place that frequently drew the city's Chicano youth. Jaime Aguilar, a key subject in Friedkin's work, stands to the left of Mundo Meza. The teens are photographed at a hot dog stand in Montebello, CA. Aguilar's fingers are entwined in his long silky hair in a subtle feminine gesture. Meza's comparably long, diminutive fingers rest close to his body, tranquil, composed, and unrestricted. *Jim and Mundo* interrogates a hypermasculine self-image pervading Chicano art through an antithetical play of feminine signifiers. Later, their gender transgressions grew

as Meza explored anthropomorphic drag expressions in art and Aguilar transistioned becoming "Arrianna" in life.

The newsprint reproduction of Meza is a rare opportunity for viewers to remember and recollect his likeness, especially as he was in the early 1970s. Here we see Meza's handsome allure, cool composure, and stylish predisposition. Friedkin's "honest" portrayal conveys the poignant conviction of these youth, in their direct posturing and intense gazes. The portrait defies Chicano barrio masculinity and urban muscularity; we are drawn to their fitted coats, scarves, and smooth pristine faces. Their self-confidence amid the arresting hostilities of the barrio cultural landscape was not lost on Friedkin, who remembered: "One of the things I found interesting was that the gangs actually accepted the gay guys … I mean, I never interviewed any of the hard-core gang guys, but from what I could tell it was like you know that's where they were coming from, its like 'leave them alone,' like 'it's okay.'"[25] These fossilized remains of Meza culled from the *Herald Examiner* provide rare insight into the transgressive genders and sexualities in East Los Angeles, the broader Chicano community's relation to these subjectivities, and a street photographer's effort to visually convey Chicano gender and sexual difference in the early 1970s. As Friedkin tells King, his series, *Gay: A Photographic Essay,* "create[s] fossils of my time."[26]

Friedkin's assertion distills how the arresting conditions of photography capture and stabilize the subject in a stationary time and place, a potentially "frozen" act. Curatorially, the newsprint attains a corporeal property. It extends Meza's physical trace in paper and thus offers a restorative correction to his material absence. Moreover, the newspaper was instrumental in his discovery of the exhibition. It was only after reading the press coverage that Meza attended, leaving a Cameravision postcard from the show for Legorreta. His tone is apologetic yet touching, saying he "went to check it out last week to find two fab pics of you very well displayed thought you might check it out! Nice show. I think about you all the time."[27]

Brandishing a photo reproduction of Friedkin's *Hustlers, Selma Avenue, Hollywood* (1971) on the reverse side, the postcard appears in the vitrine, augmenting the *Herald Examiner* article.

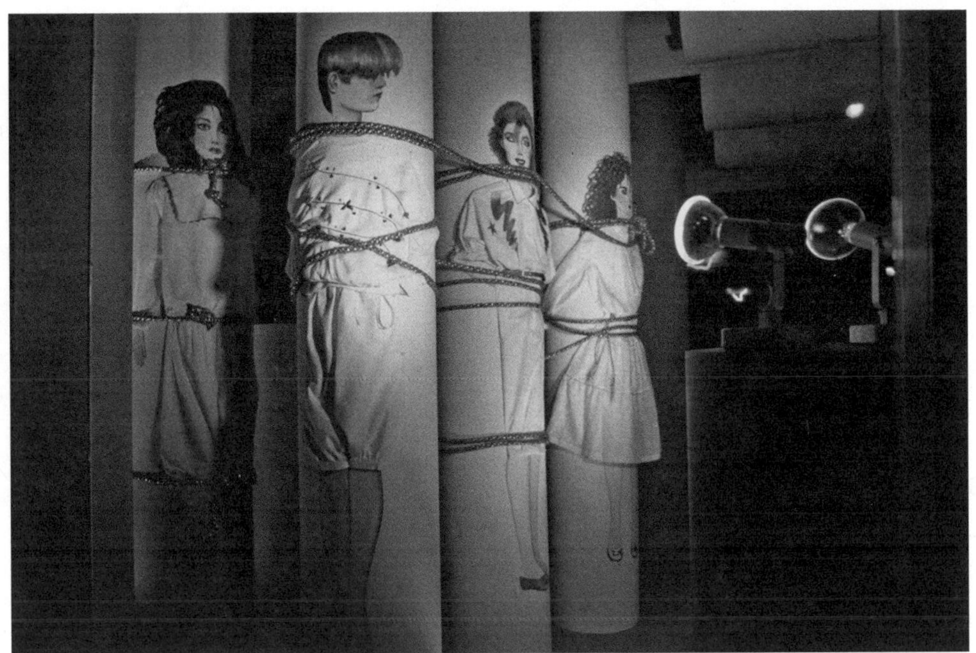

5.1 | One of Mundo Meza's first window displays for Melon's, a boutique on Melrose Avenue in Los Angeles, 1981.

Installation Relics

Print media plays a further role in the extant trace of Meza's fossilized memory as well as the retrieval of his vanished oeuvre. A newsprint clipping, a small colour photograph mounted on black card stock, and an art catalogue turned to an image of an ethereal pantomime floating in mid-air compose the next vitrine. Because of the dearth of materials documenting Meza's aesthetic, news articles emphasize another important dimension of his milieu: window dressing. Without object inventory lists, sales guides, or catalogue publications, there are few vantage points into Meza's two-dimensional work, much less into these temporary retail environments, and the importance of the window displays recovered from the pages of the *Herald* is magnified.

This "fossil," which appeared in the *Los Angeles Herald Examiner* on 30 August 1981, represents one of the few surviving images of Meza's installation art practice, a temporary form of visual merchandising resignified here as a sanctified relic. The photographs, taken by Elisa Leonelli, were published in the California Living section, paired with a brief story about striking avant-garde designs overtaking the shopping experience. The unattributed reviewer even remarks that the "stagey presentation and social drama" of the window displays incited new consumer behaviour, suggesting the storefront's theatrical possibility.[28] Meza's installation for Melon's, a boutique on Melrose Avenue, covers the entire page opposite the article (see figure 5.1). The copy lies open, inviting closer visual inspection.

In a corresponding label text at the base of the vitrine, we read:

> An *L.A. Herald Examiner* article from 1981 depicts one of Meza's first solo window designs at Melon's at 8739 Melrose Avenue, a polemic expression that defined his wildly creative and conceptual scope in the early 1980s. The display consists of four female figures painted onto spherical columns, bound and gagged with gold rope in a collective garrote. Exquisite clothing and fabrics peek out between the gilded cord. The window reveals currents of social anxiety as the fashionable captives grate against their aggressive confinements. Looping tightly around their bodies and necks, the suggestion of masochism creates a perceptual disturbance revealing the imposing tangle of beauty, violence, and social conformity.

Upon closer examination of the *Herald* article, we see that the news clipping is hand-signed by Meza, who writes, "Not too bad for one of my first windows" over the print. Just below the copy, in the marginal white space at the bottom, he playfully adds, "Fancy you buying the herald exam!," giving a sense of the intimate process by which the clipping itself was preserved by Legorreta, he, himself an eclectic collector.[29] No document of art-historical discourse, but rather a memento of Meza's career achievement, the clipping conveys intimate details about the relationship of these two artists in the personal inscription. "Fancy you buying the herald exam!" is attributed to Meza's hand, perhaps a playful recognition of Legorreta's cultural stewarding vis-à-vis his sarcastic wit. In this rare glimpse into their personal relationship, visitors might

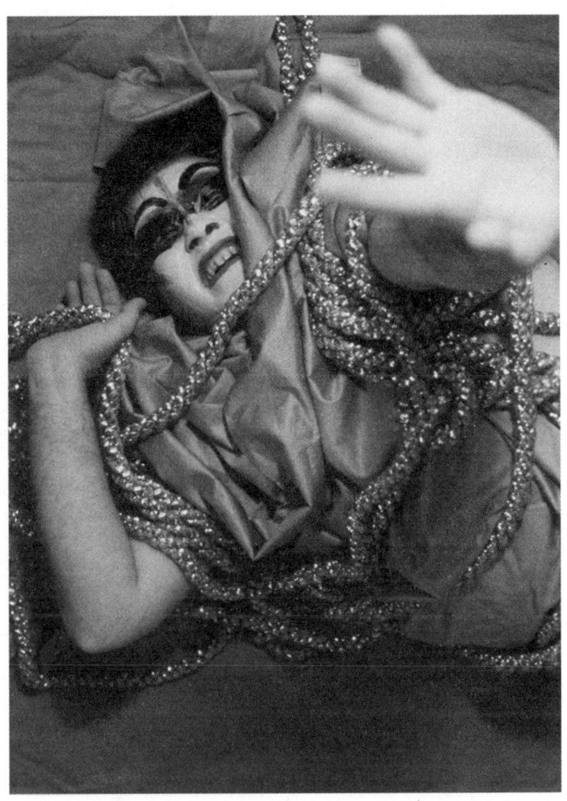

5.2 | Cyclona in *Frozen Art*, a collaborative performance with Mundo Meza (1981).

imagine Meza's discovery of the article kept among Legorreta's personal keepsakes, surprised by his friend's scavenging and consumptive behaviour ("Fancy you"), which promptly spurred his own self-reflection on his installation practice ("Not too bad"). This image of Meza's window display becomes an important moment in *Frozen World/Mundo Congelado*, revealing the commemorative investments and biographical insights gained by window dressing's queer remains.

A black-matted colour photograph contained in the vitrine punctuates Meza's penchant for the disruptive even in the stillness of window display installation. We view a comparative use of rope in Meza's collaboration with Robert "Cyclona" Legorreta from the series of experimental performances entitled *Frozen Art* in June of 1981.[30] Taken just two months before the *Herald Examiner* article, the photo documentation helps draw out the continuity of concerns across Meza's oeuvre, connecting the commercial, queer, and "outsider" domains. Re-circuiting fashion technologies, mannequin aesthetics, visual merchandising, and prop display in amorphous, transmutable embodiments for the Cyclona persona (see figure 5.2), Meza infuses early Chicano conceptual performance strategies with outrageous storefront sensibilities. Additional label text strives to make this aesthetic relationship more salient.

> In *Frozen Art*, one of his last performance exercises with Robert "Cyclona" Legorreta, Meza uses gilded rope to engulf the artist. Unlike the passive fashion brutality of Melon's Boutique window display, the Cyclona figure resists, reaching out beyond the bonds of social restriction and rebuking the impositions of body discipline. *Frozen Art* demonstrates Meza's attentions to a mannequin comportment in performance; thus, his visual composition investigates the static potentiality of artifact arrangement, set design, and the mannequin's motionless existence in shallow backdrops. Whereas the rope in the Melon's window display binds, in Cyclona's estranging choreography, the rope unwinds, freeing gender bounds, sexual restrictions, and Chicano metamorphosis.

Viewers may understand the Melon's window within Cyclona's repertoire, a performance expression indebted to Meza's forays in art installation, fabricated object environments, and merchandise design. The audience reads along a gilded rope that restricts and unravels, making a stable sex-gender social system untenable and queerly contorted.

Meza's penchant for estrangement, visual shock, and, perhaps, the paralysis wrought by perceptual disturbance found an ally in the homoerotic surreal photography of Steven Arnold. In the vitrine, his catalogue *Epiphanies* (1987) opens to the piece entitled *The Wonder of Mundo Meza*.[31] In label text, we read:

> "All is artifice, deliberate, set up," late Hollywood photographer, Steven Arnold (1943–1994) opines about his work.[32] This static expression is found in his collaborative photo-performance *The Wonder of Mundo Meza*. A geometry of squared shoulders, conic head and ballooned harem trousers structures Meza's figure, creat-

ing a voluminous silhouette. He is a pantomime taking flight. His face is washed in a familiar white stain, dark lip, and one painted eyebrow. His right eye encircled with the iconic ring perhaps cites Pete the Pup from *The Little Rascals* (1929–46) TV fame, performed originally by Pal the Wonder Dog. Arnold pairs Meza's homage to the animal performer with his magical rococo tableaux in a playful riff on American consumerism, pop culture, and circus trickery. Meza and his juggling balls freeze suspended in air. Occupying the interstices of window display and the tableau vivant form, Arnold's ethereal mediation exposes life's stagy contrivance. This photo would appear in Arnold's *Epiphanies*, published in 1987 just two years after Meza's death.

Arnold's predisposition for tableaux vivants, frozen gesture, and "freeze-frame" vision mirrors Meza's repertoire.[33] Such synchronicity is little regarded in the greater vicissitudes of Chicano avant-garde theory and aesthetics. But together, they convey a frozen world, a world predicated on Chicano performance, suspended animation, and motionless vocabularies of mannequin affectation. Though we are unable to reproduce for museum-goers the spatial and participatory experience of the original windows (aspects crucial to the completion of the art environment), the pieces assembled to form the "installation-as-relic" display conveys a sense of enduring collaborative relationships, artistic maturation, and advancing visual, material, and spatial practices in Meza's window art. All of this would, of course, reach an impasse as his illness emerged.

Phantom Gallery

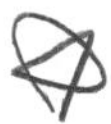

A salon-style hang of iPads stacked together in an electronic audio-visual collage of moving pictures, home video footage, and still photography faces viewers from the far wall of the gallery. Inspired by the televisual media installations of Nam June Paik, sound also emanates from multiple sources, creating a chaotic ambience that echoes the confusion, disturbance, and potential agony wrought by the AIDS crisis. Snippets from my interview with Jef Huereque on 23 August 2007, conducted at his Los Feliz apartment are heard. The correlating video shows the handsome artist, stylish in appearance and confident in his words, recounting precise moments with his former lover, Mundo. His story is at first jubilant, recollecting vignettes of lavish fashion industry parties with celebrities, designers, and photographers, a by-product of their Hollywood lifestyle. Meza had done a brief stint apprenticing for shoe designer Fred Slatten and collaborating with fashionista Simon Doonan, in popular avant-garde window display before branching out on his own at fashion boutiques like Melon's and Flip Jeans in 1981.[34] But Huereque's tale turns grim as he shares that as Meza grew ill, his close friends and family grew more distant. "So few people knew how to deal with [AIDS]," he says. "It was like, a lot of friends and family kind of disappeared because it was so unknown, you know, how you caught it, how it was transferred and stuff. Anyways, so I kind of financially nosedived taking care of him, but its something I had to do."[35]

The exact details of Meza's passing are unknown, absent in the course of the interview. Though AIDS discourse in contemporary Chicano art remains an important aim of this curatorial dream, I attempt to circumvent the objectification of AIDS cultural narratives, a visual and literary genre that has often mischaracterized people with AIDS as victims, promiscuous deviants, or diseased bodies under a biomedical gaze.[36] The video installation seeks instead to explicate the circumstances surrounding Meza's vanished body of work, highlighting for museum-goers the voids in institutional museal practice and art archiving. There may be no better way to represent this than through Huereque's own stoic words, which permeate the phantom gallery. For instance, we hear the sounds of plastic pushkeys and the hiss of audiotape overlay a truncated phone recording: "... Jef Huereque. I'm calling about, um, I needed to possibly get ahold of Patssi Valdez, um ... Mundo passed away Monday and I wanted to let her know, and you know about it, also. And you can call me back at 221-8133 and, um, or just call and leave Patssi's number on my machine if I'm not here. Thank you, bye-bye."[37] His voice, found on Harry Gamboa Jr's answering machine, is cold, nearly automated. His chilling revelation left on grainy sound recording actualizes the capacity of technology to reproduce the uncanny residues of loss, a loss similarly rehearsed by images of vanished paintings projected by LCD monitors.

Music video footage from Kim Carnes's single, "Bette Davis Eyes" (1981), flows through one iPad window. The song, however, drowns in the cheeky prose of Simon Doonan. Reading passages from his memoir,

Beautiful People (2005), in an adjoining flat screen, he recalls his creative collaborations, excursions, and life-affirming play with Meza amid AIDS. He recites: "Even though he had lesions on his feet, which necessitated the wearing of huge sheepskin scuffies, he insisted on going out dancing ... He laughed about the way he looked and at people's horrified reactions. It was a horrible negative version of that scenario where Fred and Ginger clear the floor with their expertise. We did it with a disease."[38] In the running video footage, we hear Carnes's tune faintly overlaid against Doonan's voice. Both he and Meza appear in the *mise-en-scène* as New Romantic extras adorned in Vivienne Westwood pirate drag.

His story carries over the video loop. "Two days later he went into a coma. Then, on February 11, 1985, Mundo went to join his new friends."[39] There, in the music video, the dancers vanish, a poetic turn in the edit, even if coincidental. This moment of disintegration in "Bette Davis Eyes" is a profound metaphor for Meza, for Doonan, and for the exhibition. In the phantom gallery, the non-extant lingers. It is a productive political and cultural space for thinking about the illusory resonance of AIDS in Chicano art and archive. Presence and absence grind to a freezing halt in the music video, signalling the void to come.

Such visual metaphors in my installation heighten the symbolic importance of this show, pressing the audience to consider how such archival silences occur. Viewers are confronted, visually and aurally, with the disassembling and disintegrating of Meza's painterly corpus, becoming second-hand witnesses to his erasure. By refusing fine art objects that could have performed a funerary convoy to Meza's cultural memory in a shrine-like context, I jettison material entitlements to possess and own Meza in a traditional approach to the retrospective genre. This dismal backdrop motivates the restorative effort of my curatorial dream.

While it was tragic, it is important to note that the vanishing of Meza's collection is not unusual. The dissolution of the material underpinnings of queer history and memory through the destruction and erasure of potential archival sites draws attention to the issue of violence against Mexican/Mexican American cultural heritage more broadly. Here I am reminded of early Mexican surrealist painter and set and costume designer Agustín Lazo, an artist whom Luis Cardoza y Aragón once described as "correct, neat and serene. He burns as cold as a column."[40] Sharing a similar temperament in demeanour and aesthetic, Lazo and Meza were both inspired by Picasso, who was subsequentially an influential figure in mannequin design; they also mirror an art-historical quagmire. Their obscurity is partially predicated on archival ruination and art loss. Following Lazo's death in 1971, his sisters Guadalupe and Maria Luisa are believed to have destroyed his papers and artworks, presumably to extinguish pervasive and embarrassing rumours of his close relationship with his lover, *grupo sin grupo* poet Xavier Villaurrutia.[41] In his curatorial essay about Lazo, Latin American art historian James Oles, reminds us that "archives are fragile entities, especially when fear of scandal lurks in the minds of those who survive."[42]

Like Meza, Lazo, too, left little behind. Only a few notes of personal correspondence, some self-portraits, interviews, diaries, and journals supply Oles's restorative efforts. Lazo's discreet life was perhaps a consequence of being homosexual within Mexican aristocratic society in the 1920s. His intimate relationships with a circle of other avant-garde writers, artists, and public intellectuals, known as "los Contemporáneos," can only be surmised from popular legend, including his crippling bereavement after Villaurrutia's death in 1950.[43] These affairs were likely resigned to the *alcoba* (bedchamber), a physical and symbolic place that Oles posits as a protective site for homoerotic encounters, fantasies, and of course dreams to occur, especially for Mexican surrealists of the period.[44] Whereas Meza was certainly indiscreet and unapologetically gay, facing the hostile and perilous conditions of East L.A. with glittering flair, the parallels between homosexual Mexican surrealist circles in the 1920s and their queer Chicano avant-garde counterparts in the 1970s are telling. Just as Villaurrutia's poetry inspired Lazo's fantastical painting, Legorreta's bodily poetics spurred Meza's shocking window designs and performance expressions. In either case, the non-extant conditions of Lazo and Meza encourage us to return to the allegorical and physical *alcoba* to unearth queer lives that have been confined there, and to consider the productive possibility of dreaming these lives – curatorially – into an enlarged space of public viewing and disclosure.

Though Lazo and Meza were several decades apart and separated by age, class, and geographic borders, their life narratives mirror each other, reflecting artistic invention through Mexican and Chicano avant-garde collaborations and a shared propensity for painting, performance, and set design. Moreover, and most important, both men faced devastating

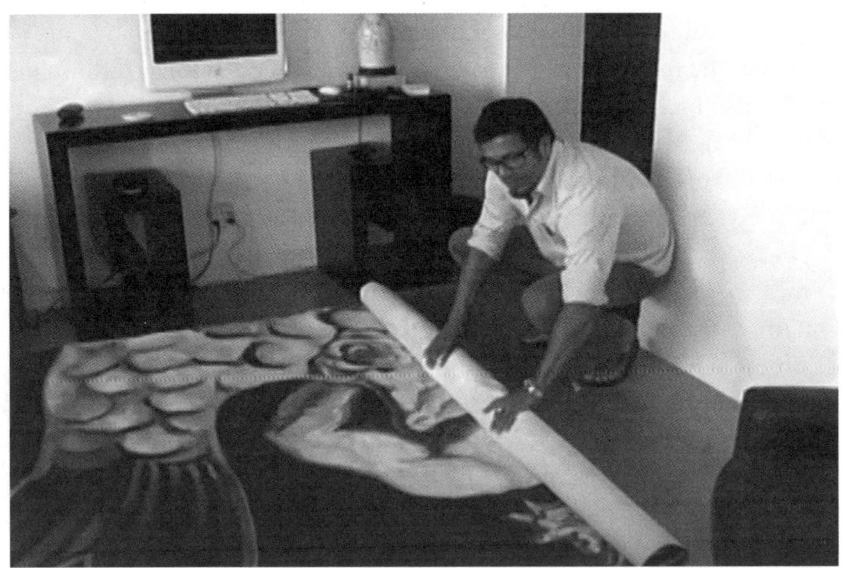

5.3 | Jef Huereque with Mundo Meza's *Merman with Mandolin* (1984) in 2007.

consequences for their archives, one by disappearance and the other by assault. Oles's dilemma is instructive in that it demonstrates how similar curatorial conundrums span Mexican and Chicano geopolitical and art-historical contexts. Silences ranging from those rooted in sexual confession to HIV/AIDS disclosure pervade the power of public records and the transformative potential of curating, and bring much to bear on the intersections of queer transnational avant-gardism(s) between East L.A. and Mexico City. Telling the stories of Lazo and Meza is arduous, requiring curatorial dreams that occupy the productive opportunities that loss allows. To tell them is to embrace, examine, and adopt insurgent curatorial practices that reveal what the "censor's flame" would otherwise destroy.[45]

Returning to the phantom gallery, we find raw home video footage of Huereque playing. Out of the ruins, we learn that just one of Meza's paintings remains in his care, dwelling in the corner of his cavernous hallway closet. In the iPad screen, we watch as he unrolls the fabric by its tattered corners (see figure 5.3). Titled *Merman with Mandolin* (1984), the unstretched canvas lies across his apartment floor. He explains how Meza was capable of producing life-size acrylic paintings very quickly.

The large-scale interpretation of a "merman" sculpture frozen in stone is a homoerotic re-visioning of the *la sirena* image seen in folk art throughout Mexico in statuary, collectibles, and the children's game *lotería*. The piece reveals Meza's agile brushwork, monochrome palette, and expedient artistic production of photorealist grand-size paintings. In the video testimony, we are told that after Meza's death, Huereque would, over the years, occasionally display the canvas in his bedroom, in a return to the *alcoba* from which his intimate and personal memories of Meza remain. After all, this piece was produced in 1984 months before Meza's death on 11 February 1985. This precious sight/site was not lost on his friends, who added to his related collection of *la sirena* collectibles on special occasions.

Perceptive gallery visitors will immediately recognize that the raw footage of *Merman with Mandolin* (1984) is conversant with another image found in the stacked iPad screens before them. The charcoal-colour pencil drawing portrays a chiseled merman, collapsed in agony on the sea floor. His head hangs low and his outstretched right hand grasps the oceanic void. It is difficult to discern what the merman struggles to clutch, and what grief paralyses him, frozen in time. Perhaps crying for all that he once had and all that he lost, *Anguish* (1991), by Jef Huereque, is a poignant end to the show.[46] Without relying on didactic label text, the digital wall collage of video interview, literary reading, documentary footage, and non-extant art creates a crucial punctuation mark for Meza's frozen world.

Huereque's piece asks viewers to meditate on just what has caused the merman's anguish, and what he strains to hold. The image distills the devastating wounds and losses of AIDS, including a tragically silenced art oeuvre emerging, albeit privately among queer facets of Chicano avant-gardists. Surviving the death of his partner, Huereque imbues the merman with his memory, keeping Meza's aesthetic safe, and enabling his symbolic future resuscitation.

Conclusion: Curating the *Frozen Afterlife*

This show offers a reconceptualization not only of the social and artistic portrait of Mundo Meza but also of the way the vanishing of his art collection engendered commemorative acts on the part of his friends, colleagues, and lovers. The cultural power of archival exhibition "queering" questions an archive's content and form, its spatial rearticulation, and the fact that the body of work faced conditions not applicable to other collections and displays. Anti-gay social hostilities, violent cultural realities, archival assaults, and the prevalence of AIDS-related vanishing all beg for curatorial approaches that interpret both the non-extant and its afterlife – a type of "afterlife analysis" that treats acts of loss, disappearance, and even disintegration as productive means of curatorial inquiry and investigation in archive theory and object biography studies. Clearly, not all dreams are pleasurable; some are violent and disturbing – and yet they, too, are necessary.

As a restorative investigation, *Frozen World/Mundo Congelado* conceives what was once deemed impossible. It partakes in new curatorial imaginaries that retrieve lost work through traces, imprints, and physical representations of the artist in fossilized remains: photo, scrapbook, art catalogue, newsprint, and commercial music video. Relics of window displays and installation designs explicate Meza's extenuated interest in performance as stillness and the freezing gesticulations of mannequin comportment. This coalescence of a lost oeuvre is a partial piece of the archival puzzle. We may never know the extent of Meza's visual vocabulary, the dynamism of his artistic productions, or just how *Frozen Art* pervaded his other aesthetic proposals. My curatorial dream uses loss to productively empower the remains of this East L.A. artist and the way his art influenced, functioned, and survived within the complex channels of the Chicano avant-garde, contemporary L.A. art and fashion, and the broader visual culture of Southern California. For this, we must go beyond the threshold of formal art collections, institutional museum venues, and conservative patrilineal genres like the retrospective, where Meza was never intended to be found. It is here that curatorial dreaming allows for a range of alternative archival tactics, some mobile and others frozen. Thus, destruction is not an end, but rather a source of creative opportunity.

Postscript

Since 2005, prompted by interviews with Doonan, Huereque, and Legorreta, I have investigated the whereabouts of Meza's lost paintings. In

2011, at the time of this writing, members from the Mundo Meza family came forward, readying several works of art from their personal collection for a proposed retrospective exhibition about their brother. Though found under variant states of physical distress likely caused by fluctuating environmental conditions and storage controls, some paintings do survive. However, the entirety of his collection, allegedly over a hundred paintings according to one account, remains at large, scattered in the aftereffects of AIDS. Meza's *Frozen World/Mundo Congelado* is found in unlikely places: networks of high school teacher retirees, the private custody of want ad respondents, and inside the immaculate wardrobe closet of a fashion celebrity. These findings demonstrate how once-abject archives may be resignified under changing perceptions of cultural worth, garnering newfound attention on the part of revered museum institutions, art foundations, and art historians. The family's conciliatory initiative shows how the writing of Chicano art history is elusive, a fractious terrain, and one always in flux. With the fortuitous recovery of Meza's art collection in parts, the narrative of Chicano avant-gardism(s) may be altered, views on AIDS perhaps shift, and the wounds of the past – hopefully – heal, making my curatorial dream a curatorial reality.

CHAPTER SIX

The Play: Reassembling African Arts in the West

JOSHUA I. COHEN

This chapter introduces *The Play*, a curatorial project juxtaposing an exhibition of masks from the Republic of Guinea, West Africa, and a multimedia stage production featuring US-based Guinean performing artists. As a hypothetical "dream" project, *The Play* responds to current conditions of display surrounding African "traditional" material culture in Western art museums. It adopts a dual platform of exhibition/performance in order to imagine a collaborative, self-reflexive, and aesthetically integrated forum for presenting Guinean arts, culture, and political history in the West. *The Play* also aims to bridge some of the classificatory divides that continue to govern Western understandings of African arts – including indigenous versus international, "traditional" versus contemporary, and material versus performing arts. The title of the project derives from a statement by Guinea art specialist Frederick Lamp, who writes: "Dance in Africa cannot be considered apart from other forms of art. In contrast to the compartmentalization of the arts in the West, with our departments of dance, theater, music and the plastic arts, there is simply one art in the traditional African setting, and that art goes by various terms often translated as 'the play,' 'medicine' (as something that effects), or 'the sacred.'"[1] Indeed, music and dance performance settings are often referred to in the Guinean Susu and Maninka languages respectively as *bere yire* and *tolon bia* – "play places."[2]

The African artistic forms featured in *The Play* – most prominently masquerades, music, and dance – belong to a genre that is typically labelled "classical," "canonical," or "traditional." I will use "traditional," here, but it is a tricky term which some criticize, others employ with apprehension, and still others reject outright. Let it be said: practitioners of "traditional" African arts do not necessarily place stock in the term either, as they may choose to describe themselves in any number of other ways. Still, overarching conceptualizations of African art in Western art history, art museums, and the art market now include categories of "modern" and "contemporary" (typically taking the form of painting, collage, sculptural construction, photography, installation, film and video, and so on) as well as "traditional" arts (typically masks, wooden sculpture, textiles, beadwork, and other forms). For pragmatic purposes, classificatory terms are needed in order to loosely distinguish these domains of artistic production. In the interest of clarity, the term "traditional" is used in what follows to refer to African arts rooted in local cultures and media – arts that have continued to evolve in contemporary, urban, and international performance settings. African artistic tradition, in other words, is bound neither by time-honoured convention nor by geographical region or ethnicity.

African Art in Museums

African "art," another heavily loaded term, emerged in the early twentieth century following European artists' "discoveries" of masks and figural sculpture from the continent. Previously, as early as the 1870s, objects from West and Central Africa had begun entering European collections through acquisitions by European explorers, colonial military personnel, businessmen, and missionaries. Yet Europeans did not initially collect these objects for aesthetic reasons. Rather, they valued the pieces (a) as exotic cultural artifacts, (b) for what they supposedly revealed about the "primitive" condition of colonized peoples, and (c) for the role they could play in justifying and promoting the purportedly "civilizing" colonial enterprise within European ethnographic institutions and universal expositions.[3] The point of departure for African "art" came in 1905–06, when avant-garde artists in Paris began looking closely at the wooden masks and figures that populated curio shops and ethnographic museums. Before long, African sculpture had become known for exerting an important influence on modernism, prompting collectors and dealers to take interest in certain of these sculptural works for their formal qualities.[4] By the 1910s and '20s, the vogue for so-called *art nègre* was in full swing, centred in Paris and extending to Germany, Belgium, New York – and Africa, where foreign demand for objects escalated.

The Western "canon" of traditional African art thus was established rather quickly, but it subsequently evolved relatively slowly, with curatorial practices evolving in a parallel way. By the 1910s, art gallery displays already consisted of masks and sculptures from West and Central Africa framed by white walls, spotlights, and pedestals.[5] This basic format, which eventually became known in other contexts as the "white cube,"[6] reflected modernism's form-based approach to African art. Today the canon has expanded to include objects from East and Southern Africa, as well as a greater diversity of objects, including textiles, furniture, beadwork, and jewelry.[7] Nevertheless, the classic "spotlight-and-pedestal" or "white cube" display paradigm persists as the standard framing for African works in art museums.[8]

Meanwhile, curatorial concerns related to contextualization have gradually made their way into some art museums, beginning in the 1950s and '60s with the emergence of African art history as an American academic and museum discipline. During that formative period, scholars and curators began to raise critical awareness around the fact that the local aesthetics of African objects and their modes of presentation – not to mention their social, cultural, and historical dimensions – could never be conveyed through formalist spotlight-and-pedestal displays. In this way, two principal paradigms – ethnographic (culturally contextualizing) and art-historical (focused primarily on form and aesthetics) – gradually converged in many art museums through the use of explanatory labels and accompanying visual materials such as photographs and in situ performance footage. Further, beginning in the 1980s, there emerged a new form of curatorial self-consciousness that began openly to consider the political and intrinsic challenges bound up in exhibiting African art.[9] Since the 1990s, curators have expanded upon this approach by focusing more attention on individual artists, and by involving African and African diasporan communities in planning exhibitions and gauging their outcomes.[10]

Following on this growing commitment to contextualization, recent decades have seen growing excitement around modern and contemporary African art. Compared with forms of art labelled "traditional," modern and contemporary African artistic production has tended to be oriented more toward the international art world and its apparatus of galleries, collectors, museums, curators, art fairs, and biennials. Many museum exhibitions of African modern and contemporary art have emphasized connections between art and radical politics – a framing that has largely remained absent from exhibitions of traditional art.[11]

Current Conditions

Notwithstanding continued breakthroughs in research, theory, and ways of exhibiting traditional African arts, a number of key assumptions have remained unaddressed. For instance, it is worth asking whether current curatorial standards – premised on the idea that African art has a didactic role in informing Western audiences about "Africa" – invariably succeed in ensuring the quality of exhibitions in terms of their potential to both challenge and inspire audiences. As should be clear, this question is by no means intended to suggest a reversion to elitism and executive decision-making in art museums. Rather, its purpose is to remind us that a crucial element of all great exhibitions is the element of surprise. Some of today's traditional African art exhibitions and permanent installations risk feeling too much like social studies – that is, too bland and didactic, devoting more attention to the works' seemingly distant cultural contexts than to their expressive modalities and recent histories. Part of what is at stake here are museum politics of identity and representation, which pose vitally necessary and important challenges. Among North American curators there is a perceived need to educate, to confront assumptions and stereotypes, and – given the problematic nature of some past exhibitions – to be sure not to offend visitors. Ambitions such as these are beyond reproach. The attendant risk, however, is of framing traditional works in ways that make them appear primarily educational, irreconcilably foreign, and, as Susan Vogel has phrased it in a parallel context, "maybe a little boring."[12]

Further, global interests in modern and contemporary African art are beginning to confront traditional art with new challenges related to public perception and display. This incipient trend raises a complex issue that must be accorded its due consideration and qualifications.[13] For, to question the importance of modern and contemporary African art, or to complain that it has somehow unfairly eclipsed the traditional, would be neither accurate nor forward-looking. At the same time, a serious concern needs to be voiced against the compartmentalization of the two genres.[14] Increasingly, traditional objects are presented alongside modern and contemporary works in permanent installations and thematic exhibitions, but the effect is not always one of substantiating continuity between them. Perversely, these juxtapositions sometimes end up subtly implying that modern and contemporary art embodies the international and up-to-date while traditional arts are comparatively hidebound and arcane.[15]

In light of such concerns, traditional objects can be framed in ways that productively connect them all at once with their artists and cultures, full aesthetic environments, and contemporary manifestations. The question of performance is central in this regard. Museum installations today tend to include performance practices via small-scale video displays, if at all. Only on rare occasions do African artists themselves present or perform with objects in museums, even though performance contexts are well understood to be the crucial, live creative spaces in which traditional works of art most often appear and engage audiences in their communities of origin.[16]

The aim of *The Play* – rather than relying on text and media within the space of the gallery – is to simultaneously combine and disaggregate, within a single production, the spotlight-and-pedestal and the contextualizing modes of display. Via the two-space forum of exhibition/performance, *The Play* seeks at once to recuperate and to critique the "white cube" as a space for exhibiting traditional African art.

The White Cube: Pros and Cons

In a classic essay of contemporary museum studies, art historian Svetlana Alpers describes a moment of revelation from her childhood when, confronted with an enormous preserved crab on display in a museum gallery, she apprehended the creature in all its magnificent detail. Within a museum environment, any wholly negative assessment of an object's

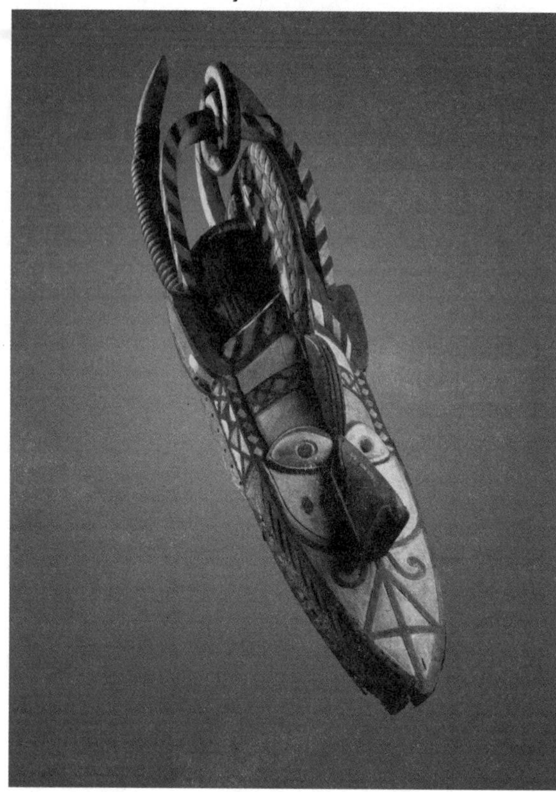

6.1 | Banda (or Kumbaruba) headdress, Baga or Nalu, Republic of Guinea, late nineteenth or early twentieth century.

death seemed impossible, Alpers states: "I could attend to a crab in this way because it was still, exposed to view, dead. Its habitat and habits of rest, eating, and moving were absent. I had no idea how it had been caught. I am describing looking at it as an artifact and in that sense like a work of art. The museum had transformed the crab – had heightened, by isolating, these aspects, had encouraged one to look at it in this way. The museum had made it an object of visual interest."[17]

This phenomenon, which Alpers calls "the museum effect – turning all objects into works of art,"[18] merits careful consideration, as museums undeniably offer a unique and valuable experience – namely a visual experience that involves close, contemplative looking. For the present purposes, Alpers's crab can be compared to an African example: a Banda (or Kumbaruba) headdress of the Baga and Nalu cultures of coastal Guinea, on permanent display at the Brooklyn Museum of Art (see figure 6.1).

The comparison is useful insofar as neither crab nor headdress was originally designed for the kind of close inspection Alpers describes. Like many African masks, this Banda would have been stored in a secret or inaccessible location when not in use. When worn for dancing, the headdress moved so quickly and with so many accompanying elements that spectators could not carefully observe its composite form: human eyes, nose, and hair; crocodile jaw and teeth; antelope horns; serpent body; and chameleon tail.[19] Further, by looking closely at the headdress, one can investigate technical and formal features. How was the headdress constructed? What strategies and techniques did the artist employ? How does the object function sculpturally? Pursuing these kinds of questions demands the close proximity and visual intelligibility afforded by the museum setting.[20]

Still, one problem with Alpers's essay is her assertion that museums "provide a place where our eyes are exercised and where we are invited to find both unexpected as well as expected crafted objects to be of visual interest to us."[21] What Alpers overlooks here are the factors determining whether and how visitors' eyes are "exercised" in museums. Two such (interrelated) factors are prior knowledge and emotional receptivity. For visitors who enter an installation or exhibition with little prior knowledge about the artworks or cultures on display, the "museum effect" alone may not be enough to spark the kind of revelatory experience Alpers enjoyed. Certainly, supplementary data can help heighten visitors' receptivity to what they see, as can discussions about how to look or what to look for. But an even more crucial curatorial responsibility is to create a sensory environment conducive to wonder and active engagement. To assume that museums inherently offer such an environment is to assume that all museum visitors are predisposed to a certain kind (Alpers's kind) of visual curiosity.

As literary scholar Henry Louis Gates Jr has argued, "The prison-house of slavery engendered a prison-house of seeing, both African peoples and their attendant cultural artifacts."[22] African objects' pathways of acquisition and recontextualization in the West are alone enough to suggest an analogy between objects and bodies, museums and incarceration.[23] We are therefore obliged to think critically about how the spotlight-and-pedestal mode of display disciplines its objects. Can the "white cube" – in which objects are typically labelled with the vague names of ethnic groups and regions – ever avoid de-historicizing African works and erasing their past trajectories of displacement? On pedestals under bright lights, African objects are framed "universally" as art, when in fact they are being elegantly misrepresented and misunderstood.

Notions of disciplinary power also extend to the very orders of knowledge – "disciplines" of another kind – that inform the practice of isolating material objects from other artistic media in the museum setting. Since at least the 1970s, Africanist art historians and curators have argued that the performance contexts of traditional objects are crucial – as much for understanding the objects' social and ritual meanings as for perceiving their overall aesthetics and modes of expression.[24] Art museum curators have responded to this basic insight by increasingly incorporating music, sound, video, photography, and moving machinery into exhibitions. These are welcome innovations in theory, but in practice they typically only serve as tokens of the multi-sensory. If the limitations of such devices are not immediately apparent, one need only think of the difference between attending a masquerade performance and watching the same on a small video screen. Still, curators seem to have reached an unspoken consensus that media interventions constitute the best possible supplementary framings for African art in museums.

Publics, Performance, and the Archive

With both benefits and drawbacks, the art museum remains a unique environment for enabling a direct, public, and collective encounter with African art, while at the same time inviting criticism for privileging visual over other sensory stimuli and for delivering an experience that is (a) minimally interactive, (b) potentially too cerebral, and (c) highly variable depending on viewers' prior levels of knowledge and ways of seeing. Meanwhile, curators' preferred means of contextualizing works of art (aside from supplementary media) include text panels, docent talks, and personal audio tours. These are all reasonable strategies for bringing specialized knowledge to bear on museum collections. At the same time, they are all premised on the idea that visitors' perceptions are singularly heightened by the ingestion of increasing amounts of discourse.

In *The Archive and the Repertoire* (2003), performance theorist Diana Taylor has argued that two forms of expressed knowledge – the performed/embodied and the textual/archived – have coexisted in reciprocity throughout world history, despite tendencies in the West to privilege the written word while dismissing performance traditions as outdated, mythic, or unconscious.[25] Following Taylor, it seems that what is most conspicuously lacking from museum galleries are the performed cultural dimensions of African objects. How can art objects, performance practices, and the archive be combined in a forum that is explicit about its own status as a contemporary reframing, while nevertheless moving significantly toward integrating, enlivening, and contextualizing traditional arts?

As the technological landscape has evolved in recent decades, many curators and institutions have added more and more media components to gallery installations. Where these innovations have occurred for African art, they have usually relied on tried-and-tested media: photographs, sound recordings, and film and video footage. Sometimes these additions are quite successful. Other times – as, for example, when video footage is displayed on small monitors, or when a mask and costume are mounted on a slowly rotating pole – such interventions arguably do a disservice to African art by making it seem old-fashioned.

With rapidly developing technologies for recording and projecting digital images on a variety of lightweight and mobile supports, it is now becoming possible to animate African objects by relying on moveable constellations of still and video footage and sound recordings gathered through archival and field research. Moreover, one aspect of the contemporary moment that is most salient for *The Play* is the significant presence of professional African traditional artists in the West. Western curators can today no longer claim that African artists are unreachable and therefore unable to be involved in museum programming. Overall, new technologies and the strong presence of African artists in the West have made geographical distance from Africa effectively obsolete.

Modernizing Tradition: Twentieth-Century Guinea

In stark contrast to old prejudicial notions of a timeless and unchanging Africa, the traditional arts of Guinea have undergone tremendous upheavals of politicization and modernization since at least the mid-twentieth century. In 1952, Les Ballets Africains, the first professional African-led performance company to tour internationally, emerged in Paris under the artistic direction of the multi-talented Guinean artist and intellectual,

Fodéba Keita.[26] Following Guinean independence in 1958, Les Ballets Africains in 1960 became Guinea's national ballet, renamed Les Ballets Africains de la République de Guinée. Through its post-independence transition, the company became one of several internationally touring ensembles at the top of a national socialist arts system designed by Guinea's first president, Sékou Touré, to integrate the country's many ethnic cultures and foster political solidarity and national pride.[27] Guinea's national arts system spawned some of Africa's most widely renowned performing artists, and it provided a model for parallel systems (often featuring ballet companies) throughout West Africa.

Having little in common with European "ballet," West African ballet produces indigenous dance, music, and masquerade for the concert stage. During the 1960s and '70s, traditional arts from throughout Guinea were adapted for ballet productions that reinterpreted historic events, folk tales, and indigenous cultural traditions to reflect political ideology and social concerns. West African ballet thus served to modernize traditional art as a global, twentieth-century genre for history telling, nation building, and trans-ethnic communication.

The death of President Touré in 1984 left Guinea a mixed legacy of generous arts patronage, divisive politics, and a crumbling economy. The next president, Lansana Conté, abandoned his predecessor's revolutionary rhetoric for deals with the IMF and World Bank. Under Conté, government arts patronage dissolved and globalization opened the country's previously sealed borders, prompting hundreds of nationally trained artists to move abroad to perform and teach. In subsequent decades, Guinean ballet arts have exploded in popularity in North America, Europe, Australia, and Japan. Today many talented Guinean performing artists live in major Western cities, but the nature of the market for "African" dance is such that artists are often required to work on an individual freelance basis or in small ensembles for teaching and performing. This limits options for large-scale collaborations among Guinean performing artists – additionally because artists must spread out geographically in order to make a living (each city can support only so many artists), and because the market rarely yields the available capital needed to coordinate large-scale events.

Meanwhile, the compartmentalization of visual and performance arts in the West has led to an apparent disconnect between Guinean music, dance, and material culture. Guinean performing artists successfully live and work in the same Western cities where Guinean sculptural works are on permanent display in museums, but sculpture and performance are worlds apart. The expertise of professional expatriate Guinean artists thus remains under-utilized, in what must be seen as a disservice to African art studies, museums, and the public. The role of *The Play* is to propose a space of interaction between Guinean performing artists, museum curators, and art objects.

The Play as Exhibition/Performance

I envision *The Play* as a hybrid project that combines an exhibition of traditional masks and a multimedia stage performance featuring professional US-based Guinean artists. The project brings together artists, art objects, and archival documentation to explore Guinean music, dance, and masquerade traditions as they have evolved from the early twentieth century to the present. It is conceived as a two-space forum in which audiences first encounter masks in a conventional "white cube" exhibition (installed in the foyer of a theatre, concert hall, or museum housing a performance space), and then take seats for a performance where, over the course of a multimedia production that incorporates digitally projected archival and field footage, Guinean artists perform the exhibition's mask genres to reveal a fuller range of expressivity and cultural context. The concept of exhibition/performance allows visitors to first encounter African art within a gallery space (the exhibition), and then to be immersed in an environment created through collaboration with Guinean artists (the performance).[28]

Within this model of exhibition/performance, audiences first experience traditional Guinean masks in the classic "white cube," which highlights material form and allows for close looking. Audiences then proceed into the performance space, where, in critical contrast, Guinean artistic traditions and cultural and political history come to life in a multimedia production featuring the same mask genres seen in the exhibition. In the performance, Guinean arts acquire a larger and more multifaceted presence. Here the aim is at once to connect and contextualize Guinean material arts and performing arts traditions by way of digitally projected translations of song lyrics, textual excerpts, and video and archival footage. The production particularly emphasizes the role of masks as embodiments of both locally and internationally significant and contested ideas.

By framing Guinean masks and their attendant arts historically and in relation to the museum, the archive, and Guinean artists' communities, *The Play* presents traditional arts as modern and contemporary forms that have been politicized, staged, and geographically displaced.

To propose *The Play* as a means of reassembling Guinean arts in the West is not to suggest a ready-made response to the challenges facing curators of African art. Far from announcing a definitive solution, *The Play* starts by posing a question: How can we conceive of Guinean arts in their broadest social, cultural, historical, geographic, political, and aesthetic dimensions? Responding to this question requires an inclusive dialogue among artists, curators, stage and exhibition designers, sponsoring institutions, and audiences.

Experiencing *The Play*

Imagine arriving for a night at the theatre. In the foyer of the theatre is an exhibition of approximately twenty Guinean masks displayed in tall, well-lit vitrines.[29] The vitrines are simple, of uniform height and style; yet the masks and headdresses displayed in them are extraordinarily diverse. As indicated on labels accompanying each vitrine, the masks hail from various regions of Guinea and date mostly from the late nineteenth century to the mid-twentieth. However, no information is given about their histories or uses. Many are familiar to collectors, who tend to class them according to their ethnic origins: Baga, Nalu, Susu, Maninka, Toma, Mano. But these names, as they appear on the object labels, mean little to unspecialized Western audiences. In addition, the labels list dimensions and materials, along with collection information. There is not much to read. This is chiefly a visual experience, an up-close encounter with sculptural form. Most of the masks appear without their accompanying costumes or regalia. Vitrines and other exhibition materials are unobtrusive.

In contrast to the "white cube" exhibition in the foyer, the performance that takes place in the theatre is impossible to outline a priori. Much of the specific archival, thematic, and traditional material to be incorporated into the production would be determined in the course of collaborations between artists, researchers, designers, and other participants. To provide an in-depth description would therefore be to undermine

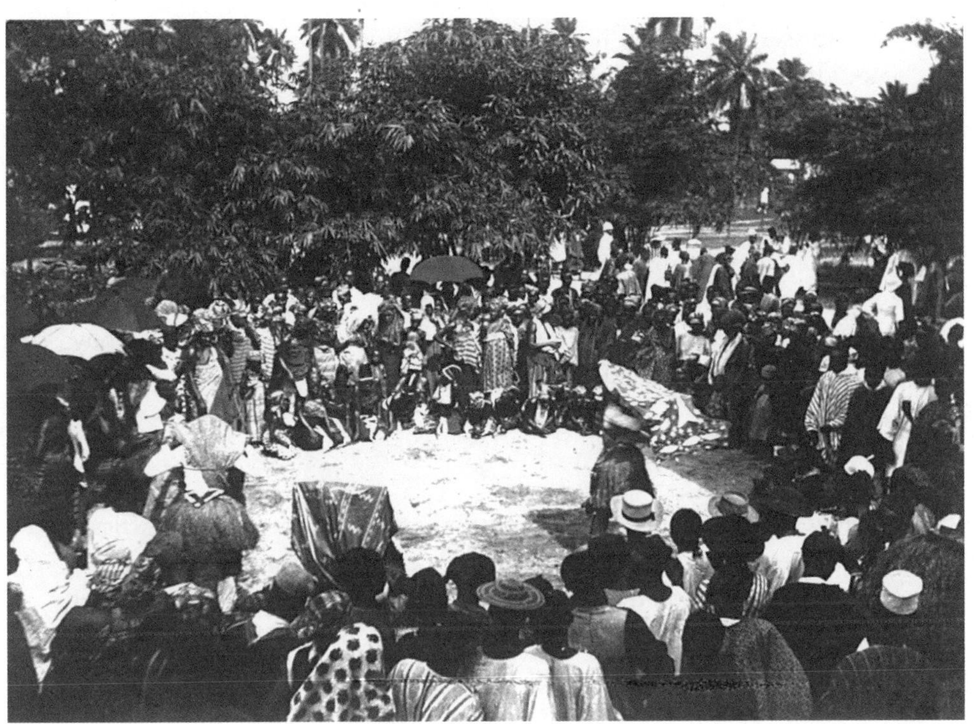

6.2 | Simo Danse (Koubadouba) in Conakry, 1899.

the project's intent. It is nevertheless possible to loosely sketch several themes that could be explored in the stage production, with the caveat that such remarks are speculative and provisional.

The stage production is conceived to present Guinean cultural history chronologically as well as by masquerade forms and themes. Each masquerade form – comprising music, dance, song(s), a mask, and costume – is explored in its local origins as well as in its historical evolution through Guinean ballet. This exploration relies on contextualizing each form with documentary elements (projected archival and field photographs and footage, digital text, audio and video interview excerpts), and by relating each artistic form to broader themes such as political change, the emergence and evolution of ballet performance, and cross-cultural encounters through the arts.

Among the forms to be explored in the stage production is the Baga/Nalu Banda headdress discussed earlier. Today, dozens of Banda headdresses are housed in museum collections worldwide, while a related dance, Sinté, was recently reinvented and popularized for international ballet dance – albeit without use of the headdress, and without the giant log drums that once accompanied it.[30] A multi-media staged production of Banda and Sinté would incorporate archival images of Banda maskers performing as early as 1899 in Conakry (see figure 6.2); photographs and film documenting performances in villages through the 1980s;[31] and recorded interviews with artists and elders commenting on the more recent transformations of these forms. Music and choreography are then arranged to interact with these documentary media components.

Conclusion

The Play takes seriously the notion that artists working within African tradition are continually developing new creative forms and styles, and that these artists should hold primary agency in presenting their cultural traditions in the West. Given the considerable financial and social capital required to realize *The Play*, I envision the project not for a single institution or site, but rather as a travelling production sponsored by multiple art museums and performing arts institutions. Because masks in museum and private collections are not permitted to be danced, *The Play* would open up a new space for a particularly controversial category of African art: the contemporary traditional object, often (reductively) labelled a "forgery" or "tourist art."[32] For *The Play* contemporary traditional masks belonging to the same or similar genres as those included in the exhibition would be commissioned or purchased to be danced on stage.

In proposing to connect Guinean material culture with Guinean performing artists and to reinterpret these works in a multi-media production, *The Play* does not purport to seamlessly recreate traditional artistic forms on the concert stage. Rather, the project is conceived as a self-conscious exploration of the modern political histories and contemporary manifestations of Guinean arts. In a collaborative framework that brings together artists, curators, and researchers, the platform of exhibition/performance emphasizes the historical and performance-based dimensions of African arts, while also calling attention to the interpersonal and cross-cultural dynamics involved in presenting these arts in the West.

CHAPTER SEVEN

But Is It Art?: *Not Really*

MATTI BUNZL

Almost ten years ago, I fell in love – with contemporary art. In some ways, it had come out of nowhere. I had been a casual museum-goer for a long time, the kind of person who has a low-level membership at the "important" institutions in town. But when my partner and I bought a house, we became properly bourgeois. Deciding we had outlived our graduate student days, we resolved not to decorate with posters. Instead, we would buy "real art." Not that we knew the first thing about what that would mean. On a trip to Chicago's Museum of Contemporary Art (MCA), the still inchoate venture became more concrete. We saw a piece that fascinated us, a text-based work by the artist Stephanie Brooks. She had removed all the letters from a group of poems, leaving only the diacritics in a smart, beautiful, eerie display. The wall label directed us to the Rhona Hoffman Gallery, and within a few days we went there and bought it. Thus began the love affair ...

Part of the appeal of the contemporary art world is the intoxicating mix of ostensibly heady intellectualism, relentless and rather entertaining showmanship, and high-end consumerism. On the one hand, you are simply shopping; on the other hand, you are doing your part to discover and promote the next generation of great artists. That, in any case, is the implicit narrative the art world presents to a newly addicted collector. Add to this the sheer exoticism of a place like New York's Chelsea – with its insider lingo, complex hierarchies, and strange behavioral codes – and this anthropologist had found not only a new love, but his next research project.

Where to go from there? As I always tell my students, good anthropology has to be based on real questions. So what was it that puzzled me as I delved into the contemporary art world, attending gallery openings, museum dinners, and even the occasional glitzy art fair? It was simply this: how do we know what is good art? The answer is far from obvious. Long gone are the days when contemporary art was judged according to the modernist standards of the avant-garde. Articulated most influentially by Alfred Barr, the key figure in the early history of New York's Museum of Modern Art, these standards were based on an obvious succession of innovations, which allowed the evaluation of artists and their works in terms of a progressive hierarchy. By the 1960s, such modernist linearity had given way to a more pluralistic field (which included Pop Art and Minimalism), and by the 1970s it was impossible to discern dominant paradigms or maintain the vision of art's ineluctable progress. Some critics spoke of a postmodern condition, while others simply announced the "end of art."[1]

Yet nothing could be farther from the truth. Over the last decades, the contemporary art world has exploded. What had been a tiny network of local avant-gardes concentrated in a few major metropolitan centres has grown into a massive global phenomenon composed of hundreds of institutions, thousands of galleries, tens of thousands of collectors, and a near infinite number of artists. The situation may seem anarchic. Yet a widespread sense that some artists are better than others, and that some works deserve special recognition for their importance, has endured. On a basic level, such value judgments are products of the interplay among the art world's various constituents: artists, gallerists, collectors, critics, curators, and art historians. But how this process actually works, particularly in a thoroughly globalized art world, remains to be examined. I had found my question, and with it my next ethnographic project.

So far, so good. But I wanted access – access to the places where the dynamics that interested me were actively negotiated. It became clear – their pronouncements on the state of the art world notwithstanding – that few writers had real access to the movers and shakers of the art world. While Larry Gagosian, who commands a gallery emporium with outposts in New York, Los Angeles, London, Paris, and Rome, was not going to invite me into any of his offices any time soon, I thought that my status as an academic might open the doors to another site of endless mystique: the inner workings of a museum, particularly its curatorial department. There, after all, sat some of the crucial taste-makers, the oracular agents who had sworn a vow of poverty (the average starting salary for a curator at a major American museum is around $30,000) in exchange for the right to pronounce on what is good and enduring in the world of contemporary art. So I went back to where my love affair began, and approached the MCA with a request to undertake ethnographic research in and on its curatorial department. Eighteen months of complex negotiations later, I was given the green light, provided with an office in the curatorial suite, and – taking advantage of a sabbatical semester in 2008 – proceeded to take up residence.

For the present purposes, I want to share the phantasmatic show *Not Really*, which I curated in my head as I observed the MCA's real curatorial staff conceiving, revising, abandoning, reconceiving, financing, and eventually installing their various exhibits. Bear in mind that, from the outset, I was fascinated with questions of inclusion and exclusion: Why are certain artists deemed worthy of display? Why are certain works considered to be better than others? Why are certain curatorial ideas plausible while others are not?

Since the mid-1990s, a – maybe even *the* – dominant paradigm in avant-garde circles was "relational aesthetics," the mode of art-making codified by French curator Nicolas Bourriaud.[2] Encompassing a varied range of practices, it is characterized primarily by an attempt to break the ossified relations between art, artist, and viewer. Rather than present spectators with finished products, the products are supposed to become activated as part of the artwork itself. The result is a blurring of various boundaries in a practice that sees itself as radically democratic and open-ended, exemplified paradigmatically in Rirkrit Tiravanija's exhibitions in which he cooks food for gallery-goers. With its progressive commitments, relational aesthetics fits into a long history of the avant-garde, a status that is further bolstered by the non-commercial, that is, not readily sellable, nature of much of the work.

The dominant gesture I encountered at the MCA was thus profoundly Duchampian: anything can be art. Following "R. Mutt's" (in)famous urinal, the curatorial champions of relational aesthetics revel in "anything goes."[3] True, the Guggenheim had beaten them to the idea of using the museum as a hotel (part of Nancy Spector's apotheosis of relational aesthetics in the 2008/09 show *Theanyspacewhatever*),[4] but they could still install couches in the galleries to instigate discussions about American foreign policy (Jeremy Deller's 2009 show *It Is What It Is: Conversations about Iraq*).[5] And they could dream about a museum that's relevant, political, transformational.

I was struck by these gestures, and the attendant notion that they would remake the museum as a genuinely democratic space. Struck, because the reality is so far from this vision. I am not talking about the difficulties of attracting a truly diverse audience (a challenge nearly all high culture institutions meet with varying degrees of success). Rather, I am intrigued with the issue on a formal level. Relational aesthetics affirms that anything can be art. What remains unexamined, however, are the frames that need to be in place for this to occur. Put differently, while anything can be art, not everything is – an issue that becomes far more pressing when the inventory of plausible art-making includes cooking food, sleeping, and discussing politics.

This problematic animates my imaginary exhibition. Is it possible to make visible the processes and criteria that separate art from non-art? The show is called *Not Really* – as in "not really art." It collects an ensemble of objects, images, texts, and situations that bear conspicuous resemblance or have a proximate relation to recently canonized pieces but fall short of being the real thing on account of the conceptual, legal, and interpretive processes animating the "originals." The items on display thus dramatize and make visible the "art function" (to echo Foucault) that is operative in the contemporary art world.[6] Such a show might not answer how the art world determines what is good and bad work; but it does expose the mechanisms that frame contemporary art's meanings.

Not Really – Works

Unauthenticated Painting by Andy Warhol

What constitutes a "real" Andy Warhol; and who gets to make the decision? These questions are far from obvious in light of Warhol's practice, which resulted in a huge output of work generated by means of mechanical reproduction, specifically silk screens. And yes – the fact that his paintings are worth millions makes the issue only more titillating.

Not Really opens with one of the paintings from the disputed Red Self Portraits series. Two of those series exist. The first, executed in 1964, contains images that are among the most widely reproduced in Warhol's oeuvre. They are considered the genuine article. A second series, created in 1965, however, does not have that imprimatur. How can this be? Both were manufactured through the silk-screen process; but in the latter case, Warhol was not personally present. It was his absence that led the Andy Warhol Foundation for the Visual Arts, Inc. and the Andy Warhol Art Authentication Board, Inc. to withhold its seal of approval. That, for all intents and purposes, makes the paintings in the second series worthless. They are neither fakes nor the real deal.

What makes this case of *Not Really* so stunning is that Warhol himself clearly considered them genuine. While he did not witness the production, he had given the printer specific instructions on the paintings' creation. He lobbied for the results to be included in his 1965 retrospective at the Institute for Contemporary Art in Philadelphia. Its curator had balked at the manufactured nature of the pieces, but that was the very reason Warhol wanted them included. To him, they pointed in a new direction of impersonal art-making (a striking proto-conceptual move). What's more, Warhol signed and inscribed one of the pieces (a sure sign of authorial acknowledgment) and authorized its reproduction on the cover (!) of his 1970 catalogue raisonné.

Portraits of Fabiola Not Included in the Collection of Francis Alÿs

Francis Alÿs is one of the leading conceptual artists working today. Much of his work interrogates notions of authorship. For example, in his Sign Painting Project, he created small images that he had had copied and enlarged by commercial painters, exhibiting the results as a quasi-collaborative form of art.

Alÿs, who is Belgian but resides in Mexico, is also known to collect art that, much like his own practice, challenges the concept of originality. Most important in this respect is his vast collection of portraits of the fourth-century saint and ascetic Fabiola. As if a trove of modern images of a fourth-century saint were not removed enough from any notion of authenticity, all of Alÿs's pictures are copies based on a now lost nineteenth-century painting by French artist Jean-Jacques Henner.

In 2007–08, Alÿs exhibited his collection of Fabiolas at the Hispanic Society under the auspices of the Dia Foundation. In effect, the installation served as one large piece of conceptual art. *Not Really* showcases portraits of Fabiola as well. They will not be culled from the collection of Alÿs, however. Given the artist's widely reported collecting zeal, it is uncertain whether any Fabiola images could be obtained. In that situation, an art student will be commissioned to execute a few paintings of Fabiola. After the show, they will be offered to Alÿs for possible inclusion in his collection.

Three Bad Paintings (Not by Karen Kilimnik)

In the current moment of contemporary art, there is a craze around bad painting. What had begun as an avant-garde gesture against the cult of beauty (Cy Twombly had to famously "unlearn" how to draw and paint) has now become routinized as one generation after another of "bad painters" is lionized for their deliberate amateurism. One of the heroes of the moment is Karen Kilimnik, whose work is said to be a conceptual position refracted through a romanticized lens of naïve youth. Kilimnik's bad paintings are art. The three bad paintings in *Not Really* will not be by Kilimnik; but the viewer will be challenged to discover that for him/herself.

A Paper Sculpture Built by Thomas Demand's Assistants

Thomas Demand is one of the world's leading photographers. His intensely conceptual practice turns on the representation of iconic historical sites. Rather than take photographs of the locations themselves, however, Demand, or rather his assistants, build(s) elaborate models of them in cardboard, which are, in turn, photographed by Demand. The resulting images, expressing multiple degrees of defamiliarization, and questioning the very possibility of "accurate" representations, form the art – the cardboard models are subsequently discarded. *Not Really* will feature one of those models.

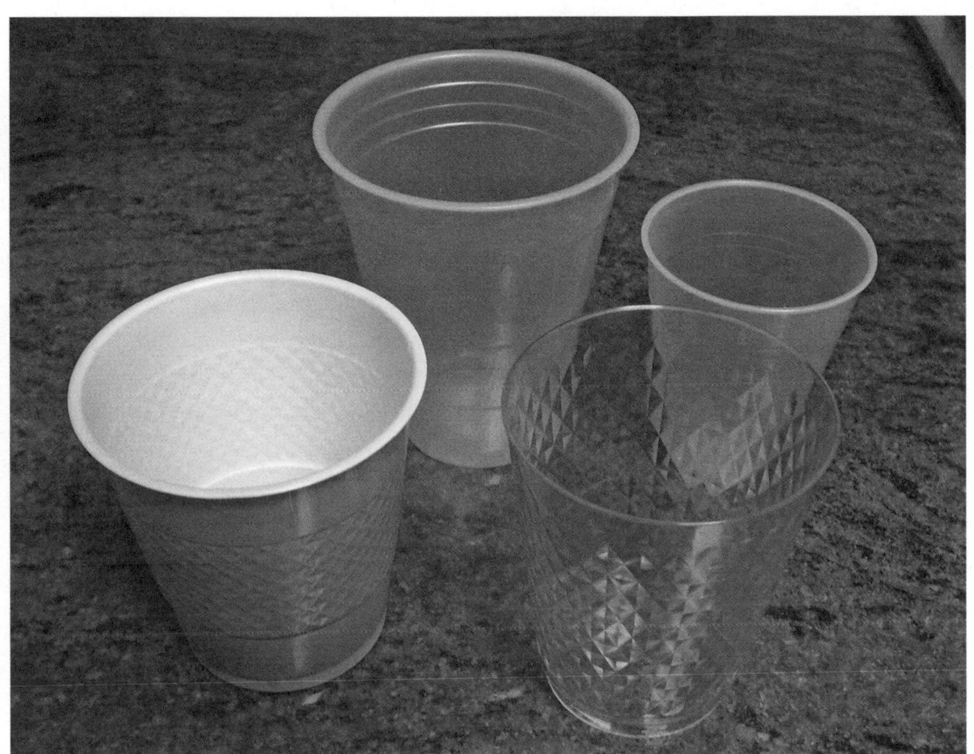

7.1 | Plastic cups.

Plastic Cups from a Tara Donovan Installation

Tara Donovan is among a group of contemporary artists (others are Tom Friedman and Chakaia Booker), who are using humble, everyday materials in mass quantities to create highly fantastical installations. In her hand (along with that of countless assistants and volunteers), hundreds of thousands of drinking straws are transformed into delicate cloudscapes and seemingly millions of pins into a large, dense cube. Donovan's work often seems like a magic trick, but it is always beautiful and memorable. Perhaps her greatest work was a mammoth piece presented in 2006 at the Pace Wildenstain Gallery in Chelsea. *Untitled (Plastic Cups)* featured three million of the titular objects, arranged into a gently undulating landscape that filled the exhibition space, leaving just enough room for visitors to walk around the installation.

All these examples raise an apparently trivial, yet fundamental question. What happens to the everyday objects, in this case the plastic cups, once a Tara Donovan installation is dismantled? Even if the piece itself were purchased by a collector or museum, it would be impossible to store it in its fully installed form. Would a collector's vault containing the millions of plastic cups be holding a Donovan piece? Analogously, would any of those individual cups, having been used in an installation by Donovan, constitute art? Not really. On view in my show are a small group of plastic cups used in a Tara Donovan installation (see figure 7.1).

Pad Thai Not Cooked by Rirkrit Tiravanija

As noted, "relational aesthetics" was the dominant avant-garde paradigm of the 1990s. Named as a quasi-movement by the French curator Nicolas Bourriaud, it subsumed various forms of art-making that resisted the traditional relationship between artists, institutions, and audiences. Artists, relational aesthetics posed, would no longer be object makers; institutions no longer repositories of rarified goods; audiences no longer passive consumers. Instead, the audience was to be activated through acts of artistic generosity that would turn galleries and museums into sites of social and political negotiation.

No artist and project embodied relational aesthetics more fully than Rirkrit Tiravanija's first solo exhibition, the 1990 *Untitled (Pad Thai)* staged at New York's Paula Allen Gallery. Instead of showing discrete objects or even undertaking a performance in front of an audience, Tiravanija simply set up a makeshift kitchen and served freshly made pad thai to visitors of the gallery. The piece was the social situation created in this context and signified by the triangulation of artist/cook, gallery/kitchen, and visitor/eater.

Over the years, Tiravanija has staged countless variations on these themes, often involving cooking, but sometimes going even further by turning gallery/museum spaces into living quarters and inviting audience members to occupy the institution in a completely novel way. But it is pad thai that remains the definitive emblem of Tiravanija's art. And, like so many other avant-garde gestures that have their origins in resistive agendas, it has been thoroughly incorporated into the contemporary art system. For some time now, equipment used in Tiravanija's pieces has been sold as art pieces (yes, these relics of relational aesthetics are unwashed) and museums pay extraordinary sums for the privilege of hosting his interventions. *Not Really* features pad thai, too. But it is not cooked by Tiravanija; it is prepared by a local restaurant.

Conversations About the Iraq War Not Staged by Jeremy Deller

Another star in the world of relational aesthetics is British artist Jeremy Deller. Like Tiravanija, Deller specializes in the creation of social situations. But while Tiravanija shines the spotlight on the everyday, Deller engages with grand historical and geopolitical themes. His most noted work was the brilliant "Battle of Orgreave" (2001). Working with hundreds of participants, Deller recreated the infamous climax of the 1984 miners' strike in South Yorkshire in a piece in which performance art met historical re-enactment. Many of the extras had been in the original confrontation (either on the side of the strikers or the police); and the film documenting Deller's action is most striking for the cathartic effects of the restaging.

More recently Deller created a piece in response to our current geopolitical moment. *It Is What It Is: Conversations About Iraq* toured through several American museums where, in terms of objects, it took the form of a small exhibit centred around the wreck of an exploded car. More important, however, was the charge to each exhibiting institution to position a group of chairs and sofas next to the vehicle and to invite experts to make themselves available for informal conversations about the Iraq war with the museum's visitors. As a result, normally quiet galleries were transformed into more or less active hubs of conversation between the audience and soldiers, expatriate Iraqis, academics, and so on. *Not Really*, too, engages visitors in conversations about the Iraq War. But they are not staged by Deller.

A Pile of Gummi Bears in the Corner

Felix Gonzalez-Torres is a great conceptual artist who died of AIDS in 1996. A leading figure during his lifetime, he has only grown in prominence in the years since his passing. His work is exhibited at major museums with extraordinary frequency; and in 2007 he was chosen to represent the United States in the American Pavilion at the Venice Biennale.

Much of Gonzalez-Torres's appeal lies in the "generosity" of his work. In a number of series that now appear as early articulations of relational aesthetics, he placed objects in galleries which visitors were encouraged to take with them. These included stacks of photocopied images and texts and, even more famously, the so-called candy spills, piles of sweets on the floor beckoning viewers to take a piece. These candy spills were portraits (the weight in candy was specified to match that of the sitter), a moving gesture, especially in pieces referring to Gonzalez-Torres's boyfriend Ross and his struggle with AIDS. But they also make for great showpieces in a museum, inserting a considerable amount of interactive whimsy as well as the *frisson* of the vaguely cannibalistic into spaces usually marked by the phrase "do not touch."

I have always been intrigued by Gonzalez-Torres's pieces. Sure, I enjoy the candy – but I have also often wondered who among the museum staff takes care of replenishing the right amount of sweets and how a museum goes about ordering fresh supplies of the right treat (all of which is specified in the piece). One thing I have noticed is that all of Gonzalez-Torres's candy spills use sweets that are wrapped – I imagine that this has to do with museum regulations, to say nothing of Americans' squeamishness about picking up food from the floor, or food that has been touched by others, let alone eating it. *Not Really* dramatizes these dynamics by placing a pile of gummi bears, with a sign, "Please help yourself" in one of the corners of the exhibition space.

Photos of Tino Sehgal's Performances

Over the last five years, Tino Sehgal has become a true art world phenomenon. At the tender age of thirty-four, he has had his work shown all over the world, including star turns at the 2005 Venice and 2006 Berlin Biennales and a much talked about solo show at the Guggenheim Museum in 2010.

Sehgal's work emerges from the intersection of conceptual traditions, performance art, and dance (he is a trained choreographer). His pieces take the form of discursive or embodied scenarios – what he calls "staged situations" – in which trained performers act out precise instructions by the artist. In *Kiss*, the viewer encounters a man and a woman contorting in a close embrace, assuming, over the course of the repeated action, the poses of four iconic couples of art history. For *This Progress*, a visitor encounters a series of progressively older interlocutors engaging the viewer in philosophical discussions. *This Is So Contemporary*, by contrast, is more lighthearted, having the guards at a museum jumping up and down declaiming the piece's title phrase.

One of the reasons for Sehgal's success, it seems to me, is that it perfectly blends the ever-increasing need for spectacle in contemporary art – museums are larger and larger, and need to be filled with audiences – with genuine avant-garde highmindedness. In regard to the latter, Sehgal insists on the imposition of strict rules. Specifically, he forbids the production of any kind of documentation, textual, visual, or otherwise. This means that his pieces are shown without wall labels, advertised without the use of paper (electronic media are allowed), and sold without contracts (!) – and yes, they are sold, in fact by some of the highest-end galleries in the world. Most stringently, Sehgal does not allow any photographic representations of his staged situations. Officially, they only exist in the here-and-now. But this being the age of the iPhone, countless photos of Sehgal's performances exist. They are sprayed all over the internet – and a selection is included in *Not Really*.

John Baldessari Notebook and Pencils

John Baldessari's *I will not make any more boring art* (1971) is one of the foundational pieces of conceptual art. It was famously conceived when Baldessari, who was based in Los Angeles, was invited by the Nova Scotia College of Art and Design to create a site-specific piece. Since the art school did not have the funds to fly Baldessari to Canada, he sent instructions for the completion of a work at a distance. The students were to write the phrase "I will not make any more boring art" on the gallery walls over and over again until they were covered.

An exceedingly funny piece, not least for its construction of those executing the work as errant school children, *I will not make any more boring art* is also iconic for its uncompromising refusal of traditional object-making and its concomitant treatment of art as a commodity. In this sense, it was fully in line with Baldessari's *Cremation Project*, the sensational 1970 action in which he burnt all the paintings he had made during an earlier artistic phase.

Baldessari, who has also had a noted career as an art teacher, continues to be a revered figure in the world of (post-)conceptual art. In 2009–10 he was honoured with a major touring retrospective that travelled from the London Tate Modern to the Los Angeles County Museum and finally to the Metropolitan Museum in New York. When I saw it there, I was almost shocked to find a gift store at the show's exit. Among the items for sale were notebooks and pencils inscribed with the phrase "I will not make any more boring art." *Not Really* concludes with an installation of similar pencils, which will be for sale.

PART THREE

Activating Art and History

CHAPTER EIGHT

Intervention/Resurrection: Intergenerational Activations of *La Cueca Sola*

LISSETTE OLIVARES and LUCIAN GOMOLL

The basic error of the translator is that he preserves the state in which his own language happens to be instead of allowing his language to be powerfully affected by the foreign tongue.
Rudolf Pannwitz[1]

Curating and Translating Chilean Performance

La cueca is a vernacular dance of uncertain origins, existing in Chile, Bolivia, Peru, and Argentina. It has become a symbol of local pride for many individuals who live in these regions. The dance is understood as an embodied and gendered interpretation of a rooster and chicken mating ritual. In its traditional formations, the man will step toward the woman and offer his arm to her in a gesture of courtship. Soon they face one another and dance to music generated by guitars, accordions, harps, and other idiophonic instruments.[2] The dancers engage in minimal physical contact, but remain intensely connected through their direct gaze and synchronized movements, such as the waving of their handkerchiefs above their heads, their percussive footwork, and their circular motions around a focal point that exists in the space between them.

In 1979 Augusto Pinochet declared *la cueca* the official dance of Chile, in an attempt to generate a sense of national pride among the country's citizens. However, in the post-dictatorship period, some Chileans have also appropriated the vernacular tradition to resist and denounce the Pinochet dictatorship's deplorable practices of intimidation and murder, as well as the social problems that have persisted. Figures who have incorporated *la cueca* into their activism include the DDHH (Group of Detained Disappearees), artist Carola Jérez, and the performance group Las Yeguas del Apocalipsis (The Mares of the Apocalypse).[3] Our "curatorial dream" is the exhibition *Intervention/Resurrection*, which explores the ways in which these Chilean artists from different generations drew from, and transformed, *la cueca* to fashion powerful public performances that simultaneously projected personal statements of loss and established lasting collaborations of resistance.

As curators of the exhibition, we take a self-reflexive approach to our own roles, attending to the ways that events and artworks maintain an "afterlife" in the collective imaginaries of contemporary Chilean society. Assuming that curatorial practice is not innocent or straightforward, we are compelled to ask a number of questions: How should these interventions be remembered? Are there curatorial techniques that would allow for a fuller "resurrection" of the events than traditional approaches would allow, alternatives that more closely represent the concerns of the artists without relying on problematic notions such as artistic originality which tend to obscure collaboration and transformation over time? What does performance in Chile teach us about its cultural institutions and the act of curating more generally? In order to critically explore the practice of curating Chilean performance, we must first look at the terms we use, regional specificities, and the material conditions that affect display techniques, all of which complicate the curator's task as a neutral "keeper" or "caretaker" of art and artifacts.[4] An analysis of the curator's role as one of mediation and translation will provide a critical toolkit for exploring this essay's specific artists and works.

We use the term "performance art" with an acute awareness of its problems. For example, the word "performance" itself is not smoothly translatable into Spanish. Theorist Diana Taylor reminds us that performance is often used in Spanish to refer explicitly to performance art, whereas *lo performático* refers to the variety of actions and embodied modes that "performance" signifies in English.[5] Furthermore, the concept of performance art in English (or performance in Spanish), carries with it the baggage of Western art history, which suggests an emergence from European traditions that may downplay subaltern and non-Western influences such as the indigenous and vernacular origins of *la cueca*.[6] Yet Taylor argues that the slipperiness and complexity of the term "performance" should be reassuring: "the untranslatability … is actually a positive one, a necessary stumbling block that reminds us that 'we' – whether in our various disciplines, or languages, or geographic locations throughout the Americas – do not simply or unproblematically understand each other."[7]

Other scholars use alternative terms to frame cultural and artistic interventions that are similar to those we explore in this essay.[8] For example, *acciones*, or actions, often refers to works by Latin American artists who stage social interventions by engaging both aesthetics and politics.[9] Additional Spanish terms used to describe performance or performance art include: *teatralidad*, *espectáculo*, and *arte dramático*, all of which refer to specific aspects of performance, but not the broad sense captured by the English definition.[10] We have chosen the term "performance art" not to emphasize a Western genealogy but precisely to contribute to its problematization. We prefer this term over alternatives such as *acciones*, because the former concept points to the understudied process of how events are framed, which is often the very factor that distinguishes performance art from "ritual," "theatre," or "everyday practices." In other words, vernacular or dramatic modes can be transformed into performance art by reframing them in a museum or gallery, which is a task of the curator.

Latin American performance art presents unique challenges for curators. Not only is performance art trivialized by national funding institutions but, because of the problems of translation and framing suggested above, it is often confused and equated with performing arts such as dance and theatre. Latin American performance artists, including Carola Jérez and others we discuss in this essay, frequently engage histories of colonial, military, and economic violence – subjects that institutions typically regard as risky and thus may not support. Thus Chilean performance art is a practical and political challenge for national exhibitors. We propose, however, that institutional resistance and risk are productive modes of discomfort that open up spaces for emerging discourses in art and politics, especially in relation to Latin America. And with this project, we hope to curate Chilean performance art in ways that help maintain degrees of the artists' intended aesthetics and politics, without domesticating their political interventionism through conservative institutional display methods.

Generally speaking, curating performance art can refer to two distinct practices: organizing a live event, and representing such an event after it has happened. We understand either type of curating performance art to be a form of translation, parallel to the way James Clifford characterizes written ethnography. He explains that, "ethnographic writing includes, minimally, a translation of experience into textual form. The process is complicated by the actions of multiple subjectivities and political constraints beyond the control of the writer."[11] Similarly, the curator of performance translates an event into an exhibitionary model – whether by framing live events for the gallery or other space of exhibition with a particular audience, writing about the events for the catalogue beforehand, or rearticulating and contextualizing its remains afterwards. In Walter Benjamin's terms, curating or translating a performance that took place in the past will produce an "echo of the original," a task that we believe must include attention to the aesthetics and politics of the intervention initially put forth by the artists. Such an approach will – as Rudolf Pannwitz called for in our chapter's epigraph also cited by Benjamin – allow the works to transform curatorial practice rather than disciplining the content to conform to more traditional display models.

Benjamin insists that "the transfer can never be total, but what reaches this region [of conceptual fidelity to an original] is that element in a translation which goes beyond transmittal of subject matter."[12] In literary translation, the poetics particular to each language makes it impossible to translate sentences by interpreting each word in isolation; we must also translate meanings from "between the lines." So too must a curator of performance art be attentive to the areas between archival materials, to represent or resurrect a form of art that was meant to be located in a social, cultural, political, conceptual, and/or performative space. One way that curators may restage these aspects of artworks is by framing objects as performative traces, rather than as static documents or art objects contained within their own material boundaries. The result may be an interactive environment that engages visitors in ways more akin to the spirit of the original intervention, a "resurrection" of an art not bound up in material object(s) to begin with, thriving instead in spaces of performance and conceptual engagement.

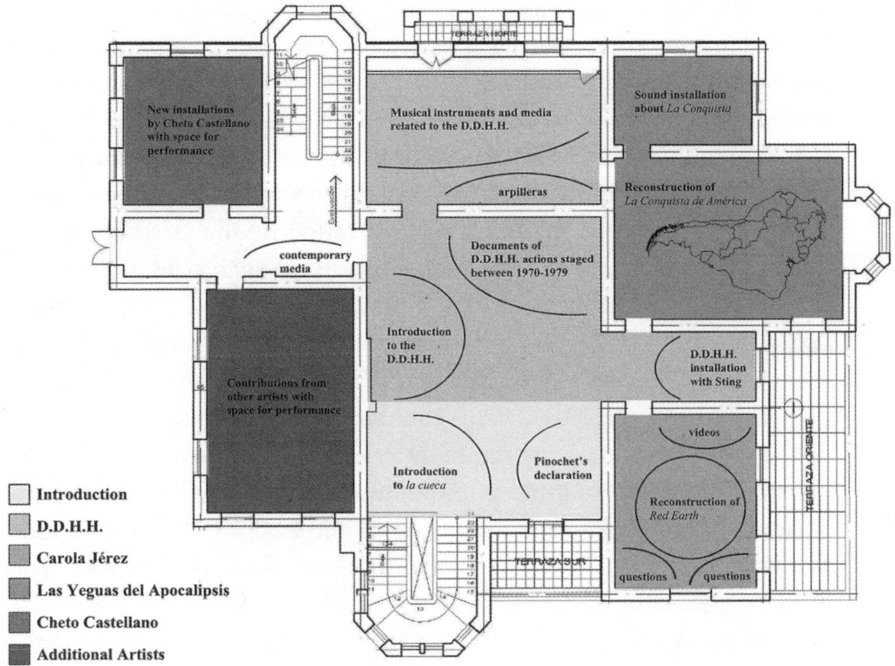

8.1 | Exhibition floor plan for the Allende Museum, designed by Lucian Gomoll (2015).

To explore curatorial risk and translation, and the ways in which curating Chilean performance can challenge and transform curatorial practice more generally, we examine the roles of dance and performance art in recalling Chile's disappeared populations. A comparative analysis of the DDHH, Carola Jérez, and Las Yeguas del Apocalipsis illustrates how *la cueca* is repeatedly cited and revisited for its power to "resurrect" the disappeared through the elimination of a physical partner in the dance.

Our exhibition is well suited for El Museo de la Solidaridad Salvador Allende (The Salvador Allende Museum of Solidarity) in Santiago, Chile. In comparison to other Chilean institutions such as the Museum of Memory and Human Rights or the Contemporary Art Museum, the Allende Museum is unique in its politics, architecture, and history. First organized in 1971 by a group of leftist intellectuals, the Allende Museum began as a solidarity organization that acquired artworks, photographs, and other cultural objects. Such materials were exhibited only twice before the 1973 coup. During the period of military rule between 1973 and 1990, the organization was shut down and dispersed into a number of underground arts and exhibition projects, while some important objects migrated abroad.[13] It was not until 1991 that the museum was reopened and reunited with many such exiled objects from the original collection. The current building was converted from a large house and thus contains intimate and uniquely situated gallery spaces. It functions as its own sort of "resurrection" of a political spirit, and is thus particularly fitting for a project such as ours, responding to the violent disturbances of the Pinochet regime and also to the inventive forms of struggle and solidarity enacted by various counter-cultural agents.

The general spatial layout of *Intervention/Resurrection* allows for interaction among multiple interpretations of *la cueca* throughout the museum in five gallery rooms, where we emphasize both collaboration and intergenerational citation. Rather than contain distinct types of performance in a single frame or room – a technique that might suggest autonomy and creative originality – we foreground exchanges among the different artists and performers. For example, visitors encounter images of Jérez dancing with DDHH members several years after the latter group staged its first interventions, and accompanying wall texts describe how *la cueca sola* transformed over time; explanatory labels in the room devoted to Las Yeguas del Apocalipsis relay to visitors the ways in which the queer performers were at once inspired by and critical of the DDHH. Our exhibition addresses the context of each version of *la cueca* throughout the intimate spaces of the Allende Museum, while allowing each iteration to appear in conversation with the others. In the sections that follow, we lay out key moments in our curatorial dream. We discuss the advantages and challenges of curating these artists during and after their performances, along with vivid descriptions of how the space looks and functions, and theorize the multiple forms of intervention and resurrection involved in curatorial processes and audience engagement.

La Cueca Sola: Dancing Alone, Mourning Collaboratively

They met while searching for their missing loved ones, crossing paths at detention sites while flashing photos of the disappeared to the prison guards. With increasing horror, they came to realize that they were not alone. In the early 1970s they were known as the families of those who had not yet been found.[14] Coming together in despair, they allied themselves with lawyers and human rights organizations, actively searching for any trace of their loved ones. A group of about two hundred, most were women whose husbands and sons were missing. In 1976 they formed an alliance with the Vicaría de la Solidaridad, holding meetings and developing a variety of tactics that would force the military state to acknowledge their presence and release information. By 1977 they began to interrupt public spaces with political demonstrations. Tollita Diaz recalls: "Every time we went out to protest, we wore the photos of our missing, and so they [too] went to the street, becoming incorporated into our protest." Their "lightning actions" required that they overcome their fear, and as the group grew, their outrage increased. Between 1977 and 1979, their public presence was impossible to ignore. They chained themselves to the gates of Congress, staged fifty-hour hunger strikes, burned themselves, and marched the streets of the city with large signs that demanded to know: "Where are they?"

Organized into small committees, the DDHH has created multiple symbolic actions during its thirty-plus years of protest. In 1978 Apolonia Ramirez, Ana Gonzalez, and Gabriela Bravo suggested creating a group that would use song to represent their struggle. Led by Gala Torres, a peasant vernacular musician, their group of approximately twenty-five women began to meet weekly, learning to play instruments and sing together for the return of their missing. "One day," recalls Tollita, "Gala arrived with a song she had written: *la cueca sola* (the solitary cueca). As she read it aloud, we offered suggestions and so it became a collective project that denounced [the situation that created] the painful experiences we were going through." More than thirty years after its first iteration, Tollita still recalls with amazement, "We didn't realize how symbolic it was." What began in the safe space of familiar allies soon became a widely recognized symbol of courage and protest for others who had also lost loved ones during the dictatorship.[15]

On 8 March 1978, International Women's Day, this vernacular segment of the DDHH was invited to perform in front of ten thousand women viewers. They prepared a special performance for this massive event. For the first time in public, they performed *la cueca sola*. As the large group of women played and sang their new interpretation of Chile's most famous vernacular music, three of the women from the group performed the steps of the song – typically danced with a partner – alone. For those watching the scene, the message could not be clearer. Traditionally performed between a man and woman as a dance of courtship, the striking new choreography, coupled with its politicized lyrics, transformed it into a dance of mourning and accusation as the women circled the stage, moving to and fro with implicit, ghostly partners.

It is this sense of mourning that we attempt to capture in *Intervention/Resurrection*. To emphasize this, we present a video of the traditional courtship *cueca*, danced by a couple, at the very beginning of the exhibition next to a larger video projection of *la cueca sola*. The solitary *cueca* video is surrounded by photographs and first-person testimonies of the DDHH women who expressed their mourning through the dance. The walls of the Allende Museum galleries are primarily white, but for this installation more somber colours are used to reflect the mood of the women's dance. Shoe prints – to suggest the steps of the dance – appear on the floor in front of the installation, beginning with the regular *cueca* and slowly transforming into the solitary version.

Gala was the director of the vernacular group and only women who had a disappeared family member could join. Those in the group who knew how to play instruments or who sang or danced would instruct those who were willing to learn. Some of these instruments are on exhibit in the space. To encourage the continued use of this symbolic dance by future generations, instructional videos made by the women expressly for the exhibition are also included. By 1979 the DDHH women had become so popular that they were invited to do three performances a day among student, worker, and political groups, and this renown is documented in our exhibition with testimonies and newspaper clippings. "There was a lot to denounce," recalls Tollita. Some of their fondest memories include visits with the British pop artist Sting in the 1980s – an impression shared by the singer, as his hit song "They Dance Alone" demonstrates.[16] Sting witnessed one of the DDHH public protests during his Amnesty Tour of 1986 and was inspired to help bring global attention to their cause, enlisting Eric Clapton as the guitarist for the song.[17] One installation in *Intervention/Resurrection* is devoted to this exchange as an example of the connections linking the women's local performances and global popular media. Engagement with global media presented the women with the possibility of establishing political alliances that might undermine the government's totalitarian efforts to isolate the Chilean populace. Headphones and explanatory captions accompany a monitor that loops the music video for "We Dance Alone," as well as interviews from Sting, the women, and television news stories from the years 1985–87 that relate to the song's content.

As the years passed and there was no sign of their family members, group members eventually began to acknowledge that their loved ones had been permanently disappeared. Many in the group have passed away, often without having received any information about the last moments of their loved ones. By 1991 Gala had withdrawn from leadership and Tollita Diaz took over the development of the DDHH. As each year passes, fewer and fewer women remain from the original group. Today there are only eight members. But our exhibition curates excerpts from the public stories of all the women, and the surviving eight members are invited to speak at the Allende Museum in panel discussions, and to perform *la cueca sola*. Audio recordings of their oral histories are also included, along with accompanying *arpilleras* (textile sculptures), which document the repertoire of this symbolic dance with delicately embroidered images. *Arpilleras* commonly depict social scenes, often outside, with fabric pieces cut into the shapes of houses, trees, mountains, and cars that have visible topstitching and constitute the background landscape. People featured in the scenes are usually sculpted three dimensionally, with stuffed or rolled body parts that pop out of the otherwise flat canvas. Additional quotidian materials such as paper, sticks, and bits of paper enhance the flat textile sculptures. For the exhibition we have selected *arpilleras* that feature incidents in which Chileans are being harassed or detained by the military, as well as scenes that explicitly reference *la cueca sola*. These emblematic works were produced by the widows as a means of raising funds for their organization, and they were sold to international allies through the Vicaria de la Solidaridad.[18] While a retrospective exhibition of the DDHH's dance has not yet been produced, the influence of the group's rearticulation of *la cueca* had a cultural influence beyond popular music. For example, artists Las Yeguas del Apocalipsis, Nako Tako (Cheto Castellano), and others cite *la cueca sola* in their own reinterpretations of the dance. In the next section, we discuss how performance artist Carola Jérez works with the women's performances, herself enacting a form of curation that frames the DDHH as art; we have also worked to curate these additional "lives" of *la cueca sola* in our exhibition at the Allende Museum.

Red Earth: Layers of Dirt, Frames of Renewal

In 1998, for the first time in Chile's post-coup period, Augusto Pinochet was charged with crimes against humanity and placed under arrest in London.[19] Chileans who had resisted the regime celebrated this legal victory in diverse global settings. For Carola Jérez, a performance artist working in Chile during the 1990s, the news came while she was in residency in Moscow. She recalls nostalgically, "I realized Pinochet was in prison, and I ran through the streets, I did a Russian dance, and I celebrated with vodka."[20] In the heat of her celebration she reached toward the ground and grasped a handful of dirt, saving it for the future. Months later, upon her return to Chile, Jérez channelled that night's emotion to create a "new" performance, by reframing the DDHH's solitary *cueca* in a museum context.

In the entrance hall of Chile's Museum of Contemporary Art, Jérez appeared dressed in black. To her left, the vernacular group of the DDHH shared the stage. At Jérez's feet was a map of La Moneda, Chile's presidential palace, which she covered with the dirt she brought home from Russia. On top of that, she added more layers of earth, coloured in red, white, and blue. Jérez took off her shoes as a cue to the musicians, who began to play the music for *la cueca*. Each of the women from the DDHH danced the steps of *la cueca sola*, in close proximity and solidarity with one another – as well as with the ghostly partners that the solitary dance "resurrects." As they danced, Jérez approached the women, her bare feet leaving tracks of dirt upon the marble floor of the museum.

Red Earth appropriates the powerful symbolic language developed by the DDHH women, but it also exceeds the women's intended expressions and interventions. Diana Taylor has speculated on many aspects of political performance in Latin America, but like other theorists in the field, she does not question the formal processes by which political performances are framed as art.[21] It is notable that in *Red Earth*, Jérez identifies the importance of political performance and uses the space of the museum to reframe the dancing women as artists. By extending this invitation to dance *la cueca sola* in the museum, Jérez critically appropriates the role of the curator, imposing her own problematization of "art" in the museum. *Red Earth* highlights Jérez's performance repertoire while simultaneously complicating the boundaries and classifications of contemporary art. Referencing historical, geographic, political, and gendered cartographies of displacement in a performative, intergenerational collaboration, the dance is at once DDHH's *cueca sola* and Jérez's own performance. Like the performance discussed in the next section, staged by Las Yeguas del Apocalípsis in 1989, Jérez trades on *la cueca sola*'s symbolic political gesture and its capacity to materialize a disappeared constituency through the absence of a companion body. In so doing, she draws renewed attention to the plight of the women and also affirms the aesthetic value of their political choreography.

By 1998, despite almost ten years of democracy in Chile, the national court system had not been able to rescind Pinochet's self-imposed immunity as a life-long Senator (*senador vitalicio*); nor had the national judiciary succeeded in trying him for crimes against humanity. Tollita Diaz recalls Pinochet's long-overdue 1998 detention in London vividly, saying, "now that was happiness, 503 days of vigil."[22] During this vigil the members of the DDHH maintained a visible presence day and night in front of Chile's courts, demonstrating their allegiance to the international human rights prosecution. This specific historical context meant that Jérez's performance fluctuated between being a dance of victorious solidarity and a collective intervention that emphasized the importance of continued resistance. As a feminist and collaborator with the women of the DDHH, Jérez related her own performing body to those of the widows, and though they all danced without partners, they danced together in a shared struggle.

In our exhibition at the Allende Museum, the Russian earth that Jérez salvaged is placed in the middle of the second gallery floor to resemble the 1998 performance environment at the Museum of Contemporary Art. The walls feature a video of the performance accompanied by autobiographical accounts of Jérez's reactions to Pinochet's detainment and her return to Chile, as well as newspaper clippings related to the event and its historical moment. By foregrounding common performers and themes, our curation of the Jérez-DDHH performance engages through cross-citationality and physical proximity the other works in the exhibition's first gallery, which focuses on the solitary *cueca*. However, it also brings attention to the ways in which the widows' actions are reframed by Jérez as art. To achieve this, we provide open-ended display labels, including:

- Compare this performance of the solitary cueca in the Museum of Contemporary Art to the other locations at which it was staged, such as in front of public buildings, or the locales featured in Gallery One. Do you feel that the meaningfulness and effectiveness of the actions change? If so, how?

- Carola Jérez insists that *la cueca sola* is art; however, only one of the women of the DDHH identifies as an artist. How would you define their roles and their actions?

- *Red Earth* was a performance that insisted on the importance of continued resistance to oppression and state injustices in 1998. Now, over a decade later, can you think of how *la cueca sola* (or a similar type of intervention) might bring needed attention to a contemporary social issue?

Despite Jérez's incorporation of the widows in the museum and her reframing of their vernacular political practice as art, in an interview with the DDHH, the women indicated that they did not feel that their work was transformed in its meaning, purpose, or impact by its performance in the museum in comparison with their other performances. Most participants in the group willingly accept the categorization of *la cueca sola* as "politics"; labelling the dance as "art" has proven more challenging. With the exception of Tollita Diaz, the women do not call themselves artists and Jérez's reframing of their work as art in the museum did not affect the women's own perceptions of themselves in relation to their work. As of yet, no past performances by Diaz and other members of the DDHH have been curated by an arts institution. Though it is of course uncertain how group members would react, their vested interest in disseminating their message would suggest the potential for collaboration across varied settings, including museums and galleries. Though the widows do not usually receive funding to support their work, part of our curatorial initiative involves raising funds for their foundation, by commissioning their performance and selling its documentation. As curators, we make a point to display the widows' varying views of themselves and their practice (in relation to their dance), along with questions for exhibition visitors, asking them to think critically about authorship and the status of artists, particularly for collaborative works.

Las Yeguas del Apocalipsis: Queering *La Cueca Sola* in *La Conquista de América*

On 12 October 1989 – el Día de la Hispanidad (The Day of "Hispanicness"), a national holiday that usually celebrates Columbus's arrival in the Americas – Pedro Lemebel and Francisco Casas, two queer artists known as Las Yeguas del Apocalipsis, staged their own resurrection of *la cueca* in a performance called *La Conquista de América* (The Conquest of America). They invited their audience to Santiago's Human Rights Commission, an institutional and activist space charged with the history of the Pinochet regime's abuses. As the audience arrived, they crowded around a large map of Latin America, devoid of national boundaries, and covered in broken glass derived from Coca-Cola bottles. Seated behind the commission's large banner, the two artists sat immobile on a bench, wearing matching uniforms of black pants, with bare feet and torsos, each holding a white handkerchief. Close-up photos of the event reveal Walkman Personal Stereos strapped to their chests beneath large "Xs" of tape that appear to feed music into each artist's headphones, but for the audience the scenario was enveloped in silence.[23]

As Las Yeguas moved together onto the territory of the map, they positioned their bodies facing each other on opposite sides, and began performing the well known national choreography of *la cueca*, each waving a white handkerchief overhead as they advanced and receded with the quarter-rhythm of the dance. A journalist covering the story describes Casas as lingering over the Southern Cone (Chile and Argentina), while Lemebel "vigorously stepped on the glass towards the other end of the map."[24] Eyewitness Isabel Larrain claims that "the silence was so acute that the audience heard and felt the shards of glass entering their bare feet, especially during the climax of the dance, during an agitated series of steps known as *el zapateo* (the kicking series).[25] After only one round of the dance, Las Yeguas exited in silence, limping, as their feet left bloodied tracks on the map.

While few audience members were present that day, eyewitness accounts, gossip, and a limited number of publicly available photographs have enabled this performance to permeate Chilean collective memory, often in highly mythologized form. In an article that documents this event, Pedro Lemebel is cited as saying that: "This performance is the first time our marginality is situated, equal to equal, at the same table of the Avanzada ("advanced scene," an artistic movement similar to the avant-garde), who were already institutionalized. We are in the street, we both live in *poblaciones* (shantytowns), while they [the Avanzada] have tried for years to speak from the street. Unlike them, we are not interested in the documentation or in the kardex (archive) of art actions."[26]

This revelation is important for understanding the intentionally ephemeral echo of *La Conquista de América*. Unlike more mainstream and institutionally supported artists, Las Yeguas positioned themselves and their performance against its potential commodification as an art object. The statement uncovers an intention less concerned with being perceived as (avant-garde or "advanced") artists, and more invested in issuing a statement about their marginality within the political and cultural realm of Chilean and Latin American civil society. Indeed, Lemebel emphasizes the layers of marginalization that *La Conquista de América* attempts to uncover: "This emphasizes all the implications of homosexuality, as a material of waste and a connotation of delinquency, we are placed alongside prostitutes, *neopreneros* (drug addicts), a margin in which homosexuality is not optional, it's a disease, and a double disease if you're Araucanian [indigenous]; homosexual and Mapuche [indigenous], and furthermore, poor, means double or triple marginalization."[27]

As is demonstrated by Lemebel's words, queerness for Las Yeguas becomes a rearticulation not only of sexual and gendered marginalization, but of class, racial, and even species abjection. Indeed, their name is constitutive of their resistance: the word *yegua*, or mare, is also a pejorative term for homosexual in Chile, and these artists transform the term's social value by distancing queer sexuality from a presumed human-animal hierarchy.

Significantly, *La Conquista de América* resurrects the subversive symbolic order manifested by the widows in *la cueca sola*. Like the widows,

Las Yeguas intervene in the military state's appropriation of *la cueca* as a cultural form representative of Chilean nationalism. Furthermore, as do the widows, Casas and Lemebel use *la cueca* to symbolically account for a disappeared and abject population subjected to violent erasure by the military state and the national republic. However, they queer the normative symbolic structure that is present within the dance's performance matrix. By disarticulating *la cueca* from a dominant meaning system that codes the dance as hetero-normative (the pair is usually coded as male-female, an expectation on which the widows relied), *La Conquista* extends the critique issued by *la cueca sola*, not only rearticulating the signifiers of dominant heteronormative ideology but dismantling the logic of this ideology as well.[28] In other words, while Las Yeguas do borrow the affect of mourning and methods for "resurrecting the disappeared" developed by the widows in their version of the dance, they alter the structure of the dance to queer the performance and the surrounding discourse. Instead of performing their version alone, Las Yeguas dance *la cueca* in proximity but not in the usual gendered pairing. Creating a statement similar to Carola Jérez's reframing of the dance via the co-presence of numerous bodies (alluding to a feminist front of solidarity and ghostly resurrection), Las Yeguas emphasize queer collectivity, which forms part of the collective marginal voice necessary to resist the transnational and neocolonial policies that made the Chilean military regime possible. Furthermore, Las Yeguas del Apocalipsis and their queer iteration of *la cueca* is equally critical of more recent national imaginaries, extending their critique to post-dictatorial transition governments, including both the Concertación presidencies and the Piñera government.

In our exhibition at the Allende Museum, we employ in-situ techniques to recreate or "resurrect" the site-specificity of *La Conquista*. Since the Allende Museum is also an institution that holds the military regime accountable for its history of oppression, the exhibition includes a reproduction of the original performance's large-scale map, with its broken Coca-Cola bottles and bloodied footprints, so that visitors can confront the ongoing legacy of neocolonial oppression persistent in Chile's post-dictatorship period. The walls include photographic and journalistic documents of Las Yeguas' performance, though they are limited in quantity due to their very partial and limited circulation during the period in which the work was produced. The installation curates sound and video recordings of viewers' descriptions of the performance, as well as second-hand accounts, such as whispered fragments of the performance's myths and memories, suggesting the underground evolution and transmission of cultural memory, and testifying to how audiences are implicated in keeping performance memories alive. Francisco Casas will visit the museum and share his own memories of the performance and read from published literary memoirs that recall the event.

Conclusion: Contemporary Activations and Endings

La cueca in its traditional form continues to be an important cultural practice for the construction of Chilean identity. During the bicentennial celebrations in September 2010, for example, the dance returned to mainstream attention, appropriated by middle- and upper-class sectors as an expression of nationalism, reframing what was once a "lowbrow" vernacular practice as a mark of bourgeois cultural pride. Also in 2010, the newly elected and ultra-conservative president Sebastian Piñera inaugurated the Chilean bicentennial celebrations by performing *la cueca*, resurrecting the nationalist meaning that Pinochet associated with the dance. This chilling refraction reminds us that, like with Pinochet, Piñera's political agenda aimed to extend the previous regime's institutionalization of neoliberalism. Thus interventions such as those discussed in this essay, with their radical critiques of the dictatorship, and in particular their resistances to the neoliberal colonization of the Americas, continue to be relevant in the contemporary context, reminding us that despite the Chilean state's formal adoption of democracy, legacies of violence from the dictatorship period remain active today.[29]

In an attempt to critique the persistence of the military regime's ideology in current Chilean political culture, the exhibition features video screenings of these new emergences of the traditional *cueca* in the hallway of the museum, before visitors enter the galleries where performances of resistant versions are resurrected. Our exhibition also includes a speaker series that addresses the construction of national identity in the post-dictatorship period. Furthermore, we will commission new performance works to be staged near the end of the exhibition's schedule, extending the collective front envisioned by the artists and cultural performers mentioned above, for continued activation at the Allende Museum.

It is our goal with this exhibition to move beyond the limitations of the art institution by integrating works, artists, and formats that critically question the shortcomings of traditional modes of display. By emphasizing solidarity over genre classifications or disciplinary boundaries, our context-specific project in the Allende Museum is free to (re)activate the life of interventions staged at various moments in Chilean history, engaging both visitors and performers from a variety of critical vantage points. Similarly, invoking a common cultural referent such as *la cueca* allows us to disarticulate its quotidian signification while resurrecting the ways it has been reworked by varying constituencies. By enabling the interplay of multiple interpretations of this dance throughout the exhibition space, we emphasize collaboration and many forms of historical citation.

Our hope is that this exhibition successfully translates different versions of *la cueca* so that visitors experience the intergenerational activations and reinterpretations characteristic of the events, at the same time as maintaining a sense of the politics during a historical period and possible connections to the current moment. By producing the exhibition specifically for the Allende Museum, as curators of both past events and live performances we maintain a commitment to the politics of the institution, the performers, and the "risky" topics they take on. Our own labour thus remains open to such risks, as we curate the works and frame them as "performance art" for the museum. We hope that the problematic aspects of this project, both in translation and politics, are put to work in ways that are productive and thought-provoking for future approaches to curating and representing political performance in Chile.

CHAPTER NINE

The Terrible Gift: Difficult Memories for the Twenty-First Century

ROGER I. SIMON

I needed some help. Typically disoriented when finding my way in large buildings, I approached a security guard and sputtered: "*The Terrible Gift*. Where can I find the exhibition: *The Terrible Gift: Difficult Memories for the Twenty-First Century*?" Directed down the hall and to the left, I wondered what I would find in the space set aside for this exhibition. I glanced again at the photograph and text on the promotional brochure. The cover contained a striking image of what seemed to be a fading, deteriorating children's playground slide, abandoned in a seemingly empty wooded terrain. It was paired with two epigraphs that promised a confrontation with possibly difficult stories. The first of these quoted from Maya Angelou's poem "On the Pulse of Morning." "History, despite its wrenching pain, cannot be unlived, and if faced with courage, need not be lived again."[1] Nicely phrased I thought, but perhaps an overly familiar sentiment too easily forgotten. Rather, it was the second quote that had been lingering with me all morning. Attributed to the philosopher Hannah Arendt, the text read as follows: "In the last analysis, our decisions about right and wrong will depend upon our choice of company, with whom we wish to spend our lives. And this company is chosen through thinking in examples, examples of persons dead or alive, and in examples of incidences, past or present."[2] This epigraph had me considering that perhaps remembrance was more a matter of *inhabitation* than representation, especially if remembrance was understood as a practice that defines how we live with and learn from images and stories from

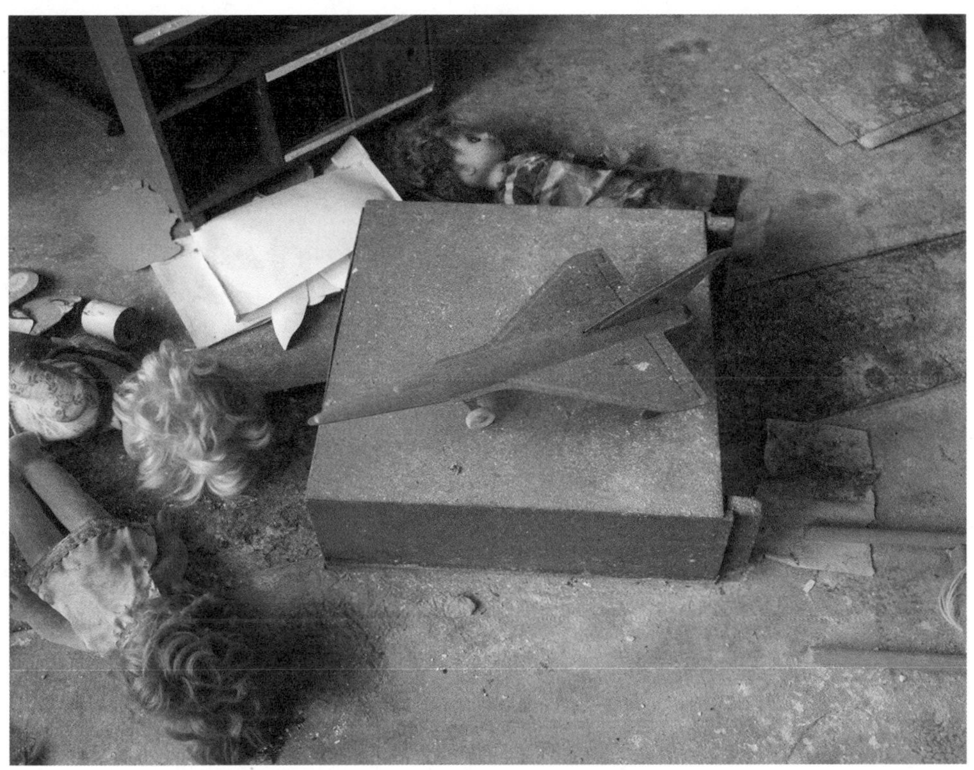

9.1 | David McMillan, *Toys on Kindergarten Floor*, Pripyat, Ukraine, October 1997.

the past, how they contribute to a sense of life's limits and possibilities, hopes and fears, identities and distinctions.

Turning into a wide passageway that served as an entranceway and antechamber to the main exhibition space, I came upon five large colour photographs, one of which I recognized as the fading playground slide on the cover of the exhibition brochure. This image and two others were mounted on the left wall of the entranceway. This triptych of photographs by David McMillan made a beautiful, haunting composition of the now deserted playgrounds and school buildings that had been situated in proximity to the Chernobyl nuclear power plant, where in 1986 a reactor exploded and subsequently leaked substantial quantities of radiation.[3]

Facing these images on the opposite wall were two very different photographs depicting massive stone carvings sited in a barren landscape, strikingly different from the irradiated Ukrainian countryside. These were photographs of monuments separately carved by Simeonie Amagoalik and Looty Pijamini, placed respectively in the Arctic communities of Resolute Bay and Grise Fiord. Together the monuments commemorate the hardships and suffering endured by the Inuit families who during the period 1953–55 were relocated by the government of Canada from the district of Inukjuak on the Eastern shore of Hudson Bay to the High Arctic.[4]

Beside these two images was a wall text. Its words were taken from the speaking notes of the Honourable John Duncan, Canadian minister of Indian affairs and northern development, at the dedication of a monument to hardships undergone by the communities of Inuit who have become known as the Arctic Exiles.[5]

> An Apology for the High Arctic Relocation – August 18, 2010
> *Inukjuak, Nunavik Elders, Inuit leaders, ladies and gentlemen, and especially those of you who were directly affected by the relocation; thank you for being here. On behalf of the Government of Canada and all Canadians, the Government of Canada would like to offer a full and sincere apology to Inuit for the relocation of families from Inukjuak and Pond Inlet to Grise Fiord and Resolute Bay during the 1950s.*
>
> *We would like to express our deepest sorrow for the extreme hardship and suffering caused by the relocation. The families were separated from their home communities and extended families by more than a thousand kilometres. They were not provided with adequate shelter and supplies. They were not properly informed of how far away and how different from Inukjuak their new homes would be, and they were not aware that they would be separated into two communities once they arrived in the High Arctic. Moreover, the Government failed to act on its promise to return anyone that did not wish to stay in the High Arctic to their old homes.*

Straight ahead, at the end of this entranceway, mounted on a narrow standing wall beyond which the main exhibition was evident, I found a video monitor on which was playing a subtitled excerpt from a theatre presentation of Malena Tytelman's *testimonio* "Cuando Ves Pasar el Tren"

(When You See the Train Pass By).[6] This performed monologue was one of a series of dramatic productions produced in collaboration with Las Abuelas de Plaza del Mayo (the Grandmothers of the Buenos Aires' Plaza del Mayo). Formed in the late 1970s, "Las Abuelas" continues today as an organization formed to demand that the children who were kidnapped as part of a method of political repression during the Argentinean dictatorship of 1976–83 be restored to their legitimate families. As the performance of Tytelman's testament unfolded, I stood witness to the pain and longing within which fantasies of recognition are enacted:

> You know when you're standing on the platform, and you see the train pass by? If you look for a while, all of a sudden you see a waterfall of faces pass in front of you. The train stops suddenly ... and out of all the faces that you saw there are a few that stay etched in your mind. Etched in detail, at least for a while, because these are the faces in which you found something.[7]

Although gathered under the sign of *The Terrible Gift*, the display in the antechamber did not make explicit why these three sets of materials were juxtaposed. This uncertainty foreshadowed the show's central question, one fundamental to consider in a world of multiplying tragedies that generate separate, at times conflicting communities of memory. Can an exhibition in which very different histories are brought together – not to compare them, but to create an atmosphere of considered cross-referencing and confrontation – engender productive new ways of inhabiting the past?

Dreaming Beyond the Politics of Recognition

The scenario above is a dream fragment of an exhibition yet to come. What might it mean to regard a proposed exhibition as a dream form? If this text is to stand as more than a simple flight of museological fantasy, we must unpack the notion of the "curatorial dream." At its most basic, a curatorial dream is a wish for something beyond the status quo in public history museums. Yet, as Ernst Bloch suggests, not all genres of dreaming are equal. Daydreams, he offers, in contrast to their self-enclosed nocturnal counterparts, can be a form of active praxis. Daydreaming ventures beyond what is, beyond existing norms and conventions in concrete plans directed at achieving something new. In this, daydreams can embody the seriousness of laying out conditions of possibility. They offer an incisive critique of the present, and a prescient, possible movement toward something better. They open windows. As such, a curatorial dream must be understood as an ambition and a form of anticipation.

In fact, the three events chosen for the curatorial dream discussed here are a subset of events that were part of planned exhibition at the Musée de la civilisation in Quebec City (MCQ). Each event selected for incorporation in the exhibition was of contemporary importance in the country in which it had taken place. In each country, the exhibition planning team had identified specific institutions that would be invited to collaborate with the MCQ as exhibition associates and thus help in identifying and securing material to be exhibited. This meant that the choice of events to be included in the exhibition was influenced by existing professional contacts with such institutions around the world. Due to a lack of funding, the final set of events and collaborative institutions was never arrived at, and the exhibition was never realized. The "dream" that constitutes this chapter is a partial imaginative version of what might have been (and might yet come to be).

Back to the gallery. Even before I had negotiated the introductory antechamber and entered the main area of the exhibition, it was apparent that my curatorial dream would be vulnerable to misrecognition. A visitor casting a cursory glance at the promotional and introductory texts could easily read this dream as a memorializing impulse – what has been caustically characterized as a "reified, stylized, fetishized, and instrumentalized" public space, providing "more bludgeons and pickaxes in the rhetorical wars of grievance against grievance."[8] A more generous gaze, alternatively, might apprehend an expression of the desire not only to memorialize those killed or subjected to extreme suffering, but to assert the memory of such suffering as an inoculation against future evil.[9] Many exhibitions share this ambition to respond to the human need for guidance and affirmation, further strengthening established notions of morality.

My curatorial dream counters both these perspectives. The fundamental ambition animating *The Terrible Gift: Difficult Memories for the*

Twenty-First Century is a rethinking of the project of public history that would take it beyond the dynamics of communal affirmation and recognition, with its resulting competitive memory politics, in which history is subject to the charge that it can only establish winners and losers.[10] My dream-work does not deploy traces of historical events in order to strengthen specific national or ethno-cultural collectivities; nor does it leverage narratives of such events to constitute and re-inscribe national identities. Rather, *The Terrible Gift* begins with a commitment to undertake public history as part of the practice of forging what Lauren Berlant has designated a "historical present" that is constantly "being made [and] lived through."[11]

In this respect, *The Terrible Gift* is dreamt as an intervention in public life that could foster new ways to live with the presence of history, not as a haunting *revenant*, but as a constitutive element in the very condition of the present, opening both contemporary practices of critique and new modes of being-in-common. In such a process, rather than being simply reduced to reference points for contemporary judgments about past or current affairs, histories are offered as resources to be worked through. As Arendt suggests, histories provide examples to think with and from which we might truly learn something that would broaden our perspectives, revise our assumptions and organizing frameworks, subject our institutional practices to critique, and form the bases for new thoughts and action.[12] This ambition for public history presents historical knowledge not only as an excavation and rendition of what was, but as a pedagogical event holding the possibility of contributing to a sense of hopefulness regarding more just and peaceful ways to cohabit our planet.

Certainly *The Terrible Gift* offers information about world events that some visitors might not be aware of, as well as material that would allow those familiar with certain aspects of these events to know them in new ways. But most important is the creation of a *mise-en-scène* that encourages people to think with (not just about) the histories presented in the exhibit.[13] As a contribution to an always-emergent historical present, the exhibition is premised not so much on the idea that exposure to chosen events will open visitors up to an empathic understanding of the suffering of others, but that recognizing the suffering of others will stimulate critical thinking about one's own historical location.[14] Thus,

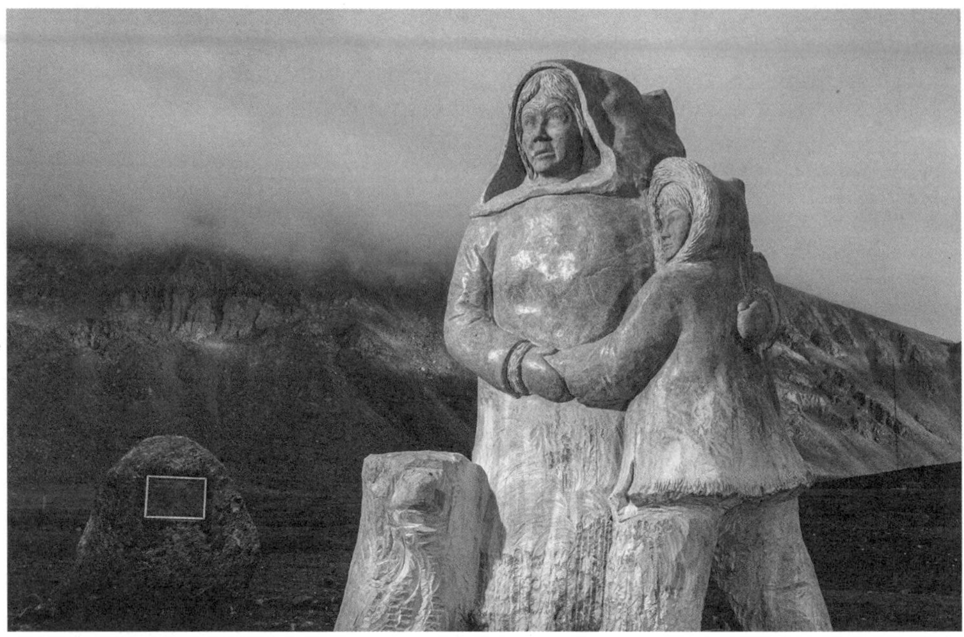

9.2 | Arctic Exile Monument (Grise Fiord), carved by Looti Pijamini.

the intent is not simply the public recognition of past suffering, but to rupture, rethink, and transform the knowledge and understanding that underwrites our patterns of living.

Exhibition Design as a Purposeful Anachronism

I entered the main space of the exhibition through an entrance at the corner of a large, rectangular room. The space contained three distinct sections, each devoted to material referencing one of the three historical events signalled in the exhibition antechamber. In the centre of the room, separated off from these three sections, was a large "Connections" table, surrounded by comfortable chairs. On this table were a number of digital monitors. Along the back wall of the exhibit space was a smaller table on which sat several large, handwritten comment books, as well as a tablet computer, also for entering comments. A series of flat screen video monitors with headphones were mounted on the wall just behind this table. These monitors continuously played edited recordings of

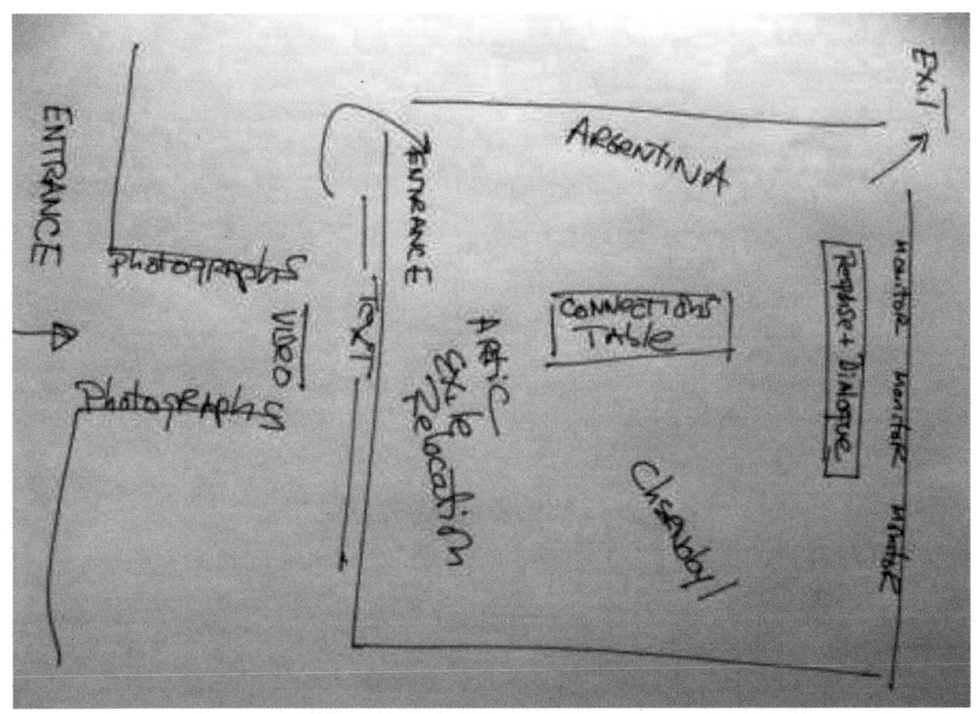

9.3 | Sketch of exhibition layout for *The Terrible Gift*.

visitor reactions to and thoughts about what they had just seen within the exhibit. This entire section was clearly marked out as a space for "Response and Dialogue" (see figure 9.3).

As I walked through the separate areas devoted to the experiences of the Inuit families transferred to the Canadian Arctic, people living in Eastern Europe who were subjected to the nuclear aftermath of the Chernobyl reactor explosion, and the families and friends whose loved one's were "disappeared" by the Argentine dictatorship, it became apparent that each of these sections was defined by a multimodal juxtaposition of material artifacts, documents, audio and video testimony, photographs, art, poetry, and music related to specific lived moments in a particular time and place.

"The Canadian High Arctic Relocation" area included: testimony provided to the Royal Commission on Aboriginal Peoples, archival government correspondence with Inuit, archival government reports, photographs of people relocated to Grise Fiord and Resolute Bay, CBC broadcasts including interviews focused on the relocation, graphic sketches by Simeonie Amagoalik regarding his relocation to Resolute Bay, documentary video excerpts from the film *Broken Promises: High Arctic Relocation* (Nutaaq Média Inc./National Film Board of Canada), songs by Madeleine Allakariallak and the Tudjaat singing duo, based on the memories of her grandmother's relocation to Resolute Bay.

The area of the exhibition dedicated to "The Chernobyl Nuclear Disaster and Its Aftermath" included: David McMillan's multi-year photograph series, which provides images of Pripyat and Chernobyl, images from the "Radiated Places" project, street art in the abandoned town of Pripyat, Russian government documents (indicating directives to suppress information), the poems of Lyubov Sirota (she and her son became gravely ill from heavy doses of radioactive contamination; to express her grief and rage, she turned to writing poems), excerpts from *Voices from Chernobyl: Oral History of a Nuclear Disaster*, photographs and video clips of residents of "dead" and "safe" villages in the region of the Ukraine near Chernobyl, excerpts from the *Sviatlana* CD-ROM project combining video, photography, music, and narrative to form a documentary that tells the broader story of the disaster as seen through the eyes of a single family.

The exhibition area "The 'Dirty War' in Argentina" included memoirs and diaries of the period of the Junta, placards carried by demonstrators protesting disappearances, memory collage posters of friends and family members who were disappeared, excerpts of video testimony of people subjected to detention and torture, government documents, photographs of protest marches (Madres del Plaza de Mayo, for instance), photographs of urban graffiti protesting events of the dictatorship, excerpts from the film *Imagining Argentina*, maps of clandestine detention centres, artwork commemorating the struggle against the dictatorship, songs of Mercedes Sosa (a voice against her government, when people were kidnapped and killed for speaking their mind).

As I roamed through the display space dedicated to the Arctic Exiles, I was able to move back and forth between the sketches of Simeonie Amagoalik regarding his experiences of relocation to Resolute Bay, oral testimony of various survivors relating their experiences of being relocated to Grise Fiord and Resolute Bay, 1954 government documentary footage of Inuit in Resolute Bay singing "Silent Night" as Christmas party entertainment for Canadian soldiers stationed there, Canadian government documents stating its rationale for initiating the relocation, and a recording of the contemporary song "Kajusita" ("My Ship Comes In") by the duo Tudjaat, composed in memory of the relocation and its traumatic consequences. Documents near songs, diaries next to poems, and photographs alongside paintings or drawings – each of the spaces was designed to create a *mise-en-scène* that enabled an intimate encounter with the past.

Such an encounter offers visitors unrestrained exposure to a life quite different from their own. The vulnerability such encounters engender allows for a heightened responsiveness, a transfixing relation. An intimate encounter is more than observing and comprehending another's life experiences. It is an openness and attentiveness to a density of detail that exceeds objectification and thematic categorization, resisting the urge to grasp or contain other lives within existing frameworks of thought.

In exhibitions that bequeath to us the traces of the experiences of others – particularly those who have been subjected to systemic violence and extreme suffering – intimacy means an unsettling of the self. This unsettling enables reflexive critique and transformative insight regarding one's relationship to the past and one's complicity with established historical certainties. This experience is a "terrible gift" – a difficult, process of inheritance that brings with it possibilities for insight and for a relationship with history's victims that reaches beyond the idealized responses of empathy, identification, and solidarity.

What each of the three spaces of parataxic display provided were juxtapositions of historical material that enabled new connections to be made, and contradictions to be apprehended.[15] While each section gave an overall sense of government actions and consequences in regard to a specific event, it highlighted the multiplicity of narratives and questions that one could generate about any given history. Not offered as self-sufficient historical accounts, these exhibit spaces enable encounters with traces of past events that initiate a desire for more information, more certainty, more conclusive judgment than they themselves could provide. As structures of possibility, each ensemble raises questions about the significance of these traces for present and future concerns.[16]

The nonlinear layout of the exhibit spaces gives *The Terrible Gift* a weak temporal frame that promotes an experiential delay and ruptures the "what's next" phenomenon fostered by the desire to take in everything on display in an exhibition. My goal is that visitors take their time.

Slowness and a frustration of visitors' desire to grasp "the point" of the exhibit seems necessary for the cultivation of doubt, uncertainty, and irony, and for a degree of suspension of knowledge or judgment about what we think we know about the events at hand.

The dream exhibit design encourages visitors to view various materials in relation to each other, at times doubling back to look again at material already seen, to make new connections. In this way, *The Terrible Gift* departs from exhibitions that offer authoritative historical narratives (or environments that claim to convey a definitive sense of "what it was like"), seeking instead to immerse visitors in a rich depository of resources for linking past and present. The exhibit becomes "a generator of a new past for new futures."[17]

While placing the three historical narratives together in one exhibition enacts an anachronism, this choice is deliberate, posing the demanding question of the relations of correspondence and contradiction that might exist among the three events. On the one hand, the events are so dissimilar that they can hardly be said to be "the same thing" without erasing the historical specificity of each. On the other hand, as Michael Rothberg suggests, such comparisons open the possibility of a "multidirectional memory" that might produce new objects and new lines of sight, rather than parcelling out entities that are either "like" or "not like" other pre-given entities.[18] While it is readily apparent that each historical event referenced in the exhibition has taken place in a different nation-state during the twentieth century, and that each differed in respect to the kind of violence sanctioned by state authorities, the very fact that they are juxtaposed opens up multiple avenues for consideration. In this respect my curatorial dream enacts a new poetics of public history in which remembrance is conceived of as both personal and social practice: the exhibition is a site of doing remembrance together.

Making Connections

After spending some time with each of the three main sections of the exhibition, somewhat tired, I gratefully sat down at the "Connections" table in the middle of the exhibit space. Tapping lightly on the digital interfaces, I was invited to learn more about the materials displayed, to share my responses to specific materials I had just seen, and to explore possible connections and distinctions among the historical events represented. First, I open a screen showing an interactive schematic of the exhibition displays I had just engaged. Tapping successive screens opened virtual displays of each of the three spaces, with all the items in the three ensembles represented. Tapping on any one of these items brought up a screen that tagged it with more contextual detail and reference information than had been provided in the display spaces. The interactive interface provided the opportunity to write and post a short "visitor tag" and thus express anything I wanted to share about my response to a specific item (including the connections I had begun making across the traces of the three historical events). Reading tags that other visitors had written, I noticed details I had missed when viewing the exhibit materials and was prompted to revisit the displays. This section of database also invited me to send reference material of various degrees of detail to my personal email account, so that I could read and view it at a later time.

As I began to think more about the relations between the three events presented, I was curious to explore possible similarities and differences in the materials displayed in connection to each event. Another set of screens helped me do just that. I discovered that all the exhibited materials, as well as other materials not physically displayed, had been cross-referenced so that, by searching on various strings of words, I could bring together particular traces of the three historical events. For example, since I was interested in learning more about how the experience of suffering and loss affected the generation born after each event, I was able to bring together all instances where this impact is made evident. Thus I could explore similarities and differences between the lyrics and music of Tudjaat's song "Kajusita," the responses of high school students to Tytelman's performance regarding the continuing anxiety for families where children were taken and subsequently were never seen again, and interviews with children whose parents were present during the explosion of the Chernobyl reactor and were subsequently struggling with various illnesses.

I was also able to pull together for careful reading various documents that provided government justifications for actions that had produced so much suffering and continuing historical trauma. Encouraged to make connections across this material, it became evident that *The Terrible Gift* was planned as a discursive event that enjoined visitors to attend to and think with an ensemble of histories in which state authorities, in the name of collective interests, acted in ways that ignored or subverted the importance of individual life and consequently resulted in extensive suffering and death. The character of these actions ranged from intentional murder, to willful ignorance of the human consequences of one's actions, to bureaucratic indifference to the means by which state policies are implemented.

As the interactive resources available at the Connections table made evident, one common element among the state actions presented was their enactment of what Henry Giroux has called a "politics of disposability."[19] This way of naming the connections among different events seemed to make sense, as each historical narrative referenced a particular form of government-sanctioned violence within which a population of people was systematically discriminated against and denied protection of the state. In these circumstances, the state disregarded the singularity of human life, subsuming some of its subjects into collective characterizations that served as a warrant for violence and a practical disregard for the social, familial, and individual consequences of suffering and death. Certainly the consequences of each form of violence were evident in the testamentary legacies on view.

The notion of "disposable life" provided a trans-historical, universal way of connecting these histories, yet the dense particularities in each of the narrative sections of the exhibition pulled against this universalizing tendency. The overall design of the exhibit was thus meant not only to encourage the making of connections but to distinguish between different possible configurations of relatedness. The goal was a notion of the universal rich with particulars, an expression of a transnational public history grounded in an ethics of singularity, intended to contest state policies and practices that justify life as abstractly classifiable – in principle, disposable. The curatorial dream envisions *The Terrible Gift* as a homeopathic experiment in which potentially toxic memories are presented so as to provoke the kind of thought and conversation essential to the health of contemporary democratic projects.

Response and Dialogue – The Exhibition as a Public-in-Formation

As I was preparing to leave the exhibition, my attention was drawn to the back wall of the exhibit space and the section entitled "Response and

Dialogue." Putting on the headphones attached to one of the monitors on the back wall, I listened to a composite video of diverse responses by people who had visited the exhibition. I also spent a few minutes leafing through the large handwritten comment books placed on the table at the back wall, noticing that many of these comments were in part responses to others who had previously written in the book or who were seen in one of the videos.

Visiting this exhibition, one is bequeathed difficult histories and asked to take them in and take care of them. This requires working to assess their significance, and subsequently taking them into account as we go about living our lives. While each visitor singularly faces this work of inheriting the memories presented, the comments registered in the "Response and Dialogue" section of the exhibit made evident that we do not do so alone. Each of us who offered our comments or even just engaged the comments of others, was part of a collectivity forged in the work of reading, viewing, listening, and thinking through the connections and distinctions present in the exhibition, making the exhibit a space of public formation.[20] The comments about the exhibition revealed convergent interests and the possibility of critical dialogue. Such a dialogical forum, and the potential for learning within it, opens and deepens the work of inheritance required by a democratic society.[21]

Conclusion: Toward a Curatorial Poetics of Public History

Constituted in the wake of a history of death and suffering, the exhibition of difficult memories in museums or galleries falls naturally under suspicion. In their disproportion to the realities of the degradation, terror, and death, as well as to the psychological and cultural traumas that still threaten to disrupt everyday relations, exhibitions as a form of public pedagogy are easy to cynically condemn. This is so even where one might attempt an exhibition that directly faces the horror. The charge is that such attempts only divert attention from realities that must be addressed in practical terms. Public history must provide something more than a version of the past that functions as a fragile "stick-it" note placed on the refrigerator to remind us of our obligations and values – a note that is always on the verge of falling off or getting lost amid the clutter of other reminders of pressing daily concerns.

Much depends on the substance of practices of remembrance; that is, the practices that constitute which traces of the past it is possible to encounter, how these traces are presented, and with what interest, epistemological framing, and reflexive awareness one might engage these inscriptions. But more than this, if practices of remembrance are to serve future life, they must pose the question of how people are to "inhabit" history. As a form for the practice of remembrance and the mediation of cultural memory, the exhibition offers a framework within which to apprehend the significance of curatorial practice as aiding in the re-articulation of the public realm and the formation of one's historical present. In this regard, the act of curating remains a much underexplored praxis for animating collective thought regarding pressing social, cultural, and political issues.

Walter Benjamin teaches us that "every image of the past that is not recognized by the present as one of its own concerns threatens to disappear irretrievably."[22] Yet recognizing the past as one of one's own concerns is no simple task. Such recognition must not be reduced to the apprehension of "relevance," to grasping from the present moment themes or issues that seem to persist through past time and into our own. One must proceed on grounds different from the typical investments one often finds at the root of the "use of history," understood as the active adaptation of history to the social, emotional, and political needs of the present.

Public history is not exclusively about authoritatively rendering and circulating a common understanding of historical events and their significance. Quite differently, it may proceed from a pedagogical practice that offers traces of the past that provide the basis for thought and conversations that render history as future-oriented, in that it offers critical resources for understanding current social life and its future possibilities. In presenting various cultural memories of lives subject to multiple forms of state violence, *The Terrible Gift* asks visitors to consider their everyday lives within the terrain of an irreconcilable tension between the singular and the universal, and between ethics and politics. Living as we do within nation-states, the exhibition challenges those attending the exhibition to be concerned not only with who belongs to the "we" of nation, but also with *how* one belongs; that is, to ask what logic and desire will animate and bind us and our communities together.

CHAPTER TEN

Reading the World: Native Histories at the Bosque Redondo Memorial, New Mexico

MARGARET A. LINDAUER

The strong marks of our colonial ... past are contradictorily present in our current reality.
Paulo Freire[1]

Entering my imagined exhibition, *Reading the World*, at the Bosque Redondo Memorial, Fort Sumner Monument – the former military site in New Mexico at which Navajo and Mescalero Apache people were imprisoned during the 1860s – visitors encounter a concave wall displaying a large photograph (see figure 10.1). Approximately four feet high and six feet wide, it depicts an armed guard who stands with his back to the camera while looking across a landscape populated by Native people huddled on a barren, stepped ground, with blankets wrapped around their shoulders. A caption in black lettering appears below the black and white image: "Navajos held under US military guard at Bosque Redondo, Fort Sumner, New Mexico, 1864." Text in red lettering is superimposed upon the photograph:

If a foreign government invaded your community, what would you do?

- *fight to your death?*
- *fight until captured?*
- *surrender upon seeing others killed?*
- *try to escape?*
- *hide your family members in a safe place?*

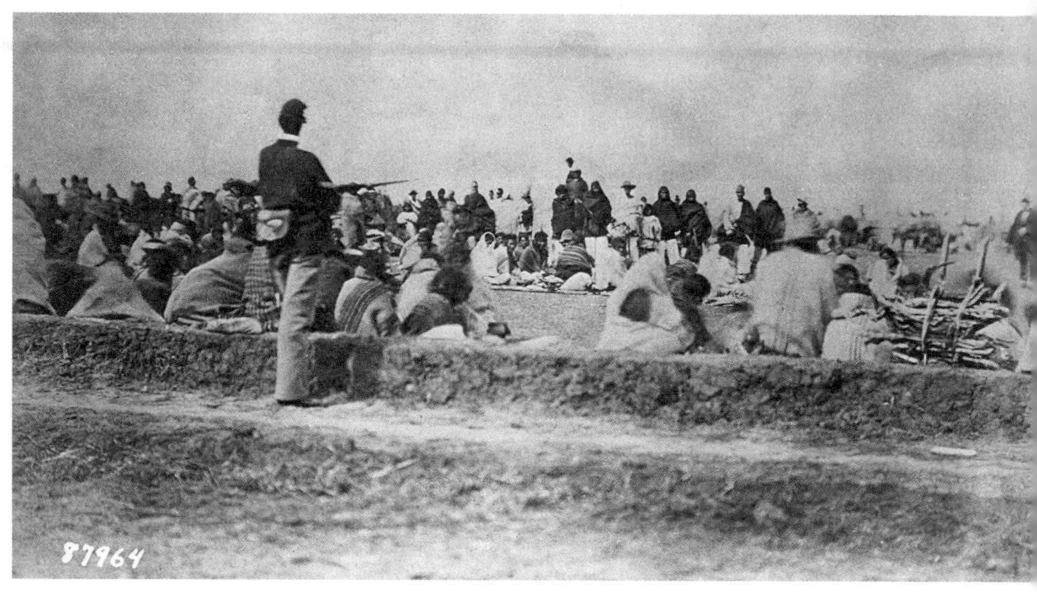

10.1 | Navajo Indian captives under guard at Fort Sumner, New Mexico.

Invited to ponder this question, visitors are ideally drawn into a contemplative, self-reflexive state of mind, thereby becoming implicitly inscribed into the exhibit narrative. The exhibit, in other words, is not only directed *toward* but also engages *with*, visitors, and with their contemporary lives. Based around this key museum-visitor relationship, *Reading the World* translates critical museum pedagogy into curatorial practice.

The overarching purpose of critical pedagogy is to engage in teaching and learning that works to redress social inequities sustained systemically through a confluence of economic, social, and political mechanisms – structures and processes of which people may not be entirely aware.[2] One objective of this pedagogy is to raise awareness of those mechanisms without imposing a predetermined educational outcome. Critical pedagogy is rooted in the educational philosophy and praxis that Paulo Freire developed while teaching non-literate, landless agricultural labourers in northeast Brazil during the late 1950s and early 1960s. He emphasized the importance of "reading the world" while learning to read the *word*, asserting that there is little purpose in textual literacy unless that ability is simultaneously applied toward a critical understanding of one's social inheritance and a hopeful determination for ongoing individual/social betterment.[3]

Freire also asserts that learning "must be forged *with*, not *for*, the oppressed," defining "oppressed" not as a particular socioeconomic class or sociocultural group, but rather as all those who have been hindered in their "pursuit of self-affirmation."[4] Elaborating on Freire's work, education theorist Henry Giroux asserts that consumers of socially constructed representations – all human-made objects, texts, and choreographed experiences (that is, theme parks, movies, television shows, websites, news media, museum exhibitions, cultural myths, political speeches, religious texts, ceremonial rituals, and fine and performing arts) – are potentially but not necessarily "oppressed" by the power relations through which and for which those representations were produced.[5] In other words, oppression depends partly upon a lack of critical reception. One of the central tenets of critical pedagogy is, accordingly, to produce curricular content that leads people to realize how their lives are shaped, in part, by socially constructed representations of current issues and past events. For example, Freire notes that the *conquest* of the Americas has historically been cast as the *discovery* of America, disavowing colonial "desire to overpower not only the physical space but also the historic and cultural spaces of the invaded."[6]

While critical of celebratory accounts of the past, Freire does not endorse an authoritarian counter-rhetoric, explaining that, "I must not, if truly progressive, arrogantly impose my knowing."[7] Instead, he proposes engaging people in provocative dialogue and analysis, through which they develop an understanding of their own cultural, historical inheritance in relationship to broader sociopolitical contexts (past and present). Self-understanding, by definition, cannot be instilled by a teacher for the benefit of a learner; indeed learners are teachers, insofar as they are "experts" in the interpretation of their own lives. He calls for teachers to present critical content in the form of problem posing, which interpolates learners as co-investigators who generate topics for further exploration. Co-investigation, according to Freire, ideally fosters critical intellect and epistemological curiosity about ways in which the past has shaped the present, but not in a determinant sense; in his words, "knowing oneself to be conditioned but not fatalistically subjected to this or that destiny opens up the way for one's intervention in the world."[8]

Freire's emphasis on dialogue and co-investigation poses a challenge to critical museum pedagogy, in that facilitators (educators/curators) do not typically accompany visitors through museum exhibitions. However, Freire notes that "the dialogical character of education ... does not begin when the teacher-student meets but rather when the ... [teacher] first asks herself or himself what she or he will dialogue with [students] *about*."[9] *Reading the World* represents this initial stage – asking questions, presenting information, and displaying provocative juxtapositions of objects, images, and text that ask viewers not only to consider the history and legacy of the historic site, but also to "perceive critically the way they *exist* in the world *with which* and *in which* they find themselves," while "com[ing] to see the world not as a static reality, but as a reality in progress, in transformation."[10]

The Memorial

Given the relative geographic isolation of the Bosque Redondo Memorial (located in a sparsely populated region of New Mexico, six miles southeast of the small town of Fort Sumner [population approximately 950] and seventy miles west of the Texas-New Mexico border), getting there requires forethought. It can therefore be assumed that by the time visitors arrive at the site, they already have at least a general knowledge of the historical internment of Navajo and Mescalero Apache people.

Among descendants of people who were imprisoned there – especially the entire tribe of Navajo people, for whom Bosque Redondo marks a defining historical moment[11] – knowledge of the past is grounded in family stories. Their stories were not told at the interpretive centre when it opened in 1971, four years after Fort Sumner became a state monument dedicated to recounting the military history of the site – which is not to say that there was no tangible marker commemorating the incarceration of native people. In 1971, before the interpretive centre opened, tribal members living in different parts of the vast Navajo Nation gathered rocks from near their homes, brought them to Bosque Redondo, and piled them together near the ruins of the fort to memorialize their ancestors who had died there. A sign installed adjacent to the rock shrine indicated that in 1968 a centennial re-enactment of the treaty signing that allowed Navajo people to return to their homeland took place at the site.

Plans for creating a more extensive formal memorial were initiated twenty years later, after nine Navajo visitors left a note at the rock shrine beseeching site administrators to tell a more thorough story about the historic internment.[12] Discussion ensued, though not without debate. Some Navajo elders caution that visiting a site where people died violates a Navajo cultural prohibition, and that the evil that resides at Bosque Redondo can attach itself to visitors and be transported back to their homes.[13] Navajo leaders nonetheless endorsed plans developed by New Mexico Department of Cultural Affairs during the late 1990s, and Navajo visitors concerned about cultural prohibition against visiting places where people died invoke protective prayers prior to entering and cleansing prayers after leaving.[14] The US Congress passed the Bosque Memorial Act in 2000, after the village of Fort Sumner donated seventy acres of land adjacent to the Fort Sumner State Monument. In the following year, the US Department of Defense allocated partial funding for design and construction, contingent upon approval of building and exhibition plans from Navajo and Mescalero Apache tribes.[15] The State of New Mexico also contributed funds, and Navajo architect David Sloan was hired to design phase one of the interpretive centre, which opened in 2005 and housed offices, a gift shop, and a small, freestanding, seven-panel exhibition that describes Navajo and Mescalero Apache life before, during, and after internment.[16]

For visitors without direct cultural or historic connections to the Bosque Redondo, pre-visit knowledge can be gleaned from two associated websites – one hosted by the Memorial's parent organization, New Mexico State Monuments, and the other by a nonprofit support group, Friends of the Bosque Redondo Memorial. The Friends' website tells potential visitors of "the dark days of suffering from 1863 to 1868 when the US Military persecuted and imprisoned 9500 Navajo (the Diné) and 500 Mescalero Apache (the N'de)," and it characterizes the purpose of the memorial as "celebrat[ing] these two cultures' dignity, resilience, endurance, courage and strength, in the face of extreme hardship, isolation, sickness and death, to emerge from Bosque Redondo to become the admired and proud people they are today."[17]

This sentiment was also expressed at the 2005 dedication ceremony, perhaps the most poignant moments of which were unscripted. During the welcoming remarks of US senator from New Mexico Pete Dominici,

Laverne Walker, a Navajo woman, jogged onto the grounds, breathlessly chanting in high-pitched song. She had run the last five miles of the historic 350-mile, militarily enforced, Long Walk from the Navajo homeland to internment at Bosque Redondo. Without pausing upon her arrival at the memorial, Walker approached the stage; the senator ceded the podium, and Navajo attendees cried as Walker briefly and breathlessly implored, "Thank you, thank you everyone. You who are Navajo out there should be proud."[18]

For Walker and the Navajo attendees, the commemoration ceremony gave an opportunity to celebrate their cultural endurance in the company of officials from the federal government that historically had ordered their incarceration. This symbolic recognition was echoed as Jeff Bingaman, a US senator from New Mexico, read a statement from the secretary of the US Department of Defense, the agency that funded the memorial. His statement proclaimed: "This Memorial pays tribute to the Native population's ability to rebound from suffering and establish the strong living communities that have long been a major influence in the State of Mexico and these United States."[19] The secretary's statement noted that the new building "faces the rising sun of the winter solstice, signaling rebirth," and entreated: "May this Memorial contribute to the healing process of the trauma, suffering and hardships endured by the Navajo and Mescalero Apache people and forge a new understanding of their strengths as Americans." Celebrating the strengths of native people *as Americans* was then reiterated: "We take pride today in honoring and restoring a respect and healing process to these great citizens of this United States, for united we stand, divided we fall." The secretary's statement thereby commemorated not only the fortitude of the survivors but also a supposed unity among all US citizens, disavowing federal policies and economic practices that have continued to oppress native people. In this sense, the memorial correlates with a relatively new type of history museum that historian Steven Conn names "therapeutic museums," which he criticizes for simplifying complex historical events while promising emotional resolution. He asserts that therapeutic museums call upon the past to "make us feel better about ourselves" as we see "just how far we humans have evolved on the moral ladder."[20]

Such self-congratulatory sentiment risks instilling a sense that oppression of native people rests in the past, thereby absolving people today of the social responsibility for recognizing and redressing current inequities rooted in past events. It also contrasts with Freire's caution against falling into a moralistic stance – whether celebratory or condemnatory. The purpose of reflecting upon the past is neither to congratulate oneself for subsequent improvements nor to condemn others for acting on (or falling prey to) greed, violence, or ignorance. Instead, Freire asserts, education ought to cultivate a sense that each of us is "an unfinished project" and thereby capable of expanding our abilities to understand how specific interpretations of past events have instilled particular assumptions, which in turn have shaped subsequent sociocultural relations.[21] *Reading the World* accordingly aims to dissuade visitors from assuming temporal distance or ethical absolution, while also commemorating the resilience of prisoners and their descendants.

Personal Stories, Multiple Histories

Freire characterizes the ideal process of learning about the world as one that includes both empirically based knowledge generated through rigorous research methods, and a reflexive analysis of personal experiences.[22] He privileges neither one over the other, noting that when epistemological curiosity extends both outward and inward, learners engage not only in awareness of how their own lives have been shaped by historic events, but also in self-criticism regarding the extent to which their current behaviours, attitudes, and activities contribute to redressing social injustices and inequities.

Self-awareness necessarily precedes self-criticism; thus *Reading the World* begins by asking visitors to imagine themselves in a situation analogous to the historic events commemorated at the memorial – to consider what they would do if a foreign government invaded their community. The exhibition then offers a personal story (as opposed to a didactic narrative), as visitors enter a small theatre to watch excerpts from *In the Footsteps of Yellow Woman*, an award-winning twenty-six-minute docudrama written and directed by Camille Manybeads Tso.[23] In the film, thirteen-year-old Tso plays both herself and her great-great-great-grandmother, Yellow Woman, who survived the Long Walk when she was a teenager. The docudrama moves back and forth from black-and-white (representing the past) to colour (representing present time), as

Tso literally walks the landscape where Yellow Woman hid her children and deliberately allowed herself to be captured in order to divert cavalrymen's attention from their hiding place. The film also represents Yellow Woman's experience of the Long Walk, and alludes to her five years of internment at Bosque Redondo before she embarked on the long path home. The film is poignant without being pedantic or moralizing, as it represents Tso's evolving sense of self while she is coming to know the past.

Immersing visitors in an autobiographical account of historical events is a curatorial strategy that respects Susan Sontag's assertion that specificity matters to the people most affected by violent events; they want to know the names of people who were killed or captured, exactly how it happened, and where.[24] But many visitors will not consider themselves (or their families) to have been directly affected by the internment. Therefore, following excerpts from Tso's film, a series of questions slowly scrolls down the screen, prompting visitors to consider the specificity of their own histories:

- *What is your connection to the history of this place?*
- *Were members of your family among the people who were imprisoned? Or did they escape capture and continue living/hiding in northeastern Arizona?*
- *Perhaps your ancestors joined the cavalry and followed orders to burn homes, destroy crops, and slaughter herds of animals – ultimately starving people into submission.*
- *Did they witness thousands of Navajo people forced on the Long Walk, over three hundred miles, from northeastern Arizona to southeastern New Mexico? Did they hear the shots that killed people consumed by physical pain or overwhelmed with fatigue? Did they know that women were being raped?*
- *Did they face food shortages as more people than expected were imprisoned?*
- *Were they related to any of the three thousand people who died from starvation or disease during the five years of internment?*
- *Perhaps your ancestors lived in another region of the United States, focusing on reconstruction and reconciliation after the Civil War? Or perhaps they lived in another country?*

- *Were they aware of what was going on?*
- *Did they sympathize with the people who were captured?*
- *Did they endorse the imprisonment?*
- *Did they admire the cavalrymen?*
- *Does your family history influence your current experience of this historic site?*

This sequence of questions introduces some historical facts, but rather than focus on those facts, it invites visitors to be cognizant of how family history and/or social affinities influence the ways in which information is received and processed. It also lets them know that other visitors' experiences might be different from their own, but it does not suggest that one experience is better, more accurate, or more important than another; nor does it ask them to hold other people's experiences in the same esteem as their own experiences. A final frame poses a rhetorical question, "Why remember the past?" and notes that a standard reply to this question cautions that those who forget history are destined to repeat it. Implicit in this response is a sense of remorse that the past is made, in part, of mistakes, errors, or actions generated out of ignorance, naïveté, greed, or some other malfeasance. However, the act of remembering historic injustices does not necessarily guard against subsequent inequities or oppression of one group of people by another.

Subsequent sections of the exhibition shift visitors' focus to an awareness of historical facts, but in a way that resists narrative closure. For example, a section introduced with the rhetorical question "Why did this happen?" contextualizes the 1860s within a larger history of governance claims that predate the Long Walk, presenting divergent accounts of why the Navajo were interned.[25] The internment accounts are drawn from US government records (as well as journals and letters of US soldiers) and from Navajo stories passed from generation to generation. Archival documents illustrate differences of opinion among US federal officials and military commanders about whether to build Fort Sumner for the purpose of establishing an Indian reservation.

A striking difference between the US government records and native narratives regards the assignment of guilt. Whereas the US government ultimately cast responsibility for ongoing raids of military outposts on the entire tribe, native narratives accused individual tribal members who ignored increasingly dire warnings of retribution. Native narratives also note that the government cavalry enlisted members of the Ute tribe, longtime adversaries of the Navajo, who were skilled at tracking people through the rugged Navajo landscapes. Warfare among native people long preceded the arrival of Europeans, especially in years of drought or other environmental events that affected food supplies. After the arrival of non-natives, some tribes continued to war against one another more than against the outsiders; other tribes treated Europeans as another competitor for resources.

European motives for engaging in warfare with native people extended beyond competition for life-sustaining resources, and ultimately influenced inter- and intra-tribal raiding. The Spanish arrived in the present-day US Southwest during the late 1500s, seeking wealth and colonizing indigenous people to mine for silver and gold.[26] The Spanish fervently believed that their religious and cultural traditions were superior to those of the native people, and demanded that the latter renounce their religious beliefs and pay a form of taxes to the Spanish crown. Native people resisted, at times effectively driving the Spanish from the region. However, as illustrated in *Reading the World* by a display of historic artifacts (seventeenth-century Spanish breastplate, helmet, and sword are juxtaposed with Navajo shield, bow, arrows, and quiver),[27] Spanish weapons of warfare were ultimately more deadly than the weapons of the indigenous people. Thus the Spanish exploited, enslaved, and killed an unprecedented number of indigenous people.

The Navajo did not surrender their cultural traditions to the will of the colonists, but by the late 1700s some bands had shifted their means of subsistence away from primary dependence upon agriculture toward an increasing emphasis on livestock, perhaps so they could better dodge raiding Utes, insofar as herds of sheep could more easily be relocated than cultivated fields.[28] However, while the Navajo shared cultural traditions, they were not a cohesive sociopolitical group with a central governance structure. Numerous bands, some of which raided other Navajo bands, resided with significant distances between one another across more than 30,000 square miles.[29] Those closest to Spanish settlements engaged in a cycle of raiding and retribution (interrupted by periodic, relatively short periods of peace), which had transpired for more than two hundred years by the time that people of Spanish heritage living in North America won the Mexican War of Independence from Spain in 1820–21. As raiding became an established tradition, wealth among Navajo and "New Mexicans" was measured by the number of sheep and captives they possessed.[30]

Twenty-five years later, in 1846, the United States laid claim to the northern territory of Mexico, acting on a belief in Manifest Destiny, which presumed that the United States was divinely destined to expand across the entire North American continent. In the 1848 treaty with Mexico, the United States promised to protect the "New Mexicans" (that is, the people of Spanish descent whose land the government had seized) against Native Americans, thereby inheriting the cycle of conflict. Periodic treaties were negotiated; however, because the Navajo bands did not operate as a cohesive tribe, only bands whose representatives agreed to the treaties recognized the agreement. Thus the cycle of raiding continued. Spanish-American settlements claimed to have lost an estimated 450,000 sheep to raiders between 1846 and 1850.[31]

In 1851 the US army established a post in Navajo territory, Fort Defiance, where they policed Navajo raiders and adjudicated Spanish-American claims (which typically required Navajo people to return stolen property and captives). The military commanders also facilitated trade and procured annuity goods from the federal government, enacting a policy of pacification that presumed that if basic needs were met, raiding would be seen as unnecessary. Relative stability ensued until 1861, when Fort Defiance was abandoned at the outset of the Civil War. Vengeance over old animosities erupted among Navajos, Utes, Kiowas, Apaches, and Spanish-Americans, while Confederate soldiers fought Union armies for control over the mineral-rich land along the overland route to California and the Pacific coast.[32] After a brief sequence of skirmishes, the Union overpowered Confederate troops, and Colonel James H. Carleton, who argued for aggressive military attacks against native people in the US Southwest, was appointed commander of the territory in 1862. In his opinion, the Navajo broke treaty agreements in part because they had not yet seen the full force of the US army. After selecting the desolate plains in southeastern New Mexico for their internment, he ordered scorched earth attacks against the Navajo. Those Navajo families who lived far from Fort Defiance had no idea why the US military was forcing them into submission.[33]

Limited Freedom

A digital looped animation included in the exhibition illustrates the historical shifting of areas of indigenous occupation and boundaries of Indian Territory and Reservations across present-day United States, reiterating the fact that the internment at Fort Sumner was part of a larger military strategy. Accompanying this visual information, a static graphic representation of changes in Native population illustrates that in 1492, approximately ten million people lived north of the Rio Grande River; by 1900, the native population had decreased to about 250,000; and by 2009 it had rebounded to 2.5 million.[34] The presentation of historic decline giving way to subsequent rise mirrors themes of survival and resilience that are noted on the Friends of Bosque Redondo Memorial website; however, it also corresponds to Freire's assertion that: "Changing the world implies a dialectic dynamic between denunciation of … a dehumanizing situation and the announcing of its being overcome."[35] Freire's characterization of "dialectic dynamic" suggests that narratives about hardship or oppression, rather than ending pronouncements that the situations in question have been overcome, should instead emphasize that past events did not determine subsequent events, and thus current oppressive situations also are not hopelessly impossible to overcome.

Reading the World represents the dialectic between oppression and resilience in a section of the exhibition that begins with a display of historic photographs taken outdoors during the internment, juxtaposed with contemporaneous photographs taken in a nondescript indoor setting. The outdoor photographs, displayed in large format, depict groups of native people seated or standing under military guard, constructing military buildings, and standing in line for food rations. These images, attributed to J.G. Gaige, who was contracted by the US military and known to have been at Bosque Redondo in 1866, depict the harsh landscape, nearly devoid of vegetation (despite its name "Bosque Redondo," a Spanish term that refers to a round area of vegetation along the flood plain of a river or stream).[36] Accompanying labels offer information that cannot be discerned from looking at the photographs alone, such as the temperature extremes from season to season and the brutal wind that blows incessantly through the cold, sometimes snowy, winter months; the paternalistic proclamation that the reservation was established in order to teach native people how to be self-sufficient; and the futility of attempted agricultural production on soil lacking sufficient nutrients. Labels also connect the shortage of natural resources to a lack of adequate housing, which forced native people to sleep in holes that they dug in the ground and covered with cloth or animal hide.

The photographs and labels clearly portray the inhumane conditions and hardship that native people endured. The message intended by photographs taken indoors is more difficult to discern. Arranged in a grid in the exhibition, they portray unidentified individual men and women, or pairs of women. The grid presentation of photographs is used in other memorial museums,[37] sometimes to feature individual headshots of murdered, displaced, or disappeared people retrieved from the victims' possessions. Some memorials, including Bosque Redondo, present staged photographs. As captives, the unnamed people portrayed would have posed as instructed. In the Bosque Redondo photographs, taken by an unknown photographer, men held weapons that would have been forbidden outside the photographic frame; individual women recline in an odalisque posture; and pairs of women, wearing finely crafted jewelry and pristinely woven textiles, embrace or lean lovingly upon one another (see figure 10.2). A total of eighty-one photographs are presented in the grid (nine rows of nine photographs) and arranged such that one or more accoutrements (blanket, necklace, weapon) appear in photographs that juxtapose one another, while no two photographs depict the same person. An accompanying exhibit label notes that the weapons and clothing are the same from one photograph to another, and it queries: "Why would captors ask prisoners to pose with weapons or dress-up in clean blankets and fine jewelry? What were they trying to accomplish with these photographs?" These questions prompt viewers to recognize that historic photographs do not offer not straightforward evidence to be taken at face value.

This point is reiterated in another group of photographs, taken in the early twentieth century, decades after native people were released from Bosque Redondo. Like the earlier photographs, they are arranged in a grid (nine rows of nine) to illustrate standard poses and visual features: women sitting at looms; men on horseback; and various people (men, women, and children, alone or in pairs) standing in front of a woven backdrop or next to a traditional hogan, a round or cone-shaped dwelling

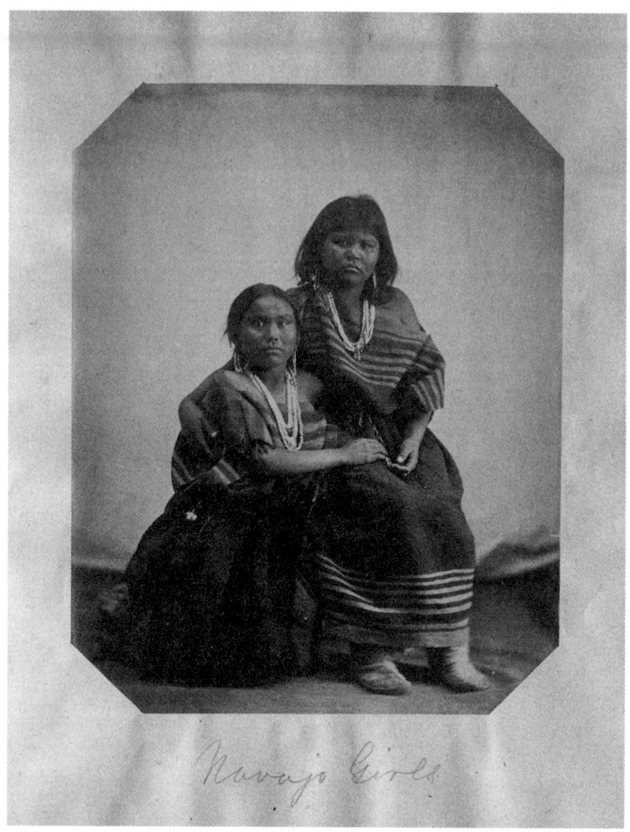

10.2 | Navajo Girls at Fort Sumner, Bosque Redondo era, New Mexico.

made of wood, sometimes covered with adobe. Accompanying text poses such questions as, "Given the visual similarity among these photographs, what can they tell us about the photographers' interests or motives?" Another question is prefaced with relevant information: "Many Native people were reluctant to have their pictures taken. They considered the camera to be a 'magic black box with an evil eye' that could inflict bad fortune upon people whose pictures were taken.[38] Given the perceived risk, why would people agree to be photographed?"

These questions, which allude to issues of objectification and agency, are implicitly addressed in a nearby display of printed advertisements featuring photographs similar to those displayed in the grid, while promoting hotels, tourist attractions, train rides and tours. Two successive sets of chronologically arranged photographs represent paradoxical aspects of the tourist industry. The first set begins with a 1915 photograph of native dancers performing for a white audience at the San Diego World's Fair. Then similar photographs taken at tourist sites in subsequent decades are presented. The sequence concludes with an undated photograph taken by David Burnett in the 1990s, which depicts a young Navajo girl, perhaps five years old, dressed in traditional ceremonial attire — velveteen blouse, long ruffled skirt, moccasins, woven waistband and stunning silver and turquoise jewelry that dwarfs her small body — and holding a sign that reads, "Taken [sic] Photo of Little Navajo Girls, $2.00 ea." The label accompanying this group of photographs asks: "What would incline this girl to sell photographs of herself? Did she have control over what the pictures looked like? What kinds of people would want to buy them, and why? What would they do with the photographs?" The second set features photographic portraits of celebrated Native American artists, who have gleaned creative and economic success in a flourishing Native American art market established upon the historic foundation of the tourist industry.[39] Selected artworks are included in the exhibition, offering tangible evidence of the artists' creative successes as well as a range of responses or attitudes toward the cross-cultural geopolitical history of the US Southwest, including the development and legacy of the tourist market.[40]

The tourist industry developed in the early twentieth century, as the cross-continental railroad expanded into the US Southwest. The construction of the railroad coincidentally began soon after the 1868 treaty negotiated by US federal agents and Navajo leaders allowed Navajo people to return to a specified portion of what had been their homeland prior to the Long Walk. The treaty (a facsimile of which is on display) required them to establish a central government and to educate their children in American schools, which ultimately were located hundreds of miles away from their homes. A map of Indian boarding schools in various locations across the United States is displayed, accompanied by portrait photographs of children when they arrived at the schools wearing their own clothing and hairstyles and again after their hair was cut and they were dressed in school uniforms or suits and dresses. Accompanying text describes standard policies and procedures among the earliest Indian schools. In addition to wearing Euro-American clothing and hairstyles, children were required to march military style from their beds to the parade grounds, cafeteria, and schoolrooms; relinquish all vestiges of their religious beliefs; and refrain from speaking their native languages. Through the schools' "outing programs" children were sent to live with white families to learn skills of domestic servants, agricultural workers, and skilled labourers.[41]

Noting that the 1868 treaty freed Navajo people from internment but also required that their children attend boarding schools, the exhibit text poses the question, "What's the difference between education and indoctrination?" At the same time, the text presents conflicting perspectives toward Indian schools. Brigadier General Richard Henry Pratt, who had fought in the Civil War before founding the first off-reservation Indian boarding school, famously asserted, "Kill the Indian and save the man," and further proclaimed, "I believe in immersing the Indians in our civilizations, and when we get them under holding them there until they are thoroughly soaked."[42] Lakota writer and activist Mary Crow Dog suggests that it is almost impossible for non-Indians to comprehend the Indian boarding school experience, explaining that it is "like the victims of Nazi concentration camps trying to tell average, middle-class Americans what their experience had been like," yet – unlike victims of the Nazi Holocaust – "we [Native Americans] owed our unspeakable boarding schools to the do-gooders, the white Indian-lovers."[43]

Not all boarding school alumni characterize their experiences as "unspeakable." Some recount long-term friendships, spirited sports rivalries, the self-reliance that comes with learning marketable skills, and knowing how to negotiate Euro-American cultural, educational, medical, and political institutions. Thus the exhibition includes photographs of prominent native people (politicians, academicians, artists, poets) who credit their boarding school experiences with contributing to their success. As historian and boarding school alumna Tsianina Lomawaima notes, "Every surviving graduate or alum of a boarding school has something to say about their education"; they might feel "pain and anger and loss or confidence and joy and security or most likely it's a combination of all of the above mixed together."[44] Yet an excerpt from Navajo poet Laura Tohe's "Letter to General Pratt," which recounts her own experience at a boarding school in the 1950s, asserts, "In the end, there are no winners, there are only the victims and the survivors of an inhumane system, whether they are the colonized or the decolonized."[45]

In addition to enumerating requirements for Navajo people, the 1868 treaty stipulated that the US government would provide food rations and two sheep per person as Navajo people returned to their homeland, and annuities (industrially produced tools, clothing, and household goods) for ten years thereafter. These provisions were essential to the Navajos' immediate survival, but they also signified a new economic system. Subsistence economies that predated internment could not be re-established because of restricted access to off-reservation arable land and ancestral hunting grounds. In the post–Fort Sumner Navajo Nation, economic production focused on wool for an external consumer market rather than agriculture for internal community consumption. Federally imposed restrictions – supposedly designed to protect American Indians from unscrupulous traders – foreclosed market competition by preventing outside sheep buyers from coming onto the reservation. Navajo sheepherders were left with little choice but to deal exclusively with a federally licensed, on-reservation trader, who typically did not pay American Indians in cash but rather in tokens that would be accepted only by that particular trader. The traders also provided raw materials and issued credit to Navajo weavers based on future rug production, ensuring acquisition of and profit from textiles before they were produced, and then supplied, in exchange for the rug, materials needed for future rug production.[46]

This information accompanies a historic photograph of the trading post at Piñon, Arizona, on the Navajo Reservation. It shows a vast supply of canned goods, boxed cereals, and bolts of fabric on shelves that extend high above the heads of the Native people, who lean on the counter separating them from the merchandise. Near the photograph, a graphic representation of quantitative differences of wealth – measured in land, crops, and sheep – among Navajo people before and immediately after their internment at Bosque Redondo is presented, as is an open ration book listing the specific amount of food and supplies that the government provided according to a set schedule. Like the earlier presentation of increases in population that followed declines, this graph also shows economic gains and losses later in the twentieth century. The most dramatic loss came in the 1930s, when the US Bureau of Indian Affairs imposed a livestock reduction program, slaughtering at least a hundred thousand sheep to mitigate overgrazing and soil erosion.[47] In subsequent decades, however, the Navajo Nation garnered significant economic gains from leasing mineral rights to mining corporations, as further described below.

Exploitation and Self-Determination

As Freire asserts, "By becoming able ... to observe, to compare, to decide, to break away, to choose, to evaluate, we have made ourselves into ethical beings, and for this very reason as well, beings capable of transgressions against ethics."[48] The exhibition accordingly acknowledges that tragedies and triumphs associated with the legacies of Navajo internment at Bosque Redondo have occurred simultaneously. The case of uranium mining on the Navajo reservation, featured in the last section of *Reading the World* exemplifies this dialectic.

Hundreds of years after the Spanish enslaved native people to mine for silver and gold, private corporations with economic interest in oil, coal, and uranium entered into contractual agreement with the centralized Navajo tribal government that had been established according to the 1868 treaty. Twentieth-century mining contracts enumerated royalties to be paid to the tribe, based on an agreed-upon percentage of corporate profits. Uranium was especially in demand during the Second World War and the subsequent nuclear arms race of the Cold War. In 1948 seven hundred thousand tons of uranium ore was produced from mines on the Navajo reservation. By 1956 production had increased to 3 million tons. In the mid-1950s, the tribe received between $600,000 and $650,000 a year in royalties, approximately 25 percent of their annual budget.[49]

While the negotiating authority of the centralized tribal government represented a post-internment triumph, the insidious, ongoing exploitation of native people was no less tragic than the overt violence enacted at Bosque Redondo. The US government and government-contracted corporations knew that uranium caused cancer (as had been discovered in Europe in 1865), yet while safety instructions and equipment were provided to miners in non-native communities, no such resources were made available to Navajo miners, who returned home from work covered in yellow uranium dust. Unaware that mining tailings were radioactive, Navajos used them to make bricks and build homes. Measurements of radioactivity in Navajo mining communities were later discovered to exceed the capabilities of Geiger counters. In 1956 the first miner died from what is believed to have been cancer (no autopsy was performed).

By 1959 ninety-one people (miners and miners' family members) had died. In the late 1960s the US government oversaw environmental cleanup of radioactive sites (including demolition and construction of contaminated residences) off the reservation, but requests to fund the razing and rebuilding of homes on the reservation that had been built with mining tailings were denied until almost forty years later. Meanwhile, from the 1970s through the late 1990s, the cancer rate among Navajos doubled at the same time that it dropped slightly among the overall US population. It was not until 1990 that Congress passed the Radiation Exposure Compensation Act, which provided funds for Navajo families suffering from radiation poisoning. At Congressional hearings in October 2007, Navajo tribal council delegate George Arthur asserted: "Navajo land is blessed with mineral resources, but the Navajo people have not benefitted much from these minerals until recently because the Navajo reservation has served, in the words of a government study, as an 'energy colony for the United States.'"[50]

The exhibit includes graphic charts presenting statistical information about economic benefits, mining capacities, numbers of miners and rates of disease and deaths across several decades; photographs of miners, at work and in old age; and available safety precautions and equipment that were not made available to Navajo miners. The exhibition then concludes, as it began, with a personal narrative presented in excerpts from a recently produced film. *The Return of Navajo Boy*, an award-winning documentary, recounts a remarkable chain of events that began in 1997 when film producer Jeff Spitz accompanied Chicago resident Bill Kennedy, son of movie director John Ford, to Monument Valley.[51] Kennedy brought a silent, black-and-white film, *Navajo Boy*, which his father had produced during the 1950s, and Spitz was interested in filming the return of the silent film to the Cly family. *Navajo Boy* focused on Jimmy Cly and featured three generations of the Cly family. The eldest family members, Happy and Willie Cly, had been pictured (though were unnamed) in countless mid-twentieth-century postcards and tourism advertisements (some of which are included in the exhibition, among the second set of photographs arranged in a grid). They also appeared as extras in numerous Hollywood Western movies.

Watching Ford's silent film, Elsie Mae Cly Begay, granddaughter of Happy and Willie and cousin to Jimmy, recognized herself as a young girl, her late mother, and her infant brother, John Wayne Cly, named after the famous actor, who had visited the Cly's home during a movie shoot. Elsie recounted that soon after the film was made, her mother died of lung cancer. Their home was located in the valley directly below the Skyline uranium mine. Unbeknownst to them at the time, radiation poisoning began fatally to affect family members. When her mother died, Elsie's brother John Wayne, then two years old, was removed from the home and taken into foster care by missionaries who lived over 250 miles away, in Continental Divide, New Mexico. They forbade him and his Navajo foster brothers and sisters from speaking their native language (mimicking the policies of Indian boarding schools). Elsie had not seen her youngest brother since the white couple had taken him.

Around the time that Ford had made *Navajo Boy*, the Kerr McGee Company created a promotional film about uranium mining near the Clys' home. Decades later, when Kennedy and Spitz were visiting Monument Valley, some members of the Cly family were testifying at congressional hearings in Washington, DC, regarding the extent of federal responsibility to Navajo victims of unsafe uranium mining practices. *The Gallup Independent* newspaper reported on the hearings and the coincidental filming of the Cly family as they watched Ford's film *Navajo Boy*. John Wayne Cly, by then an adult in his forties who ironically was working in a uranium mine, read the story and wondered if the Cly family in the news was the same as his biological family, of whom he had no memories. His subsequent homecoming is included in the 2000 film *The Return of Navajo Boy* (narrated by Elsie's son, Lorenzo Begay), as are excerpts from Ford's silent movie; mid-twentieth-century postcards, tourism advertisements, and still photographs of Happy and Willie Cly; excerpts from the Kerr McGee promotional film; and news clips about the 1999 congressional hearings.

Eight years after the film aired on Public Broadcasting Service television stations and was screened as an official selection at the 2000 Sundance Film Festival, an epilogue was added. It recounts federal legislation, mandated cleanup, and ongoing environmental activism that the film is credited with instigating or inspiring. In January 2000, the home where Elsie Begay had lived and her children had played on mining waste piles in the backyard was tested for radiation levels. The highest reading, just inside the door, was one thousand micro-Roentgens an hour; anything above eight is considered abnormal. Fifteen months later, the US

Environmental Protection Agency demolished the house, though it took eleven years for the agency to clear the uranium tailings that had continued to seep from the open Skyline Mine and into the valley below.[52] Elsie's daughter-in-law Mary Helen Begay has taken on the role of environmental activist, appearing at screenings of *The Return of Navajo Boy* and documenting ongoing efforts for environmental justice.

As excerpts from *The Return of Navajo Boy* conclude, a series of questions gradually scrolls down the screen, just as they had at the conclusion of *In the Footsteps of Yellow Woman* shown at the beginning of the exhibition. Final questions urge viewers back to a contemplative self-awareness, while also referring to overarching exhibition themes as photographs from various sections of the exhibition accompany the scrolling questions:

- *Uranium mining was fuelled by fear of attack by foreign governments. In what ways have you or your family been affected by federal policies designed to protect US citizens?*
- *What ethical dilemmas associated with exploitation or inequality have you faced?*
- *When you travel outside your community, do you take pictures of people you don't know? Do they take pictures of you?*
- *What personal or community tales of tragedy and triumph do your family members share with each other?*
- *What compels you (or would compel you) to visit the site where your ancestors were held captive?*

Curatorial Objectives, Pedagogical Goals

Reading the World implicitly casts the root cause of the historic internment at Bosque Redondo in the larger context of colonialism – understood as the invasion and/or occupation of land for the purpose of exploiting resources, including indigenous people, in order to increase the wealth of the colonizer country. The exhibition also explores selected legacies of colonialism (neocolonialist acts and attitudes), recognizing that while not as blatantly violent as the decimation of native communities, they nonetheless are fuelled by motivations similar to those that resulted in the historic internment. At the same time, the exhibition resists the trope of winners and losers (or other binary concepts such as good *versus* evil, dominant *versus* subjugated), recognizing that economic, cross-cultural, and political changes associated with the terms of the 1868 treaty between the US government and the Navajo people cannot be reduced to either tragedy or triumph. The affective goal is not to compel visitors to pity the victims or to celebrate a presumed moral evolution that has transpired since the late nineteenth century. Acts of oppression, exploitation, and inequality have continued and will continue to be enacted because all people have an innate capacity for greed, hatred, and ignorance that is not always eclipsed by their innate capacity for generosity, compassion, and curiosity. As Freire notes, "The present conquest, which does not necessarily require the conqueror's physical body, takes place through economic domination, through cultural invasion, through class domination, and through countless other instruments that the powerful, the neo-imperialists, make use of."[53]

My curatorial objective in imagining *Reading the World* is to present transgressions of what Freire calls a "universal human ethic," which recognizes that "our being in the world is far more than just 'being.' It is a 'presence,' a 'presence' that is relational to the world and to others."[54] While Freire speaks about a *universal* human ethic, he does not negate sociocultural differences among people. However, he considers people to be *conditioned* not *determined* by those differences. Transgressions of universal human ethic that were directly or indirectly related to the historic internment of native people at Bosque Redondo oppressed some people while also inspiring others to cultivate creative talents, leadership abilities, and/or activist energy. I am not concerned with whether visitors take away the very ideas I have mind. Rather, my pedagogical goals are to present a sense of dialogue; to encourage self-awareness among museum visitors, especially of their social inheritances (positive and negative, past and present); and to promote an analytical mindset. These are the features, I suggest, of critical museum pedagogy, which ideally prompts museum visitors to develop a habit of identifying aspects of economic, social, and political systems of governance, habits, and traditions (past and present) through which some people have benefited at the expense of others.

PART FOUR

Establishments Revisioned

CHAPTER ELEVEN

The World in One City: The Tropenmuseum, Amsterdam

SERENA IERVOLINO and RICHARD SANDELL

This chapter explores the potential for ethnographic museums, more particularly those based in cosmopolitan cities of ex-imperial powers, to promote intercultural understanding and dialogue by imagining *The World in One City*. In a spirit of empathy, this curatorial dream sets out to respond – in an imaginative and constructive way – to the often-strident critiques that many ethnographic museums have faced in recent years and which, in some instances, have challenged their very existence.[1] *The World in One City* is staged in the Tropenmuseum – one of Europe's most famous ethnographic museums – and in Amsterdam, where historical and contemporary patterns of migration have created a diverse, multicultural city that has been both renowned for its progressive, tolerant attitudes toward newcomers and, more recently, for the high profile, sometimes violent, clashes between people from different cultural backgrounds.

We have purposefully devised *The World in One City* as a curatorial dream that draws on and acknowledges the value of recent experimental and reflexive approaches to the display of ethnographic collections within the Tropenmuseum; approaches that have sought to respond to the shifting terrain of political sensitivities and diversity in the Netherlands. Indeed, our dream exhibition is inspired by *Travelling Tales*, one of the Tropenmuseum's semi-permanent galleries, which, focusing on the dynamics of intangible culture, attempts to represent contemporary multicultural Dutch society in ways that move "beyond notions of self and other."[2] While we have sought to firmly ground our imagined display in the history and sociopolitical realities of the Tropenmuseum, we have, at the same time, enjoyed the imagined freedom from resource constraints that inevitably shape what can be achieved in the real museum world.

The World in One City draws on the concept of hybridity[3] to support the museum in its ongoing attempts to resist established dichotomies of self and other, while developing interpretive strategies that open up ways of understanding Dutch identity and culture that are more fluid and plural, and which seek to engage visitors in challenging discussions about difference and shared experience.[4]

After examining the theoretical and contextual issues with which the chapter is centrally concerned (and with which many ethnographic museums are currently grappling), we go on to introduce the city of Amsterdam and explain our reasons for selecting the Tropenmuseum as our staging ground. In presenting *The World in One City* – both the process behind its development and the key elements of its imagined physical form – we begin by explaining how the concept of hybridity informs and guides the process of exhibition development. Then, drawing on the concept of trading zones,[5] we explore the unique (and potentially transformative) effects that might be gained by including and valuing forms of expertise alternative to those that traditionally shape exhibitions in ethnographic museums. Finally, we offer three key moments of the imagined exhibition with which visitors are confronted, focusing on interpretive strategies and interventions that, in our view, can support ethnographic museums in representing demographic and social changes, and in engaging visitors in increasingly pressing and contested conversations about difference.

Repurposing the Ethnographic Museum

In colonial times ethnographic museums stood at the crossroads between colonial heritage and scientific research.[6] They were both a product and a tool of colonialism and sought to respond to the demands of representation generated by imperial expansion. By contributing to scientific research they played a central role in the birth and development of anthropology. Ethnography became the primary research method used by anthropologists to study human societies and cultures and "provided the 'scientific' justification" for much of the colonial expansion, particularly in Africa and America.[7] Especially in recent decades, post-colonial perspectives have produced challenging critiques of ethnographic museums, posing increasingly complex and pressing questions about the way museums collect, study, and represent other cultures, and highlighting their capacity to construct and reinforce negative stereotypical images of non-Western people as primitive, savage, and inferior to a European visiting public.[8]

If during imperial times ethnographic museums functioned as instruments to exercise control and power over the non-Western other, the end of the imperial domination placed them "in a state of emerging crisis."[9] In post-colonial settings, the roles and purposes of ethnographic museums have been called into question, prompting some institutions to review their missions and fundamentally rethink their values and practices. Some have sought to change their relationships with the non-Western peoples they represented and to start developing closer collaborations with source communities from which their collections originate.[10] Some have also begun to initiate collaborations with immigrant and diaspora communities living in their proximity, many of which have connections to the collections held in the museum.[11] Nevertheless, the Eurocentric epistemological biases of ethnographic museums and the legacy of colonialism have proved difficult to overcome. Although ethnographic museums are increasingly experimenting with new modes of representation, many have faced accusations of continuing to portray formerly colonized and aboriginal peoples as primitive, unchanging, and exotic. Ciraj Rassool,[12] for example, has argued that, while recent decades have seen significant shifts in ethnology and ethnography and the development of critical, reflexive modes of practice, many ethnographic museums continue to deploy approaches to exhibition and display that remain grounded in colonial ideologies.

Recently, criticisms have focused on the failure of ethnographic museums to adequately respond to changes in contemporary society.[13] More particularly, it has been argued that European ethnographic museums find it difficult to respond to the increasingly plural and transnational character of societies shaped by globalization and international migration – societies where, increasingly, the other has become the neighbour.[14] In this respect, the five-year European project *Ethnographic Museums and World Cultures* (2008–13) also known as RIME (Réseau International des Musées d'Ethnographie) sought to facilitate constructive debate on these themes.[15] The project attempted to rethink the role of ethnographic museums within a multicultural, global, and post-colonial world "traversed by global cultural flows that are transforming the European scenario."[16] In promoting a number of international symposia, workshops, publications, as well as a collaborative touring exhibition entitled *Fetish Modernity*, RIME sought to stimulate critical reflection around ethnographic museums' crisis of mission and identity, and to redefine their priorities and strategies in a Europe that is becoming more and more multicultural.[17]

In a post-colonial, global world where cultures increasingly interact and identities are in flux, the binary dichotomy of self/other that has traditionally underpinned representational strategies in the ethnographic museum is outdated and untenable. How might strategies of display and representation be reconfigured to enable ethnographic museums to evolve from places where visitors learn about "faraway cultures" into places that equip visitors to understand and explore the diversity that increasingly characterizes their own cities? How can they engage visitors in debates surrounding the challenging questions that demographic changes have brought? Through the process of imagining our fictional exhibition, *The World in One City*, we shall see that attempts to reposition ethnographic museums demand not only changes in methodology, but, more fundamentally, a political commitment to take up (and make explicit to visitors) the museum's moral standpoint on issues relating to migration, citizenship, and belonging; issues that divide opinion and prompt heated public debate in many multicultural societies.

The Tropenmuseum

Founded in 1864, the Tropenmuseum (see figure 11.1) is one of the three Dutch ethnological museums that form the National Museum of World Cultures. This institution was established on 1 April 2014, when the Tropenmuseum became independent from the Royal Tropical Institute (KIT)[18] and merged with the Rijksmuseum Volkenkunde in Leiden (founded 1837) and the Afrika Museum in Berg en Dal (founded 1954).[19]

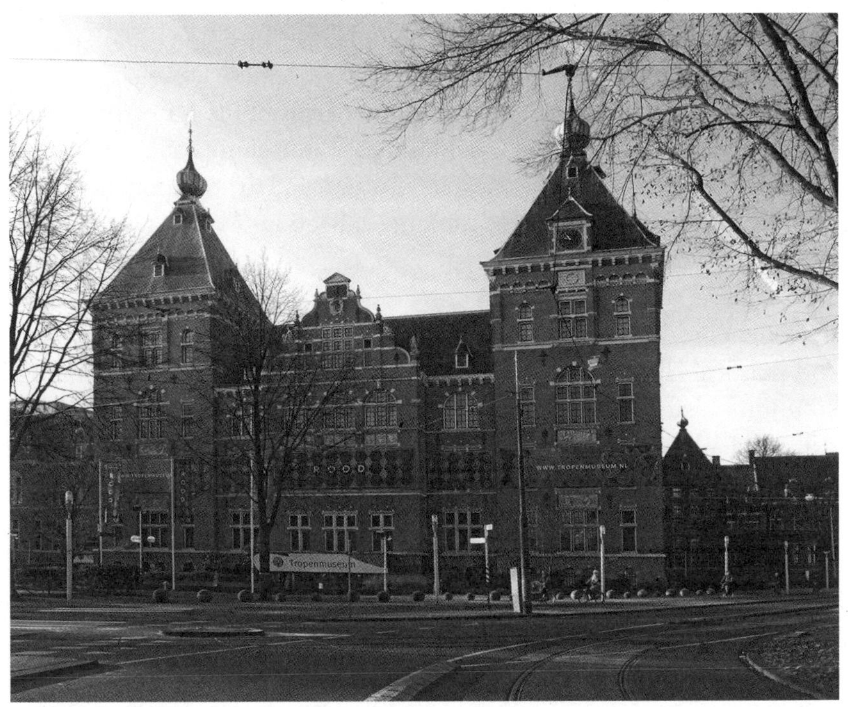

11.1 | A view of the Tropenmuseum building.

The institutions decided to join forces and form one museum that is guided by a single vision and mission, and is run by a fully integrated administration[20] but operates in the three museums' original venues in Amsterdam, Leiden, and Berg en Dal. After the merge, however, the three sites have maintained separate websites and have also continued to employ their original names in marketing communications.[21]

As Stijn Schoonderwoerd, the National Museum of World Cultures' general director, argued, the uncertain future of the Tropenmuseum was the main reason behind the merge of the three institutions and the creation of the National Museum of World Cultures (ASEMUS 2014). In October 2011 the Tropenmusem came under threat of closure when the Ministry of Foreign Affairs, which had funded the institution from the early 1970s, announced its intention to cut all its funding by the beginning of 2013.[22] Following a long period of negotiations and a large-scale internal reorganization, the Dutch government agreed to continue funding the Tropenmuseum under a number of conditions. The Tropenmuseum was asked to merge with the Rijksmuseum Volkenkunde and the Afrika Museum and to come under the aegis of the Ministry of Education, Culture and Science. In addition, the museum's collections, until then owned by the Royal Tropical Institution, had to be nationalized and become part of one centralized national collection.[23]

We chose the Tropenmuseum because, as an institution, it has sought to enhance its contemporary social relevance by re-examining its collections and approaches to display in the light of demographic and political changes in the Netherlands and globally. Although the institution's history lies in the colonial past of the country – a past that still casts a long shadow over its contemporary practices – the Tropenmuseum cannot be considered simply a relic of colonialism.[24] Indeed, the museum has undergone a number of transformations over the past century in response to shifting national and global political, cultural, and social developments,[25] most markedly after the recognition of the independence of Indonesia by the Netherlands in 1949. If before 1949 the Tropenmuseum's aim was to reflect and support colonial interests and ideologies, the second half of the twentieth century was a period during which it sought to distance itself from its colonial legacy and reorient its purpose. It widened its focus on the ex-colonies "to include the tropical and subtropical regions in their entirety,"[26] in particular Northern Africa, the Middle East, Latin America, India, and Pakistan, and sought to adopt a self-reflexive and critical approach. During this period the museum attempted to confront and problematize its colonial origin and initiated a (still ongoing) process of what Cristina Kreps describes as a "decolonization" of its practices.[27] Since then the museum has continued to evaluate its existence and transform its practices to respond to changes in Dutch society. In the early 1970s the museum shifted its attention to international development cooperation, and exhibitions took on a "social" or "emancipatory" approach[28] focusing on social problems in the developing world.

In the 1990s the emphasis changed again and the museum began to focus on cultural diversity, paying attention to the similarities and differences to be found across and between cultures, including those that commingled within Dutch society. In 1995 the museum started a major program of redisplay, which was concluded in 2008. Threaded throughout the semi-permanent galleries are stories pertaining to intercultural exchange, migration, globalization, and the rise of cultural diversity within Dutch society. In addition, the Tropenmuseum continues to take a self-reflexive approach to museum practices and seeks to stimulate debate on the contemporary social role of museums. At "Tropenmuseum for a Change," an international symposium held at the museum in December 2009, Dutch and international speakers were invited to assess the then-recently redesigned galleries and discuss the relevance of ethnographic museums and, in particular, the Tropenmuseum in the twenty-first century global world.[29] In the early 2000s the museum also sought to act as an arena for intercultural dialogue and public engagement by organizing exhibitions such as *Urban Islam*, through which it sought to stimulate and inform discussion around the contested issue of the place of Islam in Dutch society. Finally, as the Tropenmuseum has long been an institution willing to take "many bold steps in pursuing its goals,"[30] it represents a very promising laboratory in which to imagine *The World in One City* and experiment with new strategies for representing the cultural diversity that characterizes contemporary Dutch society.

Amsterdam is the capital and largest city of the Netherlands; it has experienced enormous demographic change arising from migration over the last half-century or more. After Indonesia achieved independence in 1945, many of the former Dutch residents of the colony arrived in the Netherlands.[31] In 1951 they were followed by Moluccan soldiers of the Dutch colonial army, who were housed in barracks with their families. In December 1957, Indonesia declared the remaining forty thousand Dutch nationals living in the archipelago – which included people of mixed descent (Indo-Europeans) as well as Dutch – undesirable aliens. As a result, they were forced to move to the Netherlands. People who had no relatives in the Netherlands were dispersed around the country. In the 1960s and 1970s guest workers were recruited from Southern Europe, Morocco, and Turkey.[32] While many Southern Europeans returned to their native countries in the 1970s, Turkish and Moroccan migrants tended to stay. Since the 1970s the Netherlands has increasingly received people from the Dutch overseas territories, especially Suriname and the Dutch Caribbean islands. Current minority groups include descendants of post-colonial minorities and of migrants from former guest-worker recruitment countries as well as people from other European countries and, indeed, from all over the world.[33]

Since the 1980s the Netherlands has adopted a multicultural model as its official policy for the integration of migrant and minority groups.[34] During the last decade, this policy has come under attack. Over the past ten years criticism has increasingly focused on the presence of Muslim migrants and been further fuelled by Islamophobia in the aftermath of the terrorist attacks of 9/11.[35] Tensions linked to the presence of Muslims in the country received international media attention in 2002 following the assassination of Dutch politician Pim Fortuyn, whose views on Islam and immigration had been highly controversial. The international media spotlight turned again on Amsterdam in 2004 following the murder of the film director Theo van Gogh, an event linked to the release of his film *Submission*, concerning the abuse of women in the name of Islam. Although over the past decade the country has applied more restrictive policies of integration, debates surrounding Islam and Muslim migrants continue to inflame the political sphere. Recently the fiercest challenges have come from the politician Geert Wilders, whose anti-immigration and anti-Islam Freedom party received large support in the June 2010 elections. Wilders has become famous for his overt criticism of Islam and his contentious film *Fitna*, which portrays Islam as a force seeking to destroy the West. Although Wilders remains a highly controversial figure within the Netherlands, the success of his party in 2010 highlights the challenges posed by the coexistence of a variety of worldviews within Dutch society and, worryingly, might suggest a move away from a tradition of liberalism and tolerance.[36] The controversies surrounding *Fitna* and *Submission* will be included in the media wall of our imagined exhibition.

The World in One City

The World in One City emerges from this complex and sensitive context with an explicit goal: to not only document and capture the demographic, social, political, and cultural change in the city but to provide a forum in which the pressing and difficult questions generated by those changes can be debated. Our approach to this challenging task draws on the emergence in recent years of an activist museum practice that sees curators and other practitioners adopting and eliciting support for a particular standpoint,[37] one underpinned by concepts of social justice and human rights.[38]

We envisage our curatorial dream as a concept-driven exhibition that draws on the notion of hybridity.[39] The exhibition attempts to present a more fluid and plural idea of Dutch culture and identity. Homi Bhabha uses the concept of hybridity to describe the processes of identity formation and cultural change in colonial settings. He argues that hybridity takes place when elements of the colonizer and colonized interweave, producing new hybrid identities that challenge received fixed and binary notions of identity, such as colonizer/colonized, native/foreigner, minority/majority. The concept of hybridity is helpful in thinking beyond exclusionary, fixed, binary notions of identity based on ideas of cultural, racial, and national purity and, as such, it has been widely applied by post-colonial scholars to explore processes of identity formation and intercultural negotiations in societies characterized by growing diversity.[40]

Although some have highlighted the difficulties inherent in the practical application of Bhabha's work,[41] we find it useful as a tool for exploring the underlying power relations bound up in discourses about Dutch multiculturalism.[42] Hybridity helps to highlight the contradictions within multicultural policies which, on the one hand, propose ideas of equality, but on the other perpetuate (more or less) implicit, unspoken hierarchies between Western and migrant cultures and the dominant groups' attempts to control and assimilate minorities. As Elizabeth Hallam and Brian Street argue, "conceptualising hybridity itself challenges the 'discriminatory identity effects' of the reification of 'otherness' endemic to dominant colonial and neo-colonial discourse."[43] In this sense hybridity offers a lens through which *The World in One City* can begin to unsettle entrenched notions of homogenous identity that support and justify discriminatory attitudes toward migrant and minority groups.

We envisage the audience of *The World in One City* to be drawn from the Tropenmuseum's core target groups – schoolchildren, families, and adult visitors.[44] The museum already attracts "considerable numbers of Dutch visitors with an immigrant background."[45] It also receives many school groups, especially from primary and secondary schools, as well as academic groups. Considering that half of Amsterdam schoolchildren have non-Dutch origins and Amsterdam city-dwellers include people of 110 different nationalities,[46] we imagine the core target groups of the museum to represent the most important part of the exhibition's visitors.

Complementing this theoretical framing, the realization of *The World in One City* is also reliant on a particular strategy of exhibition development: an approach to exhibition making that elicits (and gives equal value to) forms of expertise that extend, enrich, and potentially challenge the knowledge and skills that more commonly contribute to processes of exhibition development in ethnographic museums. When the Tropenmuseum produces an exhibition, it typically seeks to open up dialogue and establish a working relationship with the people whose culture the planned display seeks to represent. In addition, the museum applies a multidisciplinary approach to its exhibition production, whereby curators work with other colleagues (exhibition makers, researchers, educators, multimedia experts) and external professionals (designers and sound experts). We propose to extend this creative blend of knowledge to include inputs from individuals with alternative (but highly pertinent) expertise and insights. Our exhibition team thus includes a cross-cultural curator, an urban anthropologist, a filmmaker, a social worker, and Dutch and other national artists, as well as other individuals with lived experience of migration to and from Amsterdam. This rich mix of expertise and insight, emerging not only from disciplinary knowledge but also from lived experience, holds the potential to develop highly experimental approaches to display and public engagement.

The cross-cultural curator is neither schooled in a traditional museological discipline (such as art history, archaeology, or anthropology) nor specialized in a specific culture. Being trained, rather, in the field of cultural studies, translation studies, global studies or similar, the cross-cultural curator's expertise lies in the knowledge of the ways in which in our contemporary global world cultures interact, exchange, hybridize, and translate from one to another.

The team draws also upon the urban anthropologist's knowledge of the city of Amsterdam and its populations. This person is a sociocultural anthropologist specialized in studying city life and its dynamics. The urban anthropologist brings to the project deeper understandings of the ways in which the flows of migration to Amsterdam have affected the dynamics of the city, shaping its society and culture. Knowledge of this sort enables the team to explore the diversity of lifeways that coexist in the city and make sense of the complex and ever shifting cross-cultural expressions of its dwellers. The urban anthropologist's expertise is essential for probing deeply into the cultural expressions and everyday practices of groups (often ethnically or economically distinct, and/or socially segregated) as well as for studying how those expressions are contributing to reshape mainstream Dutch culture in the city, giving it a transnational outlook.

The filmmaker is trained in visual anthropology and their expertise lies in anthropological filmmaking. By including a filmmaker in the team we intend to realize the full potential of anthropological filmmaking to contribute to the study of contemporary Dutch culture and explore the different cultural expressions and ways of life to be found in Amsterdam. The filmmaker's expertise will be applied to finding audio-visual methods to research, represent, and produce anthropological knowledge. The films are used in the exhibition to present intangible expressions of Dutch culture (performances, music, events) as well as to bring to life some of the objects on display. Although the inclusion of ethnographic films is not a novelty in the displays of ethnographic museums, in *The World in One City* films are strategically used to show that Dutch culture is not static but fluid and dynamic, always in process. We hope to make evident that exhibitions seeking to represent contemporary Dutch culture need to be attentive both to material culture and to living, immaterial cultural phenomena.[47] By displaying material culture alongside intangible cultural expressions (using films), our intention is to challenge the existence of sharp dichotomies between material and immaterial culture.

A social worker who brings experience of working with migrants that is critical to the museum's desire to take up a more socially engaged and relevant role in contemporary society is also an essential partner in this experiment. As Lois Silverman argues,[48] social workers can bring to museum work, a "deep intuitive understanding of human frailty, strength, and resilience" that is especially important to our desire to engage more meaningfully with people with lived experiences of migration who often endure exclusion, abuses, and a sense of alienation.

Research for *The World in One City* focuses on the study, collection, and documentation of living Dutch culture. It ensures that information flows from the city into the museum, that contemporary objects are collected from a range of groups of city dwellers defined by ethnicity, nationality, or religious beliefs, as well as from intercultural meeting spaces where people with shared interests gather (such as youth clubs, book clubs, lunch clubs for elderly people, environmental organizations, and music groups); and that a variety of objects are collected that embody people's everyday practices and cultural expressions, with particular attention to objects that exemplify global interconnectedness. Here we follow Peter Jan Margry and Herman Roodenburg, who argue that "a complex and rapidly changing society like the present-day Netherlands will never be properly understood unless one looks at it from the below, from the everyday."[49] We concur with them that the study of the familiar and of everyday practices holds the potential to show the complexity and dynamism of Dutch culture. In addition, real stories and opinions of Amsterdammers (with both Dutch and non-Dutch backgrounds) are collected via recorded interviews; performances and other cultural expressions are filmed in performance spaces, community centres, migrant associations, and so on.

This collaborative approach to exhibition development reflects broader trends in the museum sector internationally toward more participatory and co-creative exhibition-making practices.[50] More particularly, we structure the collaboration in a way that ensures an equitable relationship between the diverse participants. To support us in this task we draw upon and adapt the concept of the "trading zone"[51] – an idea originating in the domain of science and technology that brings together individuals with different knowledge, skills, and perspectives. In our view, this idea can effectively sustain ethnographic museums' increasing attempts to employ interdepartmental, interdisciplinary, and ultimately collaborative approaches to processes of exhibition making. By drawing on research carried out in the field of cognitive science, in our view, (ethnographic) museums may succeed in facilitating interdisciplinary interactions among *all* the contributors to exhibition-making processes, thereby pulling experts out of a narrow focus on their specialized disciplinary knowledge. While valuing the knowledge of different fields, the notion of trading zones stresses the importance for diverse disciplines and expertise of constructively coming together in a way that facilitates the creation of new instruments and approaches to knowledge production which would not occur otherwise.[52]

We envision our process of exhibition development as constituting a "contributory" trading zone,[53] providing a framework where participants from a range of disciplines, with different worldviews and experiences of migration, dissimilar vocabulary, and unique insights come to work together. Our trading zone is a *collaborative space* where an equal exchange can be developed and where lived experience and disciplinary knowledge are equally valued. As *The World in One City* takes shape, the cross-cultural curator in our team operates as the central node of the trading zone, drawing on cultural translation skills and expertise in intercultural mediation to facilitate each participant's equal contribution. This form of collaboration, we suggest, holds unique creative potential; by learning to collaborate *despite* (and *because of*) their differences, by drawing on multiple perspectives and developing a shared language, the exhibition team can create a museum experience capable of achieving its ambitious goals.

The World in One City is situated in the Lighthall of the Tropenmuseum, the stunning atrium (some eight hundred square metres) at the heart of the museum, which up until recently was devoted to temporary exhibitions. The exhibition adopts a nonlinear narrative and resists attempts to guide visitors through a particular route. Instead, there are multiple entry points and visitors can explore each part according to their own interests, wishes, and needs. Each entrance features a brief introductory panel making explicit the exhibition's intentions: to nurture understanding and respect among people with diverse backgrounds, experience, and perspectives. Such overt public declarations of intent and ethical position may feature relatively rarely in museum displays but, we would argue, they are fundamental to the goal of stimulating dialogue on contested issues. *The World in One City* is a multi-media exhibition that includes: films; objects drawn from existing collections as well as new material derived from our program of contemporary collecting; photographs, paintings, installations, and immersive environments. The floor plan is conceived as two concentric rings. The outer ring explores the multiple factors that have made Amsterdam a multicultural city and is divided into themes such as colonization and decolonization; histories of migration; impact of the European Union. The inner circle considers the heterogeneity that characterizes contemporary Dutch culture and offers visitors opportunities to explore its multiple, often hybrid, and sometimes potentially conflicting elements, as well as the challenges and contradictions generated by increasing cultural diversity.[54] Inspired by existing galleries in the Tropenmuseum – notably *Travelling Tales* and *World of Music* – we propose including several "dwell spaces" where visitors are invited to relax and take time to reflect upon the content of the exhibition.[55] These spaces provide ideal settings in which to screen a series of short films produced by our team during the process of researching and collecting contemporary Dutch culture. Objects displayed in the exhibition may include, for example, clothes worn by Moroccan-Dutch young people to construct a metropolitan or Mediterranean identity;[56] and objects and images that represent everyday practices of Turkish-Dutch families that embody their contemporary attempts to reconcile tradition and modernity in their ways of living.[57] Consistent with our aim of framing the ways in which visitors view, understand, and debate cultural differences, the films explore the many positive implications of migration and cultural diversity as well as the associated tensions and challenges that have tended to predominate in the media.

Embodied Hybridity

At the intersection between the part of the exhibition that explores the Netherlands' colonial history and the inner circle, visitors encounter a striking statue by Dutch artist Roy Villevoye, born in 1960 in Maastricht, *Madonna* (*Omomá & Céline*) (2008), recently acquired by the museum.

Villevoye's work speaks eloquently to the exhibition's central themes as it explores cultural stereotypes and the fluid, hybrid cultural identities that grow out of processes of exchange, appropriation, and translation among cultures.[58] *Madonna* portrays a black man who carries in his hands a naked, white baby, perhaps reminiscent of the life-sized wax figures that in the museum's colonial period "were used to enliven the exhibitions on ethnography and on tropical products,"[59] such as the statue of Papuan man and child shown in figure 11.3.

The inclusion of *Madonna* is an attempt to acknowledge the museum's colonial roots and stress the contribution of Dutch colonialism to contemporary diversity. At the same time the statue is distinctively postcolonial in its perspective and meanings; the black man is not simply an abstraction, an anthropological representation of a Papuan man; he is a

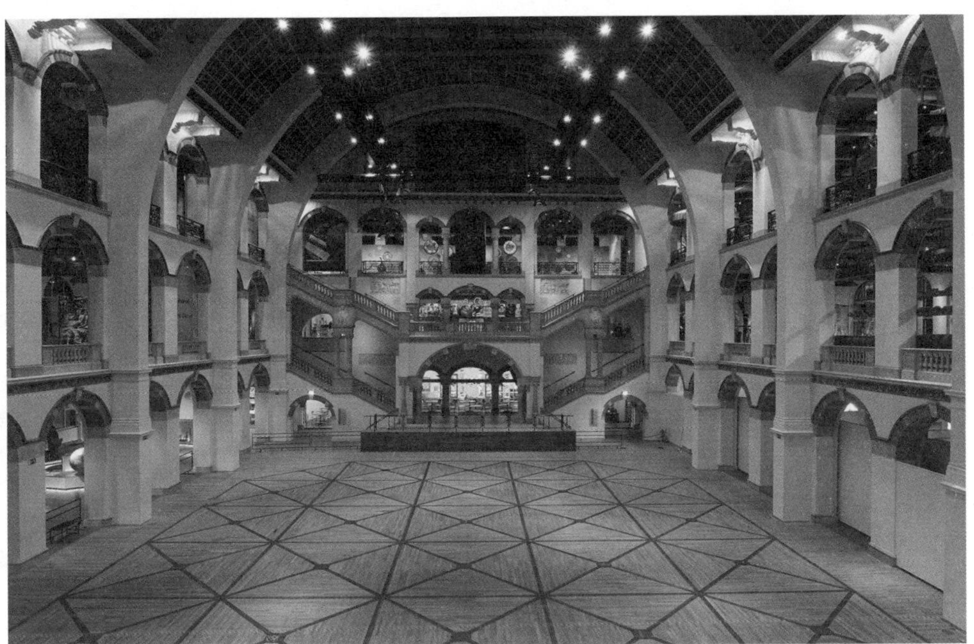

11.2 | The Lighthall of the Tropenmuseum.

portrayal of a named individual, a contemporary Papuan man – Rodan Omomá – a very good friend of Villevoye, depicted in the act of carrying Céline, the artist's baby daughter. The view of *Madonna* disrupts fixed dichotomies of us versus them, while confronting visitors with a touchstone for the idea of "exchange."[60] The statue refers to many exchanges simultaneously: to the exchange between Villevoye and Omomá and, more broadly, to historical and contemporary cultural exchanges between the West and the rest, the Netherlands and New Guinea, Dutch and non-Dutch people (happening *there*, in faraway lands and *here*, in the Netherlands). According to Lex ter Braak,[61] it was Omomá's stay in Amsterdam in 2000 and the exchanges his visit activated that inspired the statue.

In *The World in One City*, *Madonna* is exhibited in the immediate proximity of a screen showing a video-interview featuring the artist, Villevoye, and one of the subjects on display, Céline.[62] By presenting the story of the statue's creation and the personal experience of the artist as well as by giving the opportunity to one of the subjects on display

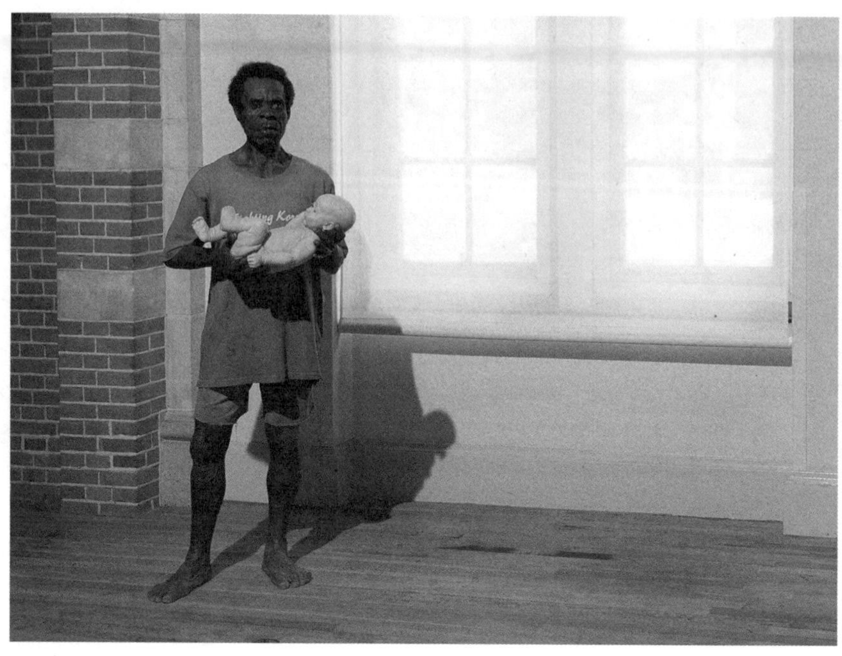

11.3 | Roy Villevoye, *Madonna (Omomá & Céline)*, 2008, a life-size statue made of synthetic resin, silicon rubber, human hair, and cloth.

to speak, we intend to enable visitors to make personal connections with the work. The video enables *Madonna* to talk to the visitors, transforming the statue from an object into a subject. This display strategy does not present the artwork as representative of a particular cultural landscape; *Madonna* represents neither Dutch nor Papuan culture but rather presents a human perspective on cultural diversity and intercultural dialogue. As Koos van Brakel, head of collections at the National Museum of World Cultures argues, "what makes this work special is the way it forces viewers to ask questions."[63] *Madonna* – like the exhibition in which it is placed – is intended to open up debates about migration and contemporary Dutch society rather than offer fixed and finite answers. Van Brakel's viewpoint could be further expanded by arguing that the statue does more than simply raise questions; it holds the potential to prompt viewers to reflect on, even confront, unconscious, deeply ingrained racial prejudices.

Debating Cultural Differences

The largest dwell space in the exhibition lies at the very centre and features a large multimedia wall that seeks to bring into the museum the fierce and ongoing debates taking place in Dutch society around multiculturalism and cultural diversity. Despite our political and ethical standpoint (explicitly stated at each entrance and embodied throughout the displays) and our underlying intention to support visitors in reaching more progressive and inclusive understandings of cultural diversity, we are mindful of the dangers of didactic displays that offer selective and partial narratives in an attempt to tell visitors how to think and behave. Accordingly, the central multimedia wall features news headlines and media coverage relating to controversies surrounding cultural clashes in the Netherlands over the past decade. Visitors can select from a series of high profile media events, and read and listen to multiple viewpoints on the contested issues each raises. The multimedia wall includes viewpoints that feature regularly in mainstream media discourse as well as those regarded as extremist or marginal. Although some of the visitors are likely to find the inclusion of these explicitly prejudiced voices offensive, our intention here is to realistically represent the character of discourses about cultural diversity to which people are exposed outside the museum. The media wall presents these extreme viewpoints with pertinent contexualizing material that makes clear the museum's ethical standpoint and unequivocal condemnation of racism and other forms of prejudice.

The goal of the display is to present multiple voices and show the different (often conflicting) perspectives that coexist in Dutch society on those themes. Our intention here is to enable visitors to understand that the same event can be represented in the media in very different ways and that representations of migrants are very often depersonalized, stigmatizing, and discriminatory. To this end, the perspectives of real individuals with lived experience of migration to and from Amsterdam (gathered as part of the fieldwork carried out by our exhibition team) will be presented. These highly personal and often moving accounts are intended to challenge the homogenized and biased portrayals of minorities favoured by mainstream news media.[64]

Somewhat controversially, the exhibit offers visitors an opportunity to view the short films *Submission* and *Fitna* and the debates that each sparked in the media both in the Netherlands and throughout the world. Accompanying the films will be interviews with Dutch people (including Muslim Dutch) who share with visitors their own views on the issues raised. Our aim is not to offer moralizing, overly simplified narratives that simply extol the virtues of cultural diversity but rather to equip visitors with more nuanced understandings of cultural difference that open up possibilities for empathy and exchange.

Personal Encounters

The final key moment in our imagined exhibition is represented by an installation that explores the personal experiences of diverse Amsterdammers, using not only objects but also personal, face-to-face encounters with individuals that – in one way or another – are linked to material on display. The installation presents personalized testimonies of migration (from and to Amsterdam), cultural change and cultural resistance, integration and marginalization. Since visitor research has highlighted that "encounters with real objects enhance museums' capabilities to offer especially engaging, emotionally intense experiences,"[65] we envision this part of the exhibition as especially object-rich. Featured objects are drawn from existing collections in the Tropenmuseum as well as being sourced through the contemporary collecting that formed part of our project. Many are loaned or donated to the museum by people with lived experience of migration and embody their experiences of cultural exchange and hybridization. Objects are important to the experience we seek to offer, as they can have intrinsic emotive and affective powers and "invite an empathetic engagement with others' life worlds and experiences."[66]

What makes this installation unique, however, is the opportunity it affords visitors to meet and interact with real individuals who can share their stories linked to the displayed objects. Inspired by the concept of the Human Library, this part of the exhibition aims to facilitate empathetic viewer/subject connections, and creates opportunities for more personal and bi-directional encounters that could transform the museum (literally in this installation) into a "sharing space"[67] for dialogue and interaction. The Human Library is an experience designed "to promote dialogue, reduce prejudices and encourage understanding."[68] In Human Libraries people can borrow "living books" – individuals who are willing to share their experiences, including those who are subjected to stereotyping and prejudices. We envision that people whose objects are displayed in the installation could act as live interpreters whom visitors can "loan" and have the opportunity to speak with informally and openly. Visitors can take part in personal, face-to-face encounters and, in the safe space of the exhibition, hear more about the meaning of the objects and their owners' experiences of migration, diversity, integration, and marginalization. The hoped-for empathetic connections between visitors and the individuals they encounter could reduce the distance between viewer and subject that usually characterizes displays in ethnographic museums. By bringing together people with different experiences and cultural backgrounds, we believe that this installation can contribute to our goals of challenging stereotypes and promote mutual understanding among different groups in Dutch society.

Conclusions

The World in One City is our attempt to respond creatively and constructively to the criticisms that many ethnographic museums have faced in recent years. In imagining the exhibition we have been guided by our interest in the social and moral agency of museums and, more particularly, our belief in the powerful role that ethnographic museums can play as forums for debate in multicultural societies. Our dream exhibition, then, is an attempt to contribute to broader discussions around the possibilities for museums to act as agents of intercultural exchange and cross-cultural understanding.[69]

In developing *The World in One City* we propose an approach that prioritizes the social agency and responsibility of museums and highlights the unique role they can play in engaging visitors in contemporary "hot" social, cultural and political debates.[70] In doing so, our curatorial dream also responds to Anthony Shelton's plea[71] for a "politically committed anthropology" that can stimulate dialogue and reflection on contemporary issues, without forgetting museums' collections and history. This position, of course, is not universally shared. Indeed, some commentators have argued that ethnographic museums should not bend to contemporary social and political concerns about diversity and multiculturalism and, instead, hold true to their origins and founding raison d'être.[72] Debates about the extent to which ethnographic museums should reorient their purposes and practices mirror broader discussions in the sector regarding the social role and responsibilities of cultural institutions.[73] Here, opposition to the notion that museums should enhance their social relevance and explore their potential to contribute to the good of society tends to suggest that such an approach is inevitably coupled with a loss of institutional authority, a dilution or distortion of purpose, and an impoverishment of scholarly research activity.[74] On the contrary, we would argue that many of the most successful attempts by museums to speak to contemporary issues and inform public debate surrounding diversity, migration, and identity are those that have drawn on the unique power of collections; that are based on robust and scholarly research (*both* on collections and on visitors), and that have blended curatorial disciplinary expertise with knowledge derived from lived experience of the issues being explored.[75]

As Robert Janes argues, museums need to become more comfortable with challenging the status quo and taking risks, being able to use their failures (when and if they come) to embrace renewal and to avoid irrelevance and resist decline.[76] Those ethnographic museums willing to embrace change and explore new roles can, we suggest, produce extraordinary exhibitions that have the potential to elicit strong emotional responses in their visitors and to actively inform our collective conversations about difference and belonging.

Acknowledgments

We would like to thank Denise Frank, freelance researcher, and Richard van Alphen, Coordinator Collection Digitalization at the National Museum of World Cultures, for their support during our imagined process of exhibition development (especially for sharing with us their insight on the museum's collection). While we remain responsible for the ideas presented in the paper, we would also like to thank Koos van Brakel, Head of Collections at the National Museum of World Cultures, for his comments on the final draft.

CHAPTER TWELVE

Museum without Walls: After *Into the Heart of Africa*

SHELLEY RUTH BUTLER

The museum is a palace of fixity we are wandering in.
Arnold Itwaru and Natahsa Ksonzek[1]

My curatorial dream, *Museum without Walls,* is a participatory, guided intervention that takes place in the African and Canadian galleries of the Royal Ontario Museum (ROM) in Toronto, Canada's most global metropolis. The ROM is a hundred-year-old "universal" museum, which is dedicated to natural history and world cultures. The yellow school buses parked outside, and the participation of influential donors and business leaders behind the scenes, are indicative of the ROM's strong ties with civic and official culture. My title, *Museum without Walls,* invokes fluidity and freedom of movement, and the potential for museums to resonate with everyday life.[2] The ROM, like comparable complex, monumental museums, is a highly planned space, though which visitors walk in prescribed ways. *Museum without Walls* encourages participants to navigate its galleries differently, in order to blur the master narratives of its geographically organized exhibitions. My subtitle refers to the famously controversial 1990 *Into the Heart of Africa* exhibition during which the ROM became a defensive fortress, blocking protestors from its entrance. The exhibition took place over two decades ago, yet it haunts the ROM and is remembered by a generation of African and Caribbean Canadians and politically engaged citizens.[3] It is canonized in museological literature as an example of inappropriate use of curatorial and institutional authority, failed community consultation, and the political and semiotic ambiguity of reflexive and ironic curatorial strategies.[4] The controversy was absent from the ROM's website until 2014, when, as part of its centenary celebrations, the museum launched an online, crowd-sourced memory project called ROM ReCollects.[5] Public engagement is a key goal expressed by ROM management in conjunction with its centenary.

Legacies and Walls

Enter *Museum without Walls.* My curatorial strategies reflect decisions made in response to the legacy of *Into the Heart of Africa.* These are: to engage and blur boundaries between the Canadian and African galleries; to establish a "curatorial collective" to create and facilitate the project; and finally, to make visible traces of the collective's work, as well as those of museum visitors who choose to participate in the project. I unpack these principles below. Having already workshopped *Museum without Walls* with an invited group of curators, scholars, and educators, I incorporate conversations and feedback on the project into my discussion below, to evoke the complex terrain that it enters, and to demonstrate the value of making visible the processes and decisions that are already shaping it.[6]

At the time of *Into the Heart of Africa,* the ROM had neither a permanent African gallery, nor a curator for its collection. This collection comprises approximately six to eight thousand objects, with strengths in central and West Africa.[7] Most were acquired in colonial and missionary contexts, with later acquisitions linked to individual collectors and travellers. A fundamental ambiguity raised by the reflexive approach of *Into the Heart of Africa* was whether its focus was on African cultures or on Canadian participation in the British Empire, including warfare, missionization, and colonial collecting. Arguably the exhibit did both, but its dominant tone of ironically re-presenting voices of missionaries and colonial propaganda angered communities who demanded respectful, sensitive accounts of African cultural worlds.

Nearly two decades later, the museum opened its first permanent African gallery, as part of its high-profile expansion called Renaissance ROM.[8] The gallery is colloquially referred to as the Triple AP gallery by museum employees since, using a classic ethnographic frame, it houses distinct displays of indigenous arts and culture from Africa, the Americas, and

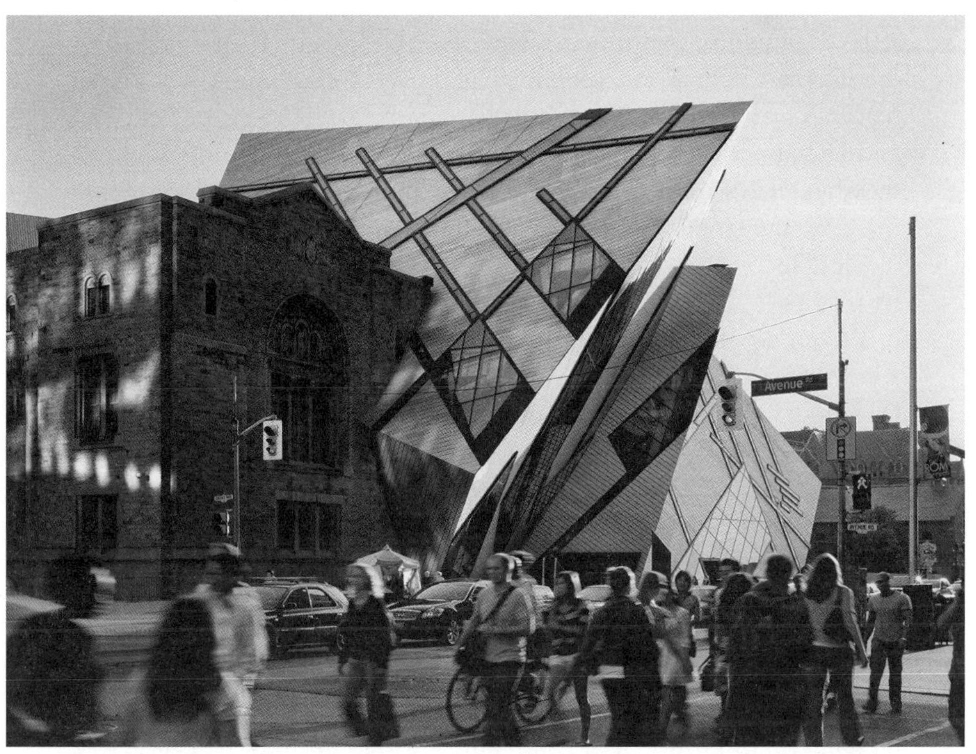

12.1 | The Michael Lee-Chin Crystal Gallery at the Royal Ontario Museum.

Asia-Pacific.[9] The African gallery displays about four hundred objects in four deep cases, using an authoritative, univocal ethnographic style. But the architectural space of the gallery is avant-garde, and this gives the ethnographic frame a cosmopolitan, edgy charge. Designed by Daniel Libeskind, the Michael Lee-Chin Crystal combines five interlocking prismatic structures that jut out of the ROM's heritage building (see figure 12.1). The interior is a maze of angled walls and surfaces, from gigantic planes protruding over the street to tiny nooks and crannies leading to dead ends. That the structure invites a sense of play was evident in June 2007 when some twenty-two thousand visitors came to explore it before the installation of any exhibitions. A documentary shows visitors leaning against and climbing the slanted walls, and tucking themselves into crevices while staff react with a mixture of enthusiasm and concern.[10] On camera, William Thorsell (director at that time) pronounces the crowds "fabulous," but thinks aloud about the need for "barriers" since the structure invites "everyone to go and play." I will discuss such issues below: *Museum without Walls* is premised on a belief in the pedagogical and affective value of moving through the museum with the intent of messing with its structures.[11] Implicit in this approach is an awareness that a monumental museum such as the ROM is both a real and "psychological space" that can welcome, forbid, exclude, dominate, or inspire its visitors.[12]

The Americas gallery does not include Canada, which is displayed in a lower level of the museum in two galleries: a Gallery of Canada and a Gallery of Canada: First Peoples.[13] I mention this detail because my curatorial dream is designed for the Canadian and African galleries. Given the legacy of *Into the Heart of Africa*, the African gallery is an obvious location for *Museum without Walls*. I suggest, however, that the Canadian gallery is equally relevant for this project. In 1990 protestors experienced several forms of alienation. They criticized the fact that Africa was portrayed largely through Occidental eyes in an era of racist evolutionism. As expressed by one visitor: "All my life I've been looking for my roots. I come here and you show me nothing." And in response to a "timeless" diorama of an Ovimbundu compound (in central Angola), a protestor lamented: "It gave you a very sad feeling. The hut looked very dark inside ... It reduced it to something rejectable that you wouldn't want to claim."[14] Protestors also voiced anger at being excluded from contemporary public culture in Canada. From the ROM's condescending last-minute community consultations to its court injunctions against protestors, the museum was not inclusive. In response, three students from York University created a six-minute video that juxtaposed voices of protestors with that of an unaccommodating officious ROM public relations employee, showing grainy guerrilla-style video images of colonial violence in the exhibition, as well as the experience of being shut out by the museum.[15]

Welcome to *Museum without Walls*: Please Meddle[16]

Participants are greeted by a few members of a diverse "curatorial collective" at the entrance of the ROM. These guides take the participants on a three-hour excursion in the museum, exploring cultural and social boundaries and exclusion in the museum, and in everyday life, in the past and present. Working in small groups with facilitators, participants interact with four museum spaces: the Canadian gallery, the "Stair of Wonders," the African gallery, and the "Spirit House."[17] Using real and virtual postcards and playlists designed by the curatorial collective, participants access the power of information and the passion of music and narrative in order to develop an analysis of the ROM's organization and logic in relation to traditional and more inclusive, contemporary, and creative ways of thinking about black/Canadian history and identity. Concluding their visit, participants create their own postcards for display in a temporary exhibition about cultural boundaries, mixing, inclusion, and exclusion. These are documented and later returned to the participants as mementos of their pedagogical experience and as catalysts for further thought and action.[18]

In contrast with the traditional practice of introducing exhibitions with anonymous textual curatorial statements, *Museum without Walls* begins with personal introductions. Members of the curatorial collective introduce themselves as educators, citizens, students, curators, and artists who want to "mine the museum" to learn, critique, reflect, and create visual culture in response to the ROM galleries and lived experience.[19] The collective does not speak in a single voice, but rather represents multiple perspectives.[20] Herein lies an epistemological and practical problem: I have authored a curatorial dream that is to be developed with a curatorial collective. How to describe a process that has not yet occurred? And despite the centrality of dialogue in the production of my curatorial dream, how to simultaneously acknowledge that this is *my* vision and that I have set its parameters (at least on paper)? While a curatorial collective will actually create and facilitate *Museum without Walls*, material that I propose here will start the conversation.

When I workshopped this curatorial dream, I expected feedback (additions, corrections, questions, critiques) on the postcards and playlists that I created and proposed to use (see below). Instead, workshop participants focused on unpacking the curatorial collective's relationship with the ROM – the project's conditions of production and power relations. I envisioned a "radical trust" model in which the curatorial collective works independently of the ROM, using the space for its own ends.[21] The collective would control both the process and the product. This is an alternative to the community consultation and advisory committee models that are often used by mainstream museums whereby, in the worst-case scenario, the institution assumes a patronizing position as it "invites" communities into the museum.[22] The museum does not relinquish its institutional authority – it remains unchallenged and unchanged. This outcome parallels the logic of state multiculturalism in Canada, which is modelled on the managed inclusion (sometimes expressed as tolerance) of racialized others, as opposed to acknowledging how global cultural flows transform and de-centre the mainstream.[23]

The radical trust model is appealing, considering the legacy of *Into the Heart of Africa*. But the workshop suggested that it would be necessary to include the museum in initial discussions, unless this was to be a guerrilla-style intervention – easy enough to carry out with digital technology and social media. I now realize that these models of curatorial collectivity and radical trust are not firm concepts, but rather, that they need to be negotiated. I am inspired by curator-artist Fred Wilson's practice of leading museums to explore change courageously. As he puts it, "It takes a village to raise a museum."[24] Working with a museum gives a project a legitimacy and presence that it cannot acquire from outside the institution.

Another related issue was voiced by workshop participants: what are the politics and outcomes associated with this curatorial dream? Can issues of equity be incorporated into the process? (I return to this question below, in the context of the ROM's Spirit House, which was designed as a lounge-cum-shrine to donors).[25] Questions of equity open a larger discussion about the value and problems of museums, and whether the institution per se is worth reforming and claiming. A person who chooses to be involved in *Museum without Walls* (either in the curatorial collective, or as a participant) likely finds the ROM to be a compelling (if problematic) environment. But critiques of the institution – even including rejection of the museum entirely – must be made a visible and audible part of the project.

What are the politics of meddling and moving unpredictably in the disciplinary space of the museum? Imagined transgressions in museums are a cinematic trope, from disaffected youth racing through the Louvre in Jean Luc Godard's *Band of Outsiders* (1964) to a wonderfully campy dance routine performed by guards at the ROM in John Greyson's *Zero*

Patience (1993).[26] Museum sleepovers, yoga, dancing and DJs, such as the ROM's Friday Night Live events, are all the rage.[27] *Museum without Walls* is neither pranksterism nor hedonistic spectacle.[28] Rather, it is an embodied and intellectual exercise that recognizes the "constitutive character and transformative possibilities of museum space as well as the ability of museum visitors and museum professionals to reshape museum spaces through practices of appropriation."[29] *Museum without Walls* focuses on space – the organization of displays, presence, and absence – and, by extension, on historical consciousness and identity.

Itinerary

The Sigmund Samuel Gallery of Canada displays some 560 paintings and objects, with an emphasis on historical, decorative, and pictorial arts from the decades preceding and following Confederation (1867). It is also relatively Ontario- (Anglo- and central-Canada-) centric. At a glance, the gallery appears conventional (though not dark and dusty), but further exploration leads to signs of curatorial experimentation. In this gallery, *Museum without Walls* participants receive a series of postcards – real and virtual (tablet-based) – with images and texts that have been created by the curatorial collective. While tablet-based browsing has a contemporary, youthful feel, real postcards are more likely to be kept and valued as souvenirs, and they have a stronger presence in the material world of the museum.[30] The postcards guide and reinforce discussions led by animators, and pose key questions. They also allow for the possibility of self-guided versions of *Museum without Walls*.

Through interaction with the guides and postcards, visitors are also introduced to *Into the Heart of Africa*, gleaning salient facts about the controversy – the goals and risks of critical museology, the legacy of Afro-Canadian exclusion, and the way in which protestors linked images of colonial violence to local racial inequalities and struggles. The possibility of making connections between exhibitions and everyday life is demonstrated and valorized.

An introductory postcard presents a floor map of the ROM and asks participants to join the curatorial collective in exploring the following ideas and questions:

The ROM, following European nineteenth-century museums, is organized according to a place-centred logic, with different galleries representing different geographic areas and historical eras. According to this model, two galleries such as the Canadian and African ones are distinct and separate. But in our era of fluid identities and global cities like Toronto, place-centred galleries have limitations.[31]

We invite you to explore two questions:

- *How is black history and culture presented in the Canadian gallery?*
- *How might the African gallery change how we think about a globalized city like Toronto?*[32]

Participants will, without doubt, notice the absence of black histories (as well as those of other racialized communities) in the Canadian gallery. However, the postcards provide visual and textual information about significant temporary exhibitions at the ROM that have tried to address this absence, on subjects such as the Underground Railway, women's quilting and community, and African Canadian identity through photography.[33] One postcard reproduces a brilliant juxtaposition, found in the catalogue of the temporary exhibition *Position as Desired: Exploring African Canadian Identity*, of a formal oil painting of philanthropist Dr Sigmund Samuel (for whom the gallery is named) with a contemporary photo portrait of a young black man dressed in a dark fur-lined hooded parka, who is positioned to recall German artist Albrecht Durer's *Self-Portrait at 28*, painted in the year 1500 (see figure 12.2).[34] Questions on this postcard read:

- *What effect does juxtaposing these portraits have?*
- *What does it suggest about Canadian identities?*
- *What does it say about the past? And the present?*

Another postcard alludes to the "elephant in the gallery," the unmentioned historical reality of slavery:

"Canada's continued forgetfulness concerning slavery here, and the nation state's attempts to record only Canada's role as a place for

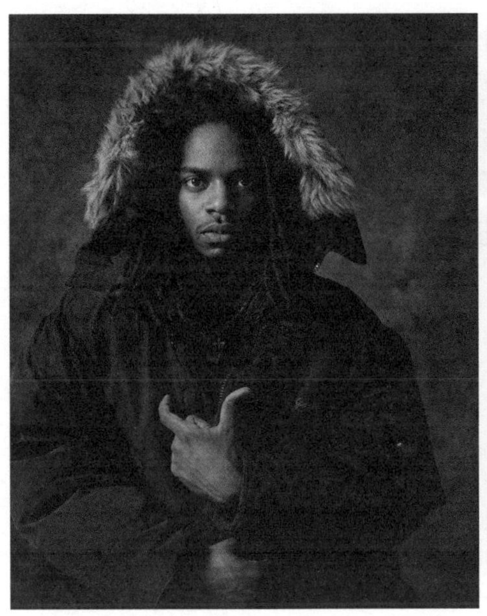

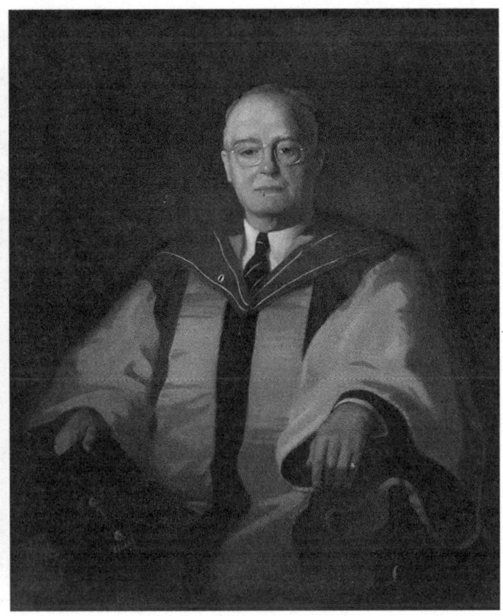

12.2 | Elements of a postcard on historical amnesia.

> *sanctuary for escaping African-Americans, is part of the story of absenting blackness from its history."*
>
> *Rinaldo Walcott*[35]

Facilitators address this subject while standing near marine history paintings that show the arrival of Loyalists in Canada. Participants are also offered electronic tablets on which they can view a "Heritage Minute" about the Underground Railway, focusing on Canada's contribution to liberating escaped American slaves.[36] Many visitors will be familiar with Heritage Minutes – one-minute, privately funded "advertisements" designed to arouse patriotic pride. They will also likely recognize the book covers reproduced on the postcard: *The Hanging of Angélique: The Untold Story of Canadian Slavery and the Burning of Old Montreal* by Afua Cooper, and the national bestseller *The Book of Negroes* by Lawrence Hill. Facilitators explain the historical contexts of both books and ask participants: To what extent has Canada acknowledged its history of slavery and racial injustice faced by eighteenth- and nineteenth-century black settlers? What further steps need to be taken?"[37] Participants have the opportunity to recognize that the Canadian gallery reinforces an official "two founding nations" narrative, with its problematic silences and distortions. A postcard highlighting interventions in the Canadian gallery by Iroquois photographer and curator Jeff Thomas models a bold, personal, and contemporary response. Thomas presents intimate, ironic, and revisionist readings of historical paintings, including the nationally iconic *Death of Wolfe* by Benjamin West (1771).

Leaving the Canadian gallery, we take the nearby "Stair of Wonders," a transition space for private and/or dialogic reflection.[38] The wide, angular white stairs lead the visitor to the third floor African gallery; landings provide natural resting points, with insertions of discreet cabinets of miniatures (toys, seashells, paperweights) in the walls. Ascending the stairs and making use of their slow, processional quality, members of the curatorial collective ask participants to reflect on the question, "Where do you come from?" which is so often posed to racialized minorities who are stigmatized as "others."[39] Participants discuss how they ask and answer this question in globalized Toronto, and in an era when hyphenated and fluid identities based on gender, race, class, origins, politics, and sexuality are possible and common. In a more fantastical version of *Museum without Walls*, participants at this point meet and interact with performance artist Camille Turner, who presents herself as black pageant queen "Miss Canadiana."[40]

Participants arrive at the African gallery. To draw attention to the way the gallery is colour-coded to demarcate distinct culture areas, facilitators present a postcard of a conventional, colourful world map. Museological themes, such as Western museums' tradition of exoticizing and "freezing" others, are discussed. Participants find in the gallery recent curatorial efforts at interrupting this tradition, thanks to the addition of vibrant, contemporary, popular African art, such as two sculptural coffins from Ghana.[41] But another postcard shows that exoticism and stereotypes still appeal to consumers. The card reproduces an excerpt from the ROM's so called "Top 10 ROM Family Favourites" which includes, in the Triple AP Gallery, a ...

> *"Shrunken Head: This is an actual human head! The Shuar culture, native to Ecuador and Peru, took their enemies' heads in battle and then shrank them, believing this would pacify the enemy's avenging soul."*

- *What does this shrunken head lead you to think about the cultures of Ecuador and Peru?*
- *What would you display to show these countries' similarities to Canada?*

In answering these questions, participants are led to assess the style and ambiance of the gallery.

The African gallery celebrates continental diversity and includes a subtle subtext about the power and presence of aesthetic objects in everyday life. Texts provide clear ethnographic information on topics such as architecture, creativity, spiritual life, everyday objects, and community relations. Although it includes artifacts from *Into the Heart of Africa*, gone is that exhibit's flawed attempt at re-presenting voices of collectors and missionaries and experiences of colonialism. It also eschews the curatorial strategy of multi-vocality, despite its effectiveness in recently updated African exhibits such as the Horniman Museum in London and the Smithsonian Institution in Washington.[42] The ROM's African gallery is the result of over two years of work with an academic advisor and advisory committee of people with professional and diasporic links to Africa, as well as ROM staff. But this process is unfortunately not acknowledged in the gallery. While providing an important foundation, the space begs to be enlivened in order to make it more personal and less abstract.[43] In response to this challenge, I propose aural playlists to stimulate critical and creative thought about this gallery in relation to the Canadian one, as well as broader themes of boundaries, belonging, and exclusion.

Participants intrigued by the history and politics of exhibitions move through the gallery while listening to an excerpt of Marlene NourbeSe Philip's *Looking for Livingstone: An Odyssey of Silence*, a powerful narrative that depicts a woman traveller in Africa confronting colonialism and colonial museology.[44] Others work with a playlist that directs them to objects chosen by members of the curatorial collective.[45] More unconventionally, facilitators introduce the history of Africville, a subject that would normally be addressed in a Canadian gallery. Facilitators orient participants to a playlist of music and narratives, noting that Africville was a nineteenth-century black settlement on the edge of Halifax that was demolished by city authorities over forty years ago, following decades of civic neglect and racial isolation. Africville is part of an Atlantic story, linked to slave routes and black loyalists. It has been a site for the struggle for social justice ever since, and many Canadian musicians have composed music to remember the atmosphere of the community that existed and to record anger about injustice.[46] Facilitators, as well as a postcard that indexes the soundtracks, pose framing questions:

- *What is the impact of listening to music about Africville in an African gallery?*
- *Does it change the way you think about the relationship of Canada and Africa?*
- *Would Africville music fit better in the Canadian gallery? What effect would it have there?*

These are not questions with right or wrong answers. Rather, they are meant to destabilize familiar notions of here and there, near and far, home and away. As participants consider the relationship between the Canadian and African galleries, some may question the absence of a Caribbean gallery in this otherwise encyclopedic museum. Perhaps the curatorial collective will invent audio and visual cues that acknowledge this absence and evoke the Caribbean's "poetics of moving."[47]

A final playlist introduces music that speaks to the influence of black cultural styles in Toronto and the fluidity of cultural and personal identities. A postcard contextualizes the music:

> *Aboriginal youth fuse hip-hop and activism. White Nova Scotian rapper Classified does "Oh Canada" (and satirizes a Heritage Minute). Kardinal Offishall asserts the diversity of black communities in Toronto. K'naan's hit "Wavin' Flag" highlights solidarity as performed by Canadian Artists for Haiti.*

- *What comes to mind on listening to this diverse music in the African gallery?*
- *How might this music change the way you look at the Canadian gallery?*
- *What music would you add to this playlist? Please write your suggestions on the whiteboard provided. The playlist will be updated periodically.*[48]

This strategy recognizes the agency of participants, who are invited to draw on their own cultural repertoires and networks to contribute to an evolving playlist.

Participants return to the first floor "Thorsell Spirit House," a sparse lounge with Daniel Libeskind's custom-designed, angular chairs and a vertical view of the Crystal's structure, to work on their own media creation in response to *Museum without Walls*. The lounge included a luminous floor-to-ceiling portrait of the museum's "New Century Founders" – seventeen donors who pledged five million dollars or more – making it an opportune site to reflect on equity and diversity at the ROM, as well as on socioeconomic inequalities experienced by blacks and racialized others in Toronto and Canada.[49] Working with a bank of images generated by the curatorial collective, and also with access to the Internet and a printer, participants create their own postcards. My contributions to the image bank highlight troubling contradictions, signs of hope and despair: a black Canadian athlete competing in the 2010 Winter Olympics in Vancouver; a cross burning on the lawn of a mixed-race couple in Nova Scotia (2010); Halifax's official apology and settlement for the destruction of Africville (2010); students parading in blackface during frosh week at the Université de Montréal (2011).[50]

After selecting an image (or images), participants choose one or more of the following messages to print on the reverse side:

- *While participating in Museum without Walls, I felt…*
- *While participating in Museum without Walls, I saw…*
- *While participating in Museum without Walls, I heard…*
- *While participating in Museum without Walls, I experienced…*
- *While participating in Museum without Walls, I thought about…*
- *While participating in Museum without Walls, I learned…*

Participants complete the sentence of their choice, self-address their postcard, and note whether they consent to its being scanned and displayed as part of a collective public conversation. The creation of such a visual and textual conversation enables participants to witness and respond to multiple perspectives.[51] An important precedent for this style of intervention at the ROM is the collaborative art project *Walls and Barriers*, co-curated by Vanessa Barnett and Elena Soni in 2010 at the same time that the museum's Institute for Contemporary Culture hosted the travelling show *El Anatsui: When I Last Wrote to You about Africa.* Inspired by the Ghanaian artist's aesthetic of using found objects to create monumental wall sculptures, a diverse group of five hundred youth worked on linked Plexiglas panels, responding to the theme of walls and barriers. Pieces included deeply personal expressions of emotions ranging from pain to well-being, as well as treatments of such global political issues as anti-immigration laws and child labour. The final product was mounted as a temporary, mobile exhibit at the ROM. Incidentally, El Anatsui's oeuvre includes a beautifully simple work alluding to legacies of slavery, constructed of driftwood and metal, entitled "Akua's Surviving Children" (1996). Since it may be familiar to ROM visitors, I would include it in the *Museum without Walls* image bank.[52] Finally, as I write this curatorial dream, the ROM has commenced an important initiative called "Of Africa" as part of its centennial celebrations.[53] Mindful of the legacy of *Into the Heart of Africa,* the ROM mounted an intimate healing ceremony. Such a ritual might also make a fitting conclusion for *Museum without Walls.*

Last Walkabout

When I workshopped *Museum without Walls*, I shifted from framing our discussion as being about "Curating Black History and Culture in Canada" and "Curating Black Canadian History and Culture." This occurred because the two frames are overlapping and interconnected; it's not easy to say where one project ends and the other begins. Yet of the two, "Curating Black History and Culture in Canada" is the more inclusive frame, as it evokes an expansive notion of identity that is central to *Museum without Walls.*

Fred Wilson argues that the "future of embedding diversity [in museums] is to further integrate what museum educators are doing with curatorial conventions."[54] *Museum without Walls* is a hybrid project that mixes pedagogy with curatorship, using both to heighten personal engagement with the ROM and cultural politics. Though I have not stated it explicitly, I hope it is obvious that I have designed this project to engage a wide audience. I do not want it to fall into an "identity politics" ghetto; nor do I think it appropriate that only black Canadians (and other racialized minorities) do the work of critically considering historical consciousness. A diverse range of participants and perspectives is necessary to ensure that the project is not reduced to, or experienced as, a "black and white" exercise.[55] The goal is to avoid racialized categories, while also encouraging deep thinking about black histories and cultures, in Toronto, Canada, and beyond.[56] African Canadian and Caribbean Canadian cultures and histories connect pedagogically – and for some, emotionally – with the African gallery. A more expansive and fluid notion of black culture can help to counter both historical and contemporary racism, which is based on exclusion, ignorance, and diminishment. More concretely, as social and economic polarization in Canada grows, it is useful for diverse individuals to cross paths in public space. This is the practice of everyday life in a global city. Done mindfully, such encounters can reshape our consciousness in subtle ways, one step at a time.[57]

CHAPTER THIRTEEN

abNormal: Bodies in Medicine and Culture

MANON PARRY

From anatomical exhibitions intended to teach the form and function of the body's major systems, to pathology specimens documenting disease or deformity, medical museums have specialized in the presentation of the normal and the abnormal.[1] Yet few of these projects have addressed the implications of this practice of exhibiting and categorizing bodies (and therefore people) as unhealthy or abnormal, or the standard by which all others should be measured. The exhibition I propose explores the role of medicine in defining human standards and diagnosing deviations from them at various historical moments. *abNormal*: *Bodies in Medicine and Culture* begins by asking: who decides what is normal, and what factors inform that decision? The goal is to equip audiences to think critically about the production of scientific knowledge, the role of medicine in shaping current attitudes towards certain bodies, and the implications for everyday, embodied living.

The exhibition is designed for the National Library of Medicine (NLM), part of the National Institutes of Health, a medical research complex funded by the US government on the outskirts of Washington, DC. Since the late 1990s, the NLM's Exhibition Program has developed a wide range of gallery, travelling, and online exhibitions on diverse topics. Although situated on a medical research campus, the exhibition team has moved beyond the simple celebration of medical accomplishments. While important medical breakthroughs that can capture the public's interest are still included, the main emphasis is now placed instead on broader issues relating to the practice of scientific research, access to health information and medical care, and the social and environmental factors that shape experiences of illness and disability. The exhibitions are intended to raise awareness of the library's collections, to encourage young people to pursue careers in the health sciences, and to contribute to consumer health by publicizing the library as a source of relevant information and resources. Projects draw on library materials but can also include objects and images from institutions around the world. Topics can thus be selected on the basis of criteria beyond the limitations of the library's holdings, and have included such disparate subjects as the development of forensic science, the history of women physicians, and recent projects I have researched and curated on global health and human rights, gender and mental illness in nineteenth-century medicine, and the experiences of Civil War veterans.[2]

While some of these topics may be considered traditional fare for a medical museum, my approach diverges from the standard narrative usually employed in such institutions. Like museums of science and technology, medical museums often present history as a linear narrative of *progress*, with current practice treated as the highpoint in a chain of breakthroughs.[3] Devices such as prosthetic limbs, surgical tools, or medical remedies might be laid out in chronological order to illustrate these steps from the past to the present. Such exhibitions tend to focus on discoveries, technologies, and the inventive minds behind them, rather than the experiences of patients or unanswered questions. The storyline thus downplays collaboration between researcher and patient, and the processes involved in the production and acceptance of medical knowledge, especially the role of doubt and failure.

As historian Ludmilla Jordanova notes, displays of medicine usually mask the processes by which knowledge is created, as they have no place for uncertainty. Instead, they highlight static products of research that are unequivocal and can be easily understood.[4] The impression then created is that changing practices are driven by objective, neutral science rather than by funding priorities, political concerns, personal and career profiles, and particular historical circumstances. Critics have argued that this approach is partly to blame for the poor public understanding of science, and have encouraged museums to focus on science as a process by revealing "unfinished" or contested research.[5] My imaginary exhibition adopts just such a strategy. The exhibition examines medical theories that were once popular but have since been disavowed and draws parallels with current research-in-progress. My intention is not to discredit medical research but to make apparent the role of social factors in the production of scientific knowledge.

The proposed exhibition draws on materials in the collections of the NLM that reflect the long history of measuring, comparing, and codifying human subjects. The scientific study of human bodies intensified in the 1800s as medical professionals sought to establish standards of appearance and behaviour and to determine the meaning of deviations from them. As historians have demonstrated, much of this work reflected the assumptions of the era and, in turn, served to underwrite social inequality by proposing scientific justifications for a hierarchical ordering of peoples.[6] American physicians embraced phrenology, for example, as a way to read the human skull for evidence of character traits. Later in the Victorian era the method was applied to the study of racial difference. Such work contributed to the professionalization of medicine by grounding a new field of expertise in the scientific study of human variation.[7]

A few exhibitions have explored the role of medicine in justifying hierarchies of race, gender, and ability, although interestingly, the most provocative of these are not to be found in medical museums. Most reinforce the "presentist" trends in traditional narratives by framing past practices as examples of quackery or pseudo-science, and sharply distinguishing "the bad old days" from the heights of modern medicine today, if they make any connection to current practices.[8] Of the group of topics I focus on, race and ethnicity are perhaps the most commonly explored, with eugenics receiving the greatest attention in museums, perhaps in part because of its status as a seemingly resolved, uncontested, and debunked area of science. *Deadly Medicine: Creating the Master Race*, the United States Holocaust Memorial Museum's travelling exhibition, for instance, describes the persecution of children with disabilities under the Nazi regime. The exhibition, launched in 2005 and booked at the time of writing until June 2015, presents this as an aberration from the usual practice of science, rather than an extension of the processes of classification that are central to medical thinking. Visitors are given the sense that social evils occasionally corrupt (otherwise neutral) scientific practice, rather than the somewhat more challenging notion that science is always informed by and constitutive of society.[9] In contrast, *Race: Are We So Different?*, an online and travelling exhibition launched by the American Anthropological Association in 2007, includes recent controversies over the scientific study of race as well as the history of scientific racism.[10]

Yet the assets in the historical section, which include the only artifacts in the exhibition, compete for the visitor's attention with video interviews calling into question the "scientific" status of those who studied racial difference in the past. The idea that scientists of an earlier time were predisposed to discover racial differences in order to confirm their beliefs – and to support the institution of slavery – is clearly made; yet there is little to link this predisposition with the ongoing scientific study of human variation today. The exhibition simply asserts that while contemporary research "tells us we share a common ancestry and the differences among people we see are natural variations, results of migration, marriage and adaptation to different environments," many people, including scientists, continue to think about race in terms of biologically based differences. When seen in combination with the design of the installation, which is very much in keeping with the style of an interactive science exhibition, the overall effect seems to celebrate "good" science – which has enabled us to appreciate our shared genetic history and origins in Africa, for example – while decrying the claims of "bad" science, which focuses on biological, rather than environmental explanations for the racial differences we see around us.[11] When *Race: Are We So Different?* visited the Smithsonian in 2011, it was installed in the National Museum of Natural History. Being housed at a site for the scientific study of humans and the natural world, and visiting mostly science centres during its national tour, it is unsurprising that the exhibition does not engage more directly with the continuing role of expert knowledge in the maintenance of discriminatory categories.

Elsewhere at the Smithsonian, at the National Museum of American History, Katherine Ott, curator in the Science, Medicine, and Society division, has addressed this phenomenon more directly. She has argued that disability has been erased from the histories told in most museums. "People present a spectrum of body types, and until recent decades, the most common physical traits included being arthritic, stooped, pock-marked, scarred, toothless, or bent and injured in some way. Difference was everywhere, yet it is missing from the history we present to the public. The healthy, idealized figures in exhibits, films, and re-enactment are as false as the landscaped and manicured grounds of a Civil War battlefield."[12]

Ott curated a major exhibition on the history of polio in 2005, which drew favourable press and large audiences. *Whatever Happened to Polio?* was intended to commemorate the fiftieth anniversary of the polio vaccine, and prior to her involvement was framed as a celebration of medical progress in the typical style of medical history exhibitions. When Ott inherited the project, she significantly reframed the main narrative from a traditional account of the trial and error of scientific research and the triumph of discovery, to instead integrate a broad range of viewpoints. The result focused equally on the experiences of those who contracted the disease or cared for a child with polio, and the impact of the illness on the lives of those who recovered. The curatorial voice of the exhibition was shared among these perspectives through the use of first-person accounts from memoirs, letters, articles, and textbooks.[13]

Disability scholars have rejected the "medical model" of disability for constructing and enforcing rigid categories of the normal and abnormal, pathologizing difference, and promoting the idea of correction or cure as the ultimate goal. The medical framework also disregards the social factors that frame the experience of disability, from inaccessible environments to discrimination in housing and employment. *Whatever Happened to Polio?* was displayed in a history museum, and approached disability as a social issue as well as a medical one. Including disability in an exhibition in a medical museum is more problematic, as these institutions have a long history of treating disability as a problem to be fixed, an unusual "case" to marvel at, or an example used to illustrate advances in modern science.[14] Reframing the medical history of disability to question such constructions of ability and disability could therefore play an important role in transforming the ways in which medical museums exhibit and interpret – and public audiences understand – bodily difference.

While medical topics have made their way into museums dealing with a wide range of topics, from the Holocaust to the history of everyday life, medical museums have largely focused on the history of their field. Yet these institutions not only have the opportunity to diversify their audiences and attract visitors without a particular interest in medicine, many must also consider how their existing exhibitions – of body parts in bottles, for example – contribute to the ordering of the normal and abnormal among their audiences.

Bodies in Medical Museums

Originally intended for the education of students or the edification of members of the profession, medical exhibitions have proven popular with non-specialist visitors, thanks largely to their fascinating collections of specimens and strange technologies and tools. However, the custodians of these institutions have long questioned the propriety of displaying the more gruesome aspects of medicine to non-medical audiences and the ethics of exhibiting human variation for the entertainment of the public.[15] In the 1990s displays of specimens illustrating bodily anomalies came under attack for perpetuating past injustices by exhibiting human remains without the permission of the subjects, and for recreating the culture of the "freak show."[16] In response, stakeholders at some of America's best-known medical museums reconfigured exhibit spaces to move away from the macabre, and to focus instead on health education and the breakthroughs of modern medicine. Mark Micozzi, at that time director of the National Museum of Health and Medicine in Washington, DC, led efforts to "modernize" their displays to reflect this changing sensibility. In 1995 he was appointed to the Mütter Museum in Philadelphia to repeat the process of "cleaning-up" the exhibitions that he had undertaken in DC.[17] Such reforms divided museum staff as well as the general public, with many bemoaning the loss of the most fascinating elements of the traditional exhibits.[18]

Industrialized, Western societies have seen a major transformation in the experience of illness and death since the nineteenth century. Public health innovations have improved childhood mortality dramatically, and medicalized care has increasingly removed serious illness and dying from the home to the hospital. This process has created a new mystique around these processes. Anatomical exhibits may allow modern audiences to indulge their curiosity and confront their own mortality in a socially acceptable way. In the void created by the invisibility of death in modern society and at the medical museum, commercial exhibitors began to capitalize on the public interest in anatomy by developing large-scale touring exhibitions of plastinated human bodies, with layers of skin and tissue removed to show the muscles, organs, and bodily systems beneath.[19]

Yet these projects contribute to some of the same processes of classifying and valuing as the traditional medical museum, and create meaning by what they leave out as well as what they include. Most of the bodies displayed are male, for example, with female bodies included primarily to highlight the reproductive system or sexual characteristics, implying that the standard human form is male and privileging childbearing as the key function of the female body. Disease and bodily difference are presented without context: the damage caused by tobacco use, for example, is highlighted by way of a disembodied set of smoker's lungs. The environmental toxins that contribute to cancerous growths and birth defects, the social factors that foster risky behaviours such as smoking, and the populations who are targeted by the tobacco industry are eclipsed by a narrow focus strictly on the physiology of health and illness.

While some commentators have wrestled with the propriety of showing flayed humans in playful poses, and questioned whether the purported educational value justifies this sensational approach, such exhibitions have proven immensely popular with audiences around the world.[20] In light of this enduring public fascination, medical museologists have sought a compromise, coming to accept that some of the appeal of their institutions lies in the illicit thrill of seeing inside different bodies. As Ken Arnold, former head of public programs at the Wellcome Trust's medical history museum in the United Kingdom, has noted, "medicine touches a special, and especially sensitive, part of our psychological make-up. Consequently, as a medical history curator, one tries in vain entirely and unequivocally to separate the 'serious' subject of medicine from the 'trivial' response to 'blood and guts.'"[21] As a result, medical museums, including the Mütter, are once again exhibiting their cabinets of curiosities, often still without much analysis of the role of these materials in codifying difference and contributing to social hierarchies.[22] In contrast, *abNormal: Bodies in Medicine and Culture* rehabilitates the medical museum by deploying the sensational aspects of these subjects in a more meaningful way than simply as a tool to attract visitors.

Theorizing Bodies on Display

Scholars and museum practitioners have recently called for a diversification of the communities represented within our cultural institutions, to promote a more inclusive society, cultivate civic engagement, and combat prejudice.[23] As a federally funded institution, the NLM has a particular responsibility to serve its tax-paying audience, although stakeholders in all sorts of institutions are increasingly prioritizing exhibitions that can offer something tangible to visitors beyond a pleasant way to spend a few hours. Perhaps one of the most relevant trends for medical museums is the effort to harness the "therapeutic" potential of history.[24] Exhibitions on the mistreatment of residents in mental health facilities, traumatic experiences in places of medical quarantine or experimentation, and encounters with illness and medical care have recently been undertaken to help visitors address their own difficult memories and to heal ill will generated by harsh practices of the past.[25]

abNormal makes a similar contribution to personal well-being by providing a thought-provoking forum for audiences to reflect on the meanings and implications of bodily difference. Throughout our lives, each of us will encounter bodies that diverge from the dominant ideals of normality and perfection in our culture: as we age, in our own and others' disabilities, and in times of pregnancy or sickness. Yet despite the universal human experience of embodiment, the diversity of bodies, and the certainty of bodily change over the course of the life cycle, public representations that counteract the dominant ideals are few and far between, and in medical museums, exist only as examples of disease or deformity. An exhibition that helps individuals to reflect upon the processes by which some bodies are highly valued while others are pathologized could have a profound effect on how visitors understand and experience both their own embodiment and the ways they view others.

Moreover, while museologists promote the importance of science museums in improving the public understanding of science, they widely acknowledge their failure thus far to equip visitors to participate in informed debate on complex issues, or to ease the culture of distrust and hostility that flourishes on both sides of the gulf between the general public and the scientific community. Despite decades of innovative exhibit strategies and interactive education activities at science museums in the United States, the public understanding of science remains low.[26]

The common exhibition narratives used in medical museums privilege celebratory narratives of discovery, technological advances, and brilliant researchers, isolating scientific accomplishments from their specific contexts, focusing on the "eureka" moment of success rather than the long and error-ridden process of research, minimizing controversy, and emphasizing medical breakthroughs while marginalizing patient experiences. As a result, as museologist Steven Conn notes, visitors have come to expect exhibitions that "present the world understood, organized, and managed, and in so doing reinforce the very idea of science" as the ultimate and conclusive tool in understanding ourselves and our surroundings.[27] As the pace and scope of research has intensified, with older theories being overturned and previously unimaginable human intervention in natural processes becoming possible, this approach may actually have increased public anxiety about the reach of science and medicine. In exhibitions where medical technologies are laid out in chronological order to convey progress, for example, the advance of science is presented as an inevitable and unstoppable march into unknown territory.[28] This format has the potential to compound controversies on a wide range of issues, from end of life care to stem cell research and climate change.[29]

History-based exhibitions have an important role to play in addressing this problem because of their particular ability to engage visitors who feel ill equipped to understand current issues. Both those with great reverence for science but little factual understanding, and skeptics critical of scientific theories, may benefit from an exhibition that illuminates the processes that shape scientific research. Curators could, for example, explicate how medical knowledge is produced, validated, applied, and revised, acknowledging the role of funding, politics, context, and individual perspectives in the selection of research topics and methodologies, and the interpretation of results. Exposure to the social aspects that shape science in this way would help audiences to better evaluate risks and benefits in the face of contradictory evidence, and to understand the dynamics of disagreement and controversy among experts.

By exploring historical examples, audiences who may resist critiques of contemporary ideas could begin to reconsider their understanding of scientific objectivity. An exploration of paradigm shifts in scientific thinking provides a valuable entrée into a new understanding of the factors that contribute to the ascent and demise of a particular theory of the body or the mind.[30] An introduction to shifting values and beliefs in the history of medicine can thus help pave the way for a more critical consideration of current ideas. In the proposed exhibition, examples from the past are juxtaposed with contemporary corollaries, and framed by provocative questions that invite visitors to consider how current research preoccupations might reflect wider contemporary social, economic, and political concerns, which support particular ways of ordering society.

Exhibition Strategies

abNormal begins with an introductory statement inviting visitors to consider how ideas about bodies have been used to justify social hierarchies, how they reflect the preoccupations of their time as well as trends in scientific research, and how the standards and beliefs of an era change. The introduction is followed by three main sections, each devoted to bodies that have, at different points in history, been labelled as inferior, deviant, or disabled. Featured artifacts include major medical texts with images or illustrations of the telltale physiology of the criminal or "feeble-minded" individual; scientific diagrams and charts laying out norms and variations from them, such as comparisons between the physical and intellectual development of people of different races; and devices used to evaluate individuals, such as phrenology charts, or to treat their so-called conditions, such as hypnosis or hyrodrotherapy for "women's diseases." These materials are complemented by other images and artifacts from the same period that convey bodily ideals and variations from them, including photographs of women in corsets and human "freaks" on display, advertisements for beauty treatments to whiten black skin from the nineteenth century and hair straightening products today, and prosthetic limbs or other assistive devices for people with disabilities.

The exhibition is not intended to provide a comprehensive chronological account of the rise and fall of particular medical ideas. Instead, the galleries will juxtapose snapshots of beliefs at specific historical moments that may provoke shock, ridicule, disbelief, or even discomfort.

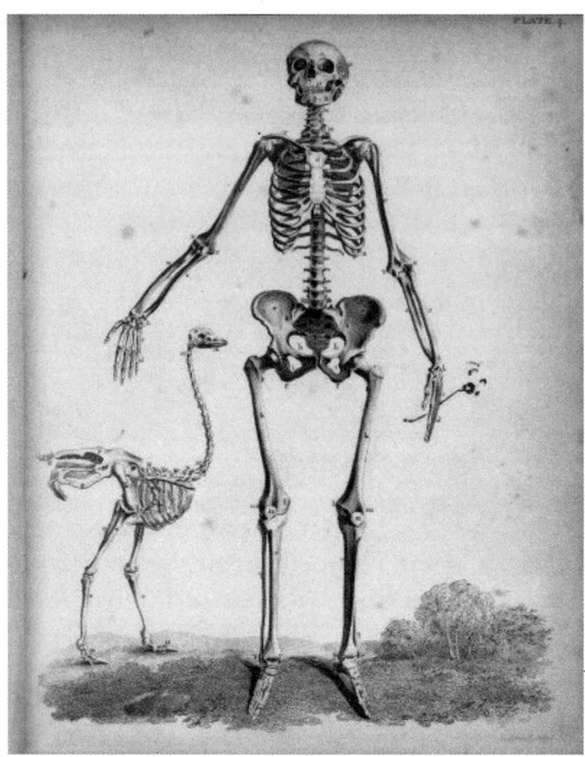

13.1 | "Female Skeleton Compared to the Ostrich," *Anatomy of the Bones of the Human Body*, Edinburgh, 1829.

Each section includes key moments in which a scientific paradigm was established or displaced, such as the definition of hysteria and the declassification of homosexuality as a disorder. One wall features a list of disease classifications and their date of origin or displacement by a new category, such as neurasthenia (1869) and chronic fatigue syndrome (1988) for example.

The first section, entitled "Inferior Bodies," will explore the representation of women's bodies and the bodies of people of color as weaker, and more susceptible to disease, than the bodies of white men. Artifacts to demonstrate past ideas include eighteenth and nineteenth-century anatomical texts that contain the first depictions of the female skeleton and which attempted to locate differences between the sexes in every part of the human body.[31] In his 1829 book *Anatomy of the Bones of the Human Body*, for example, John Barclay compared the male skeleton to that of a horse, and the female skeleton to that of an ostrich. The tiny skull and

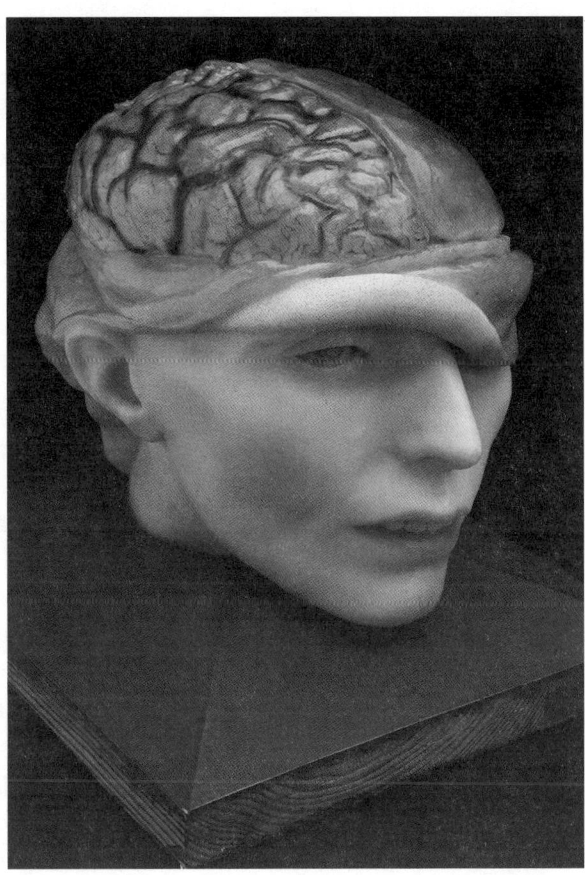

13.2 | Wax anatomical model of human head, showing the underlying structure of the brain, 1801–1900.

exaggeratedly large pelvis clearly suggest that women's bodies are designed primarily for childbearing rather than intellectual activity (see figure 13.1).

Drawing attention to the present, the exhibition relates historical examples (see figure 13.2) to recent research on the biology of sex differences in the following label and image:

> In the nineteenth century, at a time when women were arguing for a greater role in public life and equal status with men, scientists argued that their anatomy made them biologically unfit for advanced education or demanding intellectual work. Today, researchers have come to the conclusion that women and men are more

> similar than they are different, yet many remain fascinated by the subject of sex difference. Studies that claim to show how sex hormones "masculinize" or "feminize" the brain during its development in the womb mean less and less in a society where "women's work" can refer to anything from flying a plane to running a multinational corporation. Yet as women in the workplace find that their earnings and career prospects still do not match up with those of their male colleagues, should they look to social factors, or to science, for an explanation?

Visitors are also asked to consider the implications of recent research that claims that significant genetic differences "masculinize" heterosexual men's brains and "feminize" homosexual men's brains, and supposedly contribute to differences between men and women.

Other materials highlight the history of scientific racism and accounts of intellectual and physical differences between the races. Quotes describing the poor health of black soldiers in the American Civil War, for example, are contextualized by label text explaining the dire conditions these men were serving in and the reality that white soldiers were more likely to survive disease because they received more supplies and were better cared for, rather than because of any biological advantages. A present-day case study focuses on the role of genetic theory in reintroducing the idea of biologically based racial differences.[32] Genetic theories are included in each section of the exhibition, reflecting the current popularity of genetic research as a leading means of interpreting disease and bodily difference. This section also introduces the notion that explanations of difference and disease located entirely in the body exclude social factors that may also shape a person's intellectual and physical development, a theme that recurs throughout the exhibition.

Section two of the exhibit, "Deviant Bodies," focuses on the medicalization of homosexuality, and includes sexological texts that first defined "normal" heterosexuality and delineated homosexuality as a deviation from it, such as Richard von Krafft-Ebing's *Psychopathia Sexualis* (1892).[33] The exhibition notes that homosexuality was not removed from the mental health profession's encyclopedia, the *Diagnostic and Statistical Manual of Mental Disorders*, until 1973, following the emergence of the gay rights movement.[34] The present-day example for Deviant Bodies

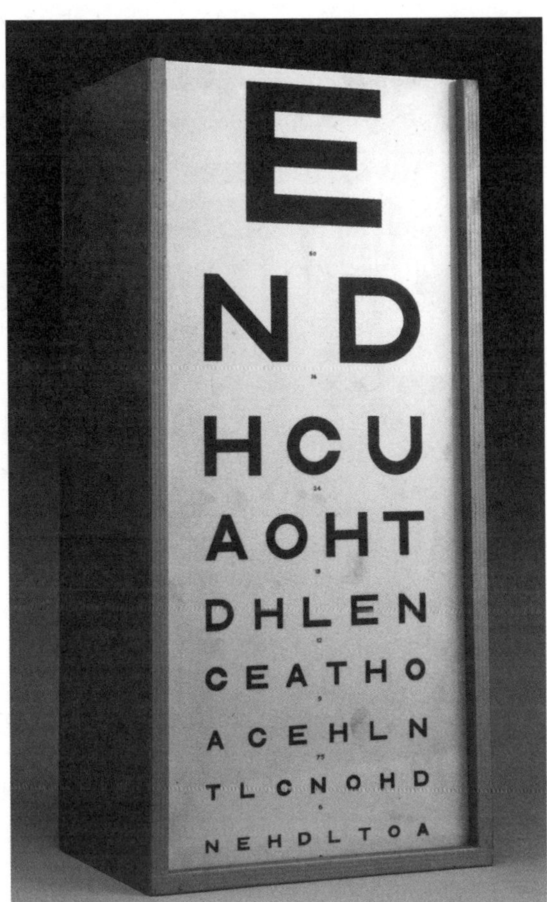

13.3 | Twentieth-century vision test based on the principles of the Snellen Eye Chart.

focuses on the search for a gay gene. An interactive kiosk poses a query about the political implications of this research, encouraging visitors to consider how medical diagnoses can be used both as empowering tools to access care and as repressive categories that invite invasive treatment efforts or cure. A display of electro-convulsive technologies used in "aversion therapy" treatments for homosexuality in the 1960s, and ephemera both endorsing and criticizing the idea of a genetic explanation for sexuality, illustrate this point.

The third section of the exhibition, "Disabled Bodies," will explore the construction of disabilities, using the introduction of the concept of 20/20 vision in 1862 by Dutch ophthalmologist Hermann Snellen as a key moment in the history of medicine that categorized the eyesight of people previously considered normal as abnormal.[35] The present-day examples of intersex conditions and genetic factors thought to predispose an individual to disease examine how new technologies reveal abnormalities that were previously undetectable. This section thus also raises the question of the purpose of diagnosing people as ill or *abnormal* when their conditions do not manifest as sickness or deformity.

The concluding section of the exhibition showcases contemporary images of idealized body types and variations from these, drawn from a wide variety of sources, from consumer advertising to plastic surgery manuals and physical fitness films, to encourage visitors to think about the ways that ideas about normal and *abnormal* bodies permeate culture (and how cultural trends may also inform medical research). (See figure 13.3.)

Engaging the Audience

Drawing on the principles of active learning and the model of the participatory museum, visitors have a series of opportunities to respond to the content of the exhibition.[36] In order to gauge their own perspectives and to enable them to explore the views of other attendees, in each section visitors are asked to assign a percentage value to the role of biology *versus* the role of society in shaping a person's intelligence, criminal tendencies, or sexuality. Individuals can cast their votes in an electronic kiosk and see how others have responded. Provocative questions are posed on the walls of each gallery, with visitor responses displayed for others to add to or comment on:

- *How can genetic explanations hurt or help individuals?*
- *Why is it important to measure physical or intellectual ability?*
- *Is there such a thing as a male or female brain?*

Visitors are also invited to comment on current trends or the changes they have noticed over the course of their lifetimes or in different contexts (from country to country, for example, among different age groups, or in various communities). Again, open-ended questions displayed in public forums where visitors can read one another's replies are used to encourage attendees to engage with each other.

In an area at the end of the exhibition, visitors are invited to apply the critical perspective cultivated in the galleries to the culture they are immersed in today. Facilitators provide materials for "culture jamming" activities, in which visitors can use art and media to deconstruct, critique, and reconstitute representations of bodies that they find offensive, stereotypical, or limiting.[37] Reproductions of historical illustrations and medical text included in the exhibition are provided, along with an array of mass culture materials, from paper dolls to magazine advertisements, as well as art supplies and computer terminals.[38] The area is staffed by young art students and activists interested or involved in culture jamming, who are on hand to offer ideas, share their own work, and help visitors use these materials to make their own pieces. Examples of submissions by previous visitors and exhibition staff are displayed in the gallery and online to give a sense of the wide range of possible approaches.

Artwork can also be submitted online, so that virtual visitors can participate in the activity, and also to allow gallery attendees to send in submissions created with their own materials and methods, perhaps incorporating their own photography or family memorabilia.[39]

Why Not? Imagining Problems and Possibilities

While some of the NLM's holdings contain materials that could illuminate personal experiences, attempts to represent the perspective of patients are relatively recent and would require expanded collection policies. The development of an exhibition provides the opportunity to build a museum's collection (of disability-related objects, for example) by moving beyond medical devices and preserving aspects of these histories that have been previously excluded. It may require additional work to locate and borrow other materials, in order to tell stories that go beyond the medical model to capture the experiences of people with disabilities.[40] The rewards of such work include the chance to engage with marginalized communities and disseminate stories that would otherwise remain unexplored, challenging standard narratives and common myths.

Exhibitions that re-evaluate an established history or include the perspective of people previously left out may also be especially appealing to visitors who have tired of the standard storyline, particularly if the topic has personal or contemporary relevance. As Carol Squiers, curator of the New York exhibition *The Body at Risk: Photography of Disorder, Illness, and Healing*, argues, "the body is now the contested point around which revolve fierce debates in the natural sciences, social sciences, religion, medicine, culture, politics, economics, and ethics about myriad issues including reproductive choice, gender discrimination, disease, aging, embryonic stem cell research, genetic modification, obesity, health care, health insurance, and the right to die."[41] The scarcity of exhibitions addressing the experience of illness and impairment thus results in missed opportunities to serve our audiences.

Museums could provide a space in which to confront fears about dying, to challenge prejudices about bodily difference, and to consider the impact of illness from the viewpoint of the sick, the healthcare profession, and the caregiver. More than being simply a site for health education on a particular topic, they might offer a cathartic environment in which visitors can consider aspects of embodiment they find frightening, confusing, or intriguing. Such practices have important implications for the experience of embodiment as well as its representation. Exhibitions on medical topics can potentially help individuals to reflect upon suffering and the nature of caregiving, and therefore have a profound effect on how we understand and experience health issues and the life cycle, as well as the way we respond to the disabilities or serious illnesses of ourselves and others.[42] Museums may even help equip visitors to participate in both policy-level debate (on the high-stakes issue of American health care reform, for example), as well as personal decision making regarding their own medical care. Curators of exhibitions on illness and impairment could play a significant role in challenging prejudice and discrimination, and in the process provide visitors with a provocative environment in which to consider fundamental questions about embodiment and mortality.

Although curatorial dreaming offers an escape from the practical constraints of real-world projects, it is also a valuable means by which to consider the kinds of restrictions that might undermine this proposal, in part to explain some of the reasons why such an exhibition might not be undertaken. In this example, it is likely that stakeholders from the medical community would be hesitant to highlight the negative uses of scientific theorizing in organizing unequal societies. Such narratives are more likely to be tolerated if they are presented as examples of a past era of ignorance, and contrasted with today's science.

Questions might also arise over the exhibition of discriminatory images and ideas, just as racist imagery – even when used to discuss the history of racism – has caused controversy and pain. While I recognize that some of the material displayed might be upsetting to visitors, part of the goal of the exhibition is to reposition these examples as sources to be critiqued.[43] By displaying such problematic artifacts representing the legacies of discrimination based on sex, race, disability, and sexuality, my intention is to illustrate the wider implications of biologically based explanations of human variation, and to encourage visitors to draw parallels across social groups, rather than drawing distinctions between them. Nevertheless, opponents might object to a discussion of sexuality for certain age groups, or argue that the representation of homosexuality in a federal institution is politically partisan and unjustifiable.[44] Yet by exploring the demedicalization of homosexuality, the exhibition focuses on incontrovertible historical events (rather than political positions) and might be defended on such grounds. Furthermore, medical museums, as opposed to science education centres, are not intended primarily to serve young audiences, and indeed, might be expected to host exhibitions containing "adult" content. Design and marketing of the exhibition could also be targeted to young adult and adult audiences rather than children.

On a practical level, the culture jamming activities could also create legal problems if the artistic use of copyrighted material was challenged by any of the companies whose advertising was re-appropriated. Given that the likely use of the material would be to criticize the attitudes and activities of such companies, attempts to censor this could be a major concern. Encouraging visitors to incorporate their own photographs or exhibit their critiques of other representations of bodies might also create a hostile or volatile environment that could prove difficult to manage. While devising a policy to prohibit pornographic imagery might be widely agreed on by museum staff, it could prove difficult to determine just what constitutes an offensive body image, especially when that may hinge, in part, on the identity of the creator of such an image – which may not be clear at the time it is submitted, or to later visitors.

As long as it remains only a curatorial dream, we can only imagine the objections and obstacles that might hinder this project. Yet the activity of musing on its possibility has a number of practical and intellectual benefits. Most simply, this exercise serves as a public pitch for an idea, and may well attract useful feedback from museum colleagues to improve the project, to bring it to fruition, or to collaborate on similar activities. Positive responses to such a proposal might be used to help justify related activities within an institution, or to raise funds. Negative responses could inform the reworking of the project to better address attitudes among visitors or to reach new target audiences. Speculative discussions of the problems in mounting such an exhibition may also allow for more honest conversations about the political forces that frame museum work than accounts of real projects ever can. This will be useful not simply to alert critics to the factors that constrain exhibition development, but also as a productive means to evaluate some of the assumptions that may inhibit particular projects. By identifying possible objections, we can begin to verify or discount them. By dreaming up exhibitions that might not yet be possible, we are taking the first steps toward their eventual realization.

CHAPTER FOURTEEN

Reel Objects: Movies in Museums[1]

JANICE BAKER

Something in the world forces us to think. This something is an object not of recognition but of fundamental encounter.
Gilles Deleuze[2]

Reel Objects: Movies in Museums is an imagined exhibition that plays with representations of museums and cultural artifacts in mainstream and high art films. The curatorial premise of the exhibition is not to didactically interpret artifacts but to complicate interpretation by presenting cinematic experiences of museum spaces. The exhibition whimsically suggests a mismatch between actual encounters with objects and the ways that visitor and artifact engagements are represented in critical literature on museums. As cinematic images, material objects often acquire an agency that is distinct from their use in the everyday. When museum artifacts are represented in films, this distinction is further heightened, with cultural objects defying all manner of common-sense expectation, most notably the notion that linear time and identity are fixed and immutable.[3]

Museums are reputed to rationally order and demarcate human and non-human worlds, yet in the cinematic realm museums and galleries become sites that variously disturb logic and common sense. There are recurring instances in movies of boundary-crossing such as visitors and artifacts time-travelling and artifacts that "come alive" and join forces with a hapless visitor. The effect is not unlike Alice in Wonderland's fall into a fantastical other world. *Reel Objects: Movies in Museums* brings together artifacts on-screen (reel) and off-screen (real) in a single exhibition space, to provoke thinking about audience-object interactions in ways that diverge from the interpretative framing of the museum in critical museology discourse.

Reel Objects is imagined installed in Hackett Hall,[4] an exhibition space that forms part of the Western Australian Museum in Perth. Originally the state's public library, the building opened in 1913. I have selected this venue for its architecture and "old world" ambiance that resonates with the way museums often feature in films as musty and antiquarian sites of adventure. Within the space of the hall, wrought iron spiral staircases access two levels of interior balconies lined with bookshelves and cabinets. The soaring upper balcony features skylights, magnificent wooden arches, and a pressed-tin ceiling with a striking art nouveau design. The venue's "atmospherics" heighten the exhibition's embrace of drama and spectacle.

Reel Objects presents a "cinematic museum," a space hovering between the narrative, diegetic world of film and the physical here and now of an exhibition. The exhibit – comprising audio-visual screenings, film stills, posters, artworks, taxidermy, and an aquarium – occupies four interconnected galleries created within the expanse of the building. Each gallery dwells on a theme: *Desires and Obsessions*; *Transgressions*; *Objects Go Wild*; and *Transformations*. These themes foreshadow the mood of each gallery, set by wall-sized projections compiled of scenes and sequences sutured together from scores of films.

The film montages depict events taking place within, or around, museums. The "real" objects installed in each gallery of the exhibition reflect or respond to these events. Some of the "reel" museums in the films exist (the Louvre), others are "modelled" on actual museums (Istanbul's Topkapi Museum), while a few are sites of fantasy (Gotham City Museum). Still images, and occasionally a film poster, appear between moving sequences; the whole is edited to present a seamless, yet temporally and generically chaotic medley of museum events – images from a recent action film cut to a dance routine from a 1940s musical comedy, followed by a scene from a 1980s horror film and so on. There are sequences drawn from silent film, Hollywood classics, and popular blockbusters, as well as arthouse and experimental cinema.

Reel Objects is intended to be accessible to a general audience. It contains pathos, humour, nostalgia, adventure, dramatic action, scary monsters, and "stars" (including Cary Grant, Audrey Hepburn, Steve Martin, and Ricky Gervais). For critically savvy museum goers, the interaction between "real" and "reel" time offers a twist on the notion of the "interactive museum," which in contemporary museology tends to refer to digitally based interactions between audiences and objects. The cinematic "immersion" of the exhibition will also appeal, for obvious reasons, to film buffs.

Concerning Theory

Connecting physical space with the "reel" space of film highlights the cinematic quality of objects within the display environment of the museum. Emphasizing the "non-didactic" aspect of objects draws attention to the disparity between what artifacts actually *do* at the level of affecting experience, and the way that objects are often interpreted in the literature of museology.[5]

In movies, museums tend to be contradictory sites; behind their classical façades and ordering taxonomies there often lurk inexplicable and uncontrollable desires. Initially museums appear as public sites where a well-behaved citizenry complies with convention in the viewing and appreciation of artifacts. This befits an institution founded on the notion that "civilizing" knowledge is acquired through objective empirical observation. Such "didactic" encounters are often exaggerated in films, with objects stereotyped within such a framing. However, invariably, this presentation is disrupted by the advent of a more serendipitous, adventurous side of the museum's Enlightenment legacy. The American Museum of Natural History in New York, and the Louvre in Paris are two paradigmatic modern museums that are particularly prone to cinematic disruption. Among other uncommon events, the Louvre has been, for example, the stage for the theft of the *Mona Lisa* in *Good Morning Boys* (directed by Marcel Varnel, 1937), a running race through the Grande Galerie in *Band of Outsiders* (directed by Jean-Luc Godard, 1964), and a key site for Opus Dei conspiracy in *The Da Vinci Code* (directed by Ron Howard, 2006).

Reel Objects generates a heightened sense of the hybridity of the museum experience, where common sense is tempered by the "irrational," strange, or unusual. The often-vivid transformations that visitors, artifacts, and sometimes the architecture of a museum undergo in a film hints at human desire for curiosity, wonder, and a touch of the macabre.

Thus we observe two school children in *The Relic* (directed by Peter Hyams, 1997) express enthusiasm about the possibility of seeing eyeballs in jars during a museum visit, recalling the desire voiced by the child in James Fenton's poem, who asks an attendant at Oxford's Pitt Rivers Museum, "Please sir, where's the withered hand?"[6]

Reel Objects demonstrates that potent encounters between museum objects and people often exceed (or even belie) the certainty of didactic messages that museums offer. The implication here is that the effect of objects to generate meaning *outside the museological staging of knowledge* requires a material mode of theoretical inquiry. Important cultural theorists, including Donna Haraway, Tony Bennett, and Mieke Bal, have focused on the relationship between the museum's construction of knowledge and the ideological and governmental power that knowledge wields. I mention these critics, specifically, because each has dwelt on knowledge-power relations in the American Museum of Natural History (AMNH) – an institution, like the Louvre, featured regularly in movies.

Donna Haraway's case study examines activities of the early years of the AMNH, arguing that the "natural sciences" were used by the museum as an antidote to what the great capitalists perceived was a looming class war. To this end, the museum's "public health role" was achieved through racial doctrines disguised as scientific knowledge and realized in activities of exhibition and conservation.[7] Tony Bennett argues that the AMNH is furthermore a vehicle for promulgating a ruling-class ethos as part of a larger social and political apparatus related to American neoliberalism.[8] Mieke Bal contributes to the critique, arguing that the museum's narrative continues to be "that of fixation, of the denial of time." Following Haraway, she situates this ahistorical monumentality with the museum's legacy of "comprehensive collecting as an activity within colonialism."[9]

The grounding of museum analyses in critical theory is a vital contribution to a rigorous cultural critique. But the powerful revelations of such analyses make it difficult to engage with museum encounters outside the contexts of critical theory. Critical theory – whether through analyses of museums' gendering of meaning, psychoanalytic concern with the relation between an object and development of the human psyche, or semiotic readings of exhibits as ideological texts – tends to frame museums in terms of their historical legacy as an authoritative Enlightenment institution. By acknowledging the agency of objects to provoke encounters that may exceed this legacy, *Reel Objects* shifts attention from overly absolutist approaches to exhibits.

Donald Preziosi gives expression to this affect when he recounts that as a child he used to lie under the dinosaur skeleton at the AMNH pretending to be wounded prey. He recalls being seduced by the exhibits, and "the visceral feeling of being pulled everywhere by the Museum and not wanting to leave."[10] The museum as a place for such wild imagining recurs in films, with outcomes distant from the concerns of Haraway, Bennett, and Bal in their critical analyses. It is tempting to consider whether other children, across the years that these critics examine, were similarly affected by artifacts, but not by the "civilizing," moral, disciplinary mandate set by the trustees of the AMNH.

A Cine/museal Folding

The film sequences are projected in each gallery to roll in continuous loops, so it is largely inconsequential at what point viewing begins. While benches are provided to enable an orderly experience of cinema viewing, people are also likely to stand and move around the space as they glimpse the screen, and visitors may come and go as they please. Referencing the ubiquity of benches as museum furniture, the presence in each gallery of "the bench" acts as a motif connecting "reel" and "real" exhibition spaces.

Reel Objects intentionally hovers between a museum exhibition and cinematic viewing. Neither clearly one nor the other, the norms of spectatorship associated with screen space and exhibition space fold together to create an unfamiliar cine/museal experience. The exhibition is not preoccupied by a film's narrative meaning or creative merit; nor is it concerned with historical analyses of artifacts. The interest lies rather in "evoking" the affecting experience of the on-screen museum visitor for the "real" visitor to the exhibition. Despite a film's genre, era, and production values, the crux is that the museum represented in each film scenario operates as a site of uncommon experience. While the specific movie encounter can obviously not be reproduced, there is nevertheless a direct cinematic impact and transference of affect between the "reel" and the "real."

Many of the film images in *Reel Objects* involve characters viewing artifacts; they sit, stand and move through exhibits, visibly transfixed, indifferent, seduced, bemused, alarmed, and sometimes even harmed. The films' protagonists move from one gallery to another, just as do the visitors in the physical space of Hackett Hall. Even when a museum in a film is the location for an apparently unremarkable meeting, the liaison ultimately hints at something unconventional or untoward – be this in Woody Allen's recurring use of galleries, such as Tate Modern for an inopportune meeting between ex-lovers in *Match Point* (2005), or criminals and lawyers conspiring in the National Gallery of Victoria in *Animal Kingdom* (directed by David Michôd, 2010).

Through the projections, visitors are confronted with artifacts, displays, and diorama influencing events and participating in the action. This phantasmagoria exemplifies the inherent ambivalence associated with museums, and responds to their "life" outside the objectivity attached to human-centred perspectives. The ahistorical, non-chronological encounters that visitors experience in galleries of the (mostly) Western world collapse the integrity of knowing the world only through linear time, marking the museum as a kind of time-less, other space. All in all, the cine/museal menagerie created in *Reel Objects* cumulatively evokes an impression that museums, through interactions between human and nonhuman subjects, are far from straightforward places.

The Exhibition

The title of the exhibition and a short introductory text panel is clearly apparent to visitors on arrival at the venue. The introductory text briefly outlines the thematic focus of the four galleries and encourages visitors to enjoy the experience. A handout provides visitors with a filmography – title, filmmaker, and year of production of the clips they will view, in the hope that it will pique curiosity prior to entering the exhibition.

Desires and Obsessions

Upon entering the first gallery, *Desires and Obsessions*, the immediate focal point is the cinematic projection. Visitors are confronted by a mashing of scenes that includes a man in the late nineteenth century gawking at a classical sculpture of Venus, a *femme fatale* in the 1960s crooning over a bejewelled dagger, and a series of cinematic seductions stimulated by encounters with objects that vary from the sentimental to the dangerous.

The evocative Venus sculpture appears in the 1898 silent film *Exhibition* (also known as *Come Along, Do!*) directed by Robert W. Paul. It is apposite to include this short film and its Victorian London art display, as this representation both resonates, and is incongruous with the cultural heritage of Hackett Hall. The link between the "reel" on-screen venue and "real" venue connects and muddies past and present, and acts as a kind of filmic talisman that attends to the unique ability of museums, as with cinema, to re-view and complicate time by the act of its representation. It also highlights that objects can be engaged by visitors in ways that do not conform to intention. In the film, having ventured off a London street a "labouring" man and his wife are seated on a bench imbibing refreshments beside the entrance to an art display. Two smartly dressed women enter the gallery, and this encourages the couple to do the same. The man is immediately entranced by a sculpture of a nude Venus, and his irritated wife attempts to drag him away. Class and gender difference are clearly apparent in the film's narrative and this was no doubt the basis of its humour for a nineteenth-century audience. Echoing the "object of attention" in the film, sculptures and images inspired by the Venus nude are displayed through the *Desires and Obsessions* section of *Reel Objects*. The presence of these nudes – classical, modern, and contemporary, including, for example, a homoerotic image of a male body by Robert Mapplethorpe – is to create a fold between the "reel" and "real" that gives the man's encounter with the nude Venus provocative expression in the present. The cultural context defining what constitutes artistic merit, creative expression, and expected audience behaviour comes into view here, not in a didactic sense, but through reel/real visitor responses to images of bodies.

The potency of (supposedly) static, non-sentient objects is enacted in the galleries via portraits and taxidermy animals that inspire the uncanny feeling of being watched. The material effect of this immaterial gaze is conveyed in a sequence from Brian de Palma's thriller *Dressed to Kill* (1980). A woman sits on a bench in a room of contemporary works in the Metropolitan Museum of Art. She stares at a vivid portrait of a woman whose painted gaze stares wistfully back at her. The empathy between the women is palpable. A painted portrait of an ape provides an additional disarming gaze. A strange man sits beside the woman. The portraits participate in the cinematic seduction that follows; intensifying the flesh-and-blood interaction between the two visitors, it seems that the pictorial images propel their affair.

The agency of a painted portrait to disturb characters' perception and motivation is also a powerful effect in Alfred Hitchcock's psychological thriller *Vertigo* (1958). Two museums are locations in *Vertigo* and both appear in *Reel Objects*. So too does the film's famous opening credit sequence, of a spiral emerging and spinning hypnotically outward from a human eye, drawing the viewer into the diegetic world of the film. This effect reverberates back into Hackett Hall with the title sequence enlarged and viewed as a sequence of frames along the gallery wall.

In the screening, the spiral sequence cuts to the classic Hitchcock scene of Scottie, an acrophobic detective, following the enigmatic Madeleine to the art gallery at the Palace of the Legion of Honor in San Francisco. Madeleine sits on a bench transfixed, viewing a portrait of Carlotta, a woman she resembles. Scottie's fascination with Madeleine is palpable, but there is clearly something not quite right. The all-encompassing nature of obsession is evoked via the spiral motif that recurs in subtle details, such as the way in which Madeleine and Carlotta's hair is similarly curled.[11]

In another excerpt from *Vertigo*, the couple climb the bell tower of the Mission San Juan Bautista, a museum outside San Francisco. The architecture in the narrow tower is cinematically conveyed as a spiral, repeating the hypnotic vision from the title sequence. The bell tower scene ends with Madeleine falling from the tower to her death. The recurring spiral imagery echoes in the architecture of Hackett Hall with its multiple spiral staircases and high ceiling.

Time experienced as spiral rather than linear is also evoked in sequences excerpted from *The Stendhal Syndrome* (directed by Dario Argento, 1996), where characters drift in and out of the pictorial plane of historical paintings. These include the film's protagonist, an undercover detective who visits the Uffizi Gallery in Florence to locate a serial killer. At first the museum is what might be expected: crowds of tourists view the art, catalogues in hand. However, as befits the illness reflected in the film's title, the detective is increasingly transfixed by the paintings. She stares intently at Caravaggio's *Medusa*, and at Piero Della Francesca's *Diptych of the Duchess and Duke of Urbino*. The Renaissance couple in the diptych are represented in profile – they will stare "forever." The intense, permanent pictorial gaze in these "static" images contrasts with the brevity of the "living" gaze. However the detective's lingering viewing disrupts the stasis by drawing the viewer into her powerful experience. Her transfixion turns into hallucination while viewing Bruegel's *The Flight of Icarus* – she/we plunge into the painting's ocean and swim amongst large fish – enormous grouper – one of which she kisses in a grotesque dream image. She wakes with her lips bleeding; having fainted, she is helped up from the floor of the gallery by the killer she is pursuing.

In response to this startling cinematic moment, a large glass aquarium is installed in the gallery. Fish swimming in the aquarium link the film narrative with the physical space of the visitor. There is a sense in which neither the fishes nor the viewing experience can be contained by the framings that normally operate to provide meaning. There is no textual information for exhibition visitors about this cross-over display. The point is not to interpret what the connection might mean, but to provoke thinking about interactions with objects by deactivating the conventional mode of experiencing them.

In movies museums are frequently imagined as sites where reason and common sense are thrown to the wind as a consequence of an intense desire or motivation. The Hollywood screwball comedy *Bringing Up Baby* (directed by Howard Hawks, 1938) enacts this scenario, climaxing in a seduction with an erotic tension symbolized by a dinosaur skeleton collapsing. A flighty socialite climbs the scaffolding supporting the enormous bony structure in the dour Stuyvesant Museum of Natural History, a private museum located somewhere in New England. She is intent on delivering the skeleton's missing bone to the museum's bemused palaeontologist, who is working at the top of the skeleton. The precious intercostal clavicle has escaped his possession for the duration of the film. As she reaches the palaeontologist, the monumental façade collapses. In this comedy of desire, obsession with a material artifact is on a par, and then replaced by the uncontrollable idiosyncrasy of human passion.

Another film that plays on obsession and desire through a museum artifact is *Topkapi* (directed by Jules Dassin, 1964). Ottoman treasures are exhibited in the labyrinth of buildings comprising Istanbul's historical Topkapi Museum (which once housed the sultanate's harem). In an opening scene from the film, a beautiful jeweller and seductress entices viewers into the museum, where she shares her obsession for an emerald-encrusted Ottoman dagger. She admits the object makes strange things happen to her and plans to steal it.

It is of course not surprising that museums in films are sites for extraordinary thefts, given the precious objects they often contain. A selection of stills and posters in *Reel Objects* provides a survey of museum thefts from films that include *Good Morning Boys*, *The Hot Rock* (directed by Peter Yates, 1972), *The Thomas Crown Affair* (directed by John McTiernan, 1999) and *Small Time Crooks* (directed by Woody Allen, 2000). The images from *Topkapi* trace a particularly breathtaking "mission impossible" museum heist. The thieves perilously cross the sprawling roof of the Topkapi Museum. The rooftop walk high above Istanbul dismays one thief, whose fear of falling takes the form of double vision; a cinematic image reminiscent of *Vertigo*'s endless spiral. Reaching the right location the thieves lower a gymnast upside down into the gallery by an ingenious rope and pulley apparatus. Using a magnet contraption, he is able to lift the glass lid of the display case, steal the coveted dagger, and exit the way he arrived.

Transgressions

From "Desires and Obsessions," visitors enter "Transgressions," a space that focuses on the fictional association of museums with the dark and macabre. The types of characters encountered range from Dr Hannibal Lecter, the cannibal/curator in *Hannibal* (directed by Ridley Scott, 2001), to the stricken museum scientist-cum-monster in *The Relic* (directed by Peter Hyams, 1996). Befitting the thematic focus of the gallery, the lighting is dim, with artifacts spotlit to starkly convey features and isolate objects within the space.

Dr Lecter is encountered in Florence presenting an erudite lecture in the fifteenth-century Palazzo Capponi, where he lives and works as a historian of its impressive art collection. He describes Dante's seventh circle of hell with the aid of renderings and paintings from the collection, works that both describe and anticipate a grisly murder at the wall of the Palazzo. From this gruesome evocation, the projection cuts to *The Da Vinci Code,* and a curator pursued by a monk through the galleries of the Louvre. The monk's cowl moves as a shadow across the walls, merging with religious images of sorrow, suffering, and death. The monk might have stepped from one of these paintings, out of place and out of time. This segues to Gotham City's Art Museum and a sequence from *Batman* (directed by Tim Burton, 1989) presenting the abject world of Batman's archrival, The Joker.

The Joker and his henchmen deface iconic works in the Gotham Collection, including paintings by Degas and Rembrandt, as well as Gilbert Stuart's portrait of George Washington. The Joker displays a penchant for contemporary art, by sparing Francis Bacon's *Figure with Meat* (1954), an image of a Pope on an electric-chair-throne, perched in front of strung up carcases. The bizarre sequence in the museum ignites The Joker's self-proclaimed "aesthetic of the homicidal artist," an abominable hysteria on a par with the papal flaying in Bacon's painting.

Like other sections of the exhibition, the transference between the narrative world in the film and the physical space of Hackett Hall is not achieved through a didactic text. It is instead manifested through connections discerned by visitors, who are led to make their own impression of strange encounters. One such encounter is a display of paintings provoking reflection on abjection and the human body, including several paintings by Francis Bacon. Transacting the exhibition's shift between "reel" and "real," Bacon's images of distorted bodies have an unsettling force that pictorially ruptures assumptions that bodies are stable forms. The paintings, with their strangely abstracted limbs and organs, twist physical features into impossible positions. They turn the body inside out, as it were, in an effect that is similar to the abject realm depicted in the film clips. As Ernst van Alphen explains of Bacon's paintings, "It is as if our skin is penetrated by affects generated by the presence of what we see: not a mediated story, but the material reality of the painting."[12]

The linkages between "reel" and "real" objects in the exhibition are an imaginative extension of the unique assemblages generated between people and museum artifacts. With this fusion the exhibitions moves toward abandoning the usual anthropocentric opposition of human subject and nonhuman object, the first supposedly possessing cognitive agency and the second lacking it. The reel/real juxtaposition also gestures to the uncommon agency of the materiality of the cinematic image. Film itself becomes noticeable as an artifact, a molecular/celluloid-digital entity with its own duration and agency.[13] Film stock/digital

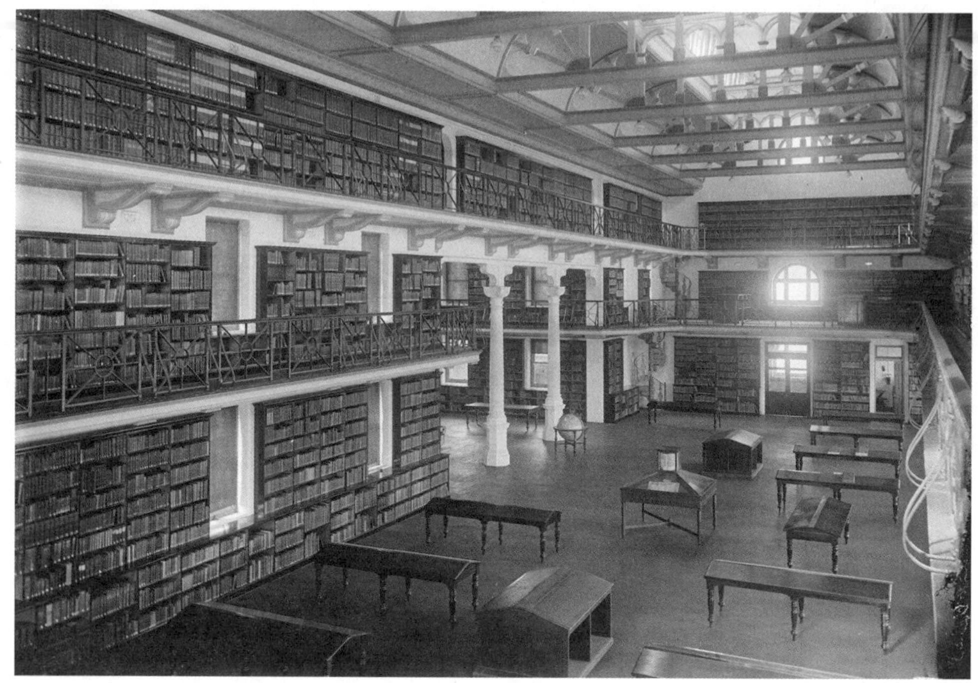

14.1 | Interior of Hackett Hall, Western Australian Museum, 1913.

bits and museum objects are both assumed to be static, yet are involved in the generation of powerful affects. The various interactions, juxtapositions, and merging in the exhibition between "reel" and "real" thus help to unlink humanist assumptions constituting the "self" as essentially separate from the object world, and to rethink relations between human and nonhuman objects.

The museum's relation to that which is deemed abject has a precursor in the horror films that appear in *Reel Objects*; *Mystery of the Wax Museum* (directed by Michael Curtiz, 1933), *The Murder in the Museum* (directed by Melville Shyer, 1934), *The Frozen Ghost* (directed by Harold Young, 1945), and *Horrors of the Black Museum* (directed by Arthur Crabtree, 1959). In these macabre images of museums, artifacts are often human bodies, coated and sculpted in wax and put on display to intrigue and entertain the public with their surprising likeness to a "real" person. Film posters and still images from these films are displayed in the gallery to simulate the *frisson* of cinematic horror and convey the tenacious curiosity that humans have for aesthetic reproductions of violence.

A selection of scenes in the audio-visual screening are drawn from *The Relic*, in which a scientist working in a North American natural history museum meddles with DNA and magic, consequently morphing into a reptilian monster. As an alien-like "relic" he inhabits the museum's basement, emerging at intervals to feed. An episode from the film shows the creature surface at a gala opening of the blockbuster exhibition *Superstition*, to an exceedingly unpleasant outcome.

As well as "supernatural" and "grisly" acts, film sequences in "Transgressions" also deal with less demonstrably demonic crimes. One is an extended chase through the galleries of the British Museum in *Blackmail* (1929), and another is a "shoot out" in the New York Guggenheim in *The International* (directed by Tom Tykwer, 2009). The black and white images from *Blackmail* show a man pursued by police through the streets of London and into the British Museum. He hides in galleries behind showcases and pillars before being forced to climb to the roof of the Library Reading Room, where he falls to his death through the glass dome. This scene curiously echoes the architecture of Hackett Hall and the library reading room with its skylights, balconies, and bookcases. The dramatic episode from *Blackmail* is followed by images from *The International*, and an extended gunfight that commences at the top of the spiral ramp and winds its way down to the foyer in a dramatic descent through the building, a counterpoint to the equally dramatic ascent of the staging in *Blackmail*.

The multimedia and video installations on display in the museum during the Guggenheim shootout augment the drama, complicating the action with images that resonate with the unfolding mayhem. These screen works add another level of viewing for the "real" visitor to the exhibition, like a body in a hall of mirrors. The violence done to the iconic building transgresses the modernist aesthetic; the modern museum exemplified by Frank Lloyd Wright's spirals is riddled with bullet holes. Following the violence, a stark silence envelops the battered space. A striking image from *Blackmail* has a similar effect, with a large Egyptian death mask in the British Museum maintaining its extraordinary presence, unperturbed by the "noise" of human misadventure.

Objects Go Wild

The third gallery, "Objects Go Wild," is a labyrinthine space suggesting a nineteenth-century museum atmosphere, where cabinets are crammed with fascinating objects. The screening accompanying "Objects Go Wild" focuses on museum objects which, for one reason or another, are no longer "tame." The exhibit space features specimens and objects in keeping with the projected imagery; however, the cultural artifacts are Australian in origin not Anglo-American.

By this stage of their visit, audiences have already confronted the potency of the "reel object" in reference to desire, obsession, and transgression. In "Objects Go Wild," the division of the "real" and the "reel" is further breached: mummies walk, talk, and suffer unrequited love, and painted portraits seek revenge and world domination.

Visitors watch as a portrait of Vigo, a seventeenth-century Carpathian magician with supernatural powers, possesses a curator at the Manhattan Museum of Art (*Ghostbusters 2*, directed by Ivan Reitman, 1989). An outcome of this transference is ... the museum coated in a living slime that reacts to human emotions. The projection shifts to an Egyptian mummy rising from his sarcophagus in the Cairo Museum (*The Mummy*, directed by Karl Freund, 1932). This introduces a montage of images from mummy films, including images that spoof these films from *Abbott and Costello Meet the Mummy* (directed by Charles Lamont, 1955) and a scene from *Night at the Museum* (directed by Shawn Levy, 2006), in which the Akhmenrah's mummy, who speaks English from its many years as an exhibit at Cambridge, is released. Enlarged screen stills and film posters from the scores of mummy films produced since the 1930s feature along the walls of the gallery.

A model dinosaur references a scene from *Night at the Museum,* in which the museum's night guard is confronted by a dinosaur skeleton absconded from its platform. This is the first of numerous encounters with taxidermy animals and historical characters who roam the museum in defiance of their static representation. Amid the taxidermy imaginary, the guard is confronted by maverick and disgruntled occupants of dioramas, including a miniature Roman legion and characters from the "wild west" American frontier, who resent their museal impotence.

Cut into this "adult" action is a sequence from the animated preschooler show "The Backyardingans" episode *The Art Is on the Loose.*[14] Children act out roles in an art gallery; one is a night security guard, the others are characters who jump in and out of paintings, where they become a part of the frame's internal landscape or event. All this activity is danced to the flamenco.

As well as coping with unruly artifacts, the guard in *Night at the Museum* has to contend with a museum director whose character parodies the elitist "old museology," which critical museologist Peter Vergo likens to "a living fossil." He expands the metaphor by comparing the museum and coelacanth, whose brain shrinks in the course of its development so that "in the end it occupies only a fraction of the space available to it."[15] The pompous museum director disdains visitors, an elitism ultimately thwarted when visitors get what they desire from the museum – encounters with "living artifacts."

Artifacts are also defiantly alive to influence the action in the gay musical *Zero Patience* (directed by John Greyson, 1993). Inexplicably the nineteenth-century explorer, fantasy writer and sexually conflicted Sir Richard F. Burton is chief taxidermist in the late twentieth century at the Royal Ontario Museum in Toronto. Artifacts in Burton's *pièce de résistance,* a Hall of Contagion, leave their dioramas to perform a routine that exposes his misconceptions about the spread of the AIDS virus and his prejudice toward sufferers of the disease. The artifacts in his displays rebel against the inappropriate way they have been utilized by scientific research.

The anarchical artifacts in *Zero Patience* are poignant talismans that preface the misuse of Native American culture in an excerpt of images from the Hollywood musical *On the Town* (directed by Gene Kelly and Stanley Donen, 1949). This sequence in the American Museum of Natural History involves an ebullient song-and-dance routine performed by sailors on twenty-four-hour leave and their "gals," set among the museum's indigenous artifacts. They incorporate musical instruments, totems, and regalia into their performance and mimic a tribal dance. As part of the routine, one character recites her infatuation with "primitive man," an obsession that endears her to a sailor who resembles a mannequin of Neanderthal man. A consequence of all this ecstatic courting is (yet another) dinosaur skeleton collapsing; the didactic museum again subverted by the antics of visitors.

The overt ethnographic stereotyping of "the primitive" in *On the Town*, besides its patent silliness, is a confrontation for exhibition visitors with a colonial mindset that frames indigenous cultures as homogenous and "uncivilized." A wall text draws attention to the insensitivity of the 1940s film, incorporating a prescient call by cultural theorist James Clifford for a new approach to the interpretation of non-Western objects: "Seen in their nomadic resistance to classification they could remind us of our lack of self-possession, of the artifices we employ to gather a world sensibly around us."[16]

Transformations

Interactions between human and nonhuman worlds evoked by visitor/artifact assemblages in movies in museums are enacted in many ways. The final gallery, in contrast to the clutter and apparent disorder of the previous room, has the ambiance of a contemporary art space: a sparse "white cube," furnished only with benches provided to view the screening.

A sequence in the Louvre from *Funny Face* (directed by Stanley Donen, 1957) shows a fashion model inspired to mimic the evocative gesture of flight of the museum's iconic Greek sculpture *The Victory of Samothrace.* Modelling a crimson *haute couture* gown, she emerges as a diminutive figure from behind the large sculpture, adopting its pose; her arms are raised as wings as she descends the museum's grand staircase to the delight of her photographer. The performance engages with the impact of the famous sculpture, as the garment of marble with its sumptuous folds and the flight of the model form an inseparable, experiential cinematic assemblage.

A similarly audacious interaction features in *The Thomas Crown Affair* (1999). Several sequences from this film are screened, including a scene in which a bench in the centre of a gallery of Impressionist art is ingeniously employed in the theft of a Monet painting. There is also a sequence in which René Magritte's surreal portrait *The Son of Man* (1964) is mimicked by art collector Thomas Crown and a group of actors. They "purloin" the pictorial image by wearing suits and donning bowler hats, traversing New York's Museum of Modern Art to create a dance of multiple identities that facilitates an art un-theft (the missing Monet reappears on the gallery wall).

A tacit belief in the ability of museum objects to effect change is part and parcel of the museum we encounter in films. In *L.A. Story* (directed by Mick Jackson, 1991), a disillusioned weatherman rollerblades unannounced, and with great panache, through the Los Angeles County Museum of Art. As he glides and pirouettes through the galleries, artworks turn or respond to his performance in approval. In *Me and Orson Welles* (directed by Richard Linklater, 2009), a writer and her friend touch a priceless Grecian Urn to bring luck; they race gleefully through the gallery to escape reprimand. Their misdemeanour proves effective as her story (of a writer inspired by museums' fracturing of time) is published in *The New Yorker*. In Jean Luc Godard's *Band of Outsiders* (1964) three disaffected young people race through the Louvre's grand gallery in an attempt to break the world record for running through the museum. A sequence from Bernardo Bertolucci's *The Dreamers* (2003) replicates the original event. In these various scenarios characters use the museum to momentarily quell the demands of their mundane, quotidian lives.

Several sequences from *Russian Ark* (directed by Alexander Sokurov, 2002) are embedded in this final screening. Filmed entirely in the Hermitage Museum in St Petersburg the movie is a single take – a long, continuous visual shot – through thirty-three rooms of the museum. In the absence of editing, there are no gaps in the film in which to create the illusion that time is constructed of a past, present, and future. In images from the film, a nineteenth-century French diplomat and art connoisseur takes the (unseen) narrator/film director and the viewer on a tour of the museum. As they drift from gallery to gallery, visitors from across three centuries are encountered. Visitors, artifacts, and the image become equally timeless; the cine/museum space collapses.

Edited between sequences in the screening are still images from Chris Marker's *La Jetée* (1962), a short science fiction film that consists almost entirely of still, black and white photographs. A man sent back in time meets a woman among the exhibits in a natural history museum. A voice-over describes them all as timeless animals. The only colour or movement in the film occurs in a solitary image of an eye that "looks"; a gaze that pierces the illusory screen space of the viewer and merges the "reel" and the "real" so they are rendered imaginatively indiscernible.

The inclusion of shots from *La Jetée* adds a certain intrigue to the screening, particularly for those aware of Marker's homage to Hitchcock's *Vertigo,* and both filmmakers' interest in Marcel Proust's evocation of time and memory. *La Jetée* cinematically enacts a doubling of the self; a sense of being as an actual present perception and at the same time a virtual memory of the present – the sense that there is a recollection of the present, contemporaneous with the present itself. It is this constant movement of the self as an interaction between two spaces/times that discerns fixed identity as an illusion. A sense of visitors and museum objects merging in reel/real space is the desired evocation of *Reel Objects.*

Coda

Reel Objects: Movies in Museums imagines visitors transported outside the conventional "knowing" of objects in museums. This "dream" accords with James Elkins's call for greater engagement with profound encounters in art museums. Elkins highlights a disdain for "feeling" in relation to art, suggesting that "tearless" art historians and academics (himself included) distrust strong emotions, seeing in them a form of manipulation. In seeking to understand why some people weep in response to an artwork, Elkins revisits theories long discarded as "false" and unfashionable, noting for example that "trance theory'" – the idea that a painting can be a bridge to another world – is "far better able to explain strong affect than well behaved, legitimate theory."[17]

Extending Elkins's notion to all museums – by way of the mysterious and magical happenings in movie museums – is not to suggest there is a lack of "spiritual" awareness in contemporary theory and curatorship. Rather, in staging these affecting encounters in the cinematic museum, *Reel Objects* demonstrates museums' inherent ability to spark radical thought about the relationship between human and nonhuman worlds. Perhaps Peter Vergo's metaphor of the old museology as a "coelacanth" is usefully complicated – cinematically – by another sea creature: the alien cephalopod in human form that races around the spiral ramp of the Guggenheim Museum to escape capture in *Men in Black* (directed by Barry

Sonnenfeld, 2002). In championing such cine/museal provocation, *Reel Objects: Movies in Museums* sees museums at the centre of inspired and sustainable interactions with nonhuman worlds, as we blithely hurtle along human-centric pathways through the twenty-first century.

AFTERWORD

BARBARA KIRSHENBLATT-GIMBLETT

I am having curatorial dreams as I write these lines in Public Central Teaching Hospital on Banacha Street in Warsaw. The room is spartan, a crucifix is affixed to the wall opposite my bed, the food is the bland fare of schools and hospitals – milk and noodles for breakfast, rice topped with apple sauce and sour cream for lunch, two slices of rye bread, a pat of butter, and slice of ham for supper, with a beaker of sweetened tea. Not far from here is Warsaw Polytechnic, a massive beaux-arts building, with its magnificent Grand Aula, the setting for a stately celebration, on Israel Independence Day, of the twenty-fifth anniversary of the restoration of Poland-Israel relations. I fainted and was left to dream, not least curatorially, from a hospital bed.

Warsaw Polytechnic, a temple to science and engineering, was one of several institutions of higher learning in Poland where antisemitic riots broke out in 1935 and where segregated seating, known as "ghetto benches," was introduced two years later. Quotas on Jewish students at Polish universities were imposed, especially in fields such as medicine and law, in which many Jewish students were enrolled, although there were rectors, professors, and Polish students who opposed such measures. These developments followed the death in 1935 of Józef Piłsudski, Poland's chief of state, and the rise of right-wing nationalists. Not far from the Warsaw Polytechnic is the newly opened POLIN Museum of the History of Polish Jews, which began as a dream in 1993. That is where I have spent almost a decade helping to turn that dream into a reality. Reading the essays in this volume, I wondered what kinds of curatorial dreams the authors might have were they to take as their starting points the hospital, the Warsaw Polytechnic, or POLIN Museum of the History of Polish Jews itself. This impulse suggests the inspirational, catalytic quality of "curatorial dreaming" proposed by the editors of this volume as a methodology for inhabiting our familiar sites of research or practice in unexpected new ways, a creative and critical mode of making meaning, an approach to integrating different ways of knowing and asking, wherever we are.

The attention to childhood experiences and memories of museums in several of this volume's essays prompted me to recall the many Saturdays that I roamed the Royal Ontario Museum, the site of Shelley Butler's curatorial dream. I grew up in a postwar immigrant neighbourhood of Toronto – more accurately, a neighbourhood defined by the post-Holocaust arrival of displaced persons, as survivors were known then. During my ultra-Orthodox religious phase, the only thing I could do on Saturday that would not violate the Sabbath was to walk to the public library or the museum. I recall no temporary exhibitions at the Royal Ontario Museum. There was only the permanent exhibition, essentially open storage. I would cycle through the six floors, a floor a week, until I tired of that routine and made my way to the new Sigmund Samuel Gallery of Canadiana, then in a nearby building – the collection was moved to the ROM's main building in 2000 and renamed the Sigmund Samuel Gallery of Canada.

Wandering the silent halls of the ROM was an *oneiric* experience. I was too young to be troubled by the troubled histories of the aboriginal Canadians rubbing sticks together to make fire in a large glass box in the basement, too young to wonder why Africa and African Canadians were nowhere to be found, too young to question the way the collections were organized and displayed, too young to ask where some of the Greek attic vases came from; they were a gift from Sigmund Samuel, a prominent Jewish philanthropist in Toronto, who was one of the founders of the ROM and a collector of Canadiana. For all of the discipline and power I later learned about from Foucault and his heirs, I was not disciplined in those galleries. I was transported. The experience in this ostensibly disciplining space was closer to Gaston Bachelard's poetics of space and Walter Benjamin's arcades than to Foucault's subjugated subject. The experience was more like a dream than a prison – and that dream was very much my own. Such dreaming was sparked by uncertainty and speculation, rather than by authoritative knowledge. Whatever the ROM's scholars and curators and designers intended, they could not discipline dreaming.

How is that possible? We know what is wrong with the older museums, and I cannot defend them other than as metamuseological artifacts of themselves, remediated art installations, or occasions for disruptive and reflexive interventions. Yet these old-fashioned and much-repudiated exhibitions turn out, paradoxically, to be in many ways more open than the tightly scripted, highly interpreted, narrative exhibitions that have supplanted them. Perhaps our curatorial dreaming might find something redemptive in outmoded practices. This is how I think about David Wilson's Museum of Jurassic Technology in Culver City in Los Angeles. This artist's project – a classic example of curation as artistic practice and vice versa – finds in scientific uncertainty an unparalleled realm of speculation and wild imagination. I cite only the exhibitions on bat echolocation, hypersymbolic cognition, obliscence, and *No One May Ever Have the Same Knowledge Again: Letters to the Mount Wilson Observatory, 1915–1935*, an exhibition of actual letters from the crank files of a scientific project that fired the untutored imagination of the public.

There are curatorial dreams in this volume that are inspired by contemporary art and curatorial practices. I see great promise here, not least because the threshold for uncertainty and indeterminacy – preconditions for dreaming – is much higher in the subjunctive space of contemporary art museums than in the constrained space of ethnographic and history museums. Contemporary art and curatorial practices more readily blur the boundaries between museum space and life space and between various media and genres. Indeed, several of the projects presented in this volume dream at the intersection of performance art and art performance.

Museums are serious business, unruly children and artists aside, and the curatorial dreams here offer correctives to current museum practice, whether by intervening in existing exhibitions or modelling alternative ways of addressing critical issues and engaging publics. The editors are to be commended for inviting scholars to cross the divide between scholarship and curation, critique and creation, and to imagine concretely what exhibitions and interventions they might make. Their approach is a welcome alternative to critiques of exhibitions made by others, though these curatorial dreams of course do mount their own critiques, not only in curatorial terms, but also discursively. Inspiration comes from the new museology – not so new anymore – and from the critical theoretical approaches that have enriched it in the course of the last forty years.

The challenge is captured in the question posed in the introduction: "How to curate 'between hope and despair' or between 'optimistic' and 'critical' museology?" This question is relevant to both curatorship and scholarship. The goal – whether we use images, objects, words, or sounds, and whether we work in the relatively hermetic world of scholarly books or in the public one of exhibitions – is to test the limits of the possible even as we dream beyond them. The essays in this volume evoke and explore this terrain.

NOTES

INTRODUCTION

1 Bloch, *The Principle of Hope,* 86. The quotation is taken from an early draft of Roger Simon's contribution to this volume.
2 Butler, "Imaginary Exhibitions."
3 Ellison, "Humanities and the Public Soul," 115.
4 See Hiatt, "We Need Humanities Labs"; Marcus and Murphy, "Ethnocharrette"; Marcus and Murphy, "Ethnography and Design," 251–68; Holmes and Marcus, "Collaboration Today," 81–101; Bendiner-Viani and Maltby, "Hybrid Ways of Doing."
5 Bruno Latour writes suggestively in relation to this urge, calling for a "*suspension* of the critical impulse" in favour of "composition" (see Latour, "Compositionist Manifesto," 475) and curated the exhibitions *Iconoclash* and *Making Things Public* as concrete expressions of it.
6 See, for example: Macdonald and Basu, *Exhibition Experiments*; Bonnell and Simon, "'Difficult' Exhibitions"; Butler, "Reflexive Museology"; Karp et al., *Museum Frictions*; Kirshenblatt-Gimblett, "The Museum as Catalyst"; Kratz, *The Ones That Are Wanted*; Lehrer et al., *Curating Difficult Knowledge.*
7 Brachear and Storch, "Controversy Closes Show at Museum."
8 Phillips, *Museum Pieces*, 302.
9 Ames, *Museums, The Public, and Anthropology*; Karp and Lavine, *Exhibiting Cultures*; Karp et al., *Museums and Communities*; Macdonald and Basu, *Exhibition Experiments*, 13.
10 Simon, "Theorizing in the Concrete," 183–95. The notion of "theorizing-in-the-concrete" was offered to us by Roger Simon in personal communica-

tion. He considered it in an early conference paper "Dramatic Portrayal as Theorizing in the Concrete."

11 In this way it is of a piece with Dewdney, Dibosa, and Walsh's notion of a "post-critical" approach, "intended not to find the museum wanting from the remote position of analytical critique," but to join "academics, museum professionals and others in productive ways in order to open up new avenues of meaning and purpose through the agency of audience" (*Post-Critical Museology*, 2).

12 See Butler, "Reflexive Museology."

13 Zussman and Misra, "Introduction," 7.

14 Artist Fernando Calzadilla and anthropologist George Marcus consider their experimental installation "a method of inquiry that opens conditions of possibility for the existence of experimental spaces within ossified disciplines" (Calzadilla and Marcus, "Artists in the Field," 109).

15 Also worth mentioning is Nobel Prize–winning author Orhan Pamuk's "Museum of Innocence" in Istanbul, which is itself an experimental concretization of an imagined love story that began as a fictional text, as well as an argument for Pamuk's belief that the role of museums should be to tell personal stories about our individual and collective humanity. Pamuk, "A Modest Manifesto for Museums." See also: Pamuk, "Orhan Pamuk on His Museum of Innocence in Istanbul"; Silverman, ed., *Museum as Process*.

16 Hooper-Greenhill, *Museums and the Interpretation of Visual Culture*, 152; Silverman, ed., *Museums as Process*.

17 Gurian, "Blue Ocean Museum," 3.

18 Spalding, *Poetic Museum*. We are also mindful of the dangers of utopian thinking in relation to museums. Museums have been conceptualized as refuges for utopian thought, but critics such as Bernadette Lynch and Samuel Alberti warn of enduring patterns of coercion and paternalism. Lynch and Alberti, "Legacies of Prejudice," 13–35.

19 See Karp and Kratz, "The Interrogative Museum"; and Welsh, "Re-configuring Museums," 103–30.

20 Ames, *Cannibal Tours*.

21 Butler, "Politics of Exhibiting Culture," 74–92.

22 We have not requested that our contributors address in detail practical issues related to budgets, design and presentation technologies, and mobilizing support, though some have done so (see below).

23 Dewdney et al., *Post-Critical Museology*, 76. Ruth Phillips recommends a case study methodology for demonstrating to students of critical museology the "distinctive quality of the network of people, politics, and resources in which each institution is situated." Phillips, *Museum Pieces*, 21.

24 Personal communication with the editors, inspired by Simon's reading of Bloch, *Principle of Hope*. "Dreaming" in various forms seems to be having a cultural moment in relation to museums. The program for a March 2012 conference at the University of Leicester School of Museum Studies entitled "Museum Utopias: Navigating the Imaginary, Ideal and Possible Museum," proposed dreaming as a way for museums to be leaders in envisioning change, rather than reacting when change comes. The visual art news digest *E-flux*'s "Agency of Unrealized Projects" considers the value of "postponed, impossible, or rejected, unrealized projects [that] form a unique testament to the speculative power of non-action." And recognizing the creativity, adventure, and intimacy of dreaming, sleep-based theatre and musical performances, as well as museum sleepovers, are proliferating. The Rubin Museum of Art in Chelsea recently held its fourth annual "Dream-Over," where visitors sleep under an artwork chosen by a curator, followed by a morning activity of dream interpretation. Ryzik, "The Entire Audience Dozed Off? Perfect!"

25 Silvia Forni, personal communication, 2012.

26 On artist-curators and museums as sites of intervention and inspiration see, Putnam, *Art and Artifact*; McShine, *The Museum as Muse*; Macdonald and Basu, *Exhibition Experiments*; Karp et al., *Museum Frictions*; Levell, "Site-specificity and Dislocation"; Wilson, *Fred Wilson: A Critical Reader*; Taylor, "A Savage Performance"; Behar and Mannheim, "The Couple in the Cage." On related attempts by artists to liberate their work from the elite framework of the museum and gallery and use it as an instrument for new modes of social participation and community engagement, see Morris and O'Neill, "Introduction."

27 Macdonald and Basu, *Exhibition Experiments*, 9.

28 Rogoff, "What is a Theorist?"

29 *Trade Is Sublime* showed at the World Trade Organization headquarters in June 2013 and was curated by Luke Cantarella and Chrstine Hegel, in collaboration with anthropologists George Marcus and Jae Chung. The video installation draws on the same ethnographic research as Marcus's curatorial dream, *Making Transparency Visible*, but the projects have no formal relationship. Thus, Marcus considers his curatorial dream to be an evolving, active project. *Trade is Sublime* can be viewed at tradeissublime.org. Marcus's unpublished manuscript *A Chronicle of Art (and Anthropology) at the World Trade Organization … In Five Not So Easy Pieces*, reflects on the use of art exhibitions to further social science research.

Lehrer's curatorial dream *Most Disturbing Souvenirs* was realized in the exhibition *Souvenir, Talisman, Toy*, which took place in the Seweryn Udziela

Ethnographic Museum in Poland, in June–July 2013. A web version of the exhibition can be found at www.luckyjews.com. For a brief consideration of the exhibit's participatory collecting strategy, see Lehrer and Ramsay, "Collecting (as) Dialogue?" For additional information about the exhibit's logistics and challenges, see Lehrer, "Exhibit Case Study."

30 Butler, *Reflexive Museology*.

31 Lehrer, "Curating Jews," 32–3.

32 Bunzl's research is described in Bunzl, *In Search of a Lost Avant-Garde*.

33 Lindauer, "Critical Museum Pedagogy," 303–14.

34 Eatman, "Engaged Scholarship," 18, cited in Ellison, "The New Public Humanists," 289.

35 Calhoun, Foreword to *Engaging Contradictions*, xviii. A related call regards the need for "research-based understandings of culture" that might compete with artists, writers, community groups, and corporate entertainment entities who have outpaced scholars "in terms of representing their cultures and brokering those representations to larger publics" (Kurin, *Reflections of a Culture Broker*, 266).

36 Lupton, "Philadelphia Dreaming," 52.

37 Frisch, *A Shared Authority;* High, "Sharing Authority," 12–34.

38 Ellison, "Lyric Citizenship," 91–114. Ellison cites both deepening social inequality, and structural unemployment in the humanities, as other drivers of the shift in academia to such public, project-based culture work.

39 Bouquet, "Thinking and Doing Otherwise," 232. Delores Hayden similarly notes that "if people's attachments to places are material, social, and imaginative, then these are necessary dimensions of new projects to extend public history in the urban landscape." Hayden, *The Power of Place*, 43.

40 On the other side of the coin, we also see visitors increasingly conceptualized as consumers, especially given cutbacks in public funding for museums.

41 Lynch and Alberti. "Legacies of Prejudice," 13–35.

42 Kurin, *Reflections of a Culture Broker*, 14.

43 Anthropologist Andrew Shryock illustrates the challenges of doing public "culture work" with members of Detroit's Arab community in the wake of 9/11, concluding that only teaching and academic writing allow him the safe space to tell certain cultural truths. "In the Double Remoteness of Arab Detroit," 279–314.

44 Kurin, *Reflections of a Culture Broker*, 20–2.

45 Karp, "Public Scholarship as a Vocation," 286, 288, 298.

46 Schneider and Wright, *Anthropology and Art Practice*; Schneider and Wright, *Between Art and Anthropology*; Schneider and Wright, *Contem-*

porary Art and Anthropology; Strohm, "When Anthropology Meets Contemporary Art," 98–124; the *Ethnographic Terminalia* curatorial collective (http://ethnographicterminalia.org/the-collective). George Marcus has most explicitly and extensively described this nascent "turn" in the discipline, as well as enacting it in his own experimental practice (Marcus, "Contemporary Fieldwork Aesthetics," 263–77). Anthropologist Nikolai Ssorin-Chiakov has also explored the research outputs of an art-infused experimental "ethnographic conceptualism," which "explicitly manufactures the social reality that it studies." Ssorin-Chiakov, "Ethnographic Conceptualism." Nirmal Puwar and Sanjay Sharma discuss curating as a way to "keep conceptual problems live." Puwar and Sharma, "Curating Sociology," 40–63. Macdonald and Basu's *Exhibition Experiments* also views exhibits as potential laboratories for the creation of new knowledge.

47 Marcus, "Contemporary Fieldwork Aesthetics," 263–77. See also Marcus, "The Uses of Complicity," 85–108.

48 One implication of this shift is that "the field" can now be created anywhere, in the form of a collaborative, participatory cultural spectacle. Marcus, "Contemporary Fieldwork Aesthetics," 41.

49 Sandell, *Museums, Prejudice and the Reframing of Difference*, 10.

50 Hernandez, this volume.

51 Rothberg, "Pedagogy and the Politics of Memory," 466–76.

52 White, "From Experimental Moment to Legacy Moment," 65–97. See also Conquergood, "Performance Studies."

53 In this spirit, the National Art Gallery of Canada has printed a series of humorous postcards called "That's Art?!" for visitors to consult in their galleries. Each card includes a reproduction of a famous abstract painting, with short quotationes from "the public," the artist, and experts, creating a dialogue about the nature of art.

54 See also Williams, *Memorial Museums*; Simon, "A Shock to Thought," 432–49; Bonnell and Simon, "'Difficult' Exhibitions," 65–85; Lehrer et al., *Curating Difficult Knowledge*; Macdonald, *Difficult Heritage*; Logan and Reeves, *Places of Pain and Shame*; Sontag, *Regarding the Pain of Others*; Silvén, "Difficult Matters," 133–46; Sevcenko, "Activating the Past," 55–64; Sevcenko, "Sites of Conscience," 20–5; Sandell and Nightingale, *Museums, Equality and Social Justice*; Busby et al., *The Idea of a Human Rights Museum*; Carter and Orange, "Contentious Terrain," 111–27; Orange and Carter, "'It's Time to Pause and Reflect,'" 259–66.

55 Arnold-de Simine, *Mediating Memory in the Museum*, 2.

56 For example: Huyssen, *Present Pasts*; Partridge, "Holocaust *Mahnmal*," 820–50; Rothberg, "Pedagogy and the Politics of Memory," 466–76.

57 Failler, Ives, and Milne, eds. "Caring for Difficult Knowledge: Prospects for the Canadian Museum for Human Rights." Special Issue, *Review of Education, Pedagogy and Cultural Studies* 37, 2–3 (2015).

58 Butler, "The Politics of Exhibiting Culture," 89.

59 Lehrer and Milton, Introduction to *Curating Difficult Knowledge: Violent Pasts in Public Places*, 1–20.

60 Butler, "The Politics of Exhibiting Culture." See also Simon et al., *Between Hope and Despair*.

61 Created in 2010, Christian Marclay's art installation *The Clock* is a video montage of thousands of clips sampled from movies and television series, demarcating, minute by minute, a twenty-four-hour loop that audiences are invited to watch and listen to. The travelling exhibition continues to mesmerize audiences and critics.

CHAPTER ONE

1 Foster, "The Artist as Ethnographer," 145–70.

2 Blustein, *Misadventures of the Most Favored Nations*.

3 Ten researchers were involved, including anthropologists and lawyers from France, Argentina, Korea, the United States, Italy, Cameroun, China, and Canada. Funding came from the French government. In late 2010 we met in Paris for a round of discussion and planning of a collaboratively written ethnography: Abélès, *Des anthropologues à l'OMC*.

4 Deeb and Marcus, "In the Green Room," 51–76.

5 Its symbolic significance is also shared by showing this famous room to WTO visitors when it is not in use. Indeed, the meetings of our team with the director-general occurred in the Green Room.

6 Marcus, *Paranoia Within Reason*.

7 The topic of transparency was the special concern of one of our team, Lynda de Matteo, who has produced a detailed paper on its various meanings and manifestations. Her ethnographic vantage point on this topic was situated within the small department of media relations at the WTO.

8 Drafting this imagined exhibition gives me the welcome opportunity to work through a similar suggestion that I made twenty years ago in and about a different venue. After a year as a scholar at the Getty Institute in Los Angeles, I wrote a critical article on this very discrete public organization (with global pretensions) that concluded with a suggestion of an exhibition that looked inward to stimulate reflection and self-critique among its own personnel. See Marcus, "The Production of European High Culture in Los Angeles." The theme of that exhibit would have been "Faking."

9 On ethnographic representation, performance, and parallel art practices from the 1980s and onward, see: Foster, "The Artist as Ethnographer;" Kaye, *Site-Specific Art*; Kwon, *One Place After Another*; Marcus, "Contemporary Fieldwork Aesthetics in Art and Anthropology"; and Suderburg, *Space, Site, Intervention.*

10 Marcus, *Lives in Trust.*

11 Clifford and Marcus, *Writing Culture.*

12 Foster, "The Artist as Ethnographer," 145–70.

13 See Wallis, "A Forum, Not a Temple" as well as the work of Neil Cummings and Marysia Lewandowska (http://www.chanceprojects.com/node/326).

14 While preparing this piece, I learned of an exhibition somewhat akin to what I have imagined for the WTO. From 15–27 February 2011, there was an exhibit at the Mount Street Galleries, London, of a series of paintings by James Hart Dyke entitled *A Year With MI6*. Once an organization that was so secret that its existence was officially unrecognized, it now is exploring degrees of exposure, if not transparency. Vetted by the controls of the Secrets Act, Hart Dyke was approved by Sir John Scarlett, then MI6 chief, to produce a series of paintings and sketches of daily activities at the headquarters of MI6, as part of the centenary observance of the service.

15 The production of the pamphlet, *The WTO Building: The Symbolic Artwork of the Centre William Rappard, Headquarters of the World Trade Organization* (2009), was overseen by the WTO's *chef de cabinet.*

16 This *chef de cabinet*, an elegant and subtle diplomat, was the primary liaison between our ethnographic project and the director-general. He has a taste for and a full understanding of the value of critical interventions within (and within the limits of!) complex organizations like the WTO. The re-display of symbolic artwork was his own (and the current director-general's) gesture at exhibition.

17 This is facilitated by innovative thinking in recent years about documents as ethnographic objects; see Riles, *Documents*. Storyboards – a basic tool of film-making – could substitute for moving images. Cartoons, calibrated to gradations of clarity and translucency in the screens, would be an ideal form for scenarios. The dialogue and thought bubbles employed in cartooning, and the alternate captioning of cartoon images (as in the competitions that occur on the back page of every issue of *The New Yorker*) are modes for commentary on transparency and its contradictions. Finally, sketches are an attractive option, inspired by the example of the artist James Hard Dyke working recently inside the headquarters of MI6 (see note 7). He produced images that might have appeared mundane to the outsider, but in their details were reported to be keenly resonant to insiders.

18 We heard more than once in our conversations with WTO staff about their duty of silence. While these experts, diplomats, and researchers often have quite acute analytic impressions and insights about the course of the organization and the moves of member countries, from which we benefited immensely in the "informant-anthropologist" relationship, their public face as mediators of negotiations and providers of trade analyses imposed a certain atmosphere of austerity that carried over to the atmosphere of the building.

19 Gallagher et al., *Managing the Challenges of WTO Participation.*

20 In considering potential images of the interior of the building to illustrate this piece, I surveyed my colleagues, and none had taken photographs of the interior or of the work that goes on there. Some had taken photos of the exterior, as well as of other places in Geneva, but there was a general neglect of the setting of ethnography, though there was no prohibition on photography per se. Perhaps, as participant observers, we were infected by the minimalism and austerity of the space and its uses, and the culture of discreet silence.

CHAPTER TWO

1 My thanks go to Shelley Butler, Cory Kratz, Ruth Phillips, and the late Roger Simon, as well as to members of our 2013 CISCC working group on Curatorial Theory and Practice at Concordia University, for constructive criticism on this curatorial dream. While begun as a dream, the vision presented in this chapter became a reality in the form of the exhibition *Souvenir, Talisman, Toy,* which took place in the Seweryn Udziela Ethnographic Museum in Krakow, Poland, in June–July 2013. A web version of the exhibition can be seen at www.luckyjews.com. For a brief consideration of the exhibition's participatory collecting strategy, see Lehrer and Ramsay, "Collecting (as) Dialogue?"

2 Greenberg, "Jews, Museums, and National Identities," 125–37.

3 Pinto, "Building a New Jewish and Polish Memory," 80.

4 Lehrer, *Jewish Poland Revisited,* 159–75.

5 Zimmerman, *Contested Memories.*

6 We lack an unproblematic vocabulary to describe the differences between the ethnic groups under discussion, without reinforcing the stereotype that Poles are essentially Catholic. Some Poles are Jewish (or: some Jews are Polish). And the cultural conflicts do not split neatly along the lines of non-Jewish Poles vs. Jews of any nationality. I use "Jews and Poles" as a catch-all term, with these issues in mind.

7 See Gruber, *Virtually Jewish*; Lehrer, *Jewish Poland Revisited*; Waligórska, *Klezmer's Afterlife*.

8 Lehrer, ibid.

9 In 2012 two articles by public intellectuals appeared in major Polish periodicals, convincing me that the moment was ripe for an exhibition: Tokarska-Bakir, "Żyd z pieniążkiem podbija Polskę," and Keff, "Żyd o imieniu Żyd podbija Polskę." In response to my exhibition, numerous additional articles in Polish, Israeli, British, and North American press have appeared on the subject.

10 The response to the letter by the Polish Minister of Tourism can be seen at www.luckyjews.com, and in the accompanying exhibit catalogue *Lucky Jews/Na Szczęscie to Żyd* (Krakow: Ha!art, 2014).

11 A talking stick is a widely used tool of aboriginal democracy, which constitutes a "symbol of [the bearer's] authority and right to speak in public" with "high ceremonial and spiritual value." More recently they have been borrowed by groups as means for spurring discussion and also as aids to resolve disputes. Wikipedia contributors, "Talking stick."

12 *Tschotschke*, Yiddish: a small object that is decorative rather than strictly functional; a trinket.

13 I am inspired here by work by Marianne Hirsch and Michael Rothberg, which suggest the creativity and generativity of memory, and particularly the way memories can be transacted and adopted beyond their ostensibly "original owners" and give rise to new kinds of community and solidarity. For the purposes of curating, my intention is to use disputed objects in participatory settings as a platform to spur memory and create debate, as well as to voice concerns and learn across boundaries of difference. I see participatory exhibitions as technologies for accessing, recombining, and recirculating marginalized memories in ways that both cut across and link communities.

14 See, for example, Clifford, *The Predicament of Culture*; Karp and Lavine, *Exhibiting Cultures*; Price, *Paris Primitive*; Iervolino and Sandell, this volume.

15 Klękot, "'Ethno' in Polish Design," 68–72. European ethnographic museums can be divided into two main types: those based on *Völkerkunde*, or studies of faraway, exotic others (prevalent in countries that had colonies), and *Volkskunde*, studies of the internal, peasant other. The latter developed in societies struggling for national recognition or emancipation under nineteenth-century imperialism, and "folk culture" continued to be nurtured as part of the emancipatory ideology shaping the "national sciences" under East European socialism. See: Lozoviuk, "Pervasive Continuities," 227–36; Stocking, "Afterword," 172–86; Vukov, "Ethnoscripts and Nationog-

raphies," 331–43. On peasant-based national mythologies, see also Baycroft and Hopkin, *Folklore and Nationalism*; Filipova, "Peasants on Display," 15–36; Hofer, "Folk Cultural Heritage," 145–70; Mihailescu, "Nation-Building Ethnology," 208–19; Peer, *France on Display*; Thiesse and Norris, "How Countries Are Made," 26–32.

16 Stauter-Halstead, *The Nation in the Village*; Robotycki, "The Anthropology of Culture in Poland," 69–86; Kroh, "Vernacular Art," 391–7.

17 Szczurek, *Sto i pół*. The second- and third-floor displays of rural lifeways, costumes, and customs were opened to the public on 19 January 1969. The ground floor display of countryside domestic and industrial interiors was established in 1951.

18 Out of more than forty thematic sections regarding Polish folklife, Jews appear as subjects (in a single image in the larger display) in only five of them; one might say they are quite conspicuously absent in displays on folk music, paper cutting, and innkeeping, domains in which Jews were widespread and influential, and remain present in popular memory.

19 For a general introduction to these folk images of Jews see Cała, *Polish Folk Culture*. See also Tokarska-Bakir, "The Hanging of Judas."

20 Strong, "Exclusive Labels," 42–56. Pauline Turner Strong uses semiotic analysis to illustrate how museum labels function to include and exclude, to assume and reinforce particular viewpoints.

21 The museum catalogue, *The Charm of Krakow Toys*, states, "We do hope that you will be captivated by the beauty of Kraków toys, intrigued by the simplicity of the handiwork, fascinated with the inventive spirit of toy-makers, and – last but not least – amused with the sometimes unintended comic character of the scenes and persons presented." Oleszkiewicz and Pyla, *Czar Zabawek Krakowskich,* 11.

22 The opening, in October 2014, of the multi-million-dollar Polin Museum of the History of Polish Jews in Warsaw, with a core exhibition team of international scholars led by New York University museum theorist Barbara Kirshenblatt-Gimblett, has made a significant, if still indeterminate, impact on the Polish museum landscape. On the one hand raising the bar for the inclusion of Jews as three-dimensional subjects of Polish history and fellow citizens of the state, it also has a potentially ghettoizing effect, suggesting that Jews already have "their" museum, and allowing other, "mainstream," Polish museums to further sidestep responsibility for including Jews in their depictions of the Polish nation.

23 This major renovation was initiated in 2012. Half of the gallery remained unfinished in August 2015, pending funding.

24 All the Jewish-themed shows have been staged in collaboration with Kraków's nine-day-long summer Jewish Cultural Festival. In 2007 there was Jerzy Dida-Gracz's cycle *Judaica*; 2009 brought photographer Wojciech Wilczyk's *There Is No Such Thing as an Innocent Eye* (documenting the state of former synagogue buildings across Poland); in 2010 *The Taming of Jerusalem: Photographs 1857–1900* was Jewish only by association; and in the summer of 2011 two more shows, *Jews on Vinyl* (showcasing Jews in mid-twentieth-century music, sponsored by the trendy, youth-oriented US-based Idelsohn society) and photographer Łukasz Baksik's *Matzevoth for Everyday Use* (depicting scavenged Jewish tombstones that have been used by Poles as building materials). The museum served only as the host for these self-contained shows; none were co-organized with the museum or based on its own collections. The 2009–10 exhibit *Islam. Orientation. Ornament* was created by the museum, largely on the basis of its collection.

25 On Poland's "post-traumatic culture" see Tokarska-Bakir, "Poland as the Sick Man of Europe?" Konstanty Gebert proposes the "phantom limb" idea in Smith, "In Poland, a Jewish Revival Thrives – Minus Jews"; on anti-semitism as a "social disease": Musiał, "Czarne jest czarne." Poland has also been described as cursed or contaminated; see Ostachowicz, *Noc Żywych Żydów*.

26 Pinto, "Can One Reconcile the Jewish World and Europe?" 25.

27 Feldman, *Above the Death Pits, Beneath the Flag*; Kugelmass, "Bloody Memories," 279–301; Sheramy, "From Auschwitz to Jerusalem," 307–26.

28 Polish literary critic Jan Błoński sketched out the repetitive schema in his classic article "Biedni Polacy patrzą na getto" ("The Poor Poles look at the Ghetto") in the Polish weekly *Tygodnik Powszechny* in 1987.

29 In this way my curatorial dream is aligned with a series of recent creative memorial provocations by Polish and Israeli artists, including Yael Bartana, Rafał Betlejewski, and Public Movement. See Lehrer and Waligórska, "Cur(at)ing History."

30 I distinguish this admittedly risky approach from, for example, the more univocally condemnatory strategy of the Jim Crow Museum of Racist Memorabilia in Big Rapids, Michigan, whose very name casts a single, strong frame that inevitably – at least symbolically – limits the interpretive space for visitors.

31 Notwithstanding Kate Wells's discussion of the relationship of care, cure, and control brought into focus by Foucault's descriptions of ostensibly "curative" institutions like Paris's seventeenth-century Hôpital Général as sites of confinement rather than aid. "Who Cares?…"

32 Clifford, *Routes*; Kurin, "The Festival of American Folklife," 7–20.

33 Polish observer Magdalena Ujma counterposed what she viewed as the Krakow Ethnographic Museum's new (post-2008) "therapeutic" approach to a "critical" one, suggesting that the former avoids reference to historical political contexts and present-day tensions. I use the notion of therapy differently, in a way that addresses her concerns (*Obieg*, "Muzeum Etnograficzne; świeże spojrzenie." 29 March 2012. http://www.obieg.pl/teksty/24505).
I am inspired by Polish artists and others who have intervened in public spaces with therapeutic mandates. Joanna Rajkowska, for example, in the context of her "oxygenator" project in Warsaw's former ghetto area, made the diagnosis that "the necrosis of urban tissue required a return to the most primal phenomena of our bodily co-being – shared breathing, situating our bodies in relation to each other, lines of sight." Rajkowska, *Where the Beast Is Buried*, 1.

34 Homeopathy is a system of treating diseases using small amounts of substances which, in larger amounts, would produce the observed symptoms.

35 Tokarska-Bakir, "Poland as the Sick Man of Europe?" Discussions of empathy have identified problematic assumptions built into the notion, including the erasure of power relations that structure emotional states, the collapsing of important social differences, the voyeuristic consumption of another's imagined experience, or the evacuation of the other's experience by the focus on one's own "empathetic" feeling. See Boler, "The Risks of Empathy"; Simon and Bonnel, "'Difficult' Exhibitions." Writing about contemporary Poland, Joanna Tokarska-Bakir suggests that a cure is needed to both "dispel the stupor" and "impart some critical awareness to the patient," and she describes empathy as "an opportunity for unearthing the truths spoken by both sides of the argument without ever annihilating the differences between them."

36 Edgar, Afterword to *Playing with Fire*, quoted in Khan, *The Road to Interculturalism*, quoted in Bodo et al., *Museums*, 23. For further discussion of Third Space, see Bhabha, *The Location of Culture*; Soja, *Thirdspace*.

37 See, for example, Peressut et al., *European Museums in the 21st Century*; Krankenhagen, "Exhibiting Europe," 269–400; Aronsson and Elgenius, "Building National Museums in Europe."

38 Schneider and Wright, *Contemporary Art and Anthropology*.

39 Léontine Meijer-van Mensch, Dorota Kawęcka, and Aleksandra Janus apply the notion of a "heritage community," developed by the Council of Europe, to describe Polish non-Jews who consider Jewish heritage part of their own heritage. Mensch et al., "Strategien zum Schutz jüdischen Kulturerbes in Polen." Similarly, Ivan Karp and Corinne Kratz talk about communities of "stakeholders" with various claims or links to museum objects. Karp and Kratz, "The Interrogative Museum."

40 Karp and Kratz, "The Interrogative Museum."
41 Julie Ellison notes the utility of uncertainty in Ellison, "Humanities and the Public Soul," 120.
42 For a consideration of the ethics of laughter in Holocaust commemoration, see Rosen, "Lunch with the Führer."
43 Ruth Phillips discusses the notion of "playability." Phillips, *Trading Identities.*
44 Appadurai, *The Social Life of Things.*
45 Karp and Kratz, "The Interrogative Museum."
46 See www.conversationmaps.org. Anthropologist Tamar Katriel noted a similar phenomenon in an Israeli gallery show of IDF soldiers' photographs of their own abuses of Palestinians. Katriel, "Showing and Telling," 109–27.

CHAPTER THREE

1 Barry Lopez hints at this kind of relentless going in "Flight" (1998), and Engseng Ho points out "absence rather than presence, everywhere shapes diasporic experiences." See Ho, *The Graves of Tarim,* 4.
2 Gilroy, *The Black Atlantic,* 4.
3 Lamming, *The Emigrants.*
4 Although, as Shannon Lee Dawdy suggests, I probably didn't know it at the time; Dawdy, "Disaster Preparedness," in *Anthrohistory*. For a discussion of anthrohistory as a way to reimagine how to be, think, write, and engage beyond scholarly disciplines, see Murphy et al, *Anthrohistory*.
5 For an analysis of hues, terrains, and the constructed image of black passengers in airline advertising, see Bhimull, *Empire in the Air.*
6 Saartjie "Sara" Baartman and Ota Benga went from Africa to Europe and the United States, coerced or by choice. Their supposedly unique physical traits led scientists to exhibit, dissect, and examine them in cases, jars, or cages.
7 In particular, I thought about imperial advertisements and exhibitions from nineteenth-century Europe: Richards, *The Commodity Culture of Victorian England* and McClintock, *Imperial Leather.*
8 For examples, see Menzies, *All Ways by Airways,* and Air France, World Map. CT 98 20158, National Air and Space Museum, Smithsonian Institution, Washington, DC (n.d., probably 1930s).
9 In this case a frequent flyer is someone who flies more than six times a year.
10 As Barbara Kirshenblatt-Gimblett points out, travel destinations have long been curated by the tourism industry. Kirshenblatt-Gimblett, *Destination Culture.*
11 The reference to the cost of this type of travel draws inspiration from the work of James Baldwin on blackness and mobility in Baldwin, *The Price*

of the Ticket. For all passages quoted in the section, see American Airlines, "Black Atlas Digital Press Kit."

12 BDS$35.00 is US$17.50. The per capita income was BDS$14,700 (US$7,350) in 2007. Central Bank of Barbados, "Barbados – Vital Statistics."

13 The question wasn't entirely unexpected. I took lots of notes during the tour.

14 Gmelch, *Behind the Smile,* 13.

15 Harriss, "The Concorde Redemption."

16 The list of permissible people includes government officials, ticketed passengers, and airport and airliner workers with security clearance.

17 Fanon, *Black Skin, White Masks*.

18 Swimming is a notable exception. It allows people to move up and down in depth.

19 For a discussion of imagination, scapes, and global flows, see Appadurai, "Disjuncture and Difference in the Global Cultural Economy"; Appadurai, "Global Ethnoscapes."

20 For Jason deCaires Taylor's work, see http://www.underwater sculpture.com.

21 Walcott, *Omeros*, 134, 168.

22 West Indian Air Transport Committee, "Report on the Opportunities for Civil Air Transport in the West Indies: British Guiana," Cmd. 2968 (September 1927), 13. CO 318/386/7, at the Public Records Office, Kew, UK.

23 Sisters, in discussion with author, May 2011.

24 Draft letter from the Labour Commissioner (Barbados) to the Permanent Secretary M.D.T.L., November 1962, Labour Department Files: Migrant Air Travel – Richard A. Williams & Co., 1960–2. E 5010/25, at the National Archives, Black Rock, Barbados.

25 Kundera makes a similar point about high speed in *Slowness*.

26 Angelou, *The Collected Poems of Maya Angelou*, 163.

27 My reference to diasporic consciousness comes from Hannah DeAngelis's "Fifteen Lessons I Learned about Race," a paper given in my seminar "Culture, Mobility, Identity: Encounters in the African Diaspora," Colby College, fall 2011.

28 Du Bois, "Of Our Spiritual Strivings," 8.

29 Morrison, *Song of Solomon*, 49.

30 Ibid., 9.

31 Ibid., 220.

32 The list of airliners operating deportation flights includes companies like British Airways and Lufthansa.

33 Lewis and Taylor, "Security Guards Accused." Carpet karaoke is a tactic that involves guards "bending deportees over in their seats and placing their head between their legs."

34 G4S Guard Diary, "Virgin Atlantic Flight 601, Heathrow to Johannesburg, May 3." This excerpt comes from a G4S guard's diary, which she gave as evidence to the British Parliament.

35 For all passages quoted in this paragraph, see witness testimony in Lewis and Taylor, "Security Guards Accused."

36 Naipaul, *The Mimic Men*.

37 Walker, "Finger-raped in Barbados."

38 For the Barbadian government's response, see *Nation News*, "Touchdown!" and *Barbados Free Press*, "Jamaican women welcome in Barbados if they submit to a finger up their vagina?"

39 NGO director, in discussion with author, April 2001.

40 Spiritual and other forms of flight have long been part of black diasporic travels.

41 For all passages quoted in the paragraph, see *Barbados Free Press* (2008); Caribbean *Net News* (2008); *Nation News* (2008). For an additional analysis, see Bhimull, "Passages."

42 For a discussion of the role of dreams in the African diaspora, see Kelley, *Freedom Dreams*.

CHAPTER FOUR

1 The launch was sponsored by the Maternal, Adolescent and Child Health (MatCH) division of the University of the Witwatersrand Health Consortium in partnership with the KZN Department of Health. A variety of groups from the private sector were also involved in this effort to inform the public about the restoration project. Children were key participants as well: a children's choir performed at the ceremony, and artwork by children involved in the Room 13 Project was on display.

2 At the time of writing in 2014, Phases One and Two of the seven-phase, projected five-year project have been completed, with backing from the KwaZulu-Natal provincial government, USAID, Save the Children, and a host of private donors.

3 Restoration of the Children's Hospital Museum has not yet begun, but it will take its own course, in some areas diverging from my dream. In particular, it seems that the actual museum will have more of a curriculum-based health sciences orientation than the arts and history emphasis that I propose here. While my curatorial dream may diverge from what is ultimately installed

in the KZN CHM, the strategies I present are relevant to any number of museum and hospital contexts interested in child-centred approaches.

4 The hospital will offer in-patient services of treatment, prevention, and care which include rehabilitation, palliative care, and psychological and social benefit support services. The precinct will include a residential facility for lodging children's caregivers, as well as NGO and social services offices providing community outreach and training. It will also host a range of research programs focused on child health issues. Walford, "Children's Hospital opens in Durban."

5 Ryan, "Facelift for Addington Children's Hospital."

6 Department of Health, Province of KwaZulu-Natal, "KwaZulu-Natal children's hospital to be unveiled."

7 Most of the historical background I present here was conveyed to me by Catherine Burns, who has worked tirelessly and against great odds to push forward the restoration project in multiple capacities: as former legal technical advisor at the Maternal, Adolescent and Child Health (MatCH) Unit, as a historian of South Africa, as a political activist, and as a concerned Durbanite. For a detailed history of the Children's Hospital and the complex circumstances of its creation, operation, and tragic closure, see her work in progress: Burns, "The Children's Hospital in Durban" (2011), paper presented at the History and African Studies Seminar at the University of KwaZulu-Natal in Durban. The following section draws primarily from interviews (12–20 August 2010) and correspondence (June 2010, ongoing) with her as well as from her foundational article.

8 Burns, "The Children's Hospital in Durban," 18.

9 Such features were first developed in Britain's influential open-air school movement for debilitated children which began in 1907 and flourished in the 1930s. See Bryder, "Wonderlands."

10 Kwa-Zulu Natal Children's Hosltpital, "Historical Overview."

11 The terms "White, "African," "Coloured," and "Indian" formed the foundation of apartheid legislation, which sought to categorize and separate its population according to an invented racial hierarchy, and while the distinctions are still used in certain contexts today, they do not (nor did they ever) accurately depict the cultural complexity or forms of identity found in South Africa. It is not my intention to reproduce these categories, perpetuate the kind of thinking from which they emerged, or contribute in any way to the pain that their invocation can induce, but I use them only in reference to the historical context that I am trying to represent. In my discussion of contemporary South Africa, I follow common usage of the term "black" to refer to people of African descent, and depending on context, this may also include people formerly classified as Coloured and Indian.

12 Coovadia et al., "Retain the Children's Hospital." Unpublished report, 28 August 1989.
13 Interviews with Catherine Burns, Durban, August 2010.
14 Burns, 20.
15 Ibid.
16 Burns, 21.
17 Following negotiations and the release of liberation leader and political detainee Nelson Mandela on 11 February 1990, the first plenary session of the Convention for a Democratic South Africa (CODESA) began on 21 December 1991, at the World Trade Centre in Johannesburg.
18 This collective included former head pediatrician at the Children's Hospital Professor Bill Winship, and doctors Imran Coovadia, Miriam Adhikari, R. Green-Thompson, and Z. Mkhize. See Burns, 21.
19 See KwaZulu-Natal Children's Hospital. "KwaZulu-Natal Children's Hospital."
20 Instead of the initial three phases identified by KZN Health MEC Sibongiseni Dhlomo, the Master Builders architectural firm in charge of renovations and constructions has identified seven phases of the project. See KwaZulu-Natal Master Builders Association, "Restoration of the Old Addington Children's hospital." Phase 1 was launched on 16 July 2013.
21 Two websites still contain descriptions of the non-operative museum, both framed within a discourse of progress over so-called primitivism: "In places this can be a maccabre [sic] exhibition, with medical equipment of a more unusual nature, illustrating the technological advances (thankfully) of more recent years. There is an underlying emphasis on the fortitude of the human spirit, patients having to overcome quite primitive treatments, early in the hospital history. Visit this museum, be amazed and be thankful for modern methods." AOL Travel, "Addington Hospital Museum, Durban." And, "The primitive history of healing highlights modern day technology's assistance in the preservation of human life ... The thought of surviving an operation in the original antique operating theatre might be enough to induce a panic attack but the knowledge that modern medicine is practised a few feet away is enough to survive the museum visit with gratitude." SA Venues, "KwaZulu Natal Things to Do: Visit the Addington Centenary Museum (Durban Beachfront)."
22 Patterson, "Constructions of Childhood."
23 As reported in a state-of-affairs summary article in the medical journal *The Lancet* in 2008: "The under-5 mortality rate is at least four times higher in the poorest quintile than the richest, and only 40% of the total health-care expenditure is spent on the public system, despite it serving 80% of the population. Such inequalities drive poverty. Millions of South Africans still

live in shacks. At the end of apartheid 6.3% of the population were living on less than US $1 a day. By 2005 this had risen to 11%." "South Africa in the Spotlight," 1215. In the subsequent issue, Clare Kapp reports that conditions have only since worsened since 2008: "There is a glaring gap between the semi-luxurious private sector which accounts for more than 56% of health expenditure for 7 million people and operates independently of the over-stretched public sector which serves 40 million people." Kapp, "New hope for Health in South Africa," 1207–8.

24 UNAIDS, *Global Report: UNAIDS Report on the global AIDS epidemic 2013*, A14.

25 This survey is based on 36,000 women attending 1,445 clinics across all nine provinces. The results were published in 2012 by the Department of Health. Republic of South Africa Department of Health, *The 2011 National Antenatal Sentinel HIV & Syphilis Prevalence Survey in South Africa*, iii.

26 Whiteside, *HIV/AIDS: A Very Short Introduction*, 1, 1087.

27 KwaZulu-Natal Children's Hospital, "About the Hospital"; Cullinan, "South Africa far from targets to reduce maternal, infant morality."

28 Known as the "twin epidemic," HIV and TB have created a global health crisis of tremendous proportions, impacting life expectancy, communities, economies, and health systems around the world. Shesgreen, "Reminder."

29 See Leonard, "Civil Society Leadership"; Wiley et al., "Democratisation and Globalisation."

30 See Coombes, *History after Apartheid*.

31 See, for instance, Newbury, "Living historically through photographs"; Solani, Noel, "The Saint of the Struggle," 42–55.

32 See, for instance, Hansen, "Public Spaces for National Commemoration," 43–60.

33 See Ross, "Interpreting the new museology," 84–103; Vergo, *The New Museology*; Macdonald, *A Companion to Museum Studies*; Witcomb, *Re-Imagining the Museum*; Marstine, *New Museum Theory and Practice*.

34 For further discussion and illustration of this concept, see Lehrer et al., *Curating Difficult Knowledge*.

35 In addition to general pediatric medicine and inpatient wards, the hospital will also provide psychological services and house a centre for HIV-positive teenagers. KwaZulu-Natal Children's Hospital, "KwaZulu-Natal Children's Hospital."

36 As MEC, Dhlomo is the head of the Health Department in the province of KwaZulu-Natal.

37 Department of Health, Province of KwaZulu-Natal, "KwaZulu-Natal children's hospital to be unveiled."

38 In a series of protracted and bitter deliberations, negotiations, and legal wranglings, advocates from MatCH and other organizations succeeding in securing the future of the hospital through the development of the Renovation Plan.

39 See, for instance, High et al., *Remembering Mass Violence*; Hurley, *Beyond Preservation*; Adair et al., *Sharing Authority*; Luchs et al., *Mapping Memories*; Igloliorte, "We Were So Far Away."

40 See, for instance, Hansen, "Public Spaces for National Commemoration," 43–60.

41 Other important partners include the Nelson Mandela Children's Hospital Trust, the Durban Office of the Reproductive Health and HIV Research Unit, and several South African universities and Colleges of Nursing. Interviews with Catherine Burns, Durban, August 2010.

42 The sheer number of factors and challenges faced by the average South African often serves to reinforce a permanent condition of poverty in which possible benefits of various initiatives are undercut and even sabotaged by other life circumstances. For example, the effectiveness of anti-retroviral medication for people who don't have enough to eat or access to adequate drinking water is severely curtailed. Similarly, what good are schools for learners who are malnourished, who have no means of getting to them, or who may be hurt or killed on their journeys between home and school?

43 Dyment et al., "Grounds for movement," 953.

44 Ibid, 957.

45 In its "Convention for the Safeguarding of the Intangible Cultural Heritage" treaty adopted in 2003, UNESCO defines intangible cultural heritage as "the practices, representations, expressions, knowledge, and skills – as well as the instruments, objects, artifacts and cultural spaces associated therewith – that communities, groups and, in some cases, individuals recognize as part of their cultural heritage." The treaty lists the following manifestations of such heritage: (a) oral traditions and expressions, including language as a vehicle of the intangible cultural heritage; (b) performing arts; (c) social practices, rituals and festive events; (d) knowledge and practices concerning nature and the universe; (e) traditional craftsmanship. UNESCO, "Safeguarding of Intangible Cultural Heritage."

46 Correspondence from Catherine Burns to members of the KZN CHRP team. No date available.

47 Ibid.

48 From "The Proposal: Jan 19, 2011 letter from Catherine to Mrs. Khumalo" on MatCH letterhead.

49 The syllabus for all primary school children in South Africa now has a health and medical theme in the integrated section from grades four to seven. Many schools are looking for spaces to take children where they can learn and work on this theme.
50 Patterson, "Constructions of Childhood."
51 Ibid., 90–163.
52 For published examples, see Crwys-Williams, *I Want Love in South Africa, Dear God*; Open School, *Two Dogs and Freedom*.
53 The International Museum of Children's Art in Oslo, Norway, is a good model. See: The International Museum of Children's Art, "The International Museum of Children's Art."
54 For an examination of the Sinomlando Memory Box Programme, the University of Cape Town's Memory Box Project in Khayelitsha, the Bambanani Group's Body Map Project, and Community-Based Theatre Projects addressing HIV/AIDS in South Africa, see Doubt, "Making Memory Work."
55 Stories and artwork of participant members of the Bambanani Women's Group in Cape Town, South Africa, were published in *Long Life: Positive HIV Stories*, 2003, a collaborative book based on the related Body Map and memory book projects. The method has also been used in the "treatment literacy" initiatives of the Treatment Action Campaign (TAC), an HIV/AIDS activist movement in South Africa. See Solomon, *'Living With X.'*
56 Denis, *Never Too Small to Remember*.
57 Clacherty et al., *The Suitcase Stories*.
58 Clacherty, "The World in a Suitcase."
59 Room 13, "Room 13."
60 Ibid.
61 Williams, *Memorial Museums*.
62 Many of the dedicated cots were named for military regiments, battles, or individuals killed in the First World War. Through the years, others were donated by families remembering their deceased children.
63 Baderoon, "How to Look."

CHAPTER FIVE

1 The author would like to thank the co-editors of this volume for their enthusiastic reception, patience, and belief in the Mundo Meza dream. This piece is deeply indebted to several fortuitous encounters, conversations, and chance meetings with museum stalwarts, archivist renegades, and art activists. Support for this research was supported in part by a gener-

ous grant from the Regents' Faculty Fellowship at University of California, Riverside.

2 Harry Gamboa Jr. Interview by Robb Hernández (with Tyler Stallings), audio recording, 9 March 2015. Los Angeles, California.

3 My thoughts here on the ephemerality of queer evidence are indebted to the polemic work of José Esteban Muñoz. For more, see Muñoz, "Ephemera as Evidence: Introductory Notes to Queer Acts." In *Women & Performance: A Journal of Feminist Theory* 8, no. 2 (1996): 5–16.

4 It would be remiss of me not to mention the extensive exhibition history of VIVA!: Gay and Lesbian Latino Artists of Los Angeles (1987–2001). Over its thirteen-year history, VIVA! created mixed-media art shows and performance-art spectacles that exposed the impact of AIDS, art censorship, and safe-sex education on queer Chicano and Latino artists. However, my ruminations over Meza and his unrecorded influence in contemporary Chicano art precede the formation of the VIVA! organization. For more, see Hernández, *VIVA Records*.

5 Adam Nagourney, "Los Angeles Stakes Its Claim."

6 More in-depth analysis about the significant contributions of Legorreta, Meza, Sandoval, and Terrill to a nascent queer visual language in the Chicano Art Movement can be found in my dissertation. See Hernández, "Archival Body/Archival Space."

7 Román, "Remembering AIDS," 283.

8 The Nixon exhibition at MoMA spurred protests and direct-action organizing by the AIDS Coalition to Unleash Power (ACT-UP), challenging exploitative portrayals of people "dying" wasted by disease as fine art objects. For more, see Reed, *Art and Homosexuality*, 207–28.

9 In the Asco exhibition catalogue, performance scholar David Román offers one account of AIDS in Gamboa Jr's video "Jetter's Jinx: A Conceptual Drama," starring Gronk and Humberto Sandoval. He reconsiders the play's ambiguous treatment of AIDS without direct references. Nevertheless, this piece comes at the end of the book, leaving much to be examined in the lives of queer Chicano avant-gardists whose careers were abruptly ended by AIDS. *Frozen World/Mundo Congelado* picks up on this fraught temporality. See Román, "Asco Wilde," 362–6.

10 Kristen Guzmán, *Self-Help Graphics & Art: Art in the Heart of East Los Angeles*, 10–11.

11 Josh Kun, "The New Chicano Movement."

12 Williams, "Creators of Censored-Art Museum Are Honored."

13 Welbon, "Immersion in Legacy."

14 Gamboa, "In the City of Angels, Chameleons, and Phantoms," 75.
15 Ibid.
16 Cyclona Scrapbook, [1973], Box 5, Folder 2, The Fire of Life: The Robert Legorreta–Cyclona Collection, 1962–2002, Collection 500. UCLA Chicano Studies Research Center Library and Archive, University of California, Los Angeles.
17 Hernández, *The Fire of Life*, 15–16.
18 Robert Legorreta, "Ed-Mundo Meza," Biographical Statement, [1989], The Gay, Chicanismo in El Arte Cyclona Art Collection, 1964–2004. The ONE National Gay and Lesbian Archives, Los Angeles.
19 Meza is but one of the visual artist provocateurs at Legorreta's apartment, which included Meza's then boyfriend, Charles, dressed as an oversize Valentine heart costume in elaborate white face make-up.
20 Gamboa, "Teddy Sandoval, Patssi Valdez, and Mundo Meza," 500.
21 Eddie Ytuarte, "Chicano Art Lives in East L.A.," *El Chicano* newspaper clipping, [1972], 9 (Box 2, Folder 7) Tomas Ybarra-Frausto research material, 1964–2004, Archives of American Art, Smithsonian Institution.
22 The events surrounding *Caca-Roaches Have No Friends* are recounted in Benavidez, *Gronk*, 19. Also, see Hernández, "Performing the Archival Body in the Robert 'Cyclona' Legorreta Fire of Life," 113–14.
23 According to Jennifer Flores Sternad's interview with Legorreta, Meza is credited with drawing masks for the performance. However, in personal communication with the author, he claims that Meza also painted the sets. For more, see Sternad, "Cyclona and Early Chicano Performance Art," 482.
24 Gamboa, "Teddy Sandoval, Patssi Valdez, and Mundo Meza," 499.
25 Anthony Friedkin. Interview by Robb Hernández, video recording, 4 September 2010. Los Angeles, California.
26 Pamela J. King, "Gay Photo-Art," G8.
27 "Anthony Enton Friedkin: The Gay Essay" Gallery Postcard, [N.D.], The Gay, Chicanismo in El Arte Cyclona Art Collection, 1964–2004. Unprocessed Papers. The ONE National Gay and Lesbian Archives, Los Angeles.
28 King, "Gay Photo-Art."
29 "Just Looking," 24. The Gay, Chicanismo in El Arte Cyclona Art Collection, 1964–2004. The ONE National Gay and Lesbian Archives.
30 "Frozen art" is often attributed to Legorreta's performance art corpus and not to Meza. Meza's training in photo-realist painting, visual merchandising, and window display design is an overlooked though defining element in this art practice, an advanced image-making that reconstituted the Cyclona image within the "frozen" performance act, still-life genre, and retail environment. For more on the topic, see Jones, "The Artist is Present,"

26–7; Sternad, "Cyclona and Early Chicano Performance Art," 482; and Hernández, "Archival Body/Archival Space."

31 See Arnold, *Epiphanies*.

32 Weiermair, 9.

33 Ibid.

34 Robert Legorreta, "Ed-Mundo Meza," Biographical Statement, [1989], The Gay, Chicanismo in El Arte Cyclona Art Collection, 1964–2004. The ONE National Gay and Lesbian Archives.

35 Jef Huereque. Interview by Robb Hernández, video recording, 23 August 2007. Los Angeles, California.

36 Crimp, "Portraits of People with AIDS," 117–33.

37 "Message: Jef Huereque," [1985], Harry Gamboa Jr Papers, Box 14. Audio Tape 4. Program h. Collection M0753, Dept. of Special Collections, Stanford University Libraries, Stanford.

38 Doonan, 249–50.

39 Ibid., 253.

40 Oles, *Agustín Lazo*, 11.

41 Ibid., 16–17.

42 Ibid., 16.

43 Ibid., 69.

44 Ibid., 14.

45 Ibid., 16.

46 "VIVA!'S MEXICO Price List," [1991], The VIVA Papers, 1985–95. Box 3. Folder 6. Collection 22, UCLA Chicano Studies Research Center Library and Archive, University of California, Los Angeles.

CHAPTER SIX

1 Lamp, "Aesthetics: African Dance Aesthetics," 13.

2 On this point I am indebted to my sister, Adrienne Cohen, who is currently completing her dissertation on contemporary traditional Guinean dance in the Department of Anthropology at Yale University.

3 On the early arrival of African objects in Paris see Paudrat, "From Africa," 125–74.

4 For more about the activities of key dealers see Biro, "Transformation de l'objet ethnographique africain en objet d'art."

5 On early exhibitions of African art in Paris and New York, see Pigearias and Hornn, "Paul Guillaume et l'art africain"; and Shannon, "African Art, 1914."

6 In actuality, "white" cubes for African art may be off-white, beige, or black. The classic text on the white cube is O'Doherty, *Inside the White Cube*.

7 For a discussion of the canon and its expansion, see Steiner, "Can the Canon Burst?," 213–17.

8 For a concise history of curatorial practices see Clarke, "From Theory to Practice."

9 This reflexive approach first took shape in a series of important exhibitions organized by the Museum for African Art. For an overview of this work see Vogel, "Portrait of a Museum in Practice," 97–123.

10 On artists and authorship in exhibitions see LaGamma, "Beyond Master Hands," and Walker, *Olowe of Ise*. On collaborations with artists and community involvement see Arnoldi et al., "Reflections on 'African Voices' at the Smithsonian's National Museum of Natural History," 16–35, 94; and McClusky, "Taming Reality," 224–40. I am grateful to curators Christine Mullen Kreamer and Pamela McClusky for sharing some of their insights and recent work.

11 For example, curator Okwui Enwezor's groundbreaking exhibition and accompanying catalogue, *The Short Century* (2001), examined African modernism and modernity in relation to anti-colonial and liberation movements. A useful section of the catalogue compiled key texts from the African independence era, including a famous speech by Guinea's first president, Sékou Touré (see Touré, "The Political Leader as a Representative of His Culture," 369–72). Still, the exhibition's focus on modern and contemporary art meant that post-independence initiatives to nationalize and modernize traditional arts – as happened in Touré's Guinea and numerous other newly independent states – fell beyond the purview of the project. Some art historians and anthropologists have explored the political dimensions of traditional art in scholarly articles and books, but such approaches have remained rare in exhibitions dealing with traditional art.

12 Vogel, "Whither African Art?," 15.

13 It is also an issue that has been raised recently for a general readership. See Cotter, "Under Threat."

14 As art historian Steven Nelson stated in a recent interview: "The past 20 years have witnessed a groundswell in studies of modern and contemporary African art. Alongside of this development, the past 20 years have also seen a lot of energy (for better or worse) spent on understanding the relationship between modern and contemporary and 'traditional' or 'classical' African art. On the one hand, some feel that the two should be considered as separate fields, with the former being a kind of offshoot of global contemporary art. On the other, some feel that the two can inform each other in exciting ways. Having done research on topics ranging from medieval Swahili architecture to contemporary art in Africa and its diasporas, I personally

ascribe to the latter view." Nelson, "A Conversation with Dr. Steven Nelson, *Grove Art Online* Guest Editor," http://blog.oup.com/2014/10/grove-art-steven-nelson-african/#sthash.Qmrttxbs.dpuf (accessed 26 January 2015).

15 In this way, there is a risk that contemporary traditional artists will remain absent from contemporary art museums. Perhaps the reasons for this absence lie not so much in museums as in the market. Since the early twentieth century, what the art market has done for traditional African objects is essentially to assign value, in art historian Z.S. Strother's analysis, "*only to the degree to which the artist can be made to disappear*," while making today's traditional artist (read: counterfeiter) "into what it presumed him to be: a carver mindlessly reproducing genre models." See Strother, "Gabama a Gingungu and the Secret History of Twentieth-Century Art," 31. Italics in original. To avoid quoting Strother's comments out of context, it is essential to note that her work also documents Pende artists who produce masks for both international markets and local performers.

16 I use the term "performance" (often implicitly in conjunction with what I understand to comprise the "traditional") in reference to corporal and collective practices serving a range of social and religious functions. Typically these practices are rooted in local creation and notions of form and style, regardless of whether manifesting in villages, urban settings, or concert halls. The phenomenon of staged traditional performance – what has become known as "ballet" in francophone West Africa and beyond – is considered here distinct from contemporary African dance (which maintains closer ties to Western modern dance), even though the project proposed in this essay ultimately seeks to bring these two genres into greater alignment. It is also worth noting that the above categories may conform more to Western than to African value systems. Among professional artists in Guinea, for example, distinctions between artistic genres lie more along rural/urban lines, according to differences between ritual and professional arts. I wish to thank my sister, Adrienne Cohen, for making this last point.

17 Alpers, "The Museum as a Way of Seeing," 25.

18 Ibid., 26.

19 Lamp, *Art of the Baga*, 44–53. Some Banda examples additionally feature small, European-influenced architectural constructions on the bridge of the nose.

20 Historically speaking, the very same museum context – initially ethnographic, then increasingly form-focused – afforded modernist painters and sculptors of diverse origins opportunities to look closely at African art objects and to study their expressive and formal principles. Notwithstanding the criticisms leveled at Picasso and other so-called "primitivists" for their

unacknowledged appropriations and racist attitudes, the museum was in the early twentieth century – and remains today – crucial for enabling practices of formal appreciation and engagement among students of both art history and studio art.

21 Alpers, "Museum as a Way of Seeing," 32 (italics mine).

22 Gates, "Europe, African Art, and the Uncanny," 23.

23 Wallace, "The Prison-House of Culture," 162; Okediji, "On Reparations," 9.

24 Cole, *African Arts of Transformation*; Thompson, *African Art in Motion*; Lamp, *See the Music, Hear the Dance.*

25 Taylor, *The Archive and the Repertoire*, 21–3.

26 This history is documented in greater detail in Cohen, "Stages in Transition," 11–48.

27 For more on national cultural policy in Guinea under Sékou Touré see [Guinea], *Cultural Policy*; and Straker, *Youth, Nationalism, and the Guinean Revolution.*

28 I theorized exhibition/performance differently in a previous essay: Cohen, "At Converging Obsolescences," 1–15.

29 The basic notion of exhibiting African art in a theatre is not new. For several months beginning in September 1879, sculptures from the Fang people of Gabon, Central Africa, were displayed in the lobby of the Théâtre du Châtelet in Paris during a production of *La Vénus noire*, a play directed by Adolphe Belot and adapted from Georg August Schweinfurth's book *Au Coeur d'Afrique* (1874). See Chalaye, *Du Noir au Nègre*, 28–9, 65–6, 72–3, 86, 259, 324–5. Z.S. Strother once cautioned me that to propose performance in conjunction with display of African objects is to risk reverting to the primitivizing displays of the late nineteenth and early twentieth centuries. While the legacy of exoticism surrounding African art is certainly pernicious and persistent, space does not here permit a full delineation of the differences between exhibition/performance and such primitivizing spectacles. My hope is that these differences are evident in the overall description and conceptualization of the project.

30 This occurred initially in the 1990s as the inspiration of artists Bangaly Bangoura in Conakry and M'Bemba Bangoura and Youssouf Koumbassa between Conakry and New York. Some artists have identified Sinté as the modernized version of the music and dance accompanying Banda. Documenting the historical relationship between the two forms will be the focus of future research in Guinea.

31 Frederick Lamp has produced excellent footage of the Banda masquerade in the late 1980s.

32 Hay, "The Value of Forgery," 5–18.

CHAPTER SEVEN

1 Kuspit, *The End of Art*; Danto, *After the End of Art*.
2 Bourriaud, *Relational Aesthetics*.
3 R. Mutt is the name Dadaist artist Marcel Duchamp signed to his famous 1917 "readymade," titled *Fountain*. Submitted to a New York gallery show of the Society of Independent Artists, it caused much debate about whether the piece was or was not art, and it was ultimately hidden from view during the show.
4 The Solomon R. Guggenheim Foundation, "theanyspacewhatever."
5 Museum of Contemporary Art Chicago, "Jeremy Deller."
6 Foucault, "What is an Author?" 113–38.

CHAPTER EIGHT

1 Quoted in Benjamin, "The Task of the Translator," 81.
2 Each region has developed its own tradition and customization of *la cueca*, and may use a variety of different instruments, such as the Peruvian *cajon peruano* (percussion box) or *cacharaina* (lower jaw of a donkey). In Chile there are at least ten different types of *cuecas* with distinct characteristics.
3 We are aware of at least two other Chilean artists who have also used *la cueca* to draw attention to the legacy of Chile's dictatorship: artist Nako Tako (Cheto Castellano) and Victor Hugo Bravo. Given space limitations, we are unable to offer extended discussion or curatorial treatment of these works at present. We hope to include their repertoires in the performance series organized at the end of our exhibition.
4 *Oxford English Dictionary*, "curator."
5 Taylor, *The Archive and the Repertoire*, 12. "Performance art" is often translated to Spanish either as simply *performance* or as *arte dramático*.
6 See Goldberg, *Performance Art*. Even though Goldberg recognizes the influences of cabaret theatre and non-Western art practices on Futurist and Dada artists, her historical frame is decidedly Eurocentric, and her explorations of other influences or precursors to performance art are minimal. While many authoritarian regimes may downplay modern and elite influences to promote an "authentic" vernacular tradition that is framed as pure and unchanged, in Chile this is more difficult to ascertain. In our opinion, the Pinochet regime was primarily concerned with coopting this regional vernacular tradition and reframing it as a distinctly Chilean (national) cultural practice. This framing initiated by the military regime has not been questioned by latter democratic leaders, and its cooptation under national

discourse continues today. For example, in the bicentennial celebrations of 2010, which are devoted to the commemoration of Chile's national identity, and which were organized under both Bachelet (socialist) and Piñera's (conservative RN) governments, both traditional and contemporary repertoires of *la cueca* proliferated. We discuss this in the conclusion of our essay.

7 Taylor, *The Archive and the Repertoire*, 15.

8 We distinguish these works from theatre because they do not follow scripts written by a playwright, and are not directed or produced in a theatrical fashion. Instead, they feature artists (and often audience members) who perform in the work, acting only as themselves, as opposed to taking on the attributes of other characters.

9 Lissette Olivares has written about the distinct genealogies of *Actions, Acciones* and *Interventions* in the forthcoming *Routledge Encyclopedia of Performance Terms.*

10 Taylor, *The Archive and the Repertoire*, 14.

11 Clifford, *The Predicament of Culture*, 25.

12 Benjamin, "The Task of the Translator," 75.

13 Museo de la Solidaridad Salvador Allende, "El Museo."

14 This denotation was given by the regime's officials, who refused to acknowledge their own culpability in the disappearance of these individuals.

15 Apart from the performances of *la cueca sola* cited here, the dance also achieved iconic status when it was performed during the post-1989 plebiscite celebrations that were staged in the National Stadium to welcome the return of democracy. Furthermore, the impact of the dance's symbolism achieved international recognition when the DDHH's performance was publicized by Sting's song "They Dance Alone."

16 The song's lyrics clearly describe the women's plight: "Why are there women here dancing on their own? Why is there this sadness in their eyes? … It's the only form of protest they're allowed; I've seen their silent faces scream so loud … They're dancing with the missing; They're dancing with the dead."

17 Sting states in the booklet for his album *Nothing Like the Sun* (1987): "On the Amnesty Tour of 1986 the musicians were introduced to former political prisoners, victims of torture and imprisonment without trial, from all over the world. These meetings had a strong effect on all of us. It's one thing to read about torture but to speak to a victim brings you a step closer to the reality that is so frighteningly pervasive. We were all deeply affected."

18 One of the most extensive collections of these works is owned by Marjorie Agosin, whose book *Tapestries of Hope, Threads of Love: Arpillera Movement of Chile 1974–1994* (1996) documents the role of these weavings in the cultural and political activism of the widows.

19 For many people around the world, this historical moment is remembered with great clarity, as it was the first and only time that the dictator was confined to prison.

20 Carola Jérez. Personal Interview with Lissette Olivares, January 15 (2008).

21 See Diana Taylor's books *The Archive and the Repertoire* (2003) and *Holy Terrors,* which she co-edited with Roselyn Costantino (2003). Taylor goes to great lengths to theorize many forms of performance across national and institutional borders. However, she does not directly question why some performances achieve the status of art and others do not.

22 Tollita Diaz. Personal interview with Lissette Olivares, 7 February (2008).

23 Very few photographs or other documents of this performance are available to the public. Some of the photographs cited here appear in: Maura, "Las Yeguas del Apocalipsis en una acción de arte," 27 (photos by Carla Moller). The photos were published more recently in *Copiar el Edén: Arte Reciente en Chile,* ed. Gerardo Mosquera (2007) and our co-authored article: Gomoll and Olivares, "Inversión de la Materia." The atmosphere of silence during the performance was confirmed by both an eyewitness account from Isabel Larrain, and the article "Las Yeguas del apocalipsis en una acción de arte" by Maura Brescia.

24 Brescia, "Las Yeguas del Apocalipsis en una acción de arte," 27.

25 Ibid.

26 French-Chilean cultural critic Nelly Richard argues that the term *Avanzada* (Advanced) is "simply operative," that it "covers the work carried out by Chileans engaged in counter-institutional practices from 1979–present," and that it is used to "avoid confusion with the nostalgic connotations of the word 'avant-garde.'" Nonetheless, Richard's term establishes boundaries between the formal and stylistic approach used by those in the *Avanzada,* and those in other realms of counter-cultural production, such as *Las Yeguas del Apocalipsis.* Richard's framing asserts that the *Avanzada* scene is distinct from the realm of other popular cultural production of the period because it "dared to gamble on a form of creativity able to disrupt the order imposed on language by the figures of authority and their grammar of power," working to gain public visibility, rather than the "spontaneous expression of rebellion" and the "temptation of anti-institutional types of resistance." For Richard, parallel cultural and popular art movements such as the Young Artists Association were mainly informed by an "aesthetics of commitment," which she describes as combative and illustrative of national crisis. She argues that this art was out of touch with the *Avanzada* because "their strategies were radically different." Ironically, this statement marked how a separation between formal and stylistic strategies used in the *Avanzada* are

used to expound the *Avanzada's* originality, and its refinement of aesthetic expression. Other Chilean art critics, such as Willy Thayer, have argued that to use the term *Avanzada* is akin to using Richard's signature. See: Richard, *Margins & Institutions*, 21–4. See also: Richard et al., *Arte y Politica 1973–1990*.

27 *Mapuche* (*mapu-* earth, *che-* people, or together "people of the earth") is an umbrella term for the indigenous groups that speak *Mapudungun*, primarily located in the South of Chile and Argentina. *Arauco* (Araucanian) is not found in the *Mapudungun* language; rather it is the name Europeans gave to this same indigenous group, due to their geographic habitation of "*Arauco*" in the South of Chile, which is a name of unknown origin that was also coined by the Europeans.

28 Hall, "The Rediscovery of Ideology."

29 See: http://www.lanacion.cl/presidente-pinera-inauguro-celebraciones-del-bicentenario/noticias/2010-09-16/213106.html. Last accessed 25 September 2015.

CHAPTER NINE

1 Angelou, "On the Pulse of the Morning."

2 As cited in Beiner, "Hannah Arendt on Judging," 113.

3 For an extensive number of David McMillan's 1994 photographs in Pripyat within the Chernobyl exclusion zone, see http://home.cc.umanitoba.ca/~dmcmill/.

4 For information on the Arctic Exile Monument Project see http://www.tunngavik.com/current-initiatives/arctic-exile- monument-project/.

5 Apology for the Inuit High Arctic Relocation: speaking notes for the Honourable John Duncan, PC MP, minister of Indian affairs and northern development and federal interlocutor for Métis and Non-Status Indians, 18 August 2010, Inukjuak, Nunavik. http://198.103.249.70/eng/1100100016115.

6 For a discussion of Malena Tytelman's *testimonio*, *Cuando Ves Pasar el Tren*, see Pauchulo, "Living with Loss," 184.

7 Ibid.

8 Symposium announcement: "Second Thoughts on the Memory Industry," New York Institute for the Humanities, New York University, 7 May 2011. http://nyihumanities.org/event/second-thoughts-on-the-memory-industry-a-symposium

9 Todorov, "Memory as Remedy for Evil," 447–62.

10 Rothberg, *Multidirectional Memory*.

11 Berlant, "Intuitionists: History and the Affective Event," 845–60.
12 King, "Arendt Between Past and Future," 250–62.
13 Britzman, *Lost Subjects, Contested Objects.*
14 Rothberg, *Multidirectional Memory,* 139.
15 Within literary study, parataxis refers to the placing of propositions or clauses one after the other, side by side, without indicating with conjunctions or connecting words, the relation (or co-ordination or subordination) between them. Adorno has a compact understanding of this form of expression; he describes parataxis as "artificial disturbances that evade the logical hierarchy of a subordinating syntax."
16 Simon et al., "Remembrance as Praxis and the Ethics of the Inter-Human."
17 Herscher, "Points of No Return."
18 Rothberg, *Multidirectional Memory,* 18–19.
19 Giroux, *Stormy Weather.*
20 Simon et al., "Heritage and Practices of Social Formation," 247–54.
21 Derrida, *Spectres of Marx.*
22 Benjamin, "Thesis on the Philosophy of History," 255.

CHAPTER TEN

1 Freire, *Pedagogy of Indignation,* 32–3.
2 Lindauer, "Critical Museum Pedagogy," 303–14.
3 Freire, *Pedagogy of the Oppressed.*
4 Ibid., 30, 32, 37.
5 See Henry Giroux, *Disturbing Pleasures: Learning Popular Culture* (New York: Routledge, 1994).
6 Freire, *Pedagogy of Indignation,* 53–4.
7 Ibid., 64.
8 Ibid., 34.
9 Freire, *Pedagogy of the Oppressed,* 74.
10 Ibid., 64.
11 By the fall of 1863, 425 Mescalero Apache people were imprisoned. In November 1965, 335 surviving detainees escaped en masse, "leaving only nine enfeebled and aged members of the tribe" (Bailey, *Bosque Redondo,* 160). An account of the historical and cultural significance of their internment is beyond the scope of this paper.
12 A copy of this note is on file at the Bosque Redondo Memorial; for a more detailed account of the history of the site as momument and memorial, see Margaret Lindauer, "Bosque Redondo: A Memorial in the Making," *Museum Management and Curatorship* 28, 3 (2013): 307–23.

13 Norbert Herrera, Plant & Facility Manager, Bosque Redondo Memorial, personal communication, 5 January 2011. See also David Roberts and Arthur Shilstone, "The Long Walk to Bosque Redondo." *Smithsonian Magazine* 28, 9 (1997): 46–55.

14 Norbert Herrera, personal communication, 5 January 2011.

15 United States Statutes at Large, Vol. 146, Part 16, 13 October through 24 October 2000, 23006.

16 Phase two of the building was built in 2009. At the time of writing, an exhibition was in the planning stage.

17 See www.bosqueredondomemorial.com (accessed 29 August 2011).

18 John Burnett, "The Navajo Nation's Own Trail of Tears," *National Public Radio*, www.npr.org/2005/06/15/4703136/the-navajo-nation-s-own-trail-of-tears (accessed 31 October 2011).

19 See Ben Moffett, "Hwééldi, the Place of Suffering," *El Palacio* (January 2006), 15.

20 Conn, *Do Museums Still Need Objects?* 46.

21 Freire, *Pedagogy of Freedom*, 26.

22 Ibid., 37.

23 *In the Footsteps of Yellow Woman*, directed/performed by Camille Manybeads Tso (Flagstaff, AZ: Outta Your Backpack Media, 2009).

24 Sontag, *Regarding the Pain of Others.*

25 Bailey, *The Long* Walk; Roessel, *Navajo Stories of the Long Walk Period.*

26 See Spicer, *Cycles of Conquest.*

27 This juxtaposition is inspired by a similar display at the Navajo Nation Museum, in Window Rock, Arizona.

28 Bailey and Bailey, *A History of the Navajo*, 17.

29 Bailey, *The Long Walk*, 21n7.

30 Ibid., 3.

31 Bailey and Bailey, *A History of the Navajo*, 18.

32 See Bailey, *The Long Walk*, 139–42.

33 See Curly Tso, in Roessel, *Navajo Stories of the Long Walk*, 92–108.

34 See Hazen-Hammond, *Timelines of Native American History.*

35 Freire, *Pedagogy of Indignation*, 62.

36 Farris, *Navajo and Photography*, 55.

37 Williams, *Memorial Museums*, 8.

38 Forrest, *With a Camera in Old Navaho Land*, 33.

39 Photographers who might be commissioned to create these portraits include Don James, whose work is published in *One Nation One Year: A Navajo Photographer's 365-Day Journey Into a World of Discovery, Life and Hope* (Rio Ranchos, NM: Rio Grande Books, 2010) and Kenji Kawamo, a

Japanese-born photographer who has worked for the Navajo Nation and *Navajo Times Today*.

40 Some artworks invoke traditional materials or patterns, such as woven textiles by Lola Cody, whose work was awarded Best of Show in the 2014 Santa Fe Indian Market. Other artworks address contemporary concerns regarding history, identity, and place – such as works by photographer Will Wilson, painter Steven Yazzie, and mixed media/installation artist Lorenzo Clayton, all of whom are represented in the Vision Project at the Museum of Contemporary Native Arts http://www.iaia.edu/museum/vision-project/.

41 Adams, *Education for Extinction.*

42 Cited in Tohe, *No Parole Today*, xi.

43 Crow Dog, "Civilize Them With a Stick," 241.

44 Lomawaima, *They Called it Prairie* Light, 159–60.

45 Tohe, *No Parole Today*, xii.

46 Weiss, *The Development of Capitalism in the Navajo* Nation, 55.

47 See Bailey and Bailey, *A History of the Navajo*, 185–93.

48 Freire, *Pedagogy of Indignation*, 109.

49 Pasternak, *Yellow Dirt.*

50 Ibid., 237–8.

51 *The Return of Navajo Boy*, directed by Jeff Spitz (Chicago: Groundswell Educational Films, 2009). See http://www.navajoboy.com.

52 See navajoboy.com/webisodes for updates on environmental cleanup of uranium in the Navajo Nation, accessed 29 August 2011.

53 Freire, *Pedagogy of Indignation*, 56.

54 Freire, *Pedagogy of Freedom*, 25.

CHAPTER ELEVEN

1 See, for example: Ames, *Museums, the Public, and Anthropology*; Dos Santos, "Don't we all have problems?"; Durrans, "The Future of the Other"; Harris and O'Hanlon, "The Future of the Ethnographic Museum"; Muñoz, "When the 'Other' Became the Neighbour"; Peers and Brown, *Museums and Source Communities*; Pieterse, "Multiculturalism and Museums"; Van Dartel, *Tropenmuseum for a Change!*

2 Legêne, "Refurbishment." Our curatorial dream is inspired by the successful efforts of *Travelling Tales* to show the complex and changing nature of cultures and their intangible expressions, including stories and ways of storytelling. *Travelling Tales* focuses on people, particularly migratory subjects, effectively presenting them as key agents in the process of cultural change and as active contributors to *Dutch* culture through singing,

dancing, performing stories, and enacting traditions from their countries of origin (Boonstra, "Conceptualising Intangible Heritage in the Tropenmuseum," 37). In the display "UnboundedNL," however, *Travelling Tales* takes a step forward by moving beyond ethnographic museums' traditional focus on the 'other.' Similarly to the *World in One City*, "UnboundedNL" concentrates on the here and now, and presents stories and performances "that are part of Dutch societies today" (van Dartel, "There's a Story behind Everything," 349). Significantly, not only migrants to the Netherlands but also a number of "ethnic" Dutch feature in "UnboundedNL." Dutch people are presented while performing both Dutch and world stories, thus effectively questioning binary dichotomies such as us and them, ourselves and the others (Iervolino, *Ethnographic Museums in Mutation*, 167).

3 Bhabha, *The Location of Culture.*

4 Sandell, *Museums, Prejudice and the Reframing of Difference.*

5 Gorman, "Levels of Expertise and Trading Zones."

6 Pimpaneau, "Quand l'ethnographie s'expose."

7 Silverman, "The Legacy of Ethnography," 9.

8 Shannon, "The Construction of Native Voice at the National Museum of the American Indian."

9 Dos Santos, "Don't we all have problems?" 41.

10 Peers and Brown, *Museums and Source Communities.*

11 See, for example, Anthony Shelton's account (2003) of the exhibition *African Worlds* at the Horniman Museum, produced with the collaboration of people of African and Caribbean descent living in or near London, and Eithne Nightingale and Deborah Swallow's narration (2003) of the show *The Arts of the Sikh Kingdoms* at the Victoria and Albert Museum created together with the Sikh community. Bodo et al., *Museums as Places for Intercultural Dialogue*, provides us with an account of a series of initiatives carried out within the European project *Museums as Places for Intercultural Dialogue* (MAP for ID), which used ethnographic collections (as well as other types of collections) of museums across Europe to engage with immigrant communities.

12 Rassool, "Ethnographic Elaborations, Indigenous Contestations."

13 Faber and van Dartel, "Introduction."

14 Muñoz, "When the 'Other' Became the Neighbour."

15 The project was funded by the Culture Program (2007–13) of the European Union and was led by Anne Marie Bouttiaux and the Musée royal de l'Afrique centrale in Tervuren, Belgium. It involved ten ethnographic and world cultures museums across Europe.

16 La Rocca, "Foreword," 3.

17 RIME culminated with a major international conference, *The Future of Ethnographic Museums*, hosted by the Pitt Rivers Museum and Keble College, University of Oxford (19–21 July 2013) (see http://www.prm.ox.ac.uk/PRMconference_details.html. Accessed 14 February 2015).

18 The Tropenmuseum and its children's museum, the Tropenmuseum Junior, were two departments of the KIT, a centre of knowledge and expertise in the areas of international and intercultural cooperation. The other departments of the KIT included Biomedical Research, Development Policy and Practice, Information Library Services, and Tropentheater.

19 The National Museum of World Cultures is one of the Netherlands' top ten museums in terms of visitor numbers and, when it was established, it held a collection of four hundred thousand items.

20 In addition, a new department of the National Museum of World Cultures, the Research Center for Material Culture, was created in Leiden, where academic and scholarly activities of the three former museums were centralized.

21 The original names were retained, as they are "brands that have a history that goes a long way back" and are well known to national and international audiences (ASEMUS 2014).

22 The Ministry of Foreign Affairs used to provide 50 percent of the institution's funding, while the remaining half was generated by the museum itself through entrance fees, etc. Since 1999 the funding provided by the Ministry of Foreign Affairs was "organised in an 'output finance' structure" (Van Beurden, *Partnership in Cultural Heritage*), as the Tropenmuseum was required to deliver certain products to the ministry, including international projects. This funding arrangement placed the Tropenmuseum in a unique position in comparison to other ethnographic museums in the Netherlands, as the institution's existence, its policies, exhibition narratives, and strategies were closely tied to Dutch policies and practices in the area of development cooperation. The Museum Volkenkunde in Leiden and the Afrika Museum in Berg en Dal were, and still are, funded by the Ministry of Education, Culture and Science, while the Municipality of Rotterdam sponsors another Dutch ethnological museum, the Wereldmuseum.

23 Hildering et al., "Visualizing Development," 310.

24 Durrans, "The Future of the Other."

25 Van Dartel, "Dilemmas of the ethnographic museum."

26 Van Brakel and Legêne, *Collecting at Cultural Crossroads.*

27 Kreps, "Decolonizing Anthropology Museums," 56.

28 Ibid., 58.

29 For further information see Van Dartel, *Tropenmuseum for a Change!*

30 Kreps, "Decolonizing Anthropology Museums," 61.

31 Although in the seventeenth and eighteenth century the country already welcomed Protestants and Jewish people escaping persecutions in other countries as well as migrants from neighbouring countries, here we focus on immigration after the Second World War.

32 Ter Wal, "The Netherlands."

33 By 2003 the six largest ethnic minority groups were, in order, Turkey, Morocco, Suriname, Netherlands Antilles and Aruba, Indonesia, and Former Yugoslavia (Ter Wal, "The Netherlands.")

34 Koopmans, *Trade-Offs between Equality and Difference.*

35 Islamophobia is understood here as the prejudice against Muslims which "involves the deployment of reductive and essentialised notions of what it means to be Muslim." Sandell, *Museums, Prejudice and the Reframing of Difference*, 92.

36 More recently, fierce debates over immigration policies and the presence of Muslims in Europe, including the Netherlands, have followed.

37 Sandell and Dodd, *Representing Disability.*

38 Sandell, *Museums, Prejudice and the Reframing of Difference.*

39 Bhabha, *The Location of Culture.*

40 Moore-Gilbert, "Spivak and Bhabha."

41 McRobbie, *The Uses of Cultural Studies*, 98.

42 In the 1980s the Netherlands was one of the first European countries to adopt an integration policy that supported an ideology of multiculturalism. However, multiculturalism "was never accepted or practiced as fully as it has often been suggested in more stereotypical depictions of Dutch integration policy" (Vink, "Dutch 'Multiculturalism' Beyond the Pillarisation Myth," 337). Especially during the last decade multiculturalism has been increasingly criticized, and more restricted policies have been applied, which have led many to declare the crisis of Dutch multicultural policies (see Carle, "Demise of Dutch Multiculturalism," and Jacobs, "Alive and kicking? Multiculturalism in Flanders"). The country's current model of multiculturalism favours a strategy of civic integration which grants rights to migrants and minorities, while clearly establishing responsibilities and duties (Prins and Saharso, "From Toleration to Repression," 88).

43 Hallam and Street, "Introduction," 5.

44 The average age of adult visitors to the Tropenmuseum is thirty-five, ten years younger than in other Dutch museums.

45 Voogt, "Presentation Discourse: Public and Presentation," 71.

46 Faber, "The Museum discourse: Museum policy."

47 Sjørslev, "Intangible cultural heritage and ethnographic museum practice in a global perspective."
48 Silverman, "Preface" in *Social Work in Museums*, xi.
49 Margry and Roodenburg, *Reframing Dutch Culture*, 2.
50 Simon, *The Participatory Museum*.
51 Gorman, "Levels of Expertise and Trading Zones."
52 The facilitation of cooperative, constructive, and egalitarian engagement among museum professionals, disciplinary experts, and invited participants remains a challenging goal in ethnographic museums, as well as in other types of museums (see, for instance Lynch, "Collaboration, Contestation and Creative Conflict"; Lynch, "Whose Cake Is It Anyway?"; Lynch and Alberti, "Legacies of Prejudice").
53 Gorman, "Levels of Expertise and Trading Zones." Gorman identifies three types of trading zones: élite, interactive, and contributory. Contributory trading zones are those where participants share a common goal and engage each other deeply in order to develop a new system/technology.
54 The exhibition might, for example, address issues generated by the presence of city dwellers whose ways of living or cultural traditions are perceived to be contradictory to Judaeo-Christian values often unquestioned in the Western world, such as those connected to travelling lifestyles, dress conventions, marriage practices, and so on.
55 During observations carried out at the Tropenmuseum in January 2010 it was noticed that many visitors to the two galleries made extensive use of the available spaces for sitting, resting, and reflection.
56 Dibbits, "Moroccan Dutch Boys and the Authentication of Clothing Styles." Inspired by Dibbits's research, we regard Moroccan-Dutch young people's clothing style as particularly relevant in the context of *The World in One City*. Dibbits argues that through their dress, Moroccan-Dutch youth seek to construct a *metropolitan* or *Mediterranean* identity more than either a Moroccan or a Dutch one. She also suggests that, thanks to Dutch fashion designers' recent incorporation of Moroccan garments into their elite designs, the broader Dutch public is also increasingly looking to Morocco for their clothing styles.
57 Van der Horst, "Appropriating Modernity and Tradition."
58 Villevoye has found inspiration in his travels to the former Dutch colony of Papua to which he regularly travelled since the end of the 1980s and, particularly, in his encounters with the Asmat people, with whom he has developed very strong ties.
59 Legêne, "Enlightenment, Empathy, Retreat," 228.

60 Ter Braak, *Zielenruil.*

61 Ibid.

62 Initially we envisaged also showing an interview with Omomá, as it was believed that the inclusion of his actual voice in the exhibition would have been particularly powerful. Unfortunately, during the process of "exhibition production" this turned out to be unfeasible as in spring 2011 Omomá sadly passed away at the age of about forty-five.

63 See http://www.tropenmuseum.nl/-/MUS/55687/Tropenmuseum/Collection/Madonna-(after-Omom-and-Cline).

64 European Institute for Comparative Cultural Research (ERICarts), "Sharing Diversity: National Approaches to Intercultural Dialogue in Europe" (An ERICarts Study for the European Commission, 2008): 28.

65 Sandell, *Museums, Prejudice and the Reframing of Difference*, 117.

66 Wehner and Sear, "Engaging the Material World," 153.

67 European Institute for Comparative Cultural Research (ERICarts), "Sharing Diversity: National Approaches to Intercultural Dialogue in Europe" (An ERICarts Study for the European Commission, 2008).

68 The history of the Human Library goes back to 1993, although it was formally born in 2000 when it was organized at the Roskilde Festival (Denmark). Nowadays most of the human libraries are hosted in public libraries, while others are located in educational institutions, festivals, book fairs, etc. See http://humanlibrary.org/what-is-the-living-library.html.

69 Bodo et al., *Museums as Places for Intercultural Dialogue.*

70 Cameron and Kelly, *Hot Topics, Public Culture and Museums.*

71 Shelton, *Museums and Source Communities,* 211.

72 See, for example, the account of the debates that occurred during the Tropenmuseum's 2009 symposium in Van Stipriaan, "Social discourse."

73 Sandell, *Museums, Prejudice and the Reframing of Difference* and Janes, *Museums in a Troubled World.*

74 Sandell, "Ethics and Activism."

75 Ibid.

76 Janes, *Museums in a Troubled World.*

CHAPTER TWELVE

1 Itwaru and Ksonzek, *Closed Entrances*, 93.

2 My title borrows the English translation of André Malraux's *Musée Imaginaire* (1965). Malraux's *Museum Without Walls* explored new ways of curating and circulating art with the advent of photography. The expression

"museum without walls" is popularly associated with virtual museums, and cultural and educational tourism, including walking tour apps such as CultureNOW. I use the expression to highlight the power of museum spaces to constitute meaning and identity, as well as utopian possibilities for meddling with such spaces.

3 See Lovell, *Betwixt, Between, Bewitched* and Royal Ontario Museum, Rahimi, "Reflecting on 'Into the Heart of Africa.'"

4 Butler, *Contested Representations,* 105–23.

5 Royal Ontario Museum, "ROM ReCollects."

6 *Curating Black History and Culture in Canada.* Centre for Ethnographic Research and Exhibition in the Aftermath of Violence. Concordia University. October 2012. Presenters included: Jenny Burman (McGill University), Irvine Carvery (Africville Genealogy Society), Afua Cooper (Dalhousie University), Warren Crichlow (York University), Ken Donovan, Silvia Forni (Royal Ontario Museum), Arlene Ghemacher (Royal Ontario Museum), Shannon Prince (Buxton National Historic Site & Museum), Charmaine A. Nelson (McGill University), Rinaldo Walcott (University of Toronto), Dorothy W. Williams (Black Community Resource Centre). Other participants included: Jennifer Carter (Université du Québec à Montréal), Julie Crooks (University of London), Dominique Fontaine (aPOSteRIORI), Kenneth Montague (Wedge Curatorial Projects), Monica Eileen Patterson (Concordia University), Cheryl Thompson (McGill University), Erica Lehrer (Concordia University). At the time of the workshop, my curatorial dream was titled *To and Fro: Belonging and Exclusion at the ROM*, to evoke movements between galleries and negotiation between communities (pace Phillips "Community Collaboration"), but the title did not resonate with many workshop participants.

7 Butler, "Review of the African Gallery." The ROM also holds a significant archeological collection from Nubia and Egypt, which is not displayed in the African gallery.

8 Butler, *Contested Representations,* 113–14.

9 The full name of the gallery is the Shreyas and Mina Aimera Gallery of Africa, the Americas and Asia-Pacific.

10 Vaughan, *The Museum.*

11 Kirshenblatt-Gimblett, "The Museum," 1; MacLeod, "Introduction," 1.

12 Fleming, "Creative Space," 55. Barriers are also class-inflected and museums reinforce social inequalities in real and symbolic ways. See Sandell, "Constructing and communicating equality," 185.

13 The gallery's full name is the Sigmund Samuel Gallery of Canada. It reopened in 2007 after a renewal process.

14 Butler, *Contested Representations*, 10, 64. On similar discomfort at the Maryland Historical Society in Baltimore, see "A Change of Heart."

15 "Into the Heart of Africa" video by Firoza Elavia, Azed Majeed, and David Sutherland. The video soundtrack is KRS-One's rap "You Must Learn." A sample lyric: "No one told you about Benjamin Banneker, a brilliant black man that invented the almanac." That its references are American does not diminish its resonance in Canada and is a testament to the transnational quality of critical pedagogy.

16 "Meddling in the Museum" was the title of Michael Nicholl Yaghgulaanus's exhibition at the Museum of Anthropology, University of British Columbia, in 2007.

17 The Canadian gallery is located on the first floor of the historical Weston Wing. The three other spaces are in the Crystal. The "Stair of Wonders" connects the first floor atrium to the African gallery.

18 Documentation prevents the fate of "ephemerality" that haunts temporary exhibitions and interventions. Thanks to Rinaldo Walcott for this suggestion.

19 Corrin, *Mining the Museum*.

20 This contrasts with the methodology of the Croatian curatorial collective *What How and for Whom* (*WHW*), which speaks in a unified voice to affirm members' equality. Bronwnell, "Croatian Curators Make Mark." Other curatorial collectives forge collaborations between differently positioned curators. See the European Biennial of Contemporary Art (2008) http://manifesta.org/2009/09/three-curatorial-collectives-in-charge-of-manifesta-8/ and the Aboriginal Curatorial Collective http://www.aboriginalcuratorialcollective.org/.

21 Simon, *The Participatory Museum*, 190–1.

22 Lynch and Alberti, "Legacies of Prejudice" and Ashley, "Negotiating Narratives of Canada."

23 Burman, "Co-Motion in the Diasporic City," 110–20.

24 "A Change of Heart."

25 Thanks to Jenny Burman, Rinaldo Walcott, and Cheryl Thompson for raising these issues.

26 On cinematic depictions of museum transgressions, see Baker, this volume.

27 Thanks to Silvia Forni for keeping me up to date on ROM activities.

28 I do not mean to suggest that the aforementioned museum programming falls into these categories, nor to deny their appeal or the quality of the interior and social experiences they may engender. Sign me up for yoga in a museum anytime!

29 MacLeod, "Introduction," 1.

30 Simon, "The Participatory Museum," 214. My use of postcards is inspired by the interventions of Erica Lehrer on Jewish heritage in Poland and the "Postcards for Tolerance" created by audiences at the Andy Warhol Museum in conjunction with its exhibition "Without Sanctuary: Lynching Photography in America" (2001–02). See Lehrer and Smotrich, "Jewish? Heritage? In Poland?" and Gogan, "The Warhol: Museum as Artist." Thanks to Dominique Fontaine, who raised the issue of virtual vs. real postcards.

31 Macdonald, "Museums, national, postnational, and transnational identities," 1–16.

32 Granted, this is not the primary mandate of the African gallery, but museums and galleries can take on multiple tasks, especially when hosting temporary exhibitions and interventions.

33 These include: *The Underground Railway: Next Stop Freedom* (2002), which was a collaboration between Parks Canada and the Ontario Black History Society; *African Quilts from Southern Ontario* (2010), for which ROM curator Silvia Forni worked closely with the Buxton National Historic Site & Museum; and *Position as Desired: Exploring African Canadian Heritage: Photography from the Wedge Collection* (Octobert 2010–March 2011), curated by Kenneth Montague, Wedge Curatorial Productions.

34 The photo portrait is entitled *Sign* and is by Dawit L. Petros, who was born in Eritrea, lived in Kenya and Saskatchewan, and is now based in New York, participating in the global art circuit. See Crooks, "*Position as Desired*," 25–6.

35 Walcott, *Black Like Who? Stitching Community* noted that slavery was only abolished in Canada after 1834. However, this was overshadowed by signage referring to Canada as a "land of freedom." Exhibits about slavery, as with other difficult histories, are ethically, emotionally, and politically complex. See Ashley, "Negotiating Narratives of Canada." *Museum without Walls* is not an exhibition about slavery, but is meant to generate awareness and reflection about its absence in the ROM.

36 Historica Canada, "Underground Railroad."

37 *The Book of Negroes* by Lawrence Hill is an extraordinarily well researched work of historical fiction about an enslaved girl who eventually joins three thousand black loyalists in moving to Nova Scotia (Canada) in 1783. Black loyalists experienced such hardships and injustice there that over twelve hundred chose in 1792 to leave, sailing for Sierra Leone in West Africa to found the colony of Freetown. *The Hanging of Angélique* by historian and poet Afua Cooper, analytically evokes the life and trial of Marie-Joseph Angélique, a slave woman found guilty of setting fire to Montreal in 1734. Another resource/postcard image for the thematic of absence and rethink-

ing African-Canadian history is artwork by Chantal Gibson. See *Ethnographic Terminalia*, "Chantal Gibson."

38 I borrow the notion of a productive "thinking walk" from writer A.A. Milne and acknowledge Michel de Certeau's utopian notion of walking as psychologically empowering, an act of claiming space: "Walking affirms, suspects, tries out, transgresses, respects, etc. the trajectories it 'speaks' (99)" Another source of inspiration is performance artist Tino Seghal's piece called "This Progress," designed for the Guggenheim Museum of Contemporary Art in New York. A series of guides accompanied museum visitors up the gallery's spiral ramp; the first was a child, then a teenager, then an adult, and finally an elderly person. Each guide engaged visitors on the question of progress. The "Stair of Wonders" is unfortunately not wheelchair accessible, so a similar exercise would need to be developed for the elevator.

39 African-Canadian historian Dorothy Williams links her experience of being "othered" in Quebec to the province's erasure of its history of slavery. See the 2010 documentary *Les Mains Noires: Procès de l'esclave incendiaire* by Tetchena Bellange. In a related vein, filmmaker Ali Kazimi states: "I want Canadians to confront the founding notion of a white Canada and how the legacy of whiteness continues to haunt us today. If we don't confront that uncomfortable truth, people like me will be 'new Canadians' forever." Tancock, "White Wash," 29.

40 Turner, "Miss Canadiana."

41 Royal Ontario Museum, "ROM Expands its African Collection."

42 Butler, *Contested Representations*, 117–18; Phillips, "Where is 'Africa'?"

43 See Butler, "Review of the African Gallery," 197–8.

44 Ideally, this would be narrated by the author Marlene NourbeSe Philip, who lives in Toronto and was an active participant in the *Into the Heart of Africa* debates.

45 This curatorial strategy is evident in the Daphne Cockwell Gallery of Canada's First Peoples, where members of an advisory committee provide textual commentary on a favourite object. The effect is eclectic and personal, though I question why ROM curators did not also participate in the exercise.

46 Africville is commemorated by folk and jazz singer-songwriter Faith Nolan (1986), jazz pianist Joe Sealy (1996), the metal/hardcore band Bucket Truck (2007), and the hip hop group Black Union (2007).

47 Philip, "Race, Space, and the Poetics of Moving."

48 The Museum without Walls workshop already generated a more diverse list of relevant artists and poets (such as Lillian Allen, D'bi Young Anitafrika, Isreal Jones) as well as a discussion regarding the potential problem of re-

inforcing a stereotype that equates black culture with hip hop and rap. On aboriginal hip hop see http://www.beatnation.org/. Accessed 15 June 2014.

49 In March 2015, the ROM removed the portrait of the donors from the Spirit House when a national newspaper published their investigation of philanthropists' unpaid pledges to the ROM, including the bulk of Michael Lee-Chin's donation, as well as that of Shreyas and Mina Ajmera. Major donors are also board members. See McArthur et al., "Behind the façade." On racialized inequality in Canada see Galabuzi, *Canada's Economic Apartheid*.

40 See "Shelley-Ann Brown"; Moore, "Burning cross"; CBC News, "Halifax Apologizes"; CBC News, "Montreal students."

51 Simon, *The Participatory Museum*, 214.

52 Binder, *El Anatsui*, 133. Also see Whyte, "El Anatsui."

53 The three-year multi-platform project was launched in October 2014. See http://www.rom.on.ca/en/about-us/newsroom/press-releases/roms-of-africa-project-explores-historical-and-contemporary-african.

54 Quoted in Marstine, "Museologically Speaking."

55 It would be especially productive to bring together school groups from different parts of the city to ensure greater socioeconomic and cultural diversity.

56 Mears and Modest, "Museums, African Collections and Social Justice"; Dewdney et al., *Post-Critical Museology*.

57 Here I paraphrase Michel de Certeau from his classic work, *The Practice of Everyday Life*.

CHAPTER THIRTEEN

1 A wide range of medical museums and other associated public history sites are listed in Lipp, *Medical Landmarks USA*. The classic "cabinet of curiosities" approach to medical history is exemplified by the Warren Anatomical Museum at Harvard. Newer institutions usually focus more on modern science and technology driven exhibitions. See, for example, *Infectious Disease: Evolving Challenges to Human Health* at the Marian Koshland Science Museum of the National Academy of Sciences, http://www.koshland-science-museum.org/exhib_infectious/ (accessed 10 April 2015), or the David J. Sencer CDC Museum at the United States Centers for Disease Control, http://www.cdc.gov/museum/index.htm (accessed 10 April 2015).

2 US National Library of Medicine, "Against The Odds"; US National Library of Medicine, "Changing the Face of Medicine"; US National Library of Medicine, "Life and Limb"; US National Library of Medicine, "The Literature of Prescription"; US National Library of Medicine, "Visible Proofs."

3 Alexander, *Museums in Motion*, 61–76.

4 Jordanova, "Medicine and Genres of Display," 211.

5 Gregory and Miller, *Science in Public*; MacDonald and Silverstone, "Science on Display."

6 Gould, *The Mismeasure of Man*.

7 As Jordanova points out, public displays of medical knowledge were crucial in asserting a credible identity for the physician in contrast to the stereotypes of quacks and charlatans; Jordanova, "Medicine and Genres of Display," 206.

8 Phrenology is now regarded as a pseudo-science but it was pursued by some eminent physicians in its time. See, for example, Carlson, "The Influence of Phrenology on Early American Psychiatric Thought," 535–8. The inclusion of phrenological tools in the Museum of Questionable Medical Devices, at the Science Museum of Minnesota, is indicative of its current status as an example of quackery. Eugenics, the broader study of improving populations, receives more serious attention, and has been the subject of numerous events at institutions hosting *Deadly Medicine* in conjunction with the display of the exhibition.

9 United States Holocaust Memorial Museum, *Deadly Medicine*.

10 American Anthropological Association, "Race."

11 A small section called "health connections" explores the role of racial discrimination, poverty, and social marginalization in hypertension.

12 Ott, "Disability and the Practice of Public History," 21; Sandell et al., *Re-Presenting Disability*, documents a range of recent projects internationally that have attempted to correct this.

13 Serlin, "Making Disability Public," 203.

14 See, for example, US National Library of Medicine, "*From 'Monsters' to Modern Medical Miracles*."

15 Brown, *Health and Medicine on Display*.

16 Garland-Thomson, *Freakery*.

17 "DC medical museum aims to shed freak-show image," *Deseret News*, 11 July 1991.

18 The clean-up was heavily criticized by attendee and journalist Alan Green in "No Guts No Glory," quoted in Margit Detweiler, "Not with My Mutter You Don't," *Philadelphia City Paper*, 25 July 1996, cover.

19 Gunther Von Hagens, MD, a German anatomist, invented the plastination technique, which allows for the preservation of the complex systems of the human body and the display of posed bodies stripped of layers of skin, muscle, and tissue. His *Body Worlds* exhibitions have been touring since 1995 and have reportedly attracted thirty-two million visitors. There are also numerous imitation exhibitions.

20 The exhibitions have continued to attract visitors despite controversy over the origins of the bodies on display. Rumours suggested that they were Chinese criminals, and Von Hagens has not produced evidence to definitively prove that all of his subjects consented to their posthumous display.
21 Bud et al., "Museums and the Making of Medical History," 161.
22 The Mütter Museum's activities show a mixed approach. They recently made a major contribution to the incorporation of patient perspectives in medical museums with a new permanent exhibition "Broken Bodies, Suffering Spirits: Injury, Death, and Healing in Civil War Philadelphia," which opened in 2013.
23 Sandell, *Museums, Prejudice and the Reframing of Difference,* and Sandell, *Museums, Society, Inequality*.
24 Dodd, "Museums and the Health of the Community," 182–9.
25 See Part IV in Logan and Reeves, "Places of Benevolent Internment."
26 Pew Research Fund, "Views on Science and Society."
27 Conn, "Science Museums and the Culture Wars," 496.
28 Gregory and Miller, *Science in Public*, 208; MacDonald and Silverstone, "Science on Display."
29 Babaian, "A Larger Reading of the Human Past," 15.
30 On paradigm shifts in science see Kuhn, *The Structure of Scientific Revolutions*.
31 Schiebinger, "Skeletons in the Closet," 42–82.
32 For a summary of the issues involved, see Carter, "Genes, Genomes, and Geneologies," 546–56.
33 Katz, "The Invention of Heterosexuality," 7–34. On the subject of medicalization more generally, see Conrad, *The Medicalization of Society*.
34 The changing landscape of mental illnesses, as represented by the various editions of this text, could form a rich exhibition in itself. For an account of current controversies over the new edition of the DSM, see Decker, "A Moment of Crisis in the History of American Psychiatry."
35 I am grateful to Katherine Ott for her suggestion of Snellen as a key example for this section.
36 Simon, *The Participatory Museum*.
37 Dery, *Culture Jamming*; Dery, "The Merry Pranksters."
38 This hands-on workspace is inspired by a "build your own cyborg" activity room I visited at the exhibition *The Uncanny: Experiments in Cyborg Culture* at the Vancouver Art Gallery in 2002.
39 Erica Lehrer also suggested a photo booth on site, where visitors could generate and annotate their own images of their bodies.
40 Anderson and O'Sullivan, "Histories of Disability and Medicine," 146.

41 Squiers, *The Body at Risk*, 9.

42 By "we" I refer here both to those within the health care profession and those outside of it.

43 For other examples of such projects, and some of their consequences, see Patterson, "Teaching Tolerance through Objects of Hatred," 55–71, and Butler, *Contested Representations*.

44 Although commentators on the controversy over *Hide/Seek: Difference and Desire in American Portraiture* at the National Portrait Gallery have argued that homophobia is behind opposition to the display of work by gay and lesbian artists, the curators suggest that the critics' focus on religious blasphemy illustrates that simple homophobia is no longer effective in stifling the representation of gay and lesbian history and culture in federally funded museums. Green, "Q&A with 'Hide/Seek' curators Jonathan Katz and David C. Ward."

CHAPTER FOURTEEN

1 *Reel Objects* owes much to the astute suggestions and editing of Shelley Butler and Erica Lehrer, for which I am very grateful.

2 Deleuze, *Difference and Repetition*, 139.

3 See my forthcoming book, *Sentient Relics: Museums and Cinematic Affect* (Aldershot: Ashgate, 2016).

4 At the time of writing, a new Western Australian Museum is planned for the site. The intention is to refurbish and integrate Hackett Hall into the contemporary, "activated" spaces of the new museum.

5 For a discussion of museums and affect see Baker, "Anarchical Artifacts."

6 Fenton, "The Pitt-Rivers Museum, Oxford."

7 Haraway, "Teddy Bear Patriarchy," 248.

8 Bennett, *Pasts Beyond Memory*, 117.

9 Bal, *Looking In*, 119, 121.

10 Preziosi, *Brain of the Earth's Body*, 5.

11 In an intertextual reference to *Vertigo*, an enlarged film still from Tom Tykwer's thriller *Run Lola Run* (1980) reveals Carlotta's portrait hanging forty years later in Berlin's Deutsches Historisches Museum.

12 Van Alphen, "Making Sense of Affect," 66.

13 Thank you to Ron Blaber for this connection.

14 Thank you to Shelley Butler for this reference.

15 Vergo, *The New Museology*, 3.

16 Clifford, "Objects and selves, an afterword," 244.

17 Elkins, *Pictures and Tears*, 73.

BIBLIOGRAPHY

"A Change of Heart: Fred Wilson's Impact on Museums." *Victoria and Albert Museum,* n.d. Accessed 15 June 2014. http://www.vam.ac.uk/content/videos/a/video-a-change-of-heart-fred-wilsons-impact-on-museums/.

Abélès, Marc. *Des anthropologues à l'OMC: Scènes de la gouvernance mondiale.* Paris: CNRS Éditions, 2011.

Adair, Bill, Benjamin Filene, and Laura Koloski, eds. *Letting Go? Sharing Authority in a User-Generated World.* Philadelphia: Pew Center for Arts & Heritage, 2011.

Adams, David Wallace. *Education for Extinction: American Indians and the Boarding School Experience, 1875–1928.* Lawrence: University of Kansas Press, 1995.

"Agency of Unrealized Projects." *E-flux,* n.d. Accessed 30 May 2014. http://www.e-flux.com/announcements/agency-of-unrealized-projects/.

Agosin, Marjorie. *Tapestries of Hope, Threads of Love: The Arpillera Movement in Chile, 1974–1994.* Albuquerque: University of New Mexico Press, 1996.

Air France. World Map. CT 98 20158, National Air and Space Museum, Smithsonian Institution, Washington, DC.

Alexander, Edward P. *Museums in Motion: An Introduction to the History and Functions of Museums.* Walnut Creek, CA: AltaMira Press, 1996.

Alpers, Svetlana. "The Museum as a Way of Seeing." In *Exhibiting Cultures: The Poetics and Politics of Museum Display,* edited by Ivan Karp and Steven Lavine, 25–32. Washington, DC: Smithsonian Institution Press, 1991.

American Airlines. "Black Atlas: Your Passport to the Black Experience," 2009. Accessed 3 July 2010. http://www.blackatlas.com/.

– "Black Atlas Digital Press Kit," 2009. Accessed 5 July 2010. http://media.blackatlas.com/.

American Anthropological Association. "Race: Are We So Different?" Accessed 10 April 2015. http://www.understandingrace.org/about/index.html.

Ames, Michael M.. *Cannibal Tours and Glass Boxes: The Anthropology of Museums*. Vancouver: UBC Press, 1992.

– *Museums, the Public, and Anthropology: A Study in the Anthropology of Anthropology*. Vancouver: UBC Press, 1986.

Anderson, Julie, and Lisa O'Sullivan. "Histories of Disability and Medicine: Reconciling Historical Narratives and Contemporary Values." In *Re-Presenting Disability: Activism and Agency in the Museum*, edited by Richard Sandell, Jocelyn Dodd, and Rosemarie Garland-Thomson, 143–54. Routledge: London and New York, 2010.

Angelou, Maya. "'On the Pulse of the Morning.'" In *The Complete Collected Poems of Maya Angelou*. 1st ed. New York: Random House, 1994.

"Anthony Enton Friedkin: The Gay Essay" Gallery Postcard, [ND], The Gay, Chicanismo in El Arte Cyclona Art Collection, 1964–2004. Unprocessed Papers. The ONE National Gay and Lesbian Archives, Los Angeles.

AOL Travel. "Addington Hospital Museum, Durban." Accessed 21 May 2014. http://travel.aol.com/travel-guide/africa/south-africa/durban/addington-hospital-museum-thingstodo-detail-213969/.

Appadurai, Arjun. "Disjuncture and Difference in the Global Cultural Economy." In *Modernity at Large: Cultural Dimensions of Globalization*, 27–47. Minneapolis: University of Minnesota Press, 1996.

– "Global Ethnoscapes: Notes and Queries for a Transnational Anthropology." In *Modernity at Large: Cultural Dimensions of Globalization*, 48–65. Minneapolis: University of Minnesota Press, 1996.

– *The Social Life of Things*. Cambridge, UK: Cambridge University Press, 1986.

Arnold, Steven. *Epiphanies*. Pasadena, CA: Twelvetrees Press, 1987.

Arnold-de Simine, Silke. *Mediating Memory in the Museum: Trauma, Empathy, Nostalgia*. New York: Palgrave Macmillan, 2013.

Arnoldi, Mary Jo, Christine Mullen Kreamer, and Michael Atwood Mason. "Reflections on 'African Voices' at the Smithsonian's National Museum of Natural History." *African Arts* 34, 2 (2001): 16–35, 94.

Aronsson, Peter, and Gabriela Elgenius. *Building National Museums in Europe 1750–2010*. Conference proceedings from EuNaMus, European National Museums: Identity Politics, the Uses of the Past and the European Citizen, Bologna, 28–30 April 2011. Linköping, Sweden: Linköping University Electronic Press, 2011.

ASEMUS (Asia-Europe Museum Network). "The Netherlands: 'The New National Museum of Worldcultures Brings Opportunities and energy.'" 11 December 2014. Accessed 14 February 2015. Available at http://asemus.museum/news/

netherlands-national-museum-of-worldcultures-opportunities/ #sthash.fxHUCroT.dpuf.

Ashley, Susan L.T. "Negotiating Narratives of Canada: Circuit of Communication Analysis of the Next Stop Freedom Exhibition." *Journal of Canadian Studies/Revue d'études canadiennes* 45, 2 (2011): 182–204.

Babaian, Sharon. "A Larger Reading of the Human Past." *The Public Historian* 27, 3 (2005): 11–26.

Baderoon, Gabeba. "How to Look." Panel discussion, "Beyond the Racial Lens: The Politics of South African Documentary Photography, Past and Present." Capetown, South Africa, 20 August 2010.

Bago, Ivana, Antonia Majača, and Vesna Vuković. "Dissociative Association, Dionysian Socialism, Non-Action and Delayed Audience: Between Action and Exodus in the Art of the 1960s and 1970s in Yugoslavia." In *Removed from the Crowd: Unexpected Encounters*, edited by Ivana Bago, Antonia Majača, and Vesna Vuković, 250–309. Zagreb: DeLVe/BLOK, 2011.

Bailey, Garrick, and Roberta Glenn Bailey. *A History of the Navajo: The Reservation Years*. Santa Fe: School of American Research Press, 1986.

Bailey, Lynn Robinson. *The Long Walk: A History of the Navajo Wars*. Los Angeles: Western Lore Press, 1964.

– *Bosque Redondo: The Navajo Internment at Fort Sumner, New Mexico, 1863–1868*. Tucson, AZ: Westernlore Press, 1998.

Baker, Janice. "Anarchical Artifacts: Museums as Sites for Radical Otherness." In *The International Handbooks of Museum Studies: Museum Theory*, edited by Andrea Witcomb and Kylie Message. New Jersey: John Wiley & Sons, 2015.

Bal, Mieke. *Looking In: The Art of Viewing*. Amsterdam: Gordon and Breach Publishing Group, 2001.

Baldwin, James. *The Price of the Ticket: Collected Nonfiction, 1948–1985*. New York: St. Martin's Press, 1985.

Barbados Free Press. "Jamaican Women Welcome in Barbados if They Submit to a Finger up Their Vagina?" *Barbados Free Press*, 8 March 2011. http://barbadosfreepress.wordpress.com/2011/03/24/jamaican-women-welcome-in-barbados-if-they-submit-to-a-finger-up-their-vagina/.

– "The Great African Tourist Scam of 2008: Ghana International Airlines Knew They Weren't Returning to Barbados!" *Barbados Free Press*, 8 December 2008. http://barbadosfreepress.wordpress.com/2008/03/08/the-great-african-tourist-scam-of-2008-ghana-international-airlines-knew-they-werent-returning-to-barbados/.

Barnett, Vanessa, Elena Soni, and Toronto Youth Artists. *Walls and Barriers: A Collaborative Project*. Toronto: Institute for Contemporary Culture and the Royal Ontario Museum, 2010.

Baycroft, Timothy, and David Hopkin. *Folklore and Nationalism in Europe During the Long Nineteenth Century*. Leiden: Brill, 2012.

Behar, Ruth, and Bruce Mannheim. "The Couple in the Cage: A Guatinaui Odyssey." *Visual Anthropology Review* 11, 1 (March 1995): 118–27.

Beiner, Ronald. "Hannah Arendt on Judging." In *Lectures on Kant's Political Philosophy*, edited by Hannah Arendt. Chicago: University of Chicago Press, 1992.

Benavidez, Max. *Gronk*. Minneapolis: University of Minnesota Press, 2007.

Bendiner-Viani, Gabrielle and Elliott Maltby. "Hybrid Ways of Doing: A Model for Teaching Public Space." Archnet-IJAR: *International Journal of Architectural Research* 4, 2–3 (January 2010). Available online: http://archnet.org/gws/IJAR/10541/files_10301/4.2-3.29-g.%20bendiner-viani,%20e.%20maltby%20-pp%20407-418.pdf.

Benjamin, Walter. *Illuminations*. New York: Schocken Books, 2007.

– "Thesis on the Philosophy of History." In *Illuminations*, edited by Hannah Arendt, 255. New York: Schocken Books, 1968.

Bennett, Tony. *Pasts Beyond Memory: Evolution, Museums, Colonialism*. London and New York: Routledge, 2004.

Berlant, Lauren Gail. "Intuitionists: History and the Affective Event." *American Literary History* 20, 4 (2008): 845–60.

Bhabha, Homi K. *The Location of Culture*. London and New York: Routledge, 1994.

Bhimull, Chandra D. *Empire in the Air: Speed, Perception, and Airline Travel in the Atlantic World*. PhD diss., University of Michigan, 2007.

Binder, Lisa, ed. *El Anatsui: When I Last Wrote to You about Africa*. New York: Museum for African Art, 2010.

Biro, Yaëlle. "Transformation de l'objet ethnographique Africain en objet d'art." PhD diss., Université Paris I–Sorbonne, 2010.

Bloch, Ernest. *The Principle of Hope*. Translated by Neville Plaice, Stephen Plaice, and Paul Knight. Cambridge, MA, and London: MIT Press, 1986.

Blustein, Paul. *Misadventures of the Most Favored Nations: Clashing Egos, Inflated Ambitions, and the Great Shambles of the World Trade System*. New York: Public Affairs, 2009.

Bodo, Simona, Kirsten Gibbs, and Margherita Sani, eds. *Museums as Places for Intercultural Dialogue: Selected Practices from Europe*. Bologna: MAP for ID, 2009.

Boler, Megan, "The Risks of Empathy: Interrogating Multiculturalism's Gaze." *Cultural Studies* 11, 2 (April 1997): 253–73.

Bonnell, Jennifer, and Roger I. Simon. "'Difficult' Exhibitions and Intimate Encounters." *Museum and Society* 5, 2 (2007): 65–85.

Boonstra, Sadiah. "Conceptualising Intangible Heritage in the Tropenmuseum, Amsterdam: The Layla and Majnun Story as a Case Study." *International Journal of Intangible Heritage* 4 (2009): 28–39.
Bouquet, Mary. "Thinking and Doing Otherwise: Anthropological Theory in Exhibitionary Practice." *Ethnos: Journal of Anthropology* 65, 2 (2000): 217–36.
Bourriaud, Nicolas. *Relational Aesthetics*. Dijon: Presses du Réel, 1998.
Brachear, Manya A., and Charles Storch. "Controversy Closes Show at Museum." *Chicago Tribune*, 21 June 2008. Accessed 3 June 2014. http://www.chicagotribune.com/news/nationworld/chi-spertus_21jun21,0,3780707.story.
Britzman, Deborah P. *Lost Subjects, Contested Objects: Toward a Psychoanalytic Inquiry of Learning*. Albany, NY: SUNY Press, 1998.
Brown, Julie K. *Health and Medicine on Display: International Expositions in the United States, 1876–1904*. Cambridge, MA: MIT Press, 2009.
Brownell, Ginanne. "Croatian Curators Make Mark By Working Together." *New York Times*, 16 October 2012. Accessed 15 June 2014. http://www.nytimes.com/2012/10/17/arts/17iht-rartzagreb17.html?pagewanted=all&_r=0.
Bryder, Linda. "'Wonderlands of Buttercup, Clover, and Daisies': Tuberculosis and the Open-Air School Movement in Britain, 1907–39." In *In the Name of the Child: Health and Welfare, 1880–1940*, edited by Roger Cooter, 72–95. London: Routledge, 1992.
Bud, Robert, Bernard Finn, and Helmuth Trischler, eds. *Manifesting Medicine: Bodies and Machines*. Australia: Harwood Academic Publishers, 1999.
Bunzl, Matti. *In Search of a Lost Avant-Garde: An Anthropologist Investigates the Contemporary Art Museum*. Chicago: University of Chicago Press, 2014.
Burman, Jeremy. "Co-motion in the Diasporic City: Transformations in Toronto's Public Culture." In *Claiming Space: Racialization in Canadian Cities*, edited by Cheryl Teelucksingh, 110–20. Waterloo, ON: Wilfrid Laurier University Press, 2006.
Burns, Catherine. "The Children's Hospital in Durban" (2011), paper presented at the History and African Studies Seminar at the University of KwaZulu-Natal in Durban.
Busby, Karen, Adam Muller, and Andrew Woolford, eds. *The Idea of a Human Rights Museum*. Winnipeg: University of Manitoba Press, 2015.
Butler, Shelley Ruth. *Contested Representations: Revisiting Into the Heart of Africa*. Toronto: University of Toronto Press, 2011. First published 2008 by Broadview Press.
– "Reflexive Museology: Lost and Found." In *Museum Theory*, edited by Andrea Witcomb and Kylie Message, 159–82. Etobicoke, ON: Wiley, 2014.
– "Review of the African Gallery at the ROM." *Anthropologica* 52 (2010): 97–8.

– "The Politics of Exhibiting Culture: Legacies and Possibilities." *Museum Anthropology* 23, 3 (December 2000): 74–92.

Cała, Alina. *The Image of the Jew in Polish Folk Culture.* Jerusalem: Hebrew University Magnes Press, 1995.

Calhoun, Craig. Foreword to *Engaging Contradictions: Theory, Politics, and Methods of Activist Scholarship*, edited by Charles R. Hale, xiii–xxv. Berkeley and Los Angeles: University of California Press, 2008.

Calzadilla, Fernando, and George Marcus. "Artists in the Field: Between Art and Anthropology." In *Contemporary Art and Anthropology*, edited by Arnd Schneider and Chris Wright, 95–115. London and New York: Berg, 2005.

Cameron, Fiona, and Lynda Kelly, eds. *Hot Topics, Public Culture, Museums.* Newcastle: Cambridge Scholars, 2010.

Caribbean Net News. "Barbados Creates History with First Flight from Africa," 2 February 2008. http://www.caribbeannewsnow.com/caribnet/archivelist.php?news_id=5810&pageaction=showdetail&news_id=5810&arcyear=2008&arcmonth=2&arcday=02=&ty=.

Carle, Robert. "Demise of Dutch Multiculturalism." *Society* 43, 3 (March 2006): 68–74.

Carlson, E.T. "The Influence of Phrenology on Early American Psychiatric Thought." *American Journal of Psychiatry* 115 (1958): 535–8.

Carter, Jennifer, and Jennifer Orange. "Contentious Terrain: Defining a Human Rights Museology." *Museum Management and Curatorship* 27, 2 (2012): 111–27.

Carter, Robert. "Genes, Genomes, and Genealogies: The Return of Scientific Racism?" *Ethnic and Racial Studies* 30, 4 (July 2007): 546–56.

CBC News. "Halifax Apologizes for Razing Africville." *CBC News Nova Scotia*, 24 February 2010. Accessed 15 June 2014. http://www.cbc.ca/news/canada/nova-scotia/halifax-apologizes-for-razing-africville-1.894944.

– "Montreal University Students Don Blackface." *CBC News Montreal*, 15 September 2011. Accessed 15 June 2014. http://www.cbc.ca/news/canada/montreal/montreal-university-students-don-blackface-1.1113695.

Chalaye, Sylvie. *Du Noir au Nègre: L'image du Noir au théâtre: De Marguerite de Navarre à Jean Genet (1550–1960)* (Images plurielles). Paris: L'Harmattan, 1998.

Clacherty, Glynis. "The World in a Suitcase: Psychosocial Support Using Artwork with Refugee Children in South Africa." *Participatory Learning and Action* 54 (2006): 121–7.

– and Diane Welvering. *The Suitcase Stories: Refugee Children Reclaim Their Identities.* Cape Town: Double Storey Books, 2006.

Clarke, Christa. "From Theory to Practice: Exhibiting African Art in the Twenty-First Century." In *Art and Its Publics: Museum Studies at the Millennium*, edited

by Andrew McClellan, 164–82. Malden, MA; Oxford, UK: Blackwell Publishing, 2003.
Clifford, James. "Objects and Selves, An Afterword." In *Objects and Others: Essays on Museums and Material Culture*, edited by George W. Stocking, 236–45. Madison: University of Wisconsin Press, 1985.
– *Routes: Travel and Translation in the Late Twentieth Century*. Cambridge, MA: Harvard University Press, 1997.
– *The Predicament of Culture: Twentieth-Century Ethnography, Literature, and Art*. Cambridge, MA: Harvard University Press, 1988.
– and George E. Marcus, eds. *Writing Culture: The Poetics and Politics of Ethnography*. Berkeley and Los Angeles: University of California Press, 1986.
Central Bank of Barbados. "Barbados – Vital Statistics." Accessed 6 December 2011. http://www.centralbank.org.bb/country_info.shtml#.
Cohen, Joshua. "At Converging Obsolescences: The Case for Exhibition-Performance in African Art-Music-Dance." *Wreck* 2, 2 (2008): 1–15.
– "Stages in Transition: Les Ballets Africains and Independence, 1959 to 1960." *Journal of Black Studies* 43, 1 (2012): 11–48.
Cole, Herbert M. *African Arts of Transformation*. Santa Barbara: The Art Galleries of the University of California, 1970.
Colunge, Rhina. "Revisiting the Tropenmuseum." In *Tropenmuseum for a Change! Present between Past and Future: A Symposium Report*, edited by Daan van Dartel. Amsterdam: KIT publishers, 2009.
Conn, Steven. *Do Museums Still Need Objects?* Philadelphia: University of Pennsylvania Press, 2010.
– "Science Museums and the Culture Wars." In *A Companion to Museum Studies*, edited by Sharon Macdonald, 494–508. Malden, MA: Blackwell, 2006.
Conrad, Peter. *The Medicalization of Society: On the Transformation of Human Conditions into Medical Disorders*. Baltimore: Johns Hopkins University Press, 2007.
Cooke, Lynne, and Peter Wollen, eds. *Visual Display: Culture Beyond Appearances*. Seattle: Bay Press, 1995.
Coombes, Annie E. *History after Apartheid: Visual Culture and Public Memory in a Democratic South Africa*. Durham, NC: Duke University Press, 2003.
Cooper, Afua. *The Hanging of Angélique: The Untold Story of Canadian Slavery and the Burning of Old Montreal*. Toronto: HarperCollins, 2006.
Coovadia, H.M., et al. "Retain the Children's Hospital." Unpublished report, 28 August 1989.
Corrin, Lisa G. "*Mining the Museum*: An Installation Confronting History." *Curator: The Museum Journal* 36, 4 (December 1993): 302–13.

Costantino, Roselyn, and Diana Taylor. *Holy Terrors: Latin American Women Perform*. Durham, NC: Duke University Press, 2003.

Cotter, Holland. "Under Threat": The Shock of the Old." *New York Times*, 17 April 2011, AR1. http://www.nytimes.com/2011/04/17/arts/design/non-western-art-history-bypasses-the-ancient.html?_r=4&ref=arts.

Crimp, Douglas. "Portraits of People with AIDS," In *Cultural Studies*, edited by Lawrence Grossberg, Cary Nelson, and Paula Treichler, 117–33. New York: Routledge, 1992.

Crooks, Julie. "Position as Desired." In *Position as Desired: Exploring African Canadian Identity: Photographs from the Wedge Collection*, 21–36. Toronto: Wedge Curatorial Projects, 2011.

Crow Dog, Mary. "Civilize Them with a Stick." In *Native American Voices: A Reader*, edited by Susan Lobo and Steve Talbot, 255–61. New York: Addison Wesley Longman, 1990.

Crwys-Williams, Jennifer, ed. *I Want Love in South Africa, Dear God*. Cape Town: Capricorn, 1987.

Cullinan, Kerry. "South Africa Far from Targets to Reduce Maternal, Infant Morality." *Health-e*, 29 October 2014. Accessed 21 May 2014. http://www.health-e.org.za/2013/10/29/south-africa-far-targets-reduce-maternal-infant-mortality/.

Danto, Arthur C. *After the End of Art: Contemporary Art and the Pale of History*. Princeton and Oxford: Princeton University Press, 1998.

Dawdy, Shannon Lee. "Disaster Preparedness." In *Anthrohistory: Unsettling Knowledge, Questioning Discipline*, edited by E.L. Murphy et al., 140–55. Ann Arbor: University of Michigan Press, 2011.

"DC Medical Museum Aims to Shed Freak-show Image." *Deseret News*, 11 July 1991.

Decker, Hannah. "A Moment of Crisis in the History of American Psychiatry." Last updated 27 April 2010. Accessed 10 April 2015. http://historypsychiatry.wordpress.com/2010/04/27/a-moment-of-crisis-in-the-history-of-american-psychiatry.

Deeb, Hadi Nicholas, and George E. Marcus. "In the Green Room: An Experiment in Ethnographic Method at the WTO." *Political and Legal Anthropology Review* 34, 1 (May 2011): 51–76.

Deleuze, Gilles. *Difference and Repetition*. Translated by Paul Patton. New York: Columbia University Press, 1994.

Denis, Philippe, ed. *Never Too Small to Remember: Memory Work and Resilience in Times of AIDS*. Pietermaritzburg, South Africa: Cluster Publications, 2005.

Department of Health, Province of KwaZulu-Natal. "Plans to Restore and Relaunch Addington Children's Hospital as the KwaZulu-Natal Children's Hospital to be Unveiled." KwaZulu-Natal Department of Health press release, 14 July 2010. KwaZulu-Natal Department of Health website. http://www.kznhealth.gov.za/mediarelease/2010/addchildhosp.htm, accessed 21 May 2014.

Derrida, Jacques. *Specters of Marx: The State of the Debt, the Work of Mourning, and the New International*. Translated by Peggy Kamuf. New York: Routledge, 1994.

Dery, Mark. *Culture Jamming: Hacking, Slashing, and Sniping in the Empire of Signs*. New Jersey: Open Magazine Pamphlet Series, 1993.

– "The Merry Pranksters and the Art of the Hoax." *New York Times Magazine*, 23 December 1990.

Detweiler, Margit. "Not with My Mutter You Don't." *Philadelphia City Paper*, 25 July 1996, cover.

Dewdney, Andrew, David Dibosa, and Victoria Walsh. *Post-Critical Museology: Theory and Practice in the Art Museum*. Oxford and New York: Routledge, 2013.

Dibbits, Hester. "Moroccan Dutch Boys and the Authentication of Clothing Styles." In *Reframing Dutch Culture: Between Otherness and Authenticity*, edited by Peter Jan Margry and Herman Roodenburg, 11–35. Aldershot: Ashgate, 2007.

Dodd, Jocelyn. "Museums and the Health of the Community." In *Museums, Society, Inequality*, edited by Richard Sandell, 182–9. London and New York: Routledge, 2002.

Doonan, Simon. *Beautiful People: My Family and Other Glamorous Varmints*. New York: Simon & Schuster Paperbacks, 2005.

Dos Santos, Paula Assunção. "Don't We All Have Problems?" In *Can We Make a Difference?: Museums, Society and Development in North and South*, edited by Paul R. Voogt, 40–53. Amsterdam: KIT Publishers, 2009.

Doubt, Jenny. "Making Memory Work: Performing and Inscribing HIV/AIDS in post-apartheid South Africa." PhD diss., Open University, 2013.

Du Bois, W.E.B. "Of Our Spiritual Strivings." In *The Souls of Black Folk*, by Farah Jasmine Griffin and W.E.B. Du Bois, 7–15. New York: Barnes & Nobles Classics, 2003.

Durrans, Brian. "The Future of the Other: Changing Cultures on Display in Ethnographic museums." In *Museum Time Machine Putting Cultures on Display*, edited by Robert Lumley, 114–69. London: Routledge, 1988.

Dyment, J.E., and A.C. Bell. "Grounds for Movement: Green School Grounds as Sites for Promoting Physical Activity." *Health Education Research* 23, 6 (2008): 952–62.

Edgar, David. *Playing with Fire*. London: Hern Books, 2005.

Elkins, James. *Pictures and Tears: A History of People Who Have Cried in Front of Paintings*. New York: Routledge, 2004.

Ellison, Julie. "Humanities and the Public Soul." In *Practising Public Scholarship: Experiences and Possibilities Beyond the Academy*, edited by Katharyn Mitchell, 113–21. Malden, MA and Oxford, UK: Wiley-Blackwell, 2008.

– "Lyric Citizenship in Post 9/11 Performance: Sekou Sundiata's the 51st (dream) State." In *American Literature's Aesthetic Dimensions*, edited by Christopher Looby and Cindy Weinstein, 91–114. New York: Columbia University Press, 2012.

– "The New Public Humanists." *PMLA*, March 2013.

Ethnographic Terminalia. "Chantal Gibson." http://ethnographicterminalia.org/2011-montreal/chantal-gibson. Accessed 1 May 2015.

European Commission against Racism and Intolerance. "Third Report on the Netherlands, 2008." Accessed 28 January 2011. http://hudoc.ecri.coe.int/XMLEcri/ENGLISH/Cycle_03/03_CbC_eng/NLD-CbC-III-2008-3-ENG.pdf.

European Institute for Comparative Cultural Research (ERICarts). "Sharing Diversity: National Approaches to Intercultural Dialogue in Europe." An ERICarts Study for the European Commission, 2008.

Faber, Paul. "The Museum Discourse: Museum Policy." In *Tropenmuseum for a Change! Present between Past and Future: A Symposium Report*, edited by Daan van Dartel, 40–50. Amsterdam: KIT Publishers, 2009.

– and Daan van Dartel. "Introduction." *Tropenmuseum for a Change! Present between Past and Future: A Symposium Report*, edited by Daan van Dartel, 7–11. Amsterdam: KIT Publishers, 2009.

Fanon, Frantz. *Black Skin, White Masks*. Translated by Richard Philcox. New York: Grove Press, 2008.

Farella, John R. *The Main Stalk: A Synthesis of Navajo Philosophy*. Tucson: University of Arizona Press, 1984.

Farris, James C. *Navajo and Photography: A Critical History of the Representation of an American People*. Albuquerque: University of New Mexico Press, 1996.

Feldman, Jackie. *Above the Death Pits, Beneath the Flag: Youth Voyages to Poland and the Performance of Israeli National Identity*. Oxford, UK, and New York: Berghahn Books, 2008.

Fenton, James. "The Pitt-Rivers Museum, Oxford." In *Children in Exile: Poems 1968–1984*. New York: Farrar, Straus and Giroux, 1984.

Filipova, Marta. "Peasants on Display: The Czechoslavic Ethnographic Exhibition of 1895." *Journal of Design History* 24, 1.

Fleming, David. "Creative Space." In *Reshaping Museum Space: Architecture, Design, Exhibitions*, edited by Suzanne MacLeod, 53–61. Abingdon and New York: Routledge, 2005.

Foucault, Michel. "What is an Author?" In *Language, Counter-Memory, Practice: Selected Essays and Interviews*, edited by Donald Bouchard, 113–38. Ithaca, NY: Cornell University Press, 1977.

Forrest, Earle R. *With a Camera in Old Navaho Land.* Norman: University of Oklahoma Press, 1970.

Foster, Hal. "The Artist as Ethnographer?" In *The Traffic in Culture: Refiguring Art and Anthropology*, edited by George E. Marcus and Fred R. Myers, 145–70. Berkeley and Los Angeles: University of California Press, 1995.

Frank, Denise. "Oceania in View." In *Oceania at the Tropenmuseum*, edited by D.A.P. van Duuren and Steven Vink, 161–78. Amsterdam: KIT Publishers, 2011.

Freire, Paulo. *Pedagogy of Freedom: Ethics, Democracy, and Civic Courage.* Lanham, MA: Rowman & Littlefield Publishers, 1998.

– *Pedagogy of Indignation.* Boulder, CO: Paradigm Publishers, 2004.

– *Pedagogy of the Oppressed.* New York: Continuum Publishing Company, 1995.

Friedkin, Anthony. Interview by Robb Hernandez, video recording, 4 September 2010. Los Angeles.

Frisch, Michael. *A Shared Authority: Essays on the Craft and Meaning of Oral and Public History.* Albany: SUNY Press, 1990.

G4S Guard Diary. 2004. "Virgin Atlantic Flight 601, Heathrow to Johannesburg, May 3." In "Staff of deportation flights played 'Russian Roulette' with lives," P. Lewis and M. Taylor. *The Guardian,* 8 February 2011. http://www.guardian.co.uk/uk2011/feb/08/staff-deportation-flights-g4s.

Galabuzi, Grace-Edward. *Canada's Economic Apartheid: The Social Exclusion of Racialized Groups in the New Century.* Toronto: Canadian Scholars' Press, 2006.

Gallagher, Peter, Patrick Low, and Andrew L. Stoler, eds. *Managing the Challenges of WTO Participation.* Cambridge, UK: Cambridge University Press, 2006.

Gamboa Jr, Harry. Interview by Robb Hernandez (with Tyler Stallings), audio recording, 9 March 2015. Los Angeles.

– "In the City of Angels, Chameleons, and Phantoms: Asco, a Case Study of Chicano Art in Urban Tones (or, Asco Was a Four-Member Word) (1991)." In *Urban Exile: Collected Writings of Harry Gamboa, Jr.*, edited by Chon A. Noriega, 71–87. Minneapolis: University of Minnesota Press, 1998.

– "In Order of Disappearance." In *Urban Exile: Collected Writings of Harry Gamboa, Jr.*, edited by Chon A. Noriega, 499–500. Minneapolis: University of Minnesota Press, 1998.

Garland-Thomson, Rosemarie, ed. *Freakery: Cultural Spectacles of the Extraordinary Body.* New York: NYU Press, 1996.

Gates, Henry Louis, Jr. "Europe, African Art, and the Uncanny." In *Africa: The Art of a Continent*, edited by Tom Phillips, 22–5. London: Royal Academy, 1995.

Gilroy, Paul. *The Black Atlantic: Modernity and Double Consciousness.* Cambridge, MA: Harvard University Press, 1993.

Giroux, Henry. *Disturbing Pleasures: Learning Popular Culture*. New York: Routledge, 1994.

– *Stormy Weather: Katrina and the Politics of Disposability*. Boulder, CO: Paradigm Publishers, 2006.

Gmelch, George. *Behind the Smile: The Working Lives of Caribbean Tourism*. Bloomington: Indiana University Press, 2003.

Gogan, Jessica. "The Warhol: Museum as Artist: Creative, Dialogic and Civic Practice." *Americans for the Arts*, n.d. Accessed 15 June 2014. http://animatingdemocracy.org/sites/default/files/documents/labs/andy_warhol_museum_case_study.pdf.

Goldberg, RoseLee. *Performance Art: From Futurism to the Present*. New York: Thames & Hudson, 2001.

Gollop, Chris. "Finger-Rape Claim Untrue." *Nation News*, 27 March 2011. http://www.nationnews.com/articles/view/finger-rape-claim-untrue/.

Gomoll, Lucian, and Lissette Olivares. "Inversión de la Materia: Reframing 1980s Chilean Conceptualism as Performance and Transnationalism." In *Removed from the Crowd: Unexpected Encounters*, edited by Ivana Bago, Antonia Majača, and Vesna Vuković, 8–51. Zagreb: DeLVe/BLOK, 2011.

Gorman, Michael E. "Levels of expertise and trading zones: A framework for multidisciplinary collaboration." *Social Studies of Science* 32, 5/6 (2002): 933–8.

Gould, Stephen Jay. *The Mismeasure of Man*. New York: W.W. Norton, 1996.

Green, Tyler. "Q&A with "Hide/Seek" curators Jonathan Katz and David C. Ward." *ArtInfo* (International edition), 8 December 2010. Accessed 10 April 2015. http://blogs.artinfo.com/modernartnotes/2010/12/qa-with-hideseek-curators-katz-ward/.

Greenberg, Reesa. "Jews, Museums, and National Identities." *Ethnologies* 24, 2 (2002): 125–37.

Gregory, Jane, and Steve E. Miller. *Science in Public: Communication, Culture, and Credibility*. New York: Plenum Trade, 1998.

Gruber, Ruth Ellen. *Virtually Jewish: Reinventing Jewish Culture in Europe*. Berkeley and Los Angeles: University of California Press, 2002.

[Guinea] – The Ministry of Education and Culture under the auspices of the Guinean National Commission for UNESCO. *Cultural Policy in the Revolutionary People's Republic of Guinea*. Paris: UNESCO, 1979.

Gurevitch, Michael. *Culture, Society and the Media*. London: Routledge, 1990.

Gurian, Elaine. "Introducing the Blue Ocean Museum: An Imagined Museum of the Nearly Immediate Future." Unpublished typescript, 2008.

Guzmán, Kristen. *Self Help Graphics & Art: Art in the Heart of East Los Angeles*. Los Angeles: UCLA Chicano Studies Research Center Press, 2005.

Hall, Stuart. "The Rediscovery of Ideology: Media Studies and the Return of the Repressed." In *Culture, Society and the Media*, edited by Michael Gurevitch, Tony Bennett, James Curran, and Janet Woollacott, 52–86. London and New York: Routledge, 1990.

Hallam, Elizabeth, and Brian V. Street. "Introduction." In *Cultural Encounters: Representing Otherness*, 1–10. London and New York: Routledge, 2000.

Hannerz, Ulf. *Exploring the City: Inquiry Toward an Urban Anthropology*. New York, Guildford: Columbia University Press, 1980.

Hansen, Birthe Rytter. "Public Spaces for National Commemoration: The Case of Emlotheni Memorial, Port Elizabeth." *Anthropology and Humanism* 28, 1 (June 2003): 43–60.

Haraway, Donna. *Simians, Cyborgs and Women: The Reinvention of Nature*. New York: Routledge, 1991.

– "Teddy Bear Patriarchy: Taxidermy in the Garden of Eden, New York City, 1908–1936." In *Grasping the World: The Idea of the Museum*, edited by Donald Preziosi and Claire J. Farago, 242–9. Aldershot, UK: Ashgate, 2004.

Harris, Claire, and Michael O'Hanlon. "The Future of the Ethnographic Museum." *Anthropology Today* 29, 1 (2013): 8–12.

Harriss, Joseph. "The Concorde Redemption: Can the superplane make a comeback?" *Air & Space Smithsonian* 16, 3 (September 2001): 16–25. http://www.airspacemag.com/flight-today/the-concorde-redemption-2394800/?all.

Hay, Jonathan. "The Value of Forgery." *RES: Anthropology and Aesthetics* 53/54 (2008): 5–18.

Hayden, Dolores. *The Power of Place: Urban Landscapes as Public History*. Cambridge, MA: MIT Press, 1997.

Hazen-Hammond, Susan. *Timelines of Native American History*. New York: Berkeley Publishing Group, 1997.

Hernández, Robb. *VIVA Records, 1970–2000: Lesbian and Gay Latino Artists of Los Angeles*. Los Angeles: UCLA Chicano Studies Research Center Press, 2013.

– "Archival Body/Archival Space: Queer Remains of the Chicano Art Movement, 1969–2009." PhD diss., University of Maryland, College Park, 2011.

– *The Fire of Life: The Robert Legorreta-Cyclona Collection*. Los Angeles: UCLA Chicano Studies Research Center Press, 2009.

– "Performing the Archival Body in the Robert 'Cyclona' Legorreta Fire of Life / El Fuego de la Vida Collection." *Aztlan* 31, 2 (2006): 113–25.

Herscher, Andrew. "Points of No Return: Cultural Heritage and Counter Memory in Post-Yugoslavia." In *Curating Difficult Knowledge: Violent Pasts in Public Places*, edited by Erica Lehrer, Cynthia E. Milton, and Monica Eileen Patterson, 147–60. New York: Palgrave Macmillan, 2011.

Hiatt, Gina. "We Need Humanities Labs." *Inside Higher Ed*, 26 October 2005. Accessed 28 May 2014. http://www.insidehighered.com/views/2005/10/26/hiatt#sthash.1mAhYTki.dpbs.

High, Steven. "Sharing Authority: An Introduction." *Journal of Canadian Studies* 43, 1 (winter 2009): 12–34.

–, Edward Little, and Thi Ry Duong, eds. *Remembering Mass Violence: Oral History, New Media and Performance*. Toronto: University of Toronto Press, Scholarly Publishing Division, 2014.

Hildering, David, Wayne Modest, and Warda Aztouti. "Visualizing development: The Tropenmuseum and international development aid." In *Museums, Heritage and International Development*, edited by Paul Basu and Wayne Modest, 310–32. New York and London: Routledge.

Hill, Lawrence. *The Book of Negroes*. Illus. ed. Toronto: HarperCollins, 2009.

Historica Canada. "Underground Railroad: From the Heritage Minutes Collection." Accessed 15 June 2014. https://www.historicacanada.ca/content/heritage-minutes/underground-railroad.

Ho, Engseng. *The Graves of Tarim: Genealogy and Mobility across the Indian Ocean*. Berkeley: University of California Press, 2006.

Hofer, Tamás. "Construction of the 'Folk Cultural Heritage' and Rival Versions of 'National' Identity in Hungary." Washington, DC: Woodrow Wilson International Center for Scholars, 2011.

Holmes, Douglas E., and George E. Marcus. "Collaboration today and the re-imagination of the classic scene of fieldwork encounter." *Collaborative Anthropologies* 1 (2008): 81–101.

Hooper-Greenhill, Eilean. *Museums and the Interpretation of Visual Culture*. Oxford and New York: Routledge, 2000.

Huereque, Jef. Interview by Robb Hernández, video recording, 23 August 2007. Los Angeles.

Hurley, Andrew. *Beyond Preservation: Using Public History to Revitalize Inner Cities*. Philadelphia: Temple University Press, 2010.

Huyssen, Andreas. *Present Pasts: Urban Palimpsests and the Politics of Memory*. Palo Alto: Stanford University Press, 2003.

Iervolino, Serena. "Ethnographic Museums in Mutation. Experiments with Exhibitionary Practices in Post/colonial Europe." PhD diss., University of Leicester, 2013.

Igloliorte, Heather. "'We were so far away': Exhibiting Inuit Oral Histories of Residential Schools." In *Curating Difficult Knowledge: Violent Pasts in Public Places*, edited by Erica Lehrer, Cynthia E. Milton, and Monica Eileen Patterson, 23–40. New York: Palgrave Macmillan, 2011.

Itwaru, Arnold, and Natasha Ksonzek. *Closed Entrances: Canadian Culture and Imperialism*. Toronto: TSAR Publications, 1994.

Jacobs, Dirk. "Alive and kicking? Multiculturalism in Flanders." *International Journal on Multicultural Societies* 6, 2 (2004): 280–99.

James, Don. *One Nation One Year: A Navajo Photographer's 365-Day Journey Into a World of Discovery, Life and Hope*. Rio Ranchos, NM: Rio Grande Books, 2010.

Janes, Robert. *Museums in a Troubled World: Renewal, Irrelevance or Collapse?* Abingdon: Routledge, 2009.

Jasmin, Jean. "Le musée, non-lieu ethnographique?" *Architecture d'aujourd'hui*, 326 (2000): 46–9.

Jones, Amelia. "'The Artist is Present': Artistic Re-enactments and the Impossibility of Presence." *TDR: The Drama Review* 55, 1 (2011): 16–45.

Jordanova, Ludmilla. "Medicine and Genres of Display." In *Visual Display: Culture beyond Appearances*, edited by Lynne Cooke and Peter Wollen, 202–17. Seattle: Bay Press, 1995.

"Just Looking." *Los Angeles Herald Examiner*, 30 August 1981, 24.

Kapp, Claire. "New Hope for Health in South Africa." *The Lancet* 372, 9645 (October 2008): 1207–8, accessed 21 May 2014.

Karp, Ivan. "Public Scholarship as a Vocation." *Arts and Humanities in Higher Learning* 11, 3 (2012): 285–99.

– and Corinne Kratz. "The Interrogative Museum." In *Museum as Process: Translating Local and Global Knowledges*, edited by Raymond Silverman, 279–98. Oxford and New York: Routledge, 2015.

–, Corinne A. Kratz, Lynn Szwaja, and Tomas Tbarra-Frausto, eds. *Museum Frictions: Public Cultures/Global Transformations*. Durham, NC: Duke University Press, 2006.

– and Steven D. Lavine, eds. *Exhibiting Cultures: The Poetics and Politics of Museum Display*. Washington: Smithsonian Institution Press, 1991.

Katriel, Tamar. "Showing and Telling: Photography Exhibitions in Israeli Discourses of Dissent." In *Curating Difficult Knowledge: Violent Pasts in Public Places*, edited by Erica Lehrer, Cynthia E. Milton, and Monica Eileen Patterson, 109–27. New York: Palgrave Macmillan, 2011.

Katz, Jonathan Ned. "The Invention of Heterosexuality." *Socialist Review* 20 (January–March 1990): 7–34.

Kaye, Nick. *Site-Specific Art: Performance, Place and Documentation*. Oxford and New York: Routledge, 2000.

Keff, Bożena. "Żyd o imieniu Żyd." *Przekrój*, 16 April 2012.

Kelley, Robin D.G. *Freedom Dreams: The Black Radical Imagination*. Boston: Beacon Press, 2002.

Khan, Neseem. *The Road to Interculturalism: Tracking the Arts in a Changing World*. London: Comedia, 2006.

Kimmelman, Michael. "Auschwitz Shifts from Memorializing to Teaching." *New York Times*, 18 February 2011.

King, Pamela J. "Gay Photo-Art." *Los Angeles Herald Examiner*, 20 January 1980, G8.

King, Richard H., and Dan Stone, eds. "Arendt Between Past and Future." In *Hannah Arendt and the Uses of History: Imperialism, Nation, Race, and Genocide*, 250–62. New York: Berghahn Books, 2007.

Kirshenblatt-Gimblett, Barbara. *Destination Culture: Tourism, Museums, and Heritage*. Berkeley: University of California Press, 1998.

– "The Museum: A Refuge for Utopian Thought." In German translation in *Die Unruhe der Kultur: Potentiale des Utopischen*, edited by Jörn Rüsen, Michael Fehr, and Annelie Ramsbrock, 187–96. Metternich: Velbrück Wissenschaft, 2004.

– "The Museum as Catalyst." Keynote address, Museums 2000: Confirmation or Challenge, organized by ICOM Sweden, the Swedish Museum Association, and the Swedish Travelling Exhibition/Riksutställningar, Vadstena, Sweden, 29 September 2000.

Klękot, Ewa. "A Journey to the Land of the People: 'Ethno' in Polish Design." *2+3D*, special edition (2013): 68–72.

Koopmans, Ruud. *Tradeoffs between equality and difference: the crisis of Dutch multiculturalism in cross-national perspective*. Copenhagen: Danish Institute for International Studies, 2006. Accessed 18 January 2011. http://www.isn.ethz.ch/isn/Digital-Library/Publications/Detail/?ots591=0c54e3b3-1e9c-be1e-2c24-a6a8c7060233&lng=en&id=26873.

Krankenhagen, Stefan, ed. "Thematic section: Exhibiting Europe." *Culture Unbound: Journal of Current Cultural Research* 3 (2011): 269–400.

Kratz, Corinne A. *The Ones That Are Wanted: Communication and the Politics of Representation in a Photographic Exhibition*. Berkeley and Los Angeles: University of California Press, 2002.

Kreps, Christina F. "Decolonizing anthropology museums: The Tropenmuseum, Amsterdam." *Museum Studies Journal* 3, Special Feature: Social Responsibility (spring–summer 1988): 56–63.

Kroh, Antoni. "Vernacular Art – Traps and Paradoxes." In *Vernacular Art in Central Europe*, edited by Jacek Purchla, 391–7. Krakow: International Cultural Centre, 2001.

Kugelmass, Jack. "Bloody Memories: Encountering the Past in Contemporary Poland." *Cultural Anthropology* 10, 3 (1995): 279–301.

Kuhn, Thomas. *The Structure of Scientific Revolutions*. Chicago: University of Chicago Press, 1962.

Kun, Josh. "The New Chicano Movement." *Los Angeles Times*, 9 January 2005.

Kundera, Milan. *Slowness*. Translated by Linda Asher. Repr. New York: HarperCollins, 1996.

Kurin, Richard. *Reflections of a Culture Broker: A View from the Smithsonian*. Washington, DC: Smithsonian Institution Press, 1997.

– "The Festival of American Folklife: Building on Tradition." *1991 Festival of American Folklife*. Washington, DC: Smithsonian Institution (1991): 7–20.

Kuspit, Donald B. *The End of Art*. Cambridge: Cambridge University Press, 2005.

KwaZulu-Natal Children's Hospital. "Historical Overview." Accessed 14 March 2014. http://www.kznchildrenshospital.org.za/Libraries/Historical_Overview/KZN_Childrens_Hospital_Pamphlet.sflb.ashx.

– "KwaZulu-Natal Children's Hospital." Accessed 7 March 2015. http://www.kznchildrenshospital.org.za.

KwaZulu-Natal Master Builders Association. "Restoration of the Old Addington Children's Hospital." Accessed 21 May 2014. http://www.masterbuilders.co.za/news/2012/December/restoration_of_the_old_addington_children_s_hospital.htm.

Kwon, Miwon. *One Place after Another: Site-Specific Art and Locational Identity*. Cambridge, MA: MIT Press, 2004.

La Rocca, Luigi. "Foreword." In *Beyond Modernity: Do Ethnographic Museums Need Ethnography?* Dedicated to the memory of Ivan Karp. International Colloquium Ethnography Museums & World Cultures. RIME. Museo Nazionale Preistorico Etnografico "Luigi Pigorini." 18–20 April 2012. http://www.pigorini.beniculturali.it/doc/RIME_EN.pdf. Accessed 14 February 2015.

LaGamma, Alisa. "Beyond Master Hands: The Lives of the Artists." *African Arts* 31, 4 (autumn 1998): 24–37, 89–90.

Lamming, George. *The Emigrants*. Ann Arbor: University of Michigan Press, 1997.

Lamp, Frederick. "Aesthetics: African Dance Aesthetics." In *International Encyclopedia of Dance, Vol. 1*, edited by Selma Jeanne Cohen, 13–15. New York: Oxford University Press, 1998.

–, ed. *See the Music, Hear the Dance: Rethinking African Art at the Baltimore Museum of Art*. New York; Munich: Prestel, 2004.

Latour, Bruno. "An Attempt at a 'Compositionist Manifesto.'" *New Literary History* 41 (2010): 471–90.

Legêne, Susan. "Enlightenment, Empathy, Retreat: The Cultural Heritage of Ethnische Politick." In *Colonial Collections Revisited*, edited by Pieter ter Keurs, 220–45. Leiden: CNWS Publications, 2007.

– "Refurbishment." In *Tropenmuseum for a Change! Present between Past and Future: A Symposium Report*, edited by Daan van Dartel, 12–22. Amsterdam: KIT Publishers, 2009.

Legorreta, Robert. Interview by Robb Hernández, video recording, 5 June 2005. Los Angeles.

Lehrer, Erica. "Curating Jews: Reflections on the Practice of Heritage." *AJS Perspectives* (spring 2010): 32–3.

– *Jewish Poland Revisited: Heritage Tourism in Unquiet Places*. Bloomington: Indiana University Press, 2013.

–, Cynthia E. Milton, and Monica Eileen Patterson, eds. *Curating Difficult Knowledge: Violent Pasts in Public Places*. New York: Palgrave Macmillan, 2011.

– and Hannah Smotrich. "Jewish? Heritage? In Poland? A Brief Manifesto and an Ethnographic Design Intervention into Jewish Tourism in Poland." *Bridges: A Jewish Feminist Journal* 12, 2 (autumn 2007): 36–41.

– and Lauren Ramsay. "Collecting (as) Dialogue? International Collaborative Collecting and 'Difficult' Objects." *Comcol International Committee for Collecting Newsletter* 22 (July 2013): 16–21.

Leonard, Llewellyn. "Civil Society Leadership and Industrial Risks: Environmental Justice in Durban, South Africa." *Journal of Asian and African Studies* 46, 2 (April 2011): 113–29.

Levell, Nicola. "Site-specificity and Dislocation: Michael Nicoll Yahgulanaas and his Haida Manga *Meddling*." *Journal of Material Culture* 18, 2 (2013): 93–116.

Lewis, Paul, and Matthew Taylor. "Security Guards Accused over Death of Man Being Deported to Angola." *The Guardian*, 14 October 2010, sec. UK news. http://www.guardian.co.uk/uk/2010/oct/14/security-guards-accused-jimmy-mubenga-death.

– "Staff on Deportation Flights Played 'Russian roulette' with lives." *The Guardian*, 8 February 2011, sec. UK news. http://www.guardian.co.uk/uk/2011/feb/08/staff-deportation-flights-g4s.

Lindauer, Margaret A. "Bosque Redondo: A Memorial in the Making." *Museum Management and Curatorship* 28, 3 (2013): 307–23.

– "Critical Museum Pedagogy: A Conceptual First Step." In *Museum Revolutions: How Museums Change and Are Changed*, edited by Simon K. Knell, Suzanne MacLeod, and Sheila Watson, 303–14. London: Routledge, 2007.

Lipp, Martin. *Medical Landmarks USA: A Travel Guide to Historic Sites, Architectural Gems, Remarkable Museums and Libraries, and Other Places of Health-Related Interest*. New York: McGraw-Hill, 1991.

Logan, William, and Keir Reeves. *Places of Pain and Shame: Dealing with 'Difficult Heritage.'* Oxford: Taylor & Francis, 2008.

Lomawaima, Tsianina. *They Called It Prairie Light: The Story of Chilocco Indian School.* Lincoln: University of Nebraska Press, 1994.

Lopez, Barry. "Flight." In *About this Life: Journeys of the Threshold of Memory*, 73–109. New York: Alfred A. Knopf, 1998.

Lovell, Lana. *Betwixt, Between, Bewitched.* Video. Innocent Cat Productions, 1992.

Luchs, Michelle, and Elizabeth Miller, eds. *Mapping Memories: Participatory Media, Place-Based Stories & Refugee Youth, Montreal.* Montreal: self-published, 2011.

Lozoviuk, Petre. "The Pervasive Continuities of Czech naordopis." In *Studying Peoples in the People's Democracies: Socialist Era Anthropology in East-Central Europe*, edited by Chris Hann, Mihally Sarkany, and Peter Skalnik, 227–36. Münster: Lit Verlag 2005.

Lupton, Julia Reinhard. "Philadelphia Dreaming." In *Practising Public Scholarship: Experiences and Possibilities Beyond the Academy*, edited by Katharyn Mitchell. Malden, MA, and Oxford, UK: Wiley-Blackwell, 2008.

Lynch, Bernadette. "Collaboration, Contestation and Creative Conflict: On the Efficacy of Museum/Community Partnerships." In *The Routledge Companion to Museum Ethics: Redefining Ethics for the Twenty-First-Century Museum*, edited by Janet Marstine, 146–63. London: Routledge, 2011.

– "Whose Cake Is It Anyway? A collaborative investigation into engagement and participation in 12 museums and galleries in the UK." Report commissioned by the Paul Hamilton Foundation. London: Paul Hamilton Foundation, 2011.

– and Samuel Alberti. "Legacies of Prejudice: Racism, Co-production and Radical Trust in the Museum." *Museum Management and Curatorship* 25, 1 (March 2010): 13–35.

Macdonald, Sharon. *Difficult Heritage: Negotiating the Nazi Past in Nuremberg and Beyond.* London and New York: Routledge, 2008.

– "Museums, National, Postnational and Transcultural identities." *Museum and Society* 1, 1 (2003): 1–16.

–, ed. *A Companion to Museum Studies.* Malden, MA, and Oxford: Wiley-Blackwell, 2011.

– and Paul Basu, eds. *Exhibition Experiments.* Oxford: Wiley-Blackwell, 2007.

– and Roger Silverstone. "Science on Display: The Representation of Scientific Controversy in Museum Exhibitions." *Public Understanding of Science* 1 (1992): 69–87.

MacLeod, Suzanne. "Introduction." In *Reshaping Museum Space: Architecture, Design, Exhibitions*, 1–8. Abingdon and New York: Routledge, 2005.

Marcus, George E. "Contemporary Fieldwork Aesthetics in Art and Anthropology: Experiments in Collaboration and Intervention." *Visual Anthropology* 23, 4 (2010): 263–77.

– "The Production of European High Culture in Los Angeles: The J. Paul Getty Trust as Artificial Curiosity." *Cultural Anthropology* 5, 3 (August 1990): 314–30.

– "The Uses of Complicity in the Changing Mise-en-Scène of Anthropological Fieldwork." *Representations* 59, 1 (1997): 85–108.

–, ed. *Paranoia Within Reason: A Casebook on Conspiracy as Explanation*. Chicago and London: University of Chicago Press, 1999.

– and Keith M. Murphy. "Ethnocharrette." 14 July 2011. Accessed 28 May 2014. http://ethnocharrette.wordpress.com.

– and Keith M. Murphy. "Ethnography and Design, Ethnography in Design … Ethnography by Design." In *Design Anthropology: Theory and Practice*, edited by Wendy Gunn, Ton Otto, and Rachel Charlotte Smith, 251–68. London, New Delhi, New York, and Sydney: Bloomsbury, 2013.

– with Peter Dobkin Hall. *Lives in Trust: The Fortunes of Dynastic Families in Late Twentieth-Century America*. Boulder, CO: Westview Press, 1992.

Margry, Peter Jan, and Herman Roodenburg. *Reframing Dutch Culture: Between Otherness and Authenticity*. Aldershot: Ashgate, 2007.

Marstine, Janet. "Museologically Speaking: An Interview with Fred Wilson." In *Museums, Equality and Social Justice*, edited by Richard Sandell and Eithne Nightingale, 38–44. Abingdon and New York: Routledge, 2012.

–, ed. *New Museum Theory and Practice: An Introduction*. Malden, MA, and Oxford: Blackwell, 2006.

Maura, Brescia. "Las Yeguas del Apocalipsis en una acción de arte." *La Época*. Santiago, 17 October 1989.

McArthur, Greg, et al. "Behind the Façade." *Globe and Mail* (Toronto), 28 March 2015. A1, A10–12.

McClintock, Anne. *Imperial Leather: Race, Gender, and Sexuality in the Colonial Context*. New York: Routledge, 1995.

McClusky, Pamela. "Taming Reality: Katherine White and the Seattle Art Museum." In *Representing Africa in American Art Museums: A Century of Collecting and Display*, edited by Kathleen Bickford Berzock and Christa Clarke, 224–40. Seattle: University of Washington Press, 2011.

McRobbie, Angela. *The Uses of Cultural Studies*. London: SAGE Publications, 2005.

McShine, Kynaston. *The Museum as Muse: Artists Reflect*. New York: Museum of Modern Art, 1999.

Mears, Helen, and Wayne Modest. "Museums, African Collections and Social Justice." In *Museums, Equality and Social Justice*, edited by Richard Sandell and Eithne Nightingale, 294–309. Abingdon and New York: Routledge, 2012.

Meijer-van Mensch, Léontine, Dorota Kawęcka, and Aleksandra Janus. "Strategien zum Schutz jüdischen Kulturerbes in Polen." In *Partizipative Erinnerungsräume: Dialogische Wissensbildung in Museen und Ausstellungen*, edited by Feliz Ackerman, Anna Boroffka, and Gregor H. Lersch, 207–20. Bielefeld, Germany: Transcript, 2013.

Menzies, H. Stuart. *All Ways by Airways*. London: Imperial Airways, 1932.

"Message: Jef Huereque," [1985], Harry Gamboa Jr Papers, Box 14. Audio Tape 4. Program h. Collection M0753, Dept. of Special Collections, Stanford University Libraries, Stanford.

Mihailescu, Vintila. "The Legacies of a 'Nation-Building Ethnology': Romania." In "Educational Histories of European Social Anthropology," *Eastern European Anthropologies*, vol. 4, edited by D. Drackle, I. Edgar, and T. Schippers, 208–19. New York and Oxford: Berghahn Books, 2003.

Moore, Oliver. "Burning Cross Ignites Racial Tension in Nova Scotia." *Global and Mail* (Toronto), 24 February 2010. Accessed 15 June 2014. http://www.theglobeandmail.com/news/national/burning-cross-ignites-racial-tension-in-nova-scotia/article561115/.

Moore-Gilbert, Bart. "Spivak and Bhabha." In *A Companion to Postcolonial Studies*, edited by Henry Schwarz and Sangeeta Ray. Malden, MA: Blackwell, 2005.

Morgan, Jonathan, and the Bambanani Women's Group. *Long Life: Positive HIV Stories*. Cape Town: Double Storey, 2004.

Morris, David, and Paul O'Neill. "Introduction: Exhibition as Social Intervention." In *Exhibition as Social Intervention: "Culture in action" 1993*, 8–13. London: In association with the Center for Curatorial Studies, Bard College, 2014.

Morrison, Toni. *Song of Solomon*. New York: Penguin Books, 1987.

Muñoz, Ariana. "When the 'Other' Became the Neighbour." In *Can We Make a Difference?: Museums, Society and Development in North and South*, edited by Paul R. Voogt, 54–62. Amsterdam: KIT Publishers, 2009.

Muñoz, José Esteban. "Ephemera as Evidence: Introductory Notes to Queer Acts." In *Women & Performance: A Journal of Feminist Theory* 8, 2 (1996): 5–16.

Murphy, E.L., D.W. Cohen, C.D. Bhimull, F. Coronil, M.E. Patterson, and J. Skurski, eds. *Anthrohistory: Unsettling Knowledge, Questioning Discipline*. Ann Arbor: University of Michigan Press, 2011.

Museo de la Solidaridad Salvador Allende. "El Museo." Accessed 30 June 2011. http://museodelasolidaridad.cl/el-museo/.

Museum of Contemporary Art Chicago. "Jeremy Deller: It Is What It Is: Conversations About Iraq." Accessed 11 June 2014. http://www2.mcachicago.org/exhibition/jeremy-deller-it-is-what-it-is-conversations-about-iraq/.

Musial, Stanislaw. "Czarne jest czarne." *Tygodnik Powszechny*, 16 November 1997. Accessed 26 May 2014. http://tygodnik.onet.pl/wiara/czarne-jest-czarne/g8xjk.

Nagourney, Adam. "Los Angeles Stakes Its Claim." *New York Times*, 13 October 2011, C1.

Naipaul, V.S. *The Mimic Men*. New York: Vintage Books, 2001.

Nation News. "Touchdown!" 1 February 2008. http://archive.nationnews.com/archive_detail.php?archiveFile=2008/February/01/LocalNews/52694.xml&start=0&numPer=20&keyword=touchdown§ionSearch=&begindate=1%2F1%2F1994&enddate=12%2F31%2F2009&authorSearch=&IncludeStories=1&pubsection=&page=&IncludePages&archive_pubname=Daily+Nation%0A%09%09%09.

Nelson, Steven. "A Conversation with Dr. Steven Nelson, Grove Art Online Guest Editor." http://blog.oup.com/2014/10/grove-art-steven-nelson-african/#sthash.Qmrttxbs.dpuf

Newbury, Darren. "Living Historically Through Photographs in Post-apartheid South Africa: Reflections on Kliptown Museum, Soweto." In *Curating Difficult Knowledge: Violent Pasts in Public Places*, edited by Erica Lehrer, Cynthia E. Milton, and Monica Eileen Patterson, 91–108. New York: Palgrave Macmillan, 2011.

Nightingale, Eithne, and Deborah Swallow. "The Arts of the Sikh Kingdoms." In *Museums and Source Communities: A Routledge Reader*, edited by Laura L. Peers and Alison K. Brown, 55–71. London and New York: Routledge, 2003.

O'Doherty, Brian. *Inside the White Cube: The Ideology of the Gallery Space*. Santa Monica, CA: Lapis Press, 1986.

Okediji, Moyo. "On Reparations: Exodus and Embodiment." *African Arts* 31, 2 (1998): 8–10.

Oles, James. *Agustín Lazo*. México, Distrito Federal: Universidad Nacional Autónoma de México, 2009.

Oleszkiewicz, Małgorzata, and Grażyna Pyla, eds. *Czar Zabawek Krakowskich*. Kraków: Muzeum Etnograficzne im. Seweryna Udzieli w Krakowie, 2007.

Open School. *Two Dogs and Freedom: Children of the Townships Speak Out*. Johannesburg: Ravan Press/The Open School, 1986.

Orange, Jennifer A., and Jennifer J. Carter. "'It's Time to Pause and Reflect': Museums and Human Rights." *Curator: The Museum Journal* 55, 3 (July 2012): 259–66.

Ostachowicz, Igor. *Noc Żywych Żydów*. Warsaw: WAB, 2012.

Ott, Katherine. "Disability and the Practice of Public History: An Introduction." *The Public Historian* 27, 2 (2005): 9–24.

Oxford English Dictionary Online. s.v. "curator." Accessed 28 January 2012. http://www.oed.com/view/Entry/45960?redirectedFrom=curator.

Oyarzún, Pablo, Nelly Richard, and Claudia Zaldívar, eds. *Arte y política*. Santiago: Universidad ARCIS, 2005.

Pamuk, Orhan. "A Modest Manifesto for Museums." *American Craft Magazine*, (June/July 2013). Accessed 28 May 2014. http://craftcouncil.org/magazine/article/modest-manifesto-museums.

– "Orhan Pamuk on His Museum of Innocence in Istanbul." *Newsweek*, 27 August 2012. Accessed 28 May 2014. http://www.newsweek.com/orhan-pamuk-his-museum-innocence-istanbul-64557.

Partridge, Damani J. "Holocaust *Mahnmal* (Memorial): Monumental Memory amidst Contemporary Race." *Comparative Studies in Society and History* 52, 4 (October 2010): 820–50.

Pasternak, Judy. *Yellow Dirt: An American Story of a Poisoned Land and a People Betrayed*. New York: Free Press, 2010.

Patterson, Monica Eileen. "Constructions of Childhood in Apartheid's Last Decades." PhD diss., University of Michigan, 2009.

– "Teaching Tolerance through Objects of Hatred: The Jim Crow Museum of Racist Memorabilia as 'Counter-Museum.'" In *Curating Difficult Knowledge: Violent Pasts in Public Places,* edited by Erica Lehrer, Cynthia E. Milton, and Monica Eileen Patterson, 55–71. New York: Palgrave Macmillan, 2011.

Pauchulo, Ana Laura. "Living with Loss: Mapping *derechos humanos* on the Landscape of Public Pemembrance of the 1976–1983 Dictatorship in Argentina." Unpublished PhD diss., University of Toronto, 2011. https://tspace.library.utoronto.ca/bitstream/1807/29840/6/Pauchulo_AnaLaura_201106_PhD_thesis.pdf

Paudrat, Jean-Louis. "From Africa." In *"Primitivism" in 20th-Century Art: Affinity of the Tribal and the Modern*, edited by William Rubin, 125–74. New York: The Museum of Modern Art, 1984.

Peer, Shanny. *France on Display: Peasants, and Folklore in the 1937 Paris World's Fair.* New York: SUNY Press, 1998.

Peers, Laura L., and Alison K. Brown, eds. *Museums and Source Communities: A Routledge Reader*. London and New York: Routledge, 2003.

Peressut, Luca, Francesca Lanz, and Gennaro Postiglione, eds. *European Museums in the 21st Century: Setting the Framework*. Vol. 2. Milan: Politecnico di Milano, 2013.

Pew Research Fund. "Public and Scientists' Views on Science and Society." Last modified 29 January 2015. Accessed 10 April 2015. http://www.pewinternet.org/2015/01/29/public-and-scientists-views-on-science-and-society.

Philip, Marlene NourbeSe. "Race, Space, and the Poetics of Moving." In *Caribbean Creolization: Reflections of the Cultural Dynamics of Language, Literature and Identity*, edited by Kathleen M. Balutansky and Marie-Agnes Sourieau, 129–54. Gainesville, FL, and Barbados: University of the West Indies Press, 1998.

Phillips, Ruth. "Community Collaboration in Exhibitions: Introduction." In *Museums and Source Communities: A Routledge Reader*, edited by Laura Peers and Alison K. Brown, 155–70. London: Routledge, 2003.

– *Museum Pieces: Toward the Indigenization of Canadian Museums*. Montreal and Kingston: McGill-Queen's University Press, 2011.

– *Trading Identities: The Souvenir in Native North American Art from the Northeast, 1700–1900*. Seattle: University of Washington Press, 1998.

– "Where Is 'Africa'?: Re-Viewing Art and Artifact in the Age of Globalization." *American Anthropologist* 104, 3 (2002): 11–19.

Pieterse, Jan Nederveen. "Multiculturalism and Museums: Discourse about Others in the Age of Globalization." In *Heritage, Museums and Galleries: An Introductory Reader*, edited by Gerard Corsane, 163–83. London and New York: Routledge, 2005.

Pigearias, Solveig, and Michèle Hornn. "Paul Guillaume et l'art africain: Histoire d'une collection à la lumière de nouvelles recherches." *Tribal Art* 59 (spring 2011): 78–91.

Pimpaneau, Sara. "Quand l'ethnographie s'expose." *Architecture d'aujourd'hui* 326 (2000): 24–7.

Pinto, Diana. "Fifty Years after the Holocaust: Building a New Jewish and Polish Memory." *East European Jewish Affairs* 26, 2 (1996): 79–95.

– "Can One Reconcile the Jewish World and Europe?" In *The New German Jewry and the European Context: The Return of the European Jewish Diaspora*, edited by Michal Y. Bodeman, 13–32. New York: Palgrave Macmillan, 2008.

Porto, Nuno. "From Exhibiting to Installing Ethnography: Experiments at the Museum of Anthropology of the University of Coimbra, Portugal, 1999–2005." In *Exhibition Experiments*, edited by Sharon Macdonald and Paul Basu, 175–96. Malden, MA: Blackwell, 2007.

Preziosi, Donald. *Brain of the Earth's Body: Art, Museums, and the Phantasms of Modernity*. Minneapolis: University of Minnesota Press, 2003.

Price, Sally. *Paris Primitive: Jacques Chirac's Museum on the Quai Branly*. Chicago: University of Chicago Press, 2007.

Prins, Bukje, and Sawitri Saharso. "From Toleration to Repression: The Dutch Backlash against Multiculturalism." In *The Multiculturalism Backlash: European Discourses, Policies, and Practices*, edited by Steven Vertovec and Susanne Wessendorf, 273–84. London: Routledge, 2009.

Putnam, James. *Art and Artifact: The Museum as Medium*. London: Thames & Hudson, 2001.

Puwar, Nirmal, and Sanjay Sharma. "Curating Sociology." *The Sociological Review* 60, Issue Supplement S1 (June 2012): 40–63.

Rahimi, Dan. "Reflecting on "Into the Heart of Africa." YouTube video, 6:58. Posted by the Royal Ontario Museum, 4 February 2014. Accessed 15 June 2014. https://www.youtube.com/watch?v=TYkByD9W5es.

Rajkowska, Joanna. *Where the Beast Is Buried*. Winchester & Washington: Zero Books, 2013.

Rassool, Ciraj. "Ethnographic Elaborations, Indigenous Contestations, and the Cultural Politics of Imagining Communities: A View from the District Six Museum in South Africa." In *Contesting Knowledge: Museums and Indigenous Perspectives*, edited by Susan Sleeper-Smith. Lincoln: University of Nebraska Press, 2009.

Reed, Christopher. *Art and Homosexuality: A History of Ideas*. New York: Oxford University Press, 2011.

Republic of South Africa Department of Health. *The 2011 National Antenatal Sentinel HIV & Syphilis Prevalence Survey in South Africa*. Pretoria: National Department of Health, 2012.

Richard, Nelly. *Margins and Institutions: Art in Chile since 1973*. Melbourne: Art and Text, 1981.

Richards, Thomas. *The Commodity Culture of Victorian England: Advertising and Spectacle, 1851–1914*. Stanford, CA: Stanford University Press, 1990.

Riles, Annelise, ed. *Documents: Artifacts of Modern Knowledge*. Ann Arbor: University of Michigan Press, 2006.

Robotycki, Czesław. "The Anthropology of Culture in Poland: A Finished Project." *Lud* 79 (1995): 69–86.

Roessel, Ruth, ed. *Navajo Stories of the Long Walk Period*. Tsaile, AZ: Navajo Community College Press, 1973.

Rogoff, Irit. "What is a Theorist?" In *Was ist ein Künstler*, edited by Katharyna Sykora. Berlin: Wilhelm Fink Verlag, 2003.

Roman, David. "Asco Wilde." In *ASCO: Elite of the Obscure*, edited by C. Ondine Chavoya and Rita Gonzalez, 362–66. Ostfildern, Germany: Hatje Cantz, 2011.

Room 13. "Room 13." Accessed 3 June 2014. http://room13.co.za/.

Rosen, Joseph. "Lunch with the Führer: Holocaust Comedy, Trauma, and the Enemy." *Poesis* 6 (2004): 30–45.

Ross, Max. "Interpreting the New Museology." *Museum and Society* 2, 2 (July 2004): 84–103.

Rothberg, Michael. *Multidirectional Memory: Remembering the Holocaust in the Age of Decolonization*. Stanford, CA: Stanford University Press, 2009.

– "Pedagogy and the Politics of Memory: 'The Countermonument Project.'" In *Teaching the Representation of the Holocaust*, edited by Marianne Hirsch and Irene Kacandes, 466–76. New York: MLA, 2004.

Royal Ontario Museum. "ROM Expands its African Collection." Royal Ontario Museum press release, 15 December 2010. Royal Ontario Museum website. Accessed 15 June 2014. http://www.rom.on.ca/en/about-us/newsroom/press-releases/rom-expands-its-african-collection.

– "ROM ReCollects." *Royal Ontario Museum*. Accessed 15 June 2014. http://www.rom.on.ca/en/romrecollects/home.

Ryan, Shaun. "Facelift for Addington Children's Hospital." NewsShare, 8 February 2012. Accessed 21 May 2014. http://news.howzit.msn.com/article.aspx?cp-documentid=160512306.

Ryzik, Melena. "The Entire Audience Dozed Off? Perfect!" *New York Times*, 16 May 2014. Accessed 28 May 2014. http://www.nytimes.com/2014/05/17/arts/dream-of-the-red-chamber-and-other-sleep-oriented-shows.html.

SA Venues. "KwaZulu Natal Things to Do: Visit the Addington Centenary Museum (Durban Beachfront)." Accessed 21 May 2014. http://www.sa-venues.com/things-to-do/kwazulunatal/visit-the-addington-centenary-museum/.

Sandell, Richard. "Constructing and Communicating Equality: The Social Agency of Museum Space." In *Reshaping Museum Space: Architecture, Design, Exhibitions*, edited by Suzanne MacLeod, 185–200. Abingdon and New York: Routledge, 2005.

– "Ethics and Activism." In *The Routledge Companion to Museum Ethics: Redefining Ethics for the Twenty-First-Century Museum*, edited by Janet Marstine, 129–45. London and New York: Routledge, 2011.

– *Museums, Prejudice and the Reframing of Difference*. London and New York: Routledge, 2007.

–, ed. *Museums, Society, Inequality*. London and New York: Routledge, 2002.

– and Eithne Nightingale, eds. *Museums, Equality and Social Justice*. Oxford and New York: Routledge, 2012.

–, Jocelyn Dodd, and Rosemarie Garland-Thomson, eds. *Re-Presenting Disability: Activism and Agency in the Museum*. London and New York: Routledge, 2010.

Sather-Wagstaff, Joy, and Rebekah Sobel. "From Memory to Action: Multisited Visitor Action at the United States Holocaust Memorial Museum." *Museums and Social Issues* 7, 2 (October 2012): 293–305.

Schiebinger, Londa. "Skeletons in the Closet: The First Illustrations of the Female Skeleton in Eighteenth-Century Anatomy." *Representations* 14 (spring 1986): 42–82.

Schneider, Arnd, and Christopher Wright, eds. *Anthropology and Art Practice*. London, New Delhi, New York, and Sydney: Bloomsbury, 2013.

– *Between Art and Anthropology: Contemporary Ethnographic Practice*. London, New Delhi, New York, and Sydney: Bloomsbury, 2010.

– *Contemporary Art and Anthropology*. London and New York: Berg, 2005.
Serlin, David. "Making Disability Public: An Interview with Katherine Ott." *Radical History Review* 94 (winter 2006): 197–211.
Sevcenko, Liz. "Activating the Past for Civic Action: The International Coalition of Historic Site Museums of Conscience." *The George Wright Forum* 19, 4 (2002): 55–64.
– "Sites of Conscience: New Approaches to Conflicted Memory." *Museum International* 62, 1–2 (May 2010): 20–5.
Shannon, Helen M. "African Art, 1914: The Root of Modern Art." In *Modern Art and America: Alfred Stieglitz and his New York Galleries*, edited by Sarah Greenough, 168–79. Washington, DC: National Gallery of Art, 2000.
Shannon, Jennifer. "The Construction of Native Voice at the National Museum of the American Indian." In *Contesting Knowledge: Museums and Indigenous Perspectives*, edited by Susan Sleeper-Smith, 218–47. Lincoln: University of Nebraska Press, 2009.
"Shelley-Ann Brown: Silver Medal Olympian 2010." Accessed 15 June 2014. http://www.shelley-annbrown.com/.
Shelton, Anthony. "Curating African Worlds." In *Museums and Source Communities: A Routledge Reader*, edited by Laura L. Peers and Alison K. Brown, 181–93. London and New York: Routledge, 2003.
Shesgreen, Deirdre. "Reminder: Thursday Briefing on Stemming the Deadly Twin Epidemics of HIV and Tuberculosis." *Science Speaks: HIV TB News (blog)*. Center for Global Health Policy, IDSA Education and Research Foundation. Accessed 21 May 2014. http://sciencespeaksblog.org/2010/05/19/reminder-thursday-briefing-on-stemming-the-deadly-twin-epidemics-of-hiv-and-tuberculosis/.
Sheramy, Rona. "From Auschwitz to Jerusalem: Re-enacting Jewish History on the March of the Living." *POLIN: Studies in Polish Jewry* 19 (2007): 307–26.
Shyrock, Andrew. "In the Double Remoteness of Arab Detroit: Reflections on Ethnography, Culture Work, and the Intimate Disciplines of Americanization." In *Off Stage/On Display: Intimacy and Ethnography in the Age of Public Culture*, edited by Andrew Shryock, 279–314. Palo Alto, CA: Stanford University Press, 2004.
Silvén, Eva. "Difficult Matters: Museums, Materiality, Multivocality." In *The Museum as Forum and Actor*, edited by Fredrik Svanberg, 133–46. Stockholm: Museum of National Antiquities, 2010.
Silverman, Lois H. *The Social Work of Museums*. London: Routledge, 2009.
Silverman, Raymond. "The Legacy of Ethnography." In *Contesting Knowledge: Museums and Indigenous Perspectives*, edited by Susan Sleeper-Smith, 9–14. Lincoln: University of Nebraska Press, 2009.

–, ed. *Museum as Process: Translating Local and Global Knowledges*. Great Britain: Taylor & Francis, 2014.

Simon, Nina. *The Participatory Museum*. Santa Cruz: Museum 2.0, 2010.

Simon, Roger I. "A Shock to Thought: Curatorial Judgment and the Public Exhibition of 'Difficult Knowledge.'" *Memory Studies* 4, 4 (October 2011): 432–49.

– "Dramatic Portrayal as Theorizing in the Concrete." In *Preservice and Inservice Education of Science Teachers*, edited by Pinchas Tamir, Avi Hofstein, and Miriam Ben-Peretz, 183–95. Rehovot, Israel, and Philadelphia: Balaban International Science Services, 1983.

–, Mario Di Paolantonio, and Mark Clamen. "Remembrance as Praxis and the Ethics of the Inter-Human." *Culture Machine* 4, 0 (February 2008). http://www.culturemachine.net/index.php/cm/article/viewArticle/272/257.

–, Sharon Rosenberg, and Claudia Eppert, eds. *Between Hope and Despair: Pedagogy and the Remembrance of Historical Trauma*. Oxford and Lanham, MD: Rowman & Littlefield, 2000.

– and Susan Ashley. "Heritage and Practices of Social Formation: Introduction." *International Journal of Heritage Studies* 16, 4 and 5 (2010): 247–54.

Sjørslev, Inger. "Intangible Cultural Heritage and Ethnographic Museum Practice in a Global Perspective." In *Scandinavian Museums and Cultural Diversity*, edited by Katherine J. Goodnow and Haci Akman, 161–71. New York: Berghahn Books, 2008.

Smith, Craig S. "In Poland, a Jewish Revival Thrives – Minus Jews." *New York Times*, 12 July 2007. Accessed 25 May 2014. http://www.nytimes.com/2007/07/12/world/europe/12krakow.html.

Soja, Edward. *Thirdspace: Journeys to Los Angeles and Other Real-and-Imagined Places*. Malden, MA: Blackwell, 1996.

Solani, Noël. "The Saint of the Struggle: Deconstructing the Mandela Myth." *Kronos* 26 (August 2000): 42–55.

Solomon, Jane. *'Living with X': A Body Mapping Journal in the time of HIV and AIDS: Facilitator's Guide*. Johannesburg: REPSSI, 2007.

Sontag, Susan. *Regarding the Pain of Others*. New York: Picador, 2004.

Spicer, Edward H. *Cycles of Conquest: The Impact of Spain, Mexico, and the United States on the Indians of the Southwest, 1533–1960*. Tucson: University of Arizona Press, 1962.

"South Africa in the Spotlight." *The Lancet* 371, 9620 (April 2008): 1215. Accessed 21 May 2014.

Squiers, Carol. *The Body at Risk: Photography of Disorder, Illness, and Healing*. New York: International Center of Photography, 2005.

Ssorin-Chiakov, Nikolai. "Ethnographic Conceptualism: An Introduction." *Laboratorium* 2 (2013). Accessed 28 May 2014. http://soclabo.org/index.php/laboratorium/article/view/336/864.

Steiner, Christopher B. "Can the Canon Burst?" *Art Bulletin* 78, 2 (1996): 213–17.
Sternad, Jennifer Flores. "Cyclona and Early Chicano Performance Art: An Interview with Robert Legorreta." *GLQ* 12, 3 (2006): 475–90.
Straker, Jay. *Youth, Nationalism, and the Guinean Revolution*. Bloomington: Indiana University Press, 2009.
Strohm, Kiven. "When Anthropology Meets Contemporary Art: Notes for a Politics of Collaboration." *Collaborative Anthropologies* 5 (2012): 98–124.
Strother, Z.S. "Gabama a Gingungu and the Secret History of Twentieth-Century Art." *African Arts* 32, 1 (1999): 18–31, 92–3.
Suderberg, Erika, ed. *Space, Site, Intervention: Situating Installation Art*. Minneapolis: University of Minnesota Press, 2000.
Stauter-Halstead, Keely. *The Nation in the Village: The Genesis of Rural National Identity in Austrian Poland, 1848–1900*. Ithaca, NY: Cornell University Press, 2001.
Stocking, George W., ed. *Objects and Others: Essays on Museums and Material Culture*. Madison: University of Wisconsin Press, 1985.
Strong, Pauline Turner. "Exclusive Labels: Indexing the National 'We' in Commemorative and Oppositional Exhibitions," *Museum Anthropology* 21, 1 (1997): 42–56.
Szczurek, Małgorzata, ed. *Sto i pół. Opowieści z Muzeum Etnograficznego w Krakowie*. Kraków: Muzeum Etnograficzne im. Seweryna Udzieli w Krakowie, 2011.
Tancock, Martha. "White Wash." *York U Magazine*, Summer 2013, 28–9. Accessed 15 June 2014. http://cpa.info.yorku.ca/files/2013/05/YorkU_Summer 20131.pdf.
Taylor, Diana. "A Savage Performance: Guillermo Gómez-Peña and Coco Fusco's 'Couple in the Cage.'" *TDR* 42, 2 (summer 1998): 160–75.
– *The Archive and the Repertoire: Performing Cultural Memory in the Americas*. Durham, NC: Duke University Press, 2003.
Ter Braak, Lex. *Zielenruil*. Amsterdam: Tropenmuseum, 2010. Accessed 27 January 2011. http://www.tropenmuseum.nl/-/MUS/55590/Tropenmuseum/Madonna---Artikel-Lex-ter-Braak.pdf.
Ter Wal, Jessika. "The Netherlands." In *European Immigration: A Sourcebook*, edited by Anna Triandafyllidou and Ruby Gropas, 249–61. Aldershot, UK, and Burlington, VT: Ashgate, 2007.
The International Museum of Children's Art. "The International Museum of Children's Art." Accessed 21 May 2014. http://www.barnekunst.no/en/.
The Solomon R. Guggenheim Foundation. "theanyspacewhatever." Accessed 11 June 2014. http://www.guggenheim.org/new-york/exhibitions/past/exhibit/1896.

Thiesse, Anne-Marie, and Sigrid Norris. "How Countries Are Made: Cultural Construction of European Nations." *Contexts* 2, 2 (May 2003): 26–32.

Thompson, Robert Farris. *African Art in Motion: Icon and Act in the Collection of Katherine Coryton White*. Los Angeles: University of California Press, 1974.

Todorov, Tzvetan. "Memory as Remedy for Evil." *Journal of International Criminal Justice* 7, 3 (2009): 447–62.

Tohe, Laura. *No Parole Today*. Albuquerque, NM: West End Press, 1999.

Tokarska-Bakir, Joanna. "'The Hanging of Judas'; or, Contemporary Jewish Subjects." *POLIN: Studies in Polish Jewry* 24 (November 2011): 281–400.

– "Żyd z pieniążkiem podbija Polskę." *Gazeta Wyborcza*, 18 February 2012. Accessed 26 May 2014. http://wyborcza.pl/1,75475,11172689,Zyd_z_pieniazkiem_podbija_Polske.html.

– "'Poland as the Sick Man of Europe?' Jedwabne, 'Post-Memory,' and Historians." *Eurozine*, 30 May 2003.

Touré, Sékou. "The Political Leader as a Representative of His Culture. Expérience Guinéenne Unité, 1962." In *The Short Century: Independence and Liberation Movements in Africa, 1945–1994*, edited by Okwui Enwezor, 369–72. Munich and New York: Prestel, 2001 [1962].

Turner, Camille. "Miss Canadiana." Accessed 15 June 2014. http://camilleturner.com/?project=miss-canadiana.

UNAIDS. *World AIDS Day Report*. Geneva: UNAIDS, 2011.

UNESCO. "Text of the Convention for the Safeguarding of Intangible Cultural Heritage." Accessed 21 May 2014. http://www.unesco.org/culture/ich/index.php?lg=EN&pg=00022.

United States Holocaust Memorial Museum. "Deadly Medicine: Creating the Master Race." Accessed 10 April 2015. http://www.ushmm.org/information/exhibitions/traveling-exhibitions/deadly-medicine.

United States National Library of Medicine. "Against the Odds: Making a Difference in Global Health." Accessed 10 April 2015. http://apps.nlm.nih.gov/againsttheodds/index.cfm.

– "Changing the Face of Medicine: Celebrating America's Women Physicians." Last modified 10 June 2013. Accessed 10 April 2015. http://www.nlm.nih.gov/changingthefaceofmedicine.

– "From 'Monsters' to Modern Medical Miracles: Selected Moments in the History of Conjoined Twins from Medieval to Modern Times." Last modified 17 September 2013. Accessed 10 April 2015. http://www.nlm.nih.gov/hmd/conjoined/index.html.

– "Life and Limb: The Toll of the Civil War." Last modified 5 February 2015. Accessed 10 April 2015. http://www.nlm.nih.gov/exhibition/lifeandlimb/index.html.

– "The Literature of Prescription: Charlotte Perkins and 'The Yellow Wall-Paper.'" Last modified 24 November 2014. Accessed 10 April 2015. http://www.nlm.nih.gov/literatureofprescription.

– "Visible Proofs: Forensic Views of the Body." Last modified 24 November 2014. Accessed 10 April 2015. http://www.nlm.nih.gov/visibleproofs.

Van Alphen, Ernst. "Making Sense of Affect." In *Francis Bacon: Five Decades*, edited by Anthony Bond, 65–78. Sydney: Art Gallery of New South Wales, 2012.

Van Beurden, Jos. *Partnership in Cultural Heritage: The International Projects of the KIT Tropenmusem in Amsterdam*. Bulletin 364. Amsterdam: KIT Publishers, 2005.

Van Brakel, K., and S. Legêne. *Collecting at Cultural Crossroads, Collection Policies and Approaches (2008–2012) of the Tropenmuseum*. Amsterdam: KIT Publishers, 2008.

Van Dartel, Daan. "Dilemmas of the Ethnographic Museum." In *Can We Make a Difference: Museums, Society and Development in North and South*, edited by Paul R. Voogt. Amsterdam: KIT Publishers, 2009.

– "There's a Story behind Everything: Moving towards the Intangible at the Tropenmusem." In *Sharing Cultures 2009: International Conference on Intangible Heritage*, edited by Sérgio Lira, Rogério Amoêda, Cristina Pinheiro, João Pinheiro, and Fernando Oliveira, 341–52. Barcelos, Portugal: Green Lines Institute for Sustainable Development, 2009.

–, ed. *Tropenmuseum for a Change: Present between Past and Future. A Symposium Report*. Amsterdam: KIT Publishers, 2009.

Van der Horst, Hilje. "Appropriating Modernity and Tradition: The Turkish-Dutch and the Imaginary Geography of East and West." In *Reframing Dutch Culture: Between Otherness and Authenticity*, edited by Peter Jan Margry and Herman Roodenburg, 83–106. Aldershot, UK: Ashgate, 2007.

Van Stipriaan, Alex. "Social discourse: Interaction between museum and society." In *Tropenmuseum for a Change! Present between Past and Future: A Symposium Report*, edited by Daan van Dartel, 55–62. Amsterdam: KIT publishers, 2009.

Vaughan, Kenton. *The Museum*. Film. National Film Board of Canada, 2008.

Vergo, Peter, ed. *The New Museology*. London: Reaktion Books, 1989.

Vink, Maarten P. "Dutch 'Multiculturalism' Beyond the Pillarisation Myth." *Political Studies Review* 5, 3 (2007): 337–50.

Vogel, Susan. "Portrait of a Museum in Practice." In *Exhibition-ism: Museums and African Art*, 97–123. New York: Museum for African Art, 1994.

– "Whither African Art? Emerging Scholarship at the End of an Age." *African Arts* 38, 4 (2005): 12–17, 91.

Voogt, Paul. "Presentation Discourse: Public and Presentation." In *Tropenmuseum for a Change! Present between Past and Future: A Symposium Report*, edited by Daan van Dartel, 70–8. Amsterdam: KIT publishers, 2009.

Vukov, Nikolai. "Ethnoscripts and Nationographies: Imagining Nations within Ethnographic Museums in East Central and Southern Europe." In *Great Narratives of the Past Traditions and Revisions in National Museums*, edited by Dominique Poulot, Felicity Bodenstein, and José María Lanzarote Guiral, 331–53. Conference proceedings from EuNaMus, European National Museums: Identity Politics, the Uses of the Past and the European Citizen, Paris, 2011.

Walcott, Derek. *Omeros*. New York: Noonday Press, 1990.

– "The Schooner Flight." In *Collected Poems, 1948–1984*, 345–61. New York: Farrar, Straus & Giroux, 1986.

Walcott, Rinaldo. *Black Like Who?* London, ON: Insomniac Press, 1997.

Walford, Lauren. "Children's Hospital Opens in Durban." *looklocal Berea*, 16 July 2013. Accessed 6 May 2014. http://www.looklocal.co.za/looklocal/content/en/berea/berea-news-general?oid=7620481&sn=Detail&pid=4197107&Children-s-Hospital-opens-in-Durban.

Waligórska, Magdalena. "Cur(at)ing History: New Genre Art Interventions and the Polish-Jewish Past." *East European Politics & Society*. Published online March 2013; paper July 2013.

– *Klezmer's Afterlife: An Ethnography of the Jewish Music Revival in Poland and Germany*. Oxford and New York: Oxford University Press, 2013.

Walker, Karyl. "Finger-raped in Barbados." *Jamaican Observer*, 14 March 2011. http://www.jamaicaobserver.com/news/Finger-raped-in-Barbados_8573453.

Walker, Roslyn Adele. *Olowe of Ise: A Yoruba Sculptor to Kings*. Washington, DC: Smithsonian Institution, 1998.

Wallace, Michelle. "The Prison-House of Culture: Why African Art? Why the Guggenheim? Why Now?" *Black Renaissance* (1997): 162–75.

Wallis, Brian. "A Forum, Not a Temple: Notes on the Return of Iconography to the Museum." *American Literary History* 9, 3 (autumn 1997): 617–23.

Wehner, Kristen, and Martha Sear. "Engaging the Material World: Object Knowledge and Australian Journeys." In *Museum Materialities: Objects, Engagements, Interpretations*, edited by Sandra H. Dudley, 143–61. London and New York: Routledge, 2010.

Weiermair, Peter, ed. *Steven Arnold: "Exotic Tableaux."* Kilchberg/Zurich, Switzerland: Edition Stemmle, 1996.

Weiss, Lawrence David. *The Development of Capitalism in the Navajo Nation: A Political-Economic History*. Minneapolis: MEP Publications, 1984.

Welbon, Yvonne. "Immersion in Legacy: Coming Home to Ourselves and One Another." *GLQ* 17, 4 (2011): 620–3.

Welsh, Peter H. "Re-configuring Museums." *Museum Management and Curatorship* 20, 2 (June 2005): 103–30.

White, Bob W. "From Experimental Moment to Legacy Moment: Collaboration and the Crisis of Representation." *Collaborative Anthropologies* 5 (2012): 65–97.

Whiteside, Alan. *HIV/AIDS: A Very Short Introduction*. Kindle Edition. Oxford: Oxford University Press, 2008.

Whyte, Murray. "El Anatsui: Finding the Meaning of Junk." *Toronto Star*, 1 October 2010. Accessed 15 June 2014. http://www.thestar.com/entertainment/2010/10/01/el_anatsui_finding_the_meaning_of_junk.html.

Wikipedia contributors. "Talking stick." *Wikipedia, The Free Encyclopedia*. Accessed 25 May 2014. http://en.wikipedia.org/w/index.php?title=Talking_stick&oldid=600971328.

Wiley, D., C. Root, and B. Peek. "Contesting the Urban Industrial Environment in South Durban in a Period of Democratisation and Globalisation." In *(D) urban Vortex*, edited by B. Freund and V. Padayachee, 223–55. Pietermaritzburg: University of KwaZulu-Natal Press. 2002.

Williams, Erin. "Creators of Censored-Art Museum Are Honored." *Washington Post*, 26 May 2011, C03.

Williams, Paul. *Memorial Museums: The Global Rush to Commemorate Atrocities*. London and New York: Berg, 2008.

Wilson, Fred. *Fred Wilson: A Critical Reader*. Edited by Doro Globus. London: Ridinghouse, 2011.

Witcomb, Andrea. *Re-Imagining the Museum: Beyond the Mausoleum*. London and New York: Routledge, 2003.

Ytuarte, Eddie. "Chicano Art Lives in East L.A." *El Chicano*, 7 December 1972, 9.

Zimmerman, Joshua, ed. *Contested Memories: Poles and Jews During the Holocaust and Its Aftermath*. New Brunswick, NJ: Rutgers University Press, 2003.

Zussman, Robert, and Joya Misra. "Introduction." In *Public Sociology*, edited by Dan Clawson, Robert Zussman, Joya Misra, Naomi Gerstel, Randall Stokes, Douglas L. Anderton, and Michael Burawoy, 3–22. Berkeley and Los Angeles: University of California Press, 2007.

CONTRIBUTORS

JANICE BAKER is a lecturer in the School of Media, Culture and Creative Arts at Curtin University, where she teaches literary and cultural studies. Her research is transdisciplinary, with an interest in sites that engage with new subjectivities, particularly cinematic representations of museums. Her book *Sentient Relics: Museums and Cinematic Affect* is forthcoming. Janice was previously a curator at the Art Gallery of Western Australia and the Lawrence Wilson Art Gallery at the University of Western Australia, and more recently a postdoctoral research fellow at Deakin University.

CHANDRA D. BHIMULL is an assistant professor of anthropology and African-American studies at Colby College. Her ethnographic and archival research focuses on racial oppression and airborne mobility. Her book *Empire in the Air: Airline Travel and the African Diaspora* will be published by New York University Press.

MATTI BUNZL is director of the Wien Museum, Vienna's municipal museum. Before taking the position in 2015, he was professor of anthropology at the University of Illinois (1998–2014) and artistic director of the Chicago Humanities Festival (2010–14). He is the author of *Symptoms of Modernity: Jews and Queers in Late-Twentieth-Century Vienna* (University of California Press, 2004), *Anti-Semitism and Islamophobia: Hatreds Old and New in Europe* (Prickly Paradigm Press/University of

Chicago Press, 2007), and *In Search of a Lost Avant-Garde: An Anthropologist Investigates the Contemporary Art Museum* (University of Chicago Press, 2014).

SHELLEY RUTH BUTLER is a cultural anthropologist and lecturer with the McGill Institute for the Study of Canada in Montreal. Her ethnographic research explores how museums and mainstream and alternative heritage sites in Canada and South Africa can become more inclusive and challenging. Her book *Contested Representations: Revisiting Into the Heart of Africa* is widely taught in the United States, the UK, and Canada. In 2013–14 she was acting director of the Centre for Ethnographic Research and Exhibition in the Aftermath of Violence at Concordia University, where she continues to be a research affiliate and consultant. Curatorial dreaming is a concept she also explores in relation to township tours in her contribution to *Slum Tourism: Poverty, Power and Ethics* (2012).

JOSHUA I. COHEN (PhD Columbia University, 2014) is assistant professor of African art history at the City College of New York, City University of New York. His interest in Guinean arts and questions of public transmission began with apprenticeships to Guinean performing artists in the United States, followed by Fulbright research conducted in Guinea. He is now working on a book that tracks appropriations of African sculpture – often encountered in museum collections – by European and then African painters between 1905 and 1980.

LUCIAN GOMOLL is an assistant professor in liberal studies and the Honors College at California State University, Los Angeles. He earned his PhD in the history of consciousness from the University of California, Santa Cruz (2012). Gomoll is a critical theorist who teaches and writes about the sciences, ability, gender, race, indigeneity, sexuality, species, museums, performance, and art. His forthcoming book, *Performativity and Difference in Museums*, historicizes and theorizes various ways that bodies have been incorporated into exhibitions and archives since the early nineteenth century.

ROBB HERNÁNDEZ is assistant professor of Latina/o literary and cultural studies in the Department of English at the University of California,

Riverside. His books, *VIVA Records 1970–2000: Lesbian and Gay Latino Artists of Los Angeles* (2013) and *The Fire of Life: The Robert Legorreta–Cyclona Collection, 1962–2002* (2009), were published by the UCLA Chicano Studies Research Center Press. His articles have appeared in *Aztlan, Collections, Museum and Curatorial Studies Review, MELUS*, and *Radical History Review*. He is currently working on his book manuscript, "Finding AIDS: Archival Body/Archival Space and the Chicano Avant-garde," which proposes a queer genealogy of Chicano avant-gardism(s) through alternative archives engendered by the AIDS crisis.

SERENA IERVOLINO is lecturer in museology and curatorial studies and degree coordinator of the MA in museum and gallery practice at UCL Qatar, Doha, an off-shore campus of University College London, where she lectures on the MA in museum and gallery practice. Her research interests include the ideologies and politics of museums and exhibitions, diversity issues, museum organizational change, and participatory heritage approaches. Her primary area of research explores how post-colonial trajectories, cultural policies and politics, migration patterns, and other factors of change are shaping current approaches to the display and interpretation of "non-Western" material culture and art in Europe and the Middle East, while instigating processes of organizational change and fuelling new museum developments. Serena holds a PhD in museum studies from the University of Leicester. In May 2015, she was awarded one of the University of Leicester's College of Arts, Humanities and Law Doctoral Prizes and Inaugural Lectures (2014–15). Serena has presented her research at international conferences and has published papers in edited books and journals, including in *Museums and Communities: Curators, Collections and Collaborations* edited by Viv Golding and Wayne Modest (2013).

BARBARA KIRSHENBLATT-GIMBLETT, university professor emerita and professor emerita of performance studies at New York University, is currently chief curator of the core exhibition at POLIN Museum of the History of Polish Jews in Warsaw. Her books include *Destination Culture: Tourism, Museums, and Heritage*; *Image before My Eyes: A Photographic History of Jewish Life in Poland, 1864–1939* (with Lucjan Dobroszycki); *The Art of Being Jewish in Modern Times* (edited with Jonathan Karp);

and *They Called Me Mayer July: Painted Memories of a Jewish Childhood in Poland Before the Holocaust*, which she co-authored with her father, Mayer Kirshenblatt. She currently serves on advisory boards for the YIVO Institute for Jewish Research, Jewish Museum Vienna, Jewish Museum Berlin, and the Jewish Museum and Tolerance Center in Moscow.

ERICA LEHRER is associate professor and Canada Research Chair in Museum and Heritage Studies in the Departments of History and Sociology-Anthropology at Concordia University, Montreal, where she is the founding director of CEREV, the Centre for Ethnographic Research and Exhibition in the Aftermath of Violence. She is the author of *Jewish Poland Revisited: Heritage Tourism in Unquiet Places* (Indiana University Press, 2013), and co-editor of *Curating Difficult Knowledge: Violent Pasts in Public Places* (Palgrave Macmillan, 2010) and *Jewish Space in Contemporary Poland* (Indiana University Press, 2015). In 2013 she curated the exhibition *Souvenir, Talisman, Toy* in Krakow, Poland's Seweryn Udziela Ethnographic Museum, along with the associated book *Lucky Jews*, and website www.luckyjews.com.

MARGARET A. LINDAUER is associate professor and department chair of art history at Virginia Commonwealth University. Her research focusing on social, cultural, and curatorial implications of the ways in which museums historically have been characterized as educational institutions has been published in several anthologies and journals including *Museum & Society* and *Journal of Museum Management and Curatorship*. She first articulated an investigation of critical museum pedagogy in an essay included in *Museum Revolutions: How Museums Change and Are Changed*.

GEORGE E. MARCUS is chancellor's professor of anthropology at University of California, Irvine, where he founded a Center for Ethnography in 2005. He has been interested in modes of experimenting with traditional methods of ethnographic research in new environments and novel understandings of fieldwork today. He was co-editor, with James Clifford, of *Writing Culture* (1986), co-author with Paul Rabinow of *Designs for an Anthropology of the Contemporary* (2008), and coeditor with James Faubion of *Fieldwork is Not What It Used to Be* (2009). At present he is at work on a volume, in collaboration with Luke Cantarella and Christina Hegel, on applications of design and art practices to ethnographic projects. A first impression of this work is in the inaugural issue of the journal *FIELD*, "A Week in Pasadena: Collaborations Toward a Design Modality for Ethnographic Research."

LISSETTE OLIVARES is the founder and director of Sin Kabeza Productions, a transmedia collective of artist-activists, and a doctoral candidate at the History of Consciousness Department at the University of California, Santa Cruz, where she is finalizing a manuscript titled "Palimpsests of Protest: Mediations of Resistance in Chile's 1980s countercultural movement." She has been awarded a curatorial fellowship from the Institute of Cultural Inquiry-Berlin and was a Helena Rubenstein fellow in critical studies at the Whitney Museum's Independent Study Program (2007–08). In 2010, together with Lucian Gomoll, she co-founded the Museum and Curatorial Studies Faculty Research Cluster at the University of California, Santa Cruz, which led to the critically acclaimed international conference, "The Task of the Curator," with keynote speaker James Clifford. In 2011, as an assistant professor and faculty fellow at the Gallatin School of Individualized Studies, she organized "A Symposium of Curatorial Interventions," an NYU cross-campus event with a keynote intervention by First Nation artist Rebecca Belmore. She has curated numerous individual and collective exhibitions, including Chile's Performance Biennial (2006, 2008), *Grotesques: Enactments of Sublime Transgression* at A Space Gallery (2008), *Writing Resistance in Crisis and Collaboration* (2010–12) at UCSC, NYU Fales, and the Queens Museum, *Consecuentes: Radical Performance from the Americas* at the Hemispheric Institute of Performance and Politics (2011), *CoEvolution and Complementarity: Encounters between Transmedia and Multispecies Storytelling* at the Institute of Cultural Inquiry-Berlin (2012), and is currently developing an "eco evo devo" SF architectural site that will display and disseminate multispecies art, design, and research.

MANON PARRY is assistant professor of public history at the University of Amsterdam. She has curated exhibitions on a wide range of topics related to the history of medicine, including global health and human rights, disability in the American Civil War, and medicinal and recreational drug use. Her travelling exhibitions have visited more than three hundred venues across the United States and in Argentina, Canada, Germany, Guam, Turkey, and the UK. She is co-editor, with Ellen S. More and Elizabeth Fee, of *Women Physicians and the Cultures of Medicine* (Johns Hopkins University Press, 2008), and author of *Broadcasting Birth Control: Mass Media and Family Planning* (Rutgers University Press, 2013). Her research interests include the public history of controversial topics and the social relevance of medical museums.

MONICA EILEEN PATTERSON is an assistant professor in the Institute of Interdisciplinary Studies at Carleton University in Ottawa, Canada. She holds a doctorate in anthropology and history from the University of Michigan. Patterson is co-editor of *Curating Difficult Knowledge: Violent Pasts in Public Places* (Palgrave Macmillan, 2011) and *Anthrohistory: Unsettling Knowledge and Questioning Discipline* (University of Michigan Press, 2011). As a scholar, curator, and activist, she is particularly interested in the intersections of memory, childhood, and violence in post-colonial Africa, and the ways in which they are represented and engaged in contemporary public spheres.

RICHARD SANDELL is professor in the School of Museum Studies at the University of Leicester. His research, frequently carried out in collaboration with museums, focuses on the potential role that museums might play in supporting human rights, social justice, and equality. He has been awarded fellowships at the Smithsonian Institution (2004/2005) and the Humanities Research Center of the Australian National University (2008) to develop projects around these themes. He has published five books; the most recent (2012) (with Eithne Nightingale) is entitled *Museums, Equality and Social Justice*. He is a trustee of the UK's Museums Association.

ROGER I. SIMON was a professor in the Department of Sociology and Equity Studies, Ontario Institute for Studies in Education at the University of Toronto. Over four decades he wrote extensively on culture, pedagogy, ethics, and social memory. His recent work addressed issues concerning the exhibition of material relating to mass violence, the implications of remembrance as a public pedagogy, and the ethics and impact of "difficult" images. His last book, entitled *A Pedagogy of Witnessing: Curatorial Practice and the Pursuit of Social Justice*, was published in 2014 by SUNY Press. Roger passed away on Rosh Hashanah of 2012.

INDEX